Equality

C0-GLO-219

Dialogues on Social Issues: Bard College and West Point

This series was created following the success of a joint venture between Bard College and West Point in 2012 on the nature of a Just War. The project included parallel seminars, joint sessions and an academic conference, many of the events videotaped for posting on *iTunes U*. Similar joint projects in 2015 and 2017 resulted in the first two volumes in the series, each containing essays by Bard and West Point faculty on a chosen theme.

The papers in these volumes cover a wide range of disciplines: Far Eastern Studies, History, Law, Middle Eastern Studies, Philosophy, Political Science, Sociology, Religious Studies, and Theology. Written by scholars from the perspective of their own discipline, the essays are intended for fellow scholars, students majoring in that discipline, and undergraduates in multi-disciplinary seminars.

Future joint projects, possibly taking different forms, can be expected to draw upon the rich intellectual resources of the two institutions. Besides academic departments, these include specialized centers, such as (at Bard College) the Hannah Arendt Center for Politics and Humanities, Levy Economics Institute, Center for Environmental Policy; and (at West Point) Center for the Rule of Law, Center for Holocaust and Genocide Studies, Army Cyber Institute, and Center for Combating Terrorism.

Volumes in the series:

Intolerance: Political Animals and Their Prey, edited by Bruce Chilton and Robert E. Tully (Hamilton Books, 2017)

Equality: More or Less, edited by Robert E. Tully and Bruce Chilton (Hamilton Books, 2019)

Equality

More or Less

Edited by
Robert E. Tully and Bruce Chilton

HAMLTON BOOKS
an imprint of
Rowman & Littlefield
Lanham • Boulder • New York • London

Published by Hamilton Books
An imprint of The Rowman & Littlefield Publishing Group, Inc.
4501 Forbes Boulevard, Suite 200, Lanham, Maryland 20706
www.rowman.com

6 Tinworth Street, London SE11 5AL, United Kingdom

Copyright © 2020 by The Rowman & Littlefield Publishing Group, Inc.

Chaper 1: "Harlen" [1]" from THE COLLECTED POEMS OF LANGSTON HUGHES by Langston Huges, edited by Arnold Rampersand with David Roessel, Associate Ediot, copyright 1994 by the Estate of Langston Hughes. Used by permission of Alfred A. Knopf Doubleday Publishing Groupe, a division of Penguin Random House LLC. All rights reserved.

Chapter 3: Excerpt(s) from SOLDATEN: ON FIGHTING, KILLING, AND DYING by Sonke Neitzel and Harald Welzer, translated by Jeffereson Chase, translation copyright 2012 by Penguin Random House LLC. Used by permission of Alfred A. Knopf, an imprint of the Knopf Doubleday Publsihing Group, a division of Penguin Random House LLC. All rights resereved.

Chapter 4: from Inequalities: Reading in Diversity and Social Life, by Betsy Lual and Morten G. Ender, ISBN 9780536924513. Printed by permission of Pearson Learning Solutions.

All rights reserved. No part of this book may be reproduced in any form or by any electronic or mechanical means, including information storage and retrieval systems, without written permission from the publisher, except by a reviewer who may quote passages in a review.

British Library Cataloguing in Publication Information Available

Library of Congress Control Number: 2019950519
ISBN 978-0-7618-7116-3 (pbk. : alk. paper)
ISBN 978-0-7618-7117-0 (electronic)

∞™ The paper used in this publication meets the minimum requirements of American National Standard for Information Sciences—Permanence of Paper for Printed Library Materials, ANSI/NISO Z39.48-1992.

Contents

List of Illustrations

Acknowledgments

The essays in this volume are based on presentations given at a three-day conference at Bard College in April 2017, the culmination of a semester-long collaboration between Bard College and the United States Military Academy at West Point. The contributors were faculty members from both institutions. A similar project in 2015 led to the creation of a series by Hamilton Books (Dialogues on Social Issues: Bard College and West Point), and the publication in 2017 of *Intolerance—Political Animals and Their Prey*, edited by Bruce Chilton and Robert Tully. A further project is planned for 2019. The editors want to thank the Deans of Bard College and West Point for their continuing strong support of an academic initiative which has been rewarding for Bard students, West Point cadets, and the participating faculty. As a result of the deepening contact that our work represents, the West Point-Bard Initiative has been formed to serve as the platform of further collaboration.

For the conference in 2017, the editors of this volume are grateful to the Director and staff of the Levy Economics Institute at Bard College for providing its fine facilities at Blithewood Manor, and to the professionalism of the Reverend Fred Cartier who videotaped the sessions there. They are also sheepishly aware that, were it not for the rigor and conscientiousness of their copyeditor, Ms. Sam Brawand, the gestation of the volume would have occurred in academic time, which is almost infinitely slower than real time.

Introduction

Robert E. Tully

Equal. Isn't that how we're created? If we've somehow lost our equality, don't we have a natural right to regain it? Meanwhile, aren't we *somewhere* on the moral arc that leads to justice?—These are rhetorical questions. They contain their own "Yes" answers, adding affirmation and a dose of assurance. Real questions about equality are more difficult to answer.

From a remote and coldly metaphysical viewpoint, however, the meaning of "equality" is simple and the *problem* of equality doesn't exist. This is because *two* things cannot be equal. Differences are what define individuals, and an individual is equal to itself alone. Two supposedly separate individuals whose characteristics are entirely the same cannot really be separate: what appear to be *they* are in fact one and the same thing. The idea of two things which are absolutely alike, even to the extent of occupying the same space at the same time, is a conceptual trick. We seem to be able to frame the idea in words, like that of "married bachelor" or "round square," only then to realize that the frame is empty. Impossibilities aren't real. To a metaphysical thinker such as Leibniz, the focus can be only on what characteristics constitute each individual and on what differences distinguish them, since the very idea of absolute equality between individuals has been explained away.

The title of this volume rightly treats equality as a matter of degree. Differences are *more* or *less* in number, *major* or *minor* in kind. Yet differences are all important to us. They mark us out as older, poorer, more entitled, less talented, more trustworthy, less respected, more powerful, less free. Certain characteristics we may be able to modify, for example our financial status. Other characteristics we might strive to modify without ever really succeeding, such as aging. Differences also mark out groups whose members are sufficiently and often recognizably similar: the poor; the elderly; the middle class; the unemployed; African Americans; mothers; soldiers; Native

Americans; the homeless; the enemy; neo-conservatives; cattle ranchers; vegans; Boston Red Sox fans. Group membership is sometimes determined by birth, sometimes strongly encouraged by others, and sometimes chosen without constraint. Many individuals belong to more than one group. It is likely impossible to belong to no group whatever, though some people resent being classified at all. Universal agreement on exactly what characteristics define a group is rare.

People draw strength and self-recognition from belonging to groups, kindling in some a sense of pride and worth, in others a sense of oppression or even a feeling of animosity towards another group. While the celebration of differences is benign and uplifting, the historical tendency to exploit differences to the disadvantage of others is unfortunately the rule rather than the exception. People have been made to suffer because of their differences. It is a glaring truth that human nature, over the course of its social evolution, has spawned groups whose size advantage and might have been sufficient to convert differences of belief, practice, color, and not least gender, into cudgels of injustice.

The sixteen essays in this volume are the work of scholars at Bard College and West Point who present cases where injustice supersedes mere inequality. The examples of their research belong to history, religion, legal theory, social science, ethics, and philosophy. The regions they cover include the Middle and Far East, Europe, and America. The periods are both contemporary and historical. Each essay is self-contained and assumes no detailed acquaintance with the topic. Although the authors show a passionate commitment to their research, they do not preach. The facts they report about injustice and the lack of equality speak for themselves and are meant to invite, even provoke, discussion.

Despite the wide variety of topics, a common thread binds these essays. It is a moral thread which lies deeper than any laws and customs which sanction injustice. The moral fault rests with those who have passed unjust laws or enforce discriminatory customs, and no less with those who condone them. Many of the essays reveal the same persistent and unappealing trait which social groups manifest in different ways and in very different circumstances: a blind willingness to perpetuate whatever advantages these groups enjoy over others and to regard themselves more equal. Being made unequal, their targets are often considered less human.

The sixteen essays can be read in different orders and combinations that expose specimens of inequality from a wide range of periods and cultures. The remainder of this Introduction, which gathers the essays into six subgroups for convenient comparison, provides just one example.

1. The process of dehumanizing a whole class of citizens is detailed by *David S. Frey* in “The Social Practice of (In)equality in Nazi Germany.” If Socialism aims to renovate a nation by dismantling the barriers of privilege,

broadening educational opportunities, eliminating poverty, opening closed professions, providing wide access to health care, protecting the family, and striving in general to ennoble work at all levels, then the National Socialist policies which were methodically introduced in Germany during the 1930s came close to fulfilling that ideal—*except* that success depended heavily on expropriations from those Germans who happened to be Jewish. The State confiscated their property, professional positions, and wealth, thereby robbing Jews of their self-respect in the eyes of fellow Germans, of their legal rights as citizens, and ultimately of their right to life. All these policies were carried out for the sake of bringing equality to the Aryan majority. The new Germany that National Socialism sought to create was called the *Volksgemeinshaft*—the community of the people (of the right sort). Moral blindness was endemic among the many Germans who were, of course, benefiting materially from the program of controlled social progress. Among those who also profited, Frey notes, were women who contributed their logistical, technical, and medical skills during the war to assist the eastward advance of the German Army (*Wehrmacht*) towards Russia, and who felt empowered by the effort. Equality for these women was shared superiority. The spoils of war—clothing, adornments and household possessions taken from dispossessed Jews—were a perk.

More than seventy-five years separate us from the benighted form of Socialism that afflicted Jews during Hitler's rule. More than fifty years have passed since new congressional laws in the United States outlawed Jim Crow discrimination against African Americans. Whereas Nazi policies of the 1930s were designed to send Germany's Jews to the sidelines and beyond, the Civil Rights legislation of the 1960s aimed to return African Americans from the periphery of society. Particularly in the southern states, the laws were intended to enable freedom to take root and flourish where for so long it had been denied. This foundation was accompanied by the hope of building a national sense of fairness. But during the decades that followed, the foundation itself became overgrown with brambles. *Robert J. Goldstein*, in his essay "Equality Deferred: A Litany of Discrimination," describes how the various practices of *de facto* discrimination in areas so fundamental as education, zoning decisions, policing, and housing, have weakened the effectiveness of the laws that banned discrimination and have allowed segregation to prevail in pernicious forms down to the present. Legal challenges to these practices will continue, but in the absence of any collective determination to correct the motives behind *de facto* segregation, genuine social improvements in American society are uncertain, as well as very unlikely while the moral leadership to do so is missing.

There is a notable and possibly surprising exception to such persistent intransigence. The armed forces of the United States have attained a level of social integration far above what is found elsewhere in America, thanks to the confluence of two powerful causes: the enactment of anti-discrimination laws for the Federal domain, and the ability of a hierarchically structured society, the military, to enforce them in the armed services. "Social Inequality and the United States Army: The (Un)lucky Seven," by *Morton G. Ender* and *Betsy Lucal*, reviews the remarkable changes that have taken place in the Army since the mid1940s. The seven important areas covered in their essay—*race, gender, class, age, ability, religion, sexual orientation*—are sensitive within today's society and variously contentious throughout human history. Answering the call to develop and introduce policies that ensure fairness and provide redress for infringements, the Army has transformed itself into a rare subculture of Americans which emphasizes tolerance and mutual respect without compromising the necessity of maintaining unity of purpose. In time, the Army's central values might have a small leavening effect within the civilian communities where veterans settle.

Yet from the standpoint of an experienced military lawyer, *LTC Christopher Jacobs*, the intrinsic hierarchy of the Army contrasts with the sense of judicial fairness that prevails elsewhere in a democracy and potentially conflicts with it. This is the problem Jacobs presents in "Selecting a Military Court-Martial Panel: A Study in Inequality." Perhaps exigency and tradition help explain why so much power is vested in the hands of the presiding officer in military trials (the so-called Convening Authority), including the power of selecting the very members of the jury. In the heat of battle, when summary decisions are needed, the rendering of justice is subordinate to the necessity of maintaining discipline, and the quick justice delivered by a court-martial trial will inevitably stand as rough justice by civilian standards. Despite well-established judicial practices in the civil domain having been gradually incorporated into military law over the past one hundred years, disproportionate powers remain with military judges. Congress has not yet successfully challenged the military's entrenched position, and full convergence between these two systems of law appears an unlikely prospect. Jacobs traces the origin of this problem to a decision made by the Supreme Court during the final year of the Civil War. The matter is not merely academic or historical. During the Obama Administration, a legislative proposal aimed to remove cases of sexual assault from the jurisdiction of the military judge in the unit where the alleged offenses occurred. The Pentagon lobbied against it on the grounds of the need to maintain military discipline. The proposal failed in the Senate.

2. By definition, the members of any hierarchy are not equal. One person's authority is more or less than another's. While it seems incongruous to describe the U.S. Army as a benevolent enterprise, one of its missions has been to promulgate and enforce standards of respectfulness concerning

relevant personal differences among its members. In that sense, even if to that extent only, the Army promotes a climate of social equality and likes to think of itself as a *family* (in a sense far more traditional than less). Indeed, by overseeing the health care of its members for life, their steady employment and training, education (for children of the military and their parents), and financial well being even after retirement, the policies and practices of the Army appear to approximate an unperverted ideal of Socialism. And so an unusual question emerges: Are hierarchies better guarantors of equality than democracies? In other words, given that relevant social differences abound in either system, are democracies less effective as *equalizers*? Two other essays show how effective some hierarchies are in enforcing their approved conceptions forms of equality.

The root meaning of "hierarchy" is priestly rule. An outstanding contemporary example is the Islamic Republic of Iran, whose official religion is Shi'ism, and where ultimate control in such areas as politics and the military lies in the hands of the Supreme Leader (Ayatollah Ali Khamenei). An insight into the nature of clerical control is provided by *Tehseen Thaver* in "The Perilous Promise of Equality: Reimagining the Qur'an in Post-Revolution Iran." Her focus is on the teachings of two contemporary Iranian scholars who argue for the need to understand the words of Muhammad, the Prophet, without dependence on official interpretation, in effect making the Qur'an a living document for the individual Shi'a believer, somewhat comparable to the Bible's role in Protestant fundamentalism. Both of these scholars cite the teachings of a famous Sufi mystic of the thirteenth century, Jalal al-Din Rumi, who emphasized the inner dimension of religious belief. Despite being anchored to religious tradition, their arguments have challenged the high place in Iran's government held by the clerics appointed to guard the words of the Prophet, with predictable results: censorship of their writings and closure of journals in which they published. One of the scholars, threatened with assassination, chose exile. In such ways, Iran's collective despotism has contrived to equalize its own citizens' *lack* of freedom. Ironically, in addition to the absence of freedom of the press, assembly and speech, freedom of religion under priestly rule even for Shi'as is also curtailed.

George W. Gawrych's "Equality and Diversity in the Late Ottoman Empire and Modern Turkey" portrays an imperial hierarchy which sought to catch up with the modern world. The Ottoman Empire included groups distinguished by ethnicity, language, region, and religion—Turks, Kurds, Egyptians, Armenians, Jews, Serbs, Greeks, Croatians (among others)—all of them subjects within a vast realm ruled from Istanbul by the sultan or caliph. During an age which saw an increasing assertion of social identity by these groups, the growing contrast between the wealth of Europe and the backwardness of Muslim countries, and (not least) the encroachment of Western imperialism on Ottoman lands, reforms were recognized to be necessary and clearly overdue. In stages during the nineteenth century, the sultanate introduced reforms in education, taxation, political representation, and legal rights. Especially for a governmental system with a proud tradition of military conquest and dominance, these various changes were ambitious and admirably far-sighted but, in the end, unsuccessful. One of the outcomes of World War I was the end of the Ottoman Empire. Less than a decade later, what rose from what remained of its once vast empire was the Republic of Turkey, under the leadership of Kemal Ataturk. His policies enshrined Turkish national identity and the Turkish language, rejected limited self-governance for ethnic groups, and no longer encouraged multiculturalism. Under his rule, and despite its official status as a democracy, Turkey began to resemble a recognizably modern form of hierarchy, a state dictatorship which holds the reins of power tightly. After a subsequent period of accommodation with Turkey's Kurdish minority, the process of consolidation and control in modern Turkey resumed, and recently even accelerated during the regime of Recep Erdogan, Ataturk's spiritual heir, who has arrogated to himself powers normally associated with parliamentary democracy.

The example of modern Turkey shows that the question, whether democracies come second to hierarchies in promoting justice, involves a false contrast. Countries that label themselves as democracies (sometimes "people's republic" is preferred), allow multiple political parties, and oversee "free and fair" voting, can yet operate under virtually one-person rule. (There are several instances in central Europe today.) Or, consider the world's largest democracy, India, which continues to tolerate a rigid social hierarchy, the caste system. *Richard H. Davis*, in his "Gandhi, Krishna, and Caste: Inequality More or Less," describes Mahatma Gandhi's effort to interpret the *Bhagavad Gita* as favoring non-violence, while nevertheless preserving the radical inequality found in the original four-layer caste system of Priest, Warrior, Worker, and Servant (to the other three). Gandhi did not attempt to overthrow the caste system itself which, after all, rested on ancient religious tradition. Instead, he tried to change his fellow Indians' attitudes towards it, particularly towards the lowest class, the Untouchables (now known as *Dalits*). A change in attitude, he urged, begins with a change towards oneself: self-reform. Being able (so to speak) to *embrace* an Untouchable is an expression of moral equality, which is where Gandhi believed the reforms needed by Indian society should begin. In this way he became a warrior for equality, but the non-violence Gandhi preached was religious in nature rather than political. Revolutionary violence against colonial British rule might well have torn much of the fabric of Indian society, whereas he sought its transformation from within. India's caste system nevertheless remains. Spiritual revolutions are compatible with a way of life that tolerates the sort of differences which many resent as paradigms of unjust inequality.

Although fighting non-violently qualifies as a form of heroism, fighting itself is commonly considered to be not the business of saints but a prerogative, often a duty, belonging to men. The manly traits of courage, physical endurance, and willing self-sacrifice are precisely those of soldiers. Given the ancient and nearly universal belief that the job of taking up arms in defense of one's own people falls necessarily to men, it seems inevitable, even natural, that the first European theorists who formulated principles for the just conduct of nations at war would adopt this belief. "Men of Fortitude: Gender and Combatant Non-Immunity in War" by *Graham Parsons* takes aim at this embedded assumption of Just War theory. Parsons argues that the gendered conception of combatants in the traditional theory of war promotes excess and also licenses injustice. His focus is on the soldierly trait of willing self-sacrifice, which is easily exploited by commanders in their planning of military operations. Those willing to sacrifice themselves for a cause become available to be sacrificed for it. Correspondingly, enemy soldiers can be killed wherever and whenever found. The game of war involves many pieces, but unlike those in board games, the pieces can be regularly replenished. Parsons offers a revision of a basic principle of just warfare that distinguishes legitimate targets (soldiers) from illegal ones (the innocent). Specifically, he proposes to extend the rules of proportionality and necessity to enemy combatants. Such a revision would reduce excessive killing; indeed, it seems intuitively correct that killing enemy soldiers during combat who pose no threat ought to be classified as illegal and therefore a war crime. How the revised principle might be put to work, however, is another question, as is how deeply such a change would affect the gendered conception of what it means to be (and be used as) a soldier, now that women are assigned combat roles. But Parsons' proposal does endow Just War theory with an enriched sense of what it means for soldiers on both sides of combat to be considered moral equals.

3. Hierarchies by nature distribute benefits proportionally and thus unequally, but not necessarily unjustly. Something similar to a hierarchy, although hardly a closed system, is a "policy subsystem" within a democracy. In the United States and other modern democracies, a policy subsystem is a social confluence of elected politicians and their staffs; appointed heads of government bureaucracies; lobbyists and the organizations they represent; the media; lawyers; and the citizens intended to benefit directly from congressional decisions. *Brandon Jason Archuleta* gives us a specimen of one such subsystem at work in his essay, "Civil War Pension Policy: The Politics of Policy Subsystems," which examines the evolution of veterans' pension policies for the Union Army in the decades following the Civil War. Except perhaps to a hard-hearted pacifist (or an unreconstructed opponent of the war in Vietnam), soldiers who have fought for their countries deserve ongoing thanks for their service when they retire. Such practical gratitude was evident

during the Revolution and continued for later wars. Even before the Civil War had ended, President Lincoln signed pension authorizations, in the first instance for wounded Union soldiers, making it predictable that the nation's thanks would be extended when victory came. But where to draw the line? Over the years following the war, the rolls of those to be thanked came to include wives, mothers, and even Union servicemen who were injured afterwards or who later suffered illnesses having no connection with the war. Confederate veterans, on the other hand, were never regarded by Congress as the equals of their Northern counterparts. As long as money was available, and organizations like the Grand Army of the Republic were able to enlarge a block of reliable voters for local and national politicians, Union veterans and their dependents were counted as more equal than others, and the policy subsystem functioned smoothly. But when revenue became an issue, voters made at least some politicians and their party pay the price. The burden on the U.S. Treasury became so large that it helped to cost President Harrison, a Civil War hero and a Republican, his reelection bid in 1892. But the policy subsystem created more than a century-and-a-half ago has remained entrenched and continues to evolve. The Department of Veterans Affairs is now the federal government's second largest agency.

Similar to a policy subsystem, although functioning outside direct democratic control, are the United Nations peace missions in Africa which *Darya Pushkina* analyzes in "United Nations Peace Missions and Protection of Civilians: Equality versus Efficiency?" In principle, there should be compatibility between two important goals: (1) fulfilling in an effective and accountable manner a UN mandate to keep the peace in a nation where armed groups are at war; (2) ensuring that innocent civilians (non-combatants) in that nation are kept as safe as possible from hostilities. Unfortunately, tensions and friction are created by efforts to achieve both of these goals equitably. Combatants often do not wear military uniforms; worse, they often disguise themselves as innocent civilians or hide among them, sometimes even making targets of the peacekeepers themselves. Further, some types of actions that fall beyond a specific UN peacekeeping mandate may nevertheless be highly relevant to it, since the responsibility to protect the rights of civilians arguably flows from the UN's own Universal Declaration of Human Rights. Hostile forces have attacked innocent civilians, as in Rwanda and, more recently, in Nigeria, Somalia, Niger and the Congo. In response to such dehumanizing strategies, international aid and medical organizations have established refugee camps and provided food and medical assistance to civilian victims. Although these organizations operate independently of the United Nations, their work must somehow be coordinated with the role of the peacekeepers, which for the sake of efficiency and equality has resulted in various alliances and working agreements. Practical needs have also required coordination in the field with the

African Union, which also maintains a peacekeeping force. Equal fulfillment of the two goals therefore seems an elusive ideal; producing an equitable balance between them seems no less daunting. Adding to this already convoluted picture, Pushkina contends, is the fact that the UN itself lacks an effective evaluation procedure of its own peacekeeping missions, but in any case has tended to set the bar of success too low. To help remedy such administrative shortsightedness, she introduces a fuller set of criteria for measuring the benefits and results of these missions.

4. Two examples from ancient history hold up a mirror in which to see ourselves, the first from Israel in the period following the destruction of the second Temple, the second from ancient Rome. The essay by *Shai Secunda*, "The Rabbinic Meritocracy and Its Discontents," illustrates how a progressive enterprise of learning can succumb to its own sense of superiority. *Hugh Liebert's* "Minding Gibbon's Manners: Unwritten Rules and the Rhetoric of Equality," describes what might be called the illusion of comity. The instructive content of both examples depends on how far we decide to keep what we recognize in the mirror at a distance.

During the second century AD, custodianship of the Torah passed from the traditional, hereditary priestly class to a group of rabbinical scholars. Membership in this group was open to any male possessing the zeal to study and the willingness to deepen his learning through interactions with fellow scholars. What came into being, as Shai Secunda describes it, was a "knowledge economy," a rabbinical meritocracy consisting of generations of teachers and their students; their *currency* was an ever-expanding record of interpretations, disputes, and rulings concerning the norms of life and observance for the larger Jewish community. These views were collected in writings known as the Midrash (which preceded the Talmud). Apart from the obvious asymmetry of teacher and student, the rabbinical society was ostensibly a respected group of equals. Yet its own rulings on matters in dispute gave precedence to the learned, the rabbis themselves, over unlearned men and women. The less equal, namely "the people," had less social value in rabbinical eyes and therefore lower legal standing. Secunda compares the arrogance of such elitism to the meritocracy found in the higher reaches of college-level education in the United States, where young aspirants are carefully filtered to ensure they merit entrance and can emerge from the educational process as social equals. That any elitist group should pride itself as authoritative and entitled to offer definitive guidance is not surprising. But if the larger community is a democracy in which such a group is an influential, progressive meritocracy, the arrogance of elitism shows itself when the people this group considers ignorant end up deciding a presidential election.

The way of Athenian democracy was never Rome's way. Mob uprisings concerned issues of daily life such as grain shortages, not national voting rights. Even at the time when Octavian became Caesar Augustus, the first Roman emperor, there remained a bond between leaders and the Senate, the time-honored assembly of influential Romans who embodied the authority of the republic on behalf of all Roman citizens. This bond was symbolized by the letters "SPQR", standing for *Senatus Populusque Romani* (The Roman Senate and People), carved in stone on triumphal monuments and carried aloft on plaques in front of columns of marching Roman soldiers, as seen in Hollywood epics. During the period covered by Edward Gibbon in the first volume of his famous *The History of the Decline and Fall of the Roman Empire*, which Hugh Liebert tracks in his essay, the very meaning of this abbreviation became empty, though not immediately, not at least in the Senate's own view which considered Octavian respectful of its authority. Augustus Caesar helped maintain the illusion that he was "one of them," and the Senate designated him "first among the senators, and first among the citizens." Allowing for the fact that theirs was a society which supported slavery and the primacy of men, he was "first among equals." Gradually, as the new Empire expanded, the Senate's influence grew less and less. Ultimate authority came to be embodied by the Emperor alone, by the man who was wily or strong enough to win that unique and coveted title during the centuries which followed the death of Augustus in 14 AD. By the time of Diocletian, who became Emperor in the year 284, who ruled from a lavish palace far from Rome itself and in the ceremonial style worthy of a traditional Syrian or Persian potentate, and who like many previous Emperors accepted the status of "god," total subservience had come to displace even the reassuring trappings of equality. While some may be inclined to compare Diocletian gold to Trumpian glitter and find inauspicious similarities in the displays of power, it is worth remembering that presidential authority in the United States, unlike Roman imperialism, remains rooted in a democracy.

4. Sometimes, what the word "equality" is taken to mean lies in the eyes of the beholder. This is a theme which underlies the essays by Dominique Townsend and Bruce Chilton. *Bruce Chilton's* "Equality in Paul of Tarsus—More *and* Less" examines the Apostle Paul's endorsement of the subordination of slaves to their masters, and of wives to their husbands. To a contemporary way of thinking, such remarks automatically brand Paul as racist and sexist. And for many Christian readers of his epistles, St. Paul's views may cause discomfort and lessen their respect for a theologian who thereby proves himself too much a prisoner of unenlightened times. How could a hierarchical body (the Church), which tolerates gender-inequality as well as slavery, ever function in harmony with Christ as its head? With parts so manifestly unequal, where is the fairness? The challenge which Chilton undertakes is not to explain Paul away but to analyze what he really meant. The central notion, frequently misunderstood by Christian readers, is that of *body*. The

word has three different senses. Two of them are familiar: the merely physical or material body, and the body in a sense which includes sensation, perception and thought. The third sense, in Paul's usage, is distinctly metaphysical and seems to have an affinity with what Descartes (many centuries later) called the *self*, the "thinking thing" which is the locus of awareness. In Paul's understanding, the resurrected Christ became a body of this sort, and when a Christian's body dies in the first two senses, there remains the body which becomes part of Christ and is equal to all those who similarly have died in Christ, no longer either slave or master, husband or wife. In this way, spiritual equality transcends—to a Christian of Paul's time—the inequalities of this world. To a secularist, on the other hand, more than enough inequality stays behind.

In "Ultimately Equal and Relatively Complicated: Questions about Equality in Teaching Buddhist Studies," *Dominique Townsend* describes the difficulty of teaching the traditional principles and practices of Buddhism to modern college students. They too, like modern Christians who read St. Paul, are inclined to be scandalized. Her students regard certain Buddhist traditions, which limit training to the intellectually superior and which rank women unequal to men in attaining the higher states of enlightenment, as not simply unfair—but also so un-Buddhist. They assume its teachings will express the Buddhist attitudes they fondly possess already. So, the pedagogical challenge for Townsend, after acquainting the students with the main streams of Buddhism (her emphasis being on the Tibetan), is to encourage an appreciation that views about intellectual capacity and gender have been disputed and interpreted since nearly the founding of Buddhism right up to the present. Nevertheless, although gender differences and the streaming of candidates are a fixed part of its tradition, Buddhism was never a theory about social progress. It aimed not to change the world but the individual. For this reason, Townsend introduces her students to the so-called Two Truths doctrine, which distinguishes relative from absolute truth. The former concerns the world (events, facts and personal relations) as most people perceive and understand them. Truth in the absolute sense is the higher-order understanding that everything in the world which is taken in the customary sense to be factual and real is no more than an unstable appearance and a deception. Absolute truth is a fact *about* what most people mistakenly consider to be real, and according to Tibetan Buddhism it is the only real truth. Yet the truth about absolute truth cannot be treated properly as the last item in a list of statements, for in that case it could not avoid being counted as merely another relative truth. Rather, absolute truth sums up, however imperfectly, what is discovered through the process of enlightenment. The implication is that it is not enough to accumulate information concerning Buddhist doctrines from the outside. The student who would understand Buddhism must internalize its teaching and follow its direction towards absolute truth, where relative inequalities no longer matter. But Townsend is a scholar and her classroom is not a monastery. She rightly has her students concentrate instead on the intractable contrast between relative and absolute truth, with emphasis on the former, since anyone who has not yet reached enlightenment must first acknowledge that inequalities exist (relatively speaking) before considering from the outside how Buddhists who are in training to reach eventual enlightenment might gain equal opportunities to learn and to progress. Meanwhile, social inequalities are part of the experience of these candidates and, although relative, do matter.

6. Some students mentioned in the Townsend essay find it "delightful" to encounter the Buddhist principle that "*the only thing that is ultimately true is that everything is relative*." Relativism is not peculiar to Buddhism but a view broadly familiar to contemporary college students. Its pedigree is traceable to ancient Greek philosophy. Sextus Empiricus, whose writings carefully arranged incompatible arguments on a wide range of philosophical issues, apparently believed that a deep immersion in their contradictions would lead the serious student to achieve a calm state of mind, an abiding resignation that truth itself cannot be reached (a state bearing some slight resemblance to Buddhist enlightenment). But the lineage has much weakened. Relativism in the contemporary sense is not concerned to pit argument against argument in an extended process leading to a settled and higher state of mind. It privileges opinion over fact, and the person who holds an opinion over evidence produced in support. Opinions are sometimes accepted as facts (truths), while evidence (the premises that support conclusions) is sometimes discounted or condemned because of the person who provides it. The result is that cynicism has become an acceptable form of wisdom. Two logical fallacies are traditionally associated with public disputes, one which attacks the arguer instead of the argument, the other which accepts (or rejects) a claim on the basis of the person who makes it (so-called arguments *ad hominem* and *ad verecundiam*). Both fallacies have enjoyed a renewed life thanks to the internet and they animate hostile interchanges on social media. *Robert Tully's* "Inequality in Skepticism" attempts to make a sharp distinction between cynicism and skepticism, defending the latter, while also further distinguishing two varieties of skepticism, one which makes science the measure of all truth, and one which recognizes a range of facts and evidence unsuited to that scale. Along the way, his essay charts the rise of skepticism in European philosophy. Despite criticizing a range of philosophers, it tries to avoid committing either of the two fallacies just mentioned.

Many disputes—perhaps most disputes—concern things judged to be right or wrong: actions, policies, laws, and the people held responsible for them. The word "equality" itself is more often used in a normative than a mathematical sense. And when it comes to *deciding* between right and wrong, people prefer to think that reason rather than emotion is or should be their guide, a belief which makes them suitable subjects of study by social scientists and advertisers. The famous philosophical champion of reason, Kant, wanted to give people facing moral choices a method that would enable them to marginalize emotion and self-interest, and thus give due weight to the role of reason. Especially in the sphere of ethics, however, no technique is able to guarantee perfect results, Kant's included. In fact, certain views he expressed have left him condemned as a racist and misogynist, in company with St. Paul (discussed in the Chilton essay), which in Kant's case magnifies the fault because his method ought to have neutralized his own unfavorable opinions about Africans and women. How could Kant focus on moral duty yet be morally blind? This is the question *Courtney Morris* investigates in her essay, "A Kantian Approach to Recognizing Privilege," and it is a sensitive one for her to ask, since she is a woman who is committed to the value of Kant's moral philosophy. Morris recognizes the risk of adopting an exculpatory answer. If Kant is treated as a creature of his own period, his blindness condescendingly dismissed, then the distinct brand of his ethical rationalism might suffer the same fate, given its failure to deliver for its inventor. The solution she offers is to find in Kant's own conception of duty adequate resources for discovering the wrongness of his racist and patriarchal views. Morris offers a deeper and richer conception of duty which draws upon Kant's own views. Although such a discovery was not made by Kant himself, the fault lies with him rather than with the principles of moral guidance that he provided, and his blindness, even if condemned as hypocritical or willful, avoids being used as a basis for rejecting his ethical doctrine itself. Nevertheless, that a thinker so intensely interested in the workings of the mind did not put his own objectionable views under the microscope remains a paradox. Perhaps Kant, because he insisted on marginalizing emotions, failed to notice the moral content of his own emotive opinions.

The sixteen essays remove much of the assurance expressed by the rhetorical questions which began this Introduction. They also reveal fundamental puzzles about equality. Several of the essays concern people who, although treated unequally, do not consider themselves victims of injustice. Who, then, should decide which inequalities count as unjust and which ones are acceptable? How can it be decided who that should be, and according to what standard of justice? Whether the system is a democracy, hierarchy, meritocracy, military dictatorship, or policy subsystem, it seems axiomatic that those in power will decide, although the decisions warranting inequality made in different systems are unlikely to match. Should one of these systems have priority? But how is *that* to be decided? Attempts to justify any choice are likely to be motivated by strong preferences and antagonisms. Cold logic does not compete well against passion. Perhaps some type of democracy—other than the spurious form of a military dictatorship—would make a good choice. Being compendious enough to include other systems, democracies seem well suited to provide the most complete means for managing inequality. Yet this answer creates a conundrum. The pursuit of equality guarantees inequality. The correction of unjust differences in a democracy will give more equality to some, inevitably less to others, and the very process of equalizing for the sake of the whole can engender discontent among the parts.

Part I

HISTORICAL PERSPECTIVES

Chapter 1

Equality Deferred

A Litany of Discrimination

Robert J. Goldstein[1]

"*What happens to a dream deferred?*" So begins a famous poem by Langston Hughes from the mid-20th Century.[2] The remainder of the poem answers the question obliquely. Hughes pictures a range of possible results, all grim, variously suggesting resignation, revulsion, quiet despair, or rage. But missing in this poem from 1951 is any glimmer of hope, and it is easy to understand why. The outlawing of slavery some eighty-five years earlier had meant little to generations of black Americans living under Jim Crow laws in the south, while a culture of unofficial segregation continued to flourish in the north. Hughes himself died in 1967, two years after Watts exploded in riots, and two months before those in Detroit.

While Hughes would not witness the steady legal progress since then of civil rights for African Americans, the poet in him would hardly have been surprised by the continuing frustration vividly displayed in today's Black Lives Matter protests, nearly seventy years after he asked his question. The long-cherished dream of freedom has indeed been steadily deferred. Many tangled reasons help explain why this is so, but they cannot justify it. In this essay I want to trace some of these tangles and to expose the knots which keep them bound.

"*Does it dry up like a raisin in the sun?*"

Every day at Angola State Penitentiary, the procession resumes of inmates walking two-by-two, watched by armed guards on horseback, making their way to work the fields in the scorching Louisiana sun. The prison was built on a former plantation. The prisoners, most of them lifers, were sentenced to hard labor. "Black bodies pepper the landscape, hunched over as they work the fields" (Atlantic 2016).[3] The plantation stretches in every direction. Their toil is closely overseen by Stetson-hatted men on horseback, heavily armed with rifles and side-arms. And the year is 2017.

Slavery has been illegal in the United States since the Thirteenth Amendment to the Constitution was passed more than 150 years ago (convicted criminals being the one significant exception); the policy of separate but equal was overruled by the Supreme Court more than sixty-three years ago; and the discriminatory laws collectively referred to as Jim Crow were prohibited by the *Civil Rights Act of 1964*, some fifty-three years ago.[4] January 2017 saw the close of the two-terms of our first African American president, and in 2003 Supreme Court Justice Sandra Day O'Connor all but declared that "racial preferences" as a form of affirmative action would no longer be needed in America by 2028[5]. In 2009, *New York Times* columnist Ross Douthat wrote that, "if affirmative action exists in the America of 2028, it will be as a spoils system for the already-successful, a patronage machine for politicians—and a source of permanent grievance among America's shrinking white population."[6]. Yet in March of 2017, Douthat, who is known as "a conservative voice" at the *Times*,[7] while describing the case for reparations for slavery an "unrealistic proposal," called it a "meaningful response to an extraordinary injustice," and concluded that reparations today "might be a better path than the one we're on right now."[8] Quite a dramatic pivot indeed.

What changed? Why do we now dredge up the subject of inequality? Legalized discrimination, embodied in Jim Crow laws has for the most part been eliminated. What remains, however, is a broad pattern of *de facto* discrimination which in many ways ensures that the legacy of legal discrimination will be perpetuated. In an attempt to identify the current extent of *de facto* discrimination, my essay looks further at what I have called the "residue of intolerance,"[9] the continuing effects of past *de jure* or legal discrimination. I will identify several areas of *de facto* discrimination and describe the mechanisms that facilitate it. However, this effort can count only as a work-in-progress, since other forms of this kind of discrimination that have not yet been recognized are bound to come into view.

What impressed on me the need for the study of contemporary discrimination were the events in Ferguson, Missouri in the summer of 2014,[10] when Michael Brown was killed by a police officer during a violent daylight encounter. My decision was based, not on any passing of judgment about the killing, but on an assessment of all the circumstances surrounding that event: the emphasis on the criminality of Brown; the alleged failure to give him immediate medical care, although he was shot and fatally wounded; and the callousness revealed by post-incident events, many of them captured on video, which pointed to the existence of a real racial divide.

Cellphone videos of other police shootings after Ferguson, many involving unarmed black men, some of them even black children, that were streamed on social media and broadcast on television news, revealed to me that this was neither a new phenomenon nor an unusual way for confrontations with police to end. In fact, reactions to such graphic videos provided compelling evidence of a great divide. As with the video of the killing of Eric Garner in Staten Island, New York,[11] our reactions serve as a kind of Rorschach test for racism. Do you look at the victim as a dangerous cigarette-peddler—a threatening animal needing to be harshly subdued; or as a human being?

There are reasons why I was especially sensitive to these videos. For more than five years, I have been engaged in research, preparation, and teaching of the West Point Civil Rights Staff Ride, an intense course on civil rights that includes two-weeks of travel to the American South. Several examples of discrimination described in this essay derive from that experience. Some of these are based on conversations with the many people we met along the way, while a few cases just played out before our very eyes. What we encountered was constant, unrelenting, and disturbing evidence of discrimination. But other examples come from books that the cadets and fellow faculty members had read for the course, as well as from my own research as a law professor with a special research interest in cases and issues involving civil rights.

Certain types of discrimination are hardly new. Smart phones, for instance, have merely exposed incidents of police brutality which before now the public at large could not witness for itself. The various forms that discrimination can be, while certainly not unfamiliar to the victims, and were a revelation to someone like me, looking in from the outside. People might think it inappropriate for me to tell this story. Admittedly, there is a definite disadvantage and discomfort to looking in from the outside. There is also the awkwardness of telling someone else's story. But regardless of the limitations of an outsider's view, it behooves us to recognize that the problems of discrimination are *not only* those of the victims *but also* those of the very society which has fostered them. In that sense none of us are outsiders. Our challenge, my challenge, is to understand why discrimination is arguably almost as pervasive as it was in 1964, when *de jure* discrimination "ended" in the United States with the passage of the *Civil Rights Act*.

"*Or crust and sugar over like a syrupy sweet?*"
[The ideal of ending discrimination: "*a syrupy sweet?*"]

When the Civil Rights Staff Ride began, at the start of President Barack Obama's second term, many people had the mistaken perception that race was no longer an issue in the United States. Accordingly, the course was planned as a largely historical assay of civil rights laws that had brought about the end of *de jure* discrimination. We would visit the sites of the great "battles" of the civil rights movement and attempt to speak with people who had witnessed those battles. One of the first people with whom I was able to share the idea, outside of my West Point colleagues, was Dr. Cornel West whose book, *Race Matters*,[12] I reread after his visit to West Point. While I cannot remember the exact words he spoke, he cautioned that having an African American president would be no panacea. The message was that race still mattered.

It took very little time on the road before we encountered confirmation of this claim. At every stop on the first Staff Ride we heard from some of the people we met that in their experience, racism was more pronounced *since* the election of President Obama. Yet there were others who lauded the president and welcomed the era of color-blindness, debating whether the time had come to end the now "purposeless" policy of affirmative action. Fifty years (since the end of *de jure* discrimination), they argued, surely is enough time for the playing field to be leveled. It should not be surprising that this bipolar vision invariably split along color lines.

Not that those who felt the end of race, or the postracial, was at hand were anything but well-intended and educated. They said that they were supportive of the African American community. My response to them was not confrontational. I described a visit to Martin Luther King's childhood home where I had seen an unfinished Monopoly game set up in the family room and had learned that Monopoly was his favorite game. I then posed a question to them: "How could the game ever be fair when the properties had already been divvied up, or when the rules discriminated against some of the players?" This made some sense to them. They had originally opined that it might take fifty years for the victims of discrimination to "catch up." But my question caused only a modest change in their estimate: perhaps not fifty years; maybe seventy-five or one hundred.

Evidence suggests that the playing field is *not* level in many critical areas, and that discrimination continues to exist and to affect practically every aspect of life. In 1965, after the passage of the *Civil Rights Act of 1964* eliminated *de jure* discrimination, it became clear that, in the absence of political power, the elimination of *de facto* discrimination was merely a pipe dream. The *Voting Rights Act of 1965* was enacted under the Fifteenth Amendment's authority to attempt to resolve the political inequality that was profoundly evident throughout the country, but particularly in the South ever since the departure of occupying Union soldiers at the close of Reconstruction.[13] Despite some progress made in the registration of minority voters and the elimination of literacy tests and poll taxes as prerequisites to voter registration, the political under-representation of minorities who actually are in the majority persists today. With the *Shelby County v. Holder* case, the U.S. Supreme Court substantially curtailed the mandate of the *Voting Rights Act* for oversight of states by the U.S. Department of Justice.[14] While this decision did not eliminate the *Act*'s protections, it eviscerated the presumption that was aimed at the protection of minority voting rights.

In due course, states with long histories of violating voter rights have tested actions that arguably would reduce minority voting. These include burdensome ID requirements, elimination of voter registration sites, and limiting early voting. States argue that these changes are necessary to thwart voter fraud, little of which, however, has been proven to exist.[15] A large part of the minority population is disenfranchised in many states where inmates cannot vote and where even released convicts who have served their time cannot reclaim their right to vote.[16] Moreover, the "art" of gerrymandering is alive and well, acting to deprive voters of their rightful influence even in areas where black and Latino voters are in the majority.[17] Gerrymandering *could* have the impact of remedying voter discrimination, but under the guise of "political" gerrymandering it can also be used to create minority districts that increase the number of non-minority districts, thereby diluting the political power of the minorities. In many states gerrymandering is merely another form of voter suppression. Because courts have thus far allowed "political" gerrymandering with little regard for its concomitant impact on minority representation, this particularly depressing problem really has no easy solution.

POVERTY: *"A SORE"* THAT FESTERS

The divide between rich and poor in America is not news, and we are made aware regularly of the ever-widening gap, but the reality is that the rate of poverty in minority communities, particularly in the African American and Latino communities, is as much as three times greater than that of the white community.[18] This should be no surprise either, since it is much more difficult for African Americans and Latinos to get good-paying jobs.[19] Even armed with a college degree, there is evidence that the job market is still tilted away from minority applicants. Studies have shown that those with "black sounding names" fare more poorly in job searches than those with "white-sounding names,"[20] and algorithms now used by web-based job search sites use programs which allegedly are biased against minority applicants.[21] Such practices could have the effect of ensuring that minority applicants will be relegated to lower paying, less desirable jobs despite having better credentials for a higher position than their non-minority competitors. Even the successful minority job applicant will face challenges as an employee. "Studies provide evidence that everyday discrimination does occur in the workplace and that it negatively affects Blacks' well-being."[22]

In a speech dedicating the Buffalo Soldier statue at West Point,[23] former Secretary of State Colin Powell, identified "The American Dream" as consisting of progress and equality. In a practical sense, the dream is often thought to include home ownership. We have in this country the express right to enjoy the privileges and immunities as citizens as well as the right to live anywhere in the country. In reality, those rights are severely limited by the practices of redlining, restrictive covenants as well as discriminatory mortgage and lending practices, which Ta-Nehisi Coates has documented in his seminal article in the *Atlantic*.[24] Exclusionary practices tolerated *and practiced* by governments at different levels have the result of ghettoizing blacks and Latinos based on nothing more than their appearance. It has been persuasively argued that the Federal Housing Administration (FHA) "went far beyond merely acquiescing to racial discrimination, and that it in fact explicitly intended to isolate black urban neighborhoods."[25] Proclaiming that "people want to live with their own" ignores the plain cold fact that minorities in America are *not* able to live where they choose, even as they become more affluent. Former Freedom Rider Hank Thomas, a proud, self-made millionaire, recounts how passersby in his affluent suburban Atlanta neighborhood would stop outside his house while he was tending his lush gardens and offer him work as a landscaper. Many other affluent minorities fare much worse in the way of insult and injury when they try to establish residence in an insular community, or succeed.[26]

These practices, carried out despite laws that might otherwise prevent them, have led to the re-segregation of schools and the concomitant inequality of those schools.[27] Given that parental decisions about where to live can be strongly influenced by the known quality of the neighborhood schools, it is axiomatic that policies which prevent people from living in the community they would otherwise choose violate their basic civil rights as Americans.

EDUCATION: *"IT JUST SAGS."*

Exacerbating the economic divide are the limited educational opportunities that face minority children. School re-segregation has shockingly made separate-and-unequal the reality more than seventy years after *Brown v. Board of Education*.[28] The result is an inferior education followed by even fewer post-educational opportunities. In some communities, school funding has been siphoned away from minority and low-income students who have been zoned-out from attending the schools in more affluent (generally non-minority) districts. Even where those school budgets might be the same, other methods of support for schools in affluent neighborhoods help ensure inequality, such as private funding, booster support from businesses, and the limited need for programs that are a necessity in low-income areas, such as school breakfast and lunch subsidies. Further, when schools are districted separately, any need for pretense is removed, since funding for the schools in affluent districts is based on tax-bases which dwarf those in low-income districts. But no judicial remedy is readily available, because federal courts have all but abandoned jurisdiction except in the most egregious cases, such as the one in Cleveland, Mississippi where, during the Obama administration, the U.S. Department of Justice found a "racial stigma" attached to one of the City's two high schools.[29].

The Civil Rights Staff Ride met Judge Roger Gregory of the Federal appeals court in 2013 and 2014. Judge Gregory bemoaned the fact that, when the *Brown* Court decided (unanimously) to overrule the decision in *Plessy v. Ferguson*, it did not put the emphasis on *equal* rather than on *separate*. Civil rights leader Bob Moses, who delivered the inaugural Medgar Evers Lecture in Jackson, Mississippi in 2014, argued for a constitutional amendment equalizing school spending per student, which would all but eliminate the efforts of state and local governments to perpetuate unequal education. In the post-Obama era, even though such an idea seems even more fragile, its purpose remains no less clear: to restore (rather, to create) the fairness that the American educational system now lacks, and to end the social divide that perpetuates inequality.

Diversity in education is no less valuable for achieving social equality than education itself. The government's compelling interest in promoting diversity in our country is really the only hope for eliminating inequality. The use of "affirmative action" has been a critical component in the limited forward progress that has been made, particularly in higher education, but the sad fact is that students—including the best and the brightest—who emerge from re-segregated schools choose to continue their education in colleges where the students are like themselves. This thwarts the goal of diversity, making it ever more difficult to bring in a class of students with the widest variety of life experience to enrich the discourse in the classroom and on campus. More evidence of a divided nation.

ENVIRONMENTAL JUSTICE: *"LIKE ROTTEN MEAT?"*

Achieving a proper solution to any particular environmental problem depends on a complex set of demanding choices. The siting of a facility that pollutes (whether private or public) routinely requires a governmental decision about location, coupled with a permit process assessing the impact on the surroundings. The stages leading to a final decision are time-consuming and costly. The decision itself may well represent the path of *least resistance*, because to challenge an unwelcome siting decision is not merely expensive, it also requires political power and legal expertise. The chosen location is more likely the one where political and financial opposition was minimal. In short, these facilities end up being located in low-income areas. The siting of facilities in such areas raises questions about the rights of the residents. They involve issues of environmental justice.[30]

If environmental justice is not outwardly based on race, its impacts are greatest on minority populations. As Coates notes in "The Case for Reparations," "black families making $100,000 typically live in the kinds of neighborhoods inhabited by white families making $30,000."[31] Such facts help explain why environmental justice cases are often characterized as involving "environmental racism." And there is much other evidence, such as studies claiming to demonstrate that "residents of chemical facility vulnerability zones are disproportionately Black (African American) or Latino, have higher rates of poverty than the U.S. as a whole, and have lower housing values, incomes and education levels than the national average."[32] and the report of the U.S. Government Accountability Office (GAO), entitled "*10 Studies in Demographics Near Waste Facilities*."[33] Despite some admitted shortcomings in the GAO report, the individual studies tend to demonstrate, over and over, that polluting facilities are located in proximity to minority communities. Even if the reports only connected environmental justice cases to socioeconomic status, the disproportionate number of minorities living in poverty in the United States noted above[34] establish a firm basis for identifying the connection as one of environmental racism.[35] Combining pollution and poverty produces many negative quality-of-life results, not the least of which is degraded health.[36]

GHETTOS: *"A SORE"* THAT RUNS

At the bottom of the economic ladder, poor minorities are trapped in segregated communities which, in the absence of the appropriate policing techniques, become havens for drugs and for violent crime. The violence in these communities is magnified by the *need* for gangs to secure the everyday protection of life, limb, and property in places where the police and government authority have failed residents. The conditions that breed gangs and violence ripen along with the poverty and hopelessness of the community. Such a debilitating phenomenon in the case of Los Angeles has been documented in *Ghettoside* by Jill Leovy, which also reveals the benefits of policing methods that lead a community to believe that gangs, who literally take the law into their own hands, are not the only way to survive.[37] But to succeed, it is necessary to demonstrate that the justice system, the whole justice system, works equally for everybody.

Such communities suffer from a multitude of inequalities, starting with dismal education systems which offer little chance of self-improvement to students and limited opportunities for legitimate local employment. This traps the residents in a cycle-of-poverty environment that includes the ready availability of drugs to use and abuse, as well as the disproportionate tendency of the police to apprehend minor offenders and other "suspicious" individuals during stop-and-frisks.[38] Minor offenders are then caught up in the criminal justice system, which initiates for them a cycle of arrest and imprisonment that runs parallel to the cycle of poverty and even accelerates its consequences. In New York City, the robust stop-and-frisk techniques used by police, known as "broken window" policing, were judged to go beyond Constitutional limitations. They involved widespread profiling of young black and Latino men for whom 'reasonable suspicion' was based on their race and ethnicity.[39] Such methods ensured that a steady stream of minority youth would be ushered into the criminal justice system for crimes for which their peers in more affluent communities would never face arrest, much less jail time.

Michelle Alexander's book, *The New Jim Crow*, highlighted the consequences of the criminal justice system for the African American male community in America's prison system.[40] The war against drug use, particularly the use of crack cocaine, filled the prisons at the expense the African American community. Bryan Stevenson's *Just Mercy* documented the treatment that African Americans receive in the criminal justice system, and the injustice of the death penalty, not merely for those sentenced to capital punishment but also for those sentenced to die in prison, to life-without-parole.[41] Many of those imprisoned, unable to receive adequate legal representation, would instead accept inequitable and inadvisable plea bargains. Some of these offenders would find themselves the victim of laws that punished "three strikes" with a term of life imprisonment without parole, a virtual sentence to die in prison. These inequities were graphically depicted in the HBO documentary *Gideon's Army*, which details the struggles of an understaffed and underfunded public defender's office attempting to ensure that poor defendants receive their Constitutional right-to-counsel in criminal matters.[42] The inadequacy of legal defense afforded to indigent defendants often results from the fact that the public defenders assigned to them carry impossible case-loads, making bad plea bargains the norm rather than the exception. What exists as, in effect, two systems of justice in America, one for the rich and one for the poor, is another glaring sign of inequality.

Here is how criminal justice works for the poor in a bifurcated system: Once someone who is poor has been drawn into the system, say by an arrest for possession of marijuana, the case is relegated to an overburdened public defender's office when the arrestee is unable to make bail or to hire a private attorney. Plea bargaining is commonplace. This means that being released from jail often requires pleading guilty to an offence, hence gaining (or adding to) a criminal record which the poor arrestee has no means to get expunged (in contrast to someone affluent, who might have escaped being arrested in the first place). And now the arrestee—a black man, let's say—because of time spent in jail and the inability to post bail, has lost his job, may become unable to pay rent or child support, and may also be hampered in landing a job in the future. In many instances, in New York City for example, the drug conviction might result in eviction from public housing.[43] and if the plea was to a felony, it might result in many states in losing the right to vote.

On the other hand, an arrestee who refuses the plea deal will expect to receive justice from a jury of his or her peers, as is guaranteed by the Constitution. The reality is that the prosecution's challenges to the selection of individuals from a pool of potential jurors can, and often does, reduce the number of minorities on any particular jury panel.[44] And when the jury brings a verdict of guilty, the penalties imposed against black and minority defendants are statistically more severe than those imposed on white defendants.[45] Some of the laws criminalizing behavior allow greater penalties for similar offenses, such as the penalties for the powder form of cocaine versus crack cocaine.[46] The result is more severe sentences for those convicted of crack cocaine possession or sales, with a high percentage of them being minority defendants.

Further, statistics for the death penalty demonstrate that a higher percentage of African Americans receive a capital sentence than do white defendants.[47] But instead of being executed, some prisoners are sentenced to die in prison: in some states, all that is needed are three strikes in order to earn a life sentence without the possibility of parole.[48] In Louisiana's Angola State Penitentiary (described in the Introduction), whose prison population is largely African American, most convicts are serving life sentences. The inordinate amount of black men imprisoned in the United States has a profound effect on families: single parents left, or none at all, to raise children, and released offenders unable to cope when they return to society with limited prospects for work and earnings.[49] Add to this the diminishing availability of health care, particularly for drug abusers, which the repeal of the *Affordable Care Act* would have exacerbated.[50]

The large and disproportionate number of minorities in prisons, particularly of African American men,[51] raises the specter of convict servitude under the Thirteenth Amendment's exception from the ban on slavery (noted earlier). This gaping loophole allows for the continuance inside prisons of a form of such labor, as in the case of Angola which has a large plantation-like farm. The prisoners I saw toiling in the field under the supervision of their horse-riding overseers, in this case armed guards, provided a surreal picture of slavery transported to the twenty-first century. This Constitutional loophole allows opportunities for abuse and also incentivizes the continued mass incarceration that Alexander documents.

THE TALK

For many minorities in this country, unabated discrimination has dictated a sense of inevitability. Coates describes the death of his Howard University friend, Prince Carmen Jones, at the hands of a police officer who, as the only witness, "claimed that Prince had tried to run him over with his jeep."[52]

I have heard too many stories of this kind before and too many times since: young black men, stopped for simply being black, and killed even though they were unarmed. Prince Jones was not the first, nor was Michael Brown in Ferguson, Missouri, but in Ferguson there was video, and that told an alarming story about the policing in this country. It was reminiscent of the thousands of lynchings, massacres, and race riots that punctuate American history. As I read Timothy B. Tyson's book, *The Blood of Emmett Till*, I recognized a story that has been playing out perhaps since the first African slaves were kidnapped and brought to America as property in 1619.[53] Young Emmett Till was no exception, he was given *the talk* by his mother as he left Chicago for Money, Mississippi that fateful summer. Even if he were not given *the talk*, as Mamie Till claimed, he would have learned about *the talk* in heavily segregated Chicago, as Tyson notes.[54]

The talk then was focused on how young Emmett should act upon encountering white people in the South; *the talk* now is the conversation that African American parents have with their children, mostly sons, on how to react if they encounter police. The grim truth is that *the talk* is as necessary today as it was when it was given to Emmett Till, Prince Jones, or Michael Brown. And that is a tragedy. No one is exempt. I have heard the same story from three senior African American leaders at West Point, members of a group engaged in discussing diversity at the United States Military Academy. All three had held distinguished assignments in the United States Army, all were well-educated, and all—like Prince Jones—were followers of "the rules."[55] Generations of Americans who have promoted or simply tolerated intolerance have created a national burden, "*a heavy load*", and there are few signs of it becoming lighter.

"OR DOES IT EXPLODE?"

The events in Ferguson, Missouri in 2014, have invigorated civil rights activists, such as those in the Black Lives Matter movement, with predictably uneven results. In Charlotte, North Carolina, the 2017 Civil Rights Staff

Ride heard from Charlotte-Mecklenburg Chief of Police Kerr Putney about the "riots" in reaction to the killing of Keith Lamont Scott in 2016. Chief Putney is not soft on crime and he characterized the unrest unequivocally as "riots," but as an African American he recognizes the underlying problems. He understands that many in the minority community lack trust in the police, and he has moved to bridge that gap in the Charlotte area. The word "riots" evokes memories of violent upheavals in urban areas like Watts and Detroit in the 1960s and in Los Angeles in 1992. These riots had profound effects on our society, but they had devastating and lasting consequences for minority populations in the urban areas in which they took place.[56] Nevertheless, these earlier riots were based on the same lack of trust and are perpetuated by the same root causes that challenge us now. The solution to this lack of trust is multi-faceted but cannot be achieved only by improving policing; it requires facing the stain of intolerance which continues to divide our society and will not disappear on its own with the passing of seventy-five or one hundred years (according to the hope mentioned above). The lynching of Emmett Till, Tyson maintains, "was caused by the nature and history of America itself and by a social system that has changed over the decades, but not as much as we pretend."[57]

This country has to go through reckoning, reconciliation, and reparations—a "revolution of the American conscience," Coates calls it.[58] How we will go about this reformation remains to be determined, but it is very clear that time is not the answer. A reckoning will require that we come clean with our past and shine a bright light on history as well as on the flaws in our social and legal systems. This will require education that does not whitewash history nor allow it to vanish from the pages of our school books. Martin Luther King Jr's words from prison are worth recalling: "It is the strangely irrational notion that there is something in the very flow of time that will inevitably cure all ills."[59]

Reconciliation will require symbolic action. The Confederacy was formed to defend the institution of slavery.[60] The Confederate flag means slavery to the descendants of slaves as much as the swastika means concentration camps and genocide to Jews, and remains a thorn in the side of reconciliation, as are the multitude of memorials honoring the Confederate cause throughout the South. At the very least, these honorifics need to be presented in their historical context, alongside memorials for those who suffered through slavery, lynchings, and Jim Crow. The example of the removal of the statue of Robert E. Lee from its high pedestal in New Orleans presents an opportunity to leave the bared pedestal as a reminder of the folly of honoring those who fought to preserve slavery. A true reconciliation must be a truthful one, however painful that might be.

Finally, as even Douthat concludes, reparations would be a necessary step.[61] The litany of problems that are mentioned in this essay are not solvable by mere cash reparations, as the direct victims of slavery are long since gone, and cash alone will not solve the problems that remain. At the very least, reparations must take the form of profound institutional changes needed to repair each problem individually along with a commitment to see it disappear. Institutional reparations will affect not only the descendants of slaves and the victims of Jim Crow, but they should also work to close the gap between rich and poor, "raising all boats," as Dr. King himself had envisioned in his Poor People's Campaign.[62] This type of reparation will be focused on achieving real equality.

Meanwhile, we cannot turn our heads while the horrors of inequality continue. The hate-crime killing of James Craig Anderson in 2010,[63] the massacre at Charleston's Emanuel African Methodist Episcopal Church in 2015,[64] the senseless killing of Timothy Caughman in Manhattan by another professed white supremacist in March of 2017, are all symptoms of our failure to directly address inequality in this country.[65] We can no longer avoid looking.

NOTES

1. Robert J. Goldstein is Professor of Law, United States Military Academy. The views expressed herein are those of the author and do not reflect the official policy of the U.S. Military Academy, Department of the Army, Department of Defense, or the U.S. Government.

2. Langston Hughes,"Harlem", *The Collected Poems of Langston Hughes*, edited by Arnold Rampersad and David Roessel (New York: Alfred A. Knopf, 1994), p. 426.

3. *Angola for Life*, dir. Jeffrey Goldberg, *Atlantic*, September 9, 2015 (Washington, DC: Atlantic Documentaries, 2016), https://www.theatlantic.com/video/index/404305/angola-prison-documentary/ (accessed March 31, 2018).

4. U.S. Congress, House, *Civil Rights Act of 1964*, HR7152, 88th Cong., 2nd sess., Public Law 88-352, *U.S. Statutes at Large* 78 (July 2, 1964): 241-50.

5. U.S. Supreme Court. *Grutter v. Bollinger*. 539 U.S. 306 (June 23, 2003).

6. Ross Douthat, "Race in 2028," *New York Times*, July 19, 2009, A19.

7. Gabriel Sherman, "The Fifth Columnist," *New Republic*. January 24, 2008, https://newrepublic.com/article/62302/the-fifth-columnist (accessed March 27, 2017).

8. Ross Douthat, "A Different Bargain on Race," *New York Times*, March 4, 2017, SR13, https://www.nytimes.com/2017/03/04/opinion/sunday/a-different-bargain-on-race.html (accessed March 27, 2017).

9. Robert J. Goldstein, "Residue of Intolerance: Polluting Civil Rights," in *Intolerance: Political Animals and Their Prey*, ed. Robert C. Tully and Bruce Chilton (Lanham, MD: Hamilton Books, 2017), 193-210.

10. William Powell, "The Roots of Violence on Ferguson," *Atlantic*, August 16, 2014, https://www.theatlantic.com/national/archive/2014/08/racial-tension-in-ferguson-isnt-over/378625/ (accessed March 31, 2018).

11. *Eric Garner Video*. Performed by N.Y. Daily News. YouTube video, posted by *New York Daily News*, July 12, 2015, https://www.youtube.com/watch?v=JpGxagKOkv8 (accessed March 31, 2018).

12. Cornel West, *Race Matters* (Boston: Beacon Press, 1993).

13. U.S Congress, House, *Voting Rights Act of 1965*, S1654, 89th Cong., 1st sess., Public Law 89-110. *U.S. Statutes at Large* 79 Stat. 437 (August 6, 1965): 437-46.

14. U.S. Supreme Court, *Shelby County v. Holder*, 570 U.S. (June 25, 2013).

15. Michael Wines, "A Texas Woman 'Voted Like a U.S. Citizen.' Only She Wasn't One," *New York Times*, March 21, 2017, A17. Online version "A Texas Woman 'Voted Like a U.S. Citizen.' Only She Wasn't." March 18, 2017. https://www.nytimes.com/2017/03/18/us/voter-fraud-fort-worth-trial-rosa-marie-ortega.html?_r=0 (Accessed March 27, 2017).

16. Michelle Alexander, *The New Jim Crow* (New York: New Press, 2012).

17. U.S. District Court, W.D. Texas, *Perez v. Abbott*, SA-11-CV-360 (March 10, 2017).

18. Stanford Center on Poverty and Inequality, "The Poverty and Inequality Report," *Pathways*, Special Issue 2015, https://inequality.stanford.edu/publications/pathway/state-states (accessed March 31, 2018).

19. Cathy O'Neil, *Weapons of Math Destruction* (New York: Crown, 2016).

20. Marianne Bertrand and Sendhil Mullainathan. *Are Emily and Greg More Employable than Lakisha and Jamal?* Working Paper (Cambridge, MA: National Bureau of Economic Research, 2003), 00.

21. O'Neil, *Weapons.*

22. Elizabeth A. Deitch et al. "Subtle Yet Significant: The Existence and Impact of Everyday Racial Discrimination in the Workplace," *Human Relations* 56, no. 11 (2003): 1299-1324.

23. Tom Willard, *Buffalo Soldiers* (New York: Tom Doherty Associates, 1997).

24. Ta-Nehisi Coates, "The Case for Reparations." *Atlantic*, June 2014, https://www.theatlantic.com/magazine/archive/2014/06/the-case-for-reparations/361631/ (accessed March 31, 2018).

25. John Kimble, "Insuring Inequality: The Role of the Federal Housing Administration in the Urban Ghettoization of African Americans," *Law & Social Inquiry* 32, no. 2 (Spring 2007): 399-434.

26. Ta-Nehisi Coates, *Between the World and Me* (New York: Spiegel & Grau, 2015).

27. Martha Minow, *In Brown's Wake: Legacies of America's Educational Landmark* (New York and Oxford: Oxford University Press, 2010).

28. U.S. Supreme Court, *Oliver Brown, et al. v. Board of Education of Topeka, et al.* 347 U.S. 483 (May 17, 1954); Minow, *In Brown's Wake*.

29. U.S. District Court, N.D. Mississippi, *Cowan v. Bolivar County Board of Education*, 2:65-CV-31-DMB (May 13, 2016).

30. Goldstein, "Residue of Intolerance."

31. Coates, "Case for Reparations."

32. Paul Orem et al., "Who's in Danger? Race, Poverty and Chemical Disasters." Environmental Justice and Health Alliance for Chemical Policy Reform. Brattleboro, VT, May 2014, http://comingcleaninc.org/assets/media/images/Reports/Who's%20in%20Danger%20Report%20FINAL.pdf (accessed March 31, 2018).

33. U.S. Government Accountability Office (GAO), *10 Studies in Demographics Near Waste Facilities* (Washington, DC: Government Accountability Office, 1995), http://www.gao.gov/products/RCED-95-158R (accessed March 31, 2018).

34. Stanford Center, "Poverty and Inequality Report."

35. Ibid.

36. Goldstein, "Residue of Intolerance."

37. Jill Leovy, *Ghettoside: A True Story of Murder in America* (New York: Spencer & Grau, 2015).

38. Ibid.

39. U.S. District Court, S.D. New York, *Floyd, et al. v. City of New York, et al.* 959 F. Supp 2d 540 (August 12, 2013).

40. Alexander, *New Jim Crow.*

41. Bryan Stevenson, *Just Mercy: A Story of Justice and Redemption* (New York: Spiegel & Grau, 2015).

42. Dawn Porter and Matthew Hamachek, *Gideon's Army*, dir. Dawn Porter (New York: HBO Documentary Films, 2013).

43. New York State/County, Supreme Court, *Matter of Sterling v. N.Y.C. Housing Authority*, 22 Misc. 3d 1129 (February 25, 2009).

44. Adam Liptak, "Exclusion of Blacks From Juries Raises Renewed Scrutiny," *New York Times*, August 17, 2015, A1, online August 15, 2015, https://www.nytimes.com/2015/08/17/us/politics/exclusion-of-blacks-from-juries-raises-renewed-scrutiny.html?_r=0 (accessed March 28, 2017)

45. American Civil Liberties Union (ACLU), *Racial Disparities in Sentencing*, Hearing on Reports on Racism in the Justice System of the United States (New York: ACLU Foundation, 2014).

46. Alexander, *New Jim Crow.*

47. ACLU, *Racial Disparities in Sentencing.*

48. Stevenson, *Just Mercy.*

49. Alexander, *New Jim Crow.*

50. U.S. Congress. House, *Patient Protection and Affordable Care Act*, HR3590, 111th Cong., 2nd sess., Public Law 111-148, *U.S. Statutes at Large* 124 (March 23, 2010): 119-1024.

51. Alexander, *New Jim Crow.*

52. Coates, *Between the World and Me.*

53. Timothy B. Tyson, *The Blood of Emmett Till* (New York: Simon & Schuster, 2017).

54. Ibid.

55. Coates, *Between the World and Me.*

56. William J. Collins and Robert A. Margo, "The Economic Aftermath of the 1960s Riots in American Cities: Evidence from Property Values," *Journal of Economic History* 67, no. 4 (2007): 849-83.

57. Tyson, *Blood of Emmett Till.*

58. Coates, "Case for Reparations." See also *Angola for Life*, dir. Goldberg.

59. Martin Luther King, Jr., "Letter From Birmingham Jail," April 16, 1963, *Love-arth Network*, https://www.drmartinlutherkingjr.com/letterfrombirminghamjail.htm (accessed March 31, 2018).

60. *Was the Civil War About Slavery?*, dir. COL Ty Seidule. YouTube video, 5:50, posted by PragerU, August 10, 2015, https://www.youtube.com/watch?v=pcy7qV-BGF4 (accessed March 31, 2018).

61. Douthat, "Different Bargain on Race."

62. Jordan Weissmann, "Remembering Martin Kuther King, Jr.'s Solution to Poverty," *Atlantic*, January 20, 2014, https://www.theatlantic.com/business/archive/2014/01/remembering-martin-luther-king-jrs-solution-to-poverty/283193/ (accessed March 31, 2018).

63. Associated Press, "Mississippi: 3 Sentenced to Prison in Racially Motivated Attack," *New York Times*, February 10, 2015, https://www.nytimes.com/2015/02/11/us/mississippi-3-sentenced-to-prison-in-racially-motivated-killing.html (accessed March 27, 2017).

64. Kevin Sack and Alan Blinder, "Killer Wrote of Race War After Charleston Shootings," *New York Times*, January 6, 2017, A11, and the online version "No Regrets From Dylann Roof in Jailhouse Manifestor." January 5, 2017, https://www.nytimes.com/2017/01/05/us/no-regrets-from-dylann-roof-in-jailhouse-manifesto.html (accessed March 31, 2018).

65. N. R. Kleinfield, "A Man Who Hated Black Men Found a Victim Who Cared for Others," *New York Times*, March 24, 2017, A1, online March 23, 2017, https://www.nytimes.com/2017/03/23/nyregion/james-harris-jackson-timothy-caughman.html?_r=0 (accessed March 27, 2017).

Chapter 2

Equality and Diversity in the Late Ottoman Empire and Modern Turkey

George W. Gawrych

Equality and diversity are dynamic concepts which require policy adjustments according to changing circumstances and evolving social consciousness.[1] The management of ethnic diversity has posed serious challenges to the unity of Middle Eastern states such as Turkey and its Kurdish population. An historical overview of Turkey from the late Ottoman Empire to the present helps to reveal the complexity of the problem.

From the 1800s to 1922, Ottoman rulers faced the monumental task of integrating a polyglot, multiethnic, and multireligious empire during an age of European nationalism and imperialism. In response, Ottoman statesmen implemented a reform program based in part on the Western notion of equality for all subjects irrespective of religion or ethnicity while at the same time accepting ethnoreligious diversity. Ultimately, Ottoman reforms failed to preserve the empire. Upon its ashes, Mustafa Kemal Atatürk (1881-1938) founded the Republic of Turkey on October 29, 1923. Rather than continue Ottoman policies, Atatürk constructed a nation-state that categorically rejected ethnic and linguistic diversity and instead required wholesale assimilation into a Turkish national identity, while allowing for equality of the individual before the law. His successors, in turn, continued this policy until Ankara finally recognized Kurdish identity in 1991. Today, Kurdish national aspirations in Turkey call for a social contract which at a minimum institutionalizes multiculturalism, but which would be accomplished in a new and explosive strategic environment in the Middle East, one that has seen much chaos and violence.

THE LATE OTTOMAN ERA

At the beginning of the nineteenth century, the Ottoman Empire (1299-1922) comprised approximately 25 million subjects, spanned three continents, and claimed 4 million square miles. Muslims formed a clear majority overall, but Christians outnumbered them in the Balkans while sizeable Christian minorities inhabited Anatolia, the Fertile Crescent, Palestine, and Egypt. Istanbul, the imperial capital, was truly a cosmopolitan city of over 391,000 people by 1844, with at least half of the inhabitants being non-Muslim, including many Europeans. The last decades of the eighteenth and the first two decades of the nineteenth centuries witnessed a decline of Ottoman imperial power. European armies and navies inflicted a series of defeats on the Sultan's forces, while local Muslim notables established semiautonomous regimes. Christian unrest began the process of creating independent nation-states. In 1804, Ottoman Serbs rebelled and eventually gained regional autonomy in 1815. Greeks followed with a rebellion in 1821 that, with the military intervention of Russia, Britain, and France, culminated in 1830 with the establishment of a small independent kingdom of Greece. Confronted with domestic unrest and military defeats, astute Ottoman officials came to appreciate the importance of winning the loyalty of all subjects if the empire was to escape further dismemberment.

At the beginning of the nineteenth century, Ottoman rule over Christians and Jews followed Islamic teaching and Ottoman traditions. Recognized as People of the Book, Christians and Jews governed themselves according to their religious laws, managed their own revenues, and ran their own schools. In return for paying the *cizye*, or poll tax, they maintained their protected status and were exempt from military service. The Ottoman state officially recognized three main religious communities, or *millets*: Jews, the Rum (Greek) Orthodox, and the Armenian Orthodox, although the number of *millets* did increase in the nineteenth century. The *millet* system thus legally recognized and protected religious and linguistic pluralism for Christians and Jews.

By Western standards of the early nineteenth century, however, Christians and Jews were second-class subjects, unequal before the law. Muslims monopolized the government and the army, and criminal matters fell under the jurisdiction of Islamic and Sultanic Laws. Further, Christians and Jews faced discriminatory practices, among them having to wear distinctive clothing, being prohibited from proselytizing, and encountering restrictions on the repair or new construction of their places of worship. Yet, despite these restrictions, Christians and Jews dominated the empire's banking and international trade and contributed various skills to the empire's economic activities.

In the first half of the nineteenth century, both the internal and external challenges to the empire's territorial integrity eventually spawned a major reform movement, called the *Tanzimat* [Reorganization], which covered the period from 1839 to 1876. On November 3, 1839, in the presence of top government officials and members of foreign missions, the Grand Vezir proclaimed the Imperial Rescript of Gülhane, which guaranteed security of life, honor, and property; committed the state to establishing a regular system of taxation, as well as a fair system of conscripting, training, and maintaining soldiers for defense of the *vatan* [fatherland]; and promised fair and public trials. The Rescript clearly incorporated a nascent concept of equality, a concept with clear European influences: "All the subjects of our illustrious Sultanate, both Muslims and the members of the other *millets*, shall benefit from these concessions without exception."[2] Initially, the Tanzimat reformers were more interested in bringing the Sultan under the rule of law and thus preventing arbitrary acts, such as the summary execution of officials, than in enforcing equality for all. However, the next eighty or so years of Ottoman history saw the development of reforms designed to gain the loyalty of non-Muslim subjects under the principle of an expanding notion of equality.

In 1840, the *Tanzimat* reformers implemented a new Penal Code that articulated the principle of equality before the law for both Muslims and non-Muslims in criminal matters, although judicial bias favoring Muslims remained a common complaint of court proceedings. However, on February 18, 1856 near the end of the Crimean War (1853-1856), the *Tanzimat* reformers produced a second Imperial Rescript, written with the assistance of the British and French ambassadors. The principle of equality was now clearly articulated. This time, the reform program promised integration of non-Muslims into state schools and bureaucracy; it also required military service for all, and equal taxation. One year later, the government abolished *jizye* [poll tax], although it sanctioned an exemption fee to replace military service, which most Christians and Jews readily paid.[3]

Tanzimat reformers also took steps to promote equal opportunity for non-Muslims in the imperial system. Founded in 1859, the Imperial School of Administration (*Mekteb-i Mülkiye*), which sought to produce bureaucrats for the empire on the basis of a modern curriculum, admitted non-Muslim students. In 1895, the school had an enrollment of 415 Muslims and 31 non-Muslims. By the yardstick of integration, the foreign ministry fared the best among the various ministries. By the end of the nineteenth century, non-Muslims, mainly Greeks and Armenians, occupied some 40 percent of the top positions, including ambassadorial postings.[4] A handful of Christians even attained cabinet positions, such as ministers of public works and foreign affairs. Moreover, the Provincial Law of 1864, while strengthening the powers of government-appointed governors mandated the inclusion of non-Muslims on the following provincial institutions: the governor's advisory council, the province's commercial and criminal courts, and the elected provincial assembly.[5] The whole Tanzimat period thus witnessed concrete steps to enlist non-Muslims in the business of imperial governance.

The Tanzimat reformers also sought to create a new identity under the principle of Ottomanism (*Osmanlılık*), i.e., Ottoman nationalism or supra-nationalism. The word "Ottoman" had earlier been associated with the dynasty alone; now, all of the empire's subjects could be identified as Ottomans. The Sultan had medallions struck with the august title of "L'Empereur des Ottomans." The Nationality Law of 1869 went further with the idea of equality by granting citizenship to every Ottoman, regardless of their ethnic or religious affiliation. Every Ottoman was now a citizen with individual rights rather than a subject.[6] Despite these various reforms, however, the *millets* remained in force, and the imperial system still favored Muslim dominance.

In 1868, the central government founded the Imperial Galatasaray Lycée, the best state advanced high school in the empire, cosmopolitan in both education and enrollment. It was designed to foster Ottomanism and an Ottoman identity. Most instructors were foreign, though the faculty also included Turks, Greeks, and Armenians. Both non-Muslims and Muslims received government scholarships to study at this prestigious school. Initially, the school attracted many more non-Muslim than Muslim students. In 1869, Galatasaray numbered 277 Muslim and 345 non-Muslim students, whereas by 1901 the student body of 724 Muslims and 221 non-Muslims reflected the religious composition of the empire's overall population.[7] With its religious and ethnic diversity, Galatasaray Lycée stood as an example of Ottoman "religious desegregation."[8] It also educated many of the empire's political and intellectual elites.

During two brief periods, the Ottoman Empire even embraced a constitutional, representative form of government. Non-Muslim minorities played a role in each endeavor. The 1876 Constitution ushered in the First Constitutional Period, which covered the years 1876 to 1878. Parts of this document read like a *U.S. Bill of Rights*. All subjects were Ottomans, without distinction of religion, equal before the law, and citizens. Admission to public office depended on knowledge of and facility in Turkish, the official language. The Senate, appointed by the Sultan, had twenty-six senators of whom twenty-one were Muslims and five non-Muslims. Voting for the Assembly was limited to a small number of citizens. The 1877 elections produced a religiously diverse parliament: seventy- one Muslim, forty-four Christian, and four Jewish deputies. A Christian served briefly as provisional president and Christians chaired several committees. This legal arrangement granted Christians "undoubted responsibility for a major decision."[9]Unfortunately, too much power resided with the Ottoman Sultan, who in less than two years dissolved both chambers in what would prove to be a thirty-year closure. The Second Constitutional Period from 1908 to 1920 reinstituted a modicum of parliamentary government with similar religious diversity among its deputies and senators, but Muslims continued to dominate political power in the state.

Despite Ottomanism, the *millet* system experienced increased "ethnicization of confessional identity" among Ottoman Christians with different ethnic groups seeking their own *millet* status.[10] Very few non-Muslims attended state primary and secondary schools but instead selected their own communal schools, which often offered a more advanced curriculum. Moreover, nationalist currents flowed inside the various Ottoman Christian communities, especially among Serbs, Greeks, Bulgarians, Macedonians, and Armenians. European powers often intervened on behalf of Christian populations and forced administrative reforms. Russia even went to war against the Ottoman Empire in 1876 on behalf of the Slavic population in the Balkans. Defeated in war, the Ottoman government was forced to recognize the independence of Serbia, Montenegro, and Rumania, autonomy for the principality of Bulgaria, and the Habsburg occupation of Bosnia and Hercegovina. In subsequent decades, these new nation-states, as well as Greece, pursued their own expansionist policies in what remained of the Ottoman Empire in the Balkans. Finally, Bulgaria, Serbia, Greece, and Montenegro defeated the Ottoman Empire in the Balkan Wars (1912-1913), leaving only Eastern Thrace and Istanbul on the empire's European side. Ottomanism had thus failed to triumph over the ethnic nationalism of the various *millets*. Only a small minority of the Ottoman elites were fully committed to its full implementation.

To complicate matters, ethnic nationalism made inroads in the Muslim population. By 1900, small numbers of Muslim Albanians, who formed about 70 percent of the Albanian community, joined fellow Catholics and Orthodox in seeking cultural rights, such as schools and publications in their native language. Muslim Arabs, Turks, and Kurds for their part also began expressing their own national sentiments, by which time the word *millet* had taken on a second meaning of "nation." This change in meaning represented the ethnicization of the Muslim community in the Ottoman Empire.[11]

By World War I, all that remained of the Ottoman Empire in the Balkans was Istanbul and Eastern Thrace. Meanwhile, in North Africa, France occupied Tunisia (1882), Britain seized Egypt (1882), and Italy absorbed Libya (1913). Losses of territory in the Balkans and the Russian expansion into the Caucasus brought ethnic cleansing of Muslim populations, transforming Anatolia into a peninsula of refugees and making the empire more Muslim in composition, upwards of 75 percent. In the second half of the nineteenth century, the Ottoman Empire had gained the popular designation as "The Sick Man of Europe," a part of Europe relegated to second-class status.

During World War I (1914-1918), the Ottoman government, led by the Committee of Union and Progress (CUP), revived the process of ethnic cleansing. In 1914, it expelled some 300,000 Greek Orthodox Christians to Greece. In May 1915, in response to an Armenian rebellion in Van and guerrilla actions, the CUP implemented an internal deportation policy that resulted in mass atrocities of upwards of 700,000 to 800,000 Armenians. During this period, Mustafa Kemal, who would later become the first President of the Republic of Turkey, served in senior command positions in the Gallipoli campaign and was thus not involved in the Armenian Genocide.

The Great War virtually ended the Ottoman Empire. The victorious Entente states helped implement its final dismemberment. Arab regions of Iraq, Syria, and Palestine eventually fell under British and French Mandates sanctioned by the League of Nations. Anatolia also faced a division of spoils among the victors. The Treaty of Sèvres of August 10, 1920, forced upon the Ottoman Sultan-Caliph, essentially dissolved the empire. Greece received western Anatolia centered on the city of Izmir, Eastern Thrace, and several Aegean islands. An independent Armenia was assigned territory in parts of eastern Anatolia. Kurds were granted a small but autonomous Kurdistan with the promise of a plebiscite for independence within a year of the treaty's implementation. France gained zones of influence in south and south-eastern Anatolia, while Italy was rewarded with southwestern Anatolia. Istanbul and the Straits fell under international control. A small territory in the middle of Anatolia would form an independent Turkey. Sèvres thus represented the height of European imperialism in the Ottoman Empire. But the victors of World War I failed to implement the treaty.

THE KEMALIST REVOLUTION

Meanwhile, even before the Treaty of Sèvres, as Allied troops occupied Istanbul and areas in Anatolia, Mustafa Kemal had begun organizing a national resistance movement to prevent the partition of Anatolia and Thrace. He built his struggle mainly on Muslim nationalism, specifically identifying Turks and Kurds as two *millets*. Kurds now formed the largest Muslim ethnic group after the Turks, upwards of 20 percent of the population. By 1923, Atatürk had forced the withdrawal of all foreign troops from Anatolia and Eastern Thrace and thereby ensured the independence and territorial integrity of Turkey with the Treaty of Lausanne on July 27, 1923.

Three months later, on October 29, 1923, Kemal founded the Republic of Turkey, and over the next fifteen years, as its President, he implemented major reforms worthy of the label "revolution." He abolished the Ottoman caliphate and created a secular state with no official religion; changed the alphabet from Arabic to Latin characters; imported Western legal codes to replace Islamic law; closed all Islamic mystical orders; expanded the role and rights of women in society; implemented the Western calendar, the weekend, and the metric system; and compelled the adoption of surnames. In 1934, he chose Atatürk, or Father of the Turks, as his own surname, the name by which he would become widely known.

Under his leadership, Turkey developed as a *Turkish* nation-state. During the nineteenth century, nationalism had clearly emerged as the most effective ideology in both state consolidation and state formation, and Atatürk fully embraced this reality. He regarded the diversity and pluralism of the Ottoman era as a weakness that European states had exploited to their advantage and the empire's disadvantage, leading ultimately to its demise, while non-Muslim minorities had used ethnoreligious nationalism to undermine the empire from within. Atatürk focused on what weakened the empire rather than on what had kept it together despite the ethnic and religious differences. In his worldview, a quest for homogeneity trumped acceptance of diversity and pluralism.

To facilitate national unity, Atatürk had reached an agreement with Greece in January 1923 for a population exchange even before he established the Republic. Both countries were essentially on the same sheet of music in seeking national unity and homogeneity. Nine hundred thousand Greeks ended up settling in Greece, while 400,000 Muslims relocated to Turkey. Atatürk was determined to prevent European states from using Christians as leverage with which to intervene in the Ottoman empire's internal affairs, as had been the practice in the last century.

Yet, despite population transfers of this kind, homogeneity was an impossible goal. Although the Republic of Turkey's Muslim majority numbered 97.5 percent, Muslims split along sectarian lines: 75 to 80 percent Sunni, 20 to 25 percent Alevi (related to Shiites). For their part, Kurds constituted a large ethnic minority, in 1923 forming around 15 to 20 percent of the country's 11.5 million inhabitants. The Republic also had various other ethnic Muslim groups: Laz, Arabs, Georgians, Circassians, Bosnians, Albanians, and others. Religious and ethnic diversity failed to disappear but merely changed its complexion.

Inheriting an Ottoman legacy of ethnoreligious conflict exploited by European powers, Atatürk viewed cultural and religious diversity as an existential threat to the new country's unity and integrity, and he therefore set out to inculcate a uniform Turkish national identity among the various peoples of Turkey. Article 88 of the 1924 Constitution set forth a principle of civic nationalism: "The people of Turkey, regardless of religion and race, are Turks as regards citizenship."[12] But Atatürk also promoted assimilation based on one nation and one language.[13] His nation-state embraced hegemonic Turkish nationalism. A Turkish identity now clearly and unequivocally replaced an Ottoman one as the official state ideology. Atatürk wanted Turkish nationalism to permeate every aspect of society. In a school textbook issued in

1931, this aim translated into everyone "speaking the same language, raised with the same culture and the same ideal," as well as rejecting "privilege for groups, class, family, or individual."[14]

In 1930, Atatürk, with the assistance of European scholars, helped formulate the "Turkish History Thesis," which depicted Turks as the founders and disseminators of world civilization. From their original home in Central Asia in the Neolithic Age, ancient Turks had spread to all regions of the world bringing with them a developed civilization.[15] In 1931, Atatürk founded the Society for the Examination of Turkish History, to spread the nationalist creed. On October 29, 1933, in his speech commemorating the tenth anniversary of the founding of the Republic, Atatürk uttered the phrase that became a nationalist mantra for future generations, a mantra designed to instill individual and national pride: "How fortunate is he who says I am a Turk."[16] Turkish pride blossomed with the establishment of the nation-state. In 1936, the Sun Language Theory appeared in print which argued that the Turkish language constituted the source for all the existing languages in the world.[17] The Sun Language Theory thus complemented the Turkish History Thesis. Atatürk used these two theories to help instill national pride by placing Turks at the center of human history, and together they served as an antidote to the Ottoman legacy of being regarded the Sick Man of Europe.

Language was to serve as a glue to unite the people of Turkey. Atatürk believed that the Turkish language would facilitate a common conscience, morality, and world view when combined with an official history and educational system that indoctrinated a belief of "common roots and descent."[18] Kurds and other non-Turkish Muslims would eventually assimilate and embrace being Turks, although Christians and Jews faced a general prejudice in gaining full acceptance as Turks. There were many examples of successful assimilation in Atatürk's era. Two standouts in his generation were İsmet İnönü (1884-1973) and Ziya Gökalp (1876-1924). İnönü served as Atatürk's chief of staff in World War I, front commander in the War of Independence, foreign minister for the Treaty of Lausanne, and prime minister during much of the Republic. Then he became president of the Republic upon Atatürk's death in 1938. Gökalp was an important ideologue of Turkish nationalism. Both men possessed some Kurdish background.

In its quest for assimilation, however, the Kemalist Republic quickly came to deny the Kurdish identity and officially regarded Kurds as a fallen away Turks or as mountain Turks. Kurds were prohibited from using their language. "Atatürk never mentioned the Kurds by name in his public speeches after the proclamation of the Republic."[19] Assimilation of the entire Kurdish population, however, was an impossible proposition, and Kurds constituted the greatest challenge. They spoke an Indo-European language related to Farsi or Persian; Turkish, on the other hand, belongs to the Ural-Altaic language family. The official 1935 census reported a total of 16,157,450 inhabitants in Turkey, with 13,899,073 (86.02%) identifying Turkish as their mother tongue and 1,480,246 (9.16%) Kurdish.[20] This figure was low, since many Kurds spoke Turkish but avoided identifying Kurdish as their mother tongue in a state hostile to their ethnic identity.

Geography and history created an insurmountable barrier for Kurdish assimilation and also hindered the development of a strong Kurdish national movement in the twentieth century. Kurds formed a clear majority in the largely mountainous region in east and southeastern Anatolia. Many lived in a fragmented society divided along tribal loyalties, with a centuries-old warlike tradition resistant to government control and taxes. Kurds spoke two dialects of the Kurdish language: Kurmanji and Zaza. Zaza is essentially a separate language from Kurmanji, but its native speakers identify themselves as Kurds and are generally seen as such by other Kurds. Religiously, Kurds divide between Sunnis and Alevis, but many belonged to Sufi orders, most prominent being the Naqshbandi or its offshoots. These tribal, religious, and linguistic divisions have helped prevent the emergence of a strong national movement among Turkey's Kurds. Nevertheless, the Kemalist regime confronted a dozen or so minor Kurdish rebellions; a few were significant for their Kurdish national sentiment and Islamic ideology. Cooperation of competing Kurdish tribes helped the Ankara government suppress the revolts and led to the relocation of rebellious Kurds to Turkish-speaking areas of Turkey and the settlement of Turkish-speaking citizens in Kurdish areas. The Turkish army also perpetrated a number of massacres of civilians.[21]

Atatürk feared that any acceptance of Kurdish cultural rights would lead to demands for Kurdish independence. The Treaty of Sèvres had underscored for him how European states could continue using diversity to undermine the state from within by supporting an independent Kurdistan. But Atatürk made assimilation relatively easy and open to all Muslims. Assimilation only depended on accepting a Turkish identity and speaking the language. In a period that was noted for hostile racist ideology, Atatürk's approach seems benign. "Race referred not to a biological community, but to a national one ... defined through language and not genetic factors."[22] Assimilation ensured an "equality" available to all Muslims living in Turkey.

As for his global politics, Atatürk championed a Turkish nationalism neither xenophobic nor expansionist. He viewed the world as "one civilization," not a clash of civilizations. For him, Turkish nationalism was compatible with a universalism and humanism based on knowledge, science, and culture. In his Republic, Turkey welcomed a steady stream of foreign experts who came to provide their scientific knowledge. The American educator John Dewey, for example, visited the country and gave his recommendations for educational reform. In 1933, Atatürk opened the door to three dozen Jewish professors who had fled Nazi Germany. Their mission was to help modernize Istanbul University, Turkey's only university at the time. Universalism and humanism thus stood in sharp contrast to the policies of social engineering carried out elsewhere in Europe. Atatürk advocated a homogeneous society based on the hegemony of one identity, one language, one nation, and an authoritarian state. In his way of thinking, Westernization and Turkish nationalism complemented each other. A recalibration of the status of Kurds in Turkey would have to await the 1990s.

KURDS IN THE POST-KEMALIST ERA

In keeping with Atatürk's legacy of unity without diversity, subsequent Ankara governments maintained a ban on the development of a Kurdish identity into the 1990s. Nevertheless, equality for all Turkish citizens before the law remained a stated principle of government, so the door stayed open for the assimilation of non-Turkish Muslims. Turks accepted non-Turk Muslims who embraced the mantle of assimilation. Democracy came to Turkey with the 1950 elections, eventually leading to public discussion of the Kurds as a separate people with their distinct language, culture, and history.

But how did the Kurds fare in the post-Kemalist period? Kurdish areas in eastern and southeastern Anatolia remained economically disadvantaged compared to other parts of the country, but many Kurds benefited from the modernization and urbanization of the 1960s and 1970s that helped create a better educated society overall. Many Kurds moved into the major cities, transforming Istanbul itself into the city with the largest Kurdish population in the world. As in other parts of the globe, the same two decades in Turkey witnessed the emergence of leftist movements with socialist goals. Kurdish intellectuals participated in these movements, often championing under the banner of socialism the imperative of addressing regional economic inequalities, thus promoting a transethnic agenda. At the same time, Kurdish publications and associations emerged from the shadows without government suppression. On November 27, 1978, Abdullah Ocalan, a student at the prestigious Faculty of Political Science in Ankara University from a poor Kurdish peasant family in southeastern Turkey, founded the Kurdistan Workers' Party, the PKK, a Marxist-Leninist organization which combined resurgent Kurdish national sentiments with socialist ideology. First generation Kurdish university students were its main members.[23]

The Ankara government remained entrenched in its refusal to give official recognition to Kurdish identity. Frustrated at this impasse, Ocalan launched a guerrilla terror campaign in 1984 aimed at destabilizing Turkey and establishing an independent Kurdistan, first in Turkey and then by incorporating

Kurdish areas in neighboring countries. At its height in the 1990s, the PKK numbered 15,000 fighters. In response to the PKK's military threat, Ankara unleashed the army to wage a counterinsurgency campaign and ruled the east and southeast of the country with special decrees not subject to the purview of regular courts. The war became quite brutal, claiming as many 40,000 lives, mostly civilians, between 1984 and 2017. Moreover, between 1986 to 2006, Turkish security forces evacuated 3,000 villages and hamlets and relocated approximately 800,000 Kurds, many of them forcibly moved to western Anatolia. To help keep boots on the ground, the Turkish army trained and armed 40,000 to 60,000 Village Guards, who then became targets for the PKK. Extreme Turkish nationalist groups reacted by arming themselves as vigilantes who set about killing Kurds.[24]

The PKK's armed insurrection, among other factors, brought about a change in Ankara's policy toward the Kurdish Question. In 1991, Prime Minister Turgut Özal (1927-1993), himself partly of Kurdish background, officially recognized the Kurds as a separate nationality and negotiated a cease-fire with the PKK. His steps proved a turning point for Kurds in their relations with the government of Ankara. Kurds found some political expression in political parties for brief periods until the government clapped down, often under pressure from the army. During the 1990s, the PKK declared several unilateral ceasefires.[25] The 1990s witnessed the emergence of a Kurdish historiography that challenged both the Turkish History Thesis and the Sun Language Theory by claiming that Kurds predated Turks in the Middle East, their homeland being the eastern Tarsus region and the Zagros Mountains.[26]

Despite some moderation on Ankara's part, Özal died suddenly in 1993 and the PKK resumed its armed fight for independence, aided by the Hafez al-Assad regime in Damascus with training bases and supplies in both Syria and Syrian-controlled Lebanon.[27] But in 1998, Turkey threatened to invade Syria if Assad continued to provide safe havens. Damascus complied with Turkish demands and banished Ocalan from the country. Iraqi Kurdistan then became the PKK's main base. In February 1999, Turkish Special Forces captured Ocalan in Kenya, and he has remained in a Turkish prison since.

Recep Tayyip Erdoğan, prime minister from 2002 to 2014 and president from 2014 to today, instituted a liberalization of government policy toward the Kurds. He appeared willing to reach a negotiated settlement on the Kurdish Question. During Turkish elections in this period, several political parties expressed pro-Kurdish sentiments. In 2004, the PKK even declared a unilateral five-year ceasefire. However, Ankara still considered the PKK a terrorist organization, as did the United States and the European Union, and would not negotiate with its leaders. In June 2012, Erdoğan allowed the Kurdish language to become an elective in state schools, and Kurds even gained a state television station in Kurdish. In the last few years, the Peoples'

Democratic Party (HDP) emerged as an umbrella organization for the rights Kurds and other minorities. In the national elections on November 1, 2015, the HDP won over the ten percent (10.76%) threshold to gain fifty-nine seats in the Grand National Assembly of Turkey composed of 550 deputies. Kurds now fielded urban, educated politicians and intellectuals, both men and women, on behalf of the Kurdish cause. Meanwhile, Ocalan moderated his position. He rejected independence as the goal and instead supported negotiations, opposed violence, and appeared to champion a federalism that would incorporate a Kurdish nation within a larger Turkish nation-state, achieving thereby a separate but equal status for Kurds.

All the above progress suffered a major setback that has left the future of the Kurds in Turkey ominous. Erdoğan expected the HDP to support his bid to change the Constitution to create a strong presidency for him without the checks and balances of a mature democracy. He dreamed of replacing Atatürk as the new icon of Turkish national historiography, the founder of a new and powerful Turkey with an Islamist orientation. For this he needed the HDP's support to change the Constitution, but Kurdish leaders of the HDP feared a return to authoritarian rule that would eventually turn against them and they refused to support him.

Meanwhile, in 2015, the PKK returned to a campaign of violence and terror. This time, the violence moved from the mountainous regions of southeastern Turkey to urban areas. Intense fighting converted sections of towns into war zones, including Diyarbakir with its population of approximately one million. Since July 2015, some 500,000 people have been displaced and 2,500 killed in clashes between the Turkish military and the PKK. A failed military coup in July 2016, as well as PKK's armed insurrection, gave Erdoğan the excuse to move against opponents and pull back on Kurdish rights. He used emergency powers granted by the Grand National Assembly of Turkey to incarcerate 40,000 Kurds, to remove 100,000 government officials and teachers, to arrest 120 journalists, and to close numerous television channels, radio stations, and newspapers. Security forces also arrested twenty-nine Kurdish deputies in parliament, including Selahattin Demirtaş, the charismatic leader of the HDP, and replaced dozens of elected Kurdish mayors.

Complicating matters, Turkey's Kurdish Question has mushroomed into a regional, destabilizing issue. Today, some 30 million Kurds live in the Middle East. Kurds still form the largest ethnic minority in Turkey, some 20 percent (15 million) of a total population of 75 million. They also constitute the largest stateless ethnic group in the world, dispersed among the four countries of Turkey, Syria (2 million), Iraq (6 million), and Iran (7 million). All four countries have opposed Kurdish independence or even regional autonomy. With such unanimous opposition in the neighborhood, no Western country has wanted to endorse Kurdish aspirations for a single independent nation.

The first Gulf War, however, had changed the strategic environment by creating an Iraqi Kurdistan as an autonomous region within Iraq. Iraqi Kurdistan has remained steadfastly pro-West and the most stable region in Iraq, yet Washington has consistently opposed Kurdish independence and supported a unified Iraq. However, the rise of ISIS (Islamic State of Iraq and Syria), has compelled a recalibration of US strategy. Washington came to depend on Kurdish Syrian fighters in Syria from the Democratic Union Party (PYD), established in 2003. But the PKK essentially controls the PYD. Ankara thus considers the PYD as an instrument of the PKK and views the establishment of an autonomous Kurdish region in Syria as an existential threat to Turkey's unity. Erdoğan dispatched the Turkish Army to Syria in order to prevent the emergence of a large, contiguous Kurdish-controlled region in the northern part of the country. The United States, on the other hand, has come to rely on the military forces provided by Iraqi Kurdistan and the Syrian Kurds in fighting ISIS. This has helped put the United States and Turkey at odds. Erdoğan regards Kurdish nationalist aspirations as a greater threat than is ISIS.[28]

CONCLUSION

Contemporary Turkey has inherited a checkered history in regard to ethnoreligious equality and diversity. The *Tanzimat* reformers of the mid-nineteenth century embarked on policies designed to transform the Ottoman Empire's tradition of religious autonomy based on the *millet system* into a society based on equality before the law. Their efforts evolved into the ambitious program known as Ottomanism, which created a new Ottoman identity for citizens of the Empire. The old *millet* system, however, continued to provide a separate ethnic identity for non-Muslim, ethnoreligious communities, and the nationalist aspirations of these communities heightened rivalries, tensions, and violence during the 1880s and 1890s. Defeated in World War I, the Ottoman Empire essentially disappeared because of a century-old process of ethnoreligious discrimination, aspirations for independence, the harsh suppression of resistance, and Western imperialism.

Rather than continue policies of Ottomanism, Atatürk and subsequent regimes in Ankara imposed assimilationist policies based on Turkish nationalism—one language, one identity, one nation—which promised equality for everyone in the Republic. Nevertheless, their endeavors failed to create a single national identity for Turkey, and by the 1960s Kurdish national sentiments began stirring with new force in urban areas. In 1984, the PKK renewed what has proven to be for over fifty years an armed struggle against the Turkish state. Western Powers rejected Kurdish national aspirations until the two Gulf Wars unsettled the region and transformed the Kurdish Question into a major regional issue. Out of the resultant chaos has emerged a regional government for Iraqi Kurdistan, but also the Syrian civil war, and ISIS. To defeat ISIS, the United States has come to rely on Kurdish fighters, both in Syria and in Iraq. Nevertheless, Kurdish nationalist aspirations now pose the threat of fragmenting the region even further by challenging the unity of Turkey and Iraq and inviting interventions to preserve their unity.

A historical perspective on equality and ethnoreligious diversity reveals a pattern in modern Middle East history. Once again, Western intervention and ethnoreligious diversities have set forces into motion that threaten the further weakening and possible dismemberment of political states in the region. Turkey under Erdoğan's leadership faces the immense challenge of maintaining the unity of the country while enabling the integration of Kurds based on equality and the nurturing of ethnic diversity. Meanwhile, the United States bears responsibility for the regional chaos caused by launching the second Gulf War. Turkey and the Kurds have become our problem. Washington must look beyond its own national interests and forge a wise long-range strategy on Turkey and the Kurdish Question. But at the present time, the prospects for hearing a proud new mantra—"How fortunate is the person who can say 'I am a citizen of Turkey.'"—are quite poor.

NOTES

1. This paper covers the period to the beginning of 2017 and is designed as a broad overview on how the late Ottoman Empire and Turkey struggled with equality within the context of ethnic, religious, and linguistic diversity.

2. Stanford J. Shaw and Ezel Kural Shaw, *History of the Ottoman Empire and Modern Turkey. Reform, Revolution, and Republic, the Rise of Modern Turkey, 1808-1975* (Cambridge: Cambridge University Press, 1977), vol. 2, 61.

3. Roderic H. Davidson, *Reform in the Ottoman Empire, 1856-1876*, 2nd ed. (New York: Gordian Press, 1973), 52-60; and Niyazi Berkes, *The Development of Secularism in Turkey* (Montreal: McGill University Press, 1964), 152-59.

4. Carter H. Findley, *Bureaucratic Reform in the Ottoman Empire: The Sublime Porte, 1789-1922* (Princeton, NJ: Princeton University Press, 1980), 206.

5. Shaw and Shaw, *History*, 88-90.

6. Derya Bayir, *Minorities and Nationalism in Turkish Law* (New York: Routledge, 2016), 42.

7. Kemal H. Karpat, *The Politicization of Islam: Reconstructing Identity, State, Faith, and Community in the Late Ottoman Empire* (Oxford: Oxford University Press, 2001), 101.

8. Bernard Lewis, *The Emergence of Modern Turkey*, 3rd ed. (Oxford: Oxford University Press, 2002), 122.

9. Robert Devereux, *The First Ottoman Constitutional Period: A Study of the Midhat Constitution and Parliament* (Baltimore: Johns Hopkins University Press, 1963), 169.

10. Howard Eissenstat, "Modernization, Imperial Nationalism, and the Ethnicization of Confessional Identity in the Late Ottoman Empire," in *Nationalizing Empires*, ed. Alexei Miller and Stefan Berger (Budapest: Central European University Press, 2015), 429-59.

11. George W. Gawrych, *The Crescent and the Eagle: Ottoman Rule, Islam and the Albanians, 1874-1913* (London: I. B. Tauris, 2006).

12. Edward Meade Earle, "The New Constitution of Turkey," *Political Science Quarterly* 40, no. 1 (March 1925): 58.

13. For an opposing argument for integration rather than assimilation, see Metin Heper, *The State and the Kurds in Turkey: The Question of Assimilation* (New York: Palgrave, 2007), 83-89.

14. *Tarih* IV: *Türkiye Cumhuriyeti* (İstanbul: Devlet Matbaası, 1931), 199-200.

15. M. Şükrü Hanioğlu, *Atatürk: An Intellectual Biography* (Princeton, NJ: Princeton University Press, 2011), 163-66.

16. *Atatürk'ün Söylev ve Demeçleri, I-III* (Ankara: Atatürk Araştırma Merkezi, 2006), vol. 2, 319.

17. Hanioğlu, *Atatürk*, 176-80.

18. Heper, *State and the Kurds in Turkey*, 86-87.

19. Andrew Mango, *Atatürk: The Biography of the Founder of Modern Turkey* (Woodstock, NY: Overlook Press, 2000), 428.

20. Servet Mutlu, "Ethnic Turks in Turkey: A Demographic Study," *International Journal of Middle East Studies* 28, no. 4 (November 1996): 520.

21. Uğur Ümit Üngör, *The Making of Modern Turkey: Nation and State in Eastern Anatolia, 1913-1950.* Oxford: Oxford University Press, 2011), 123-69.

22. Soner Çağaptay, "Race, Assimilation and Kemalism: Turkish Nationalism and the Minorities in the 1930s," *Middle Eastern Studies* 40, no. 3 (May 2004): 86-101, at 97.

23. Cengiz Güneş, *The Kurdish National Movement in Turkey: From Protest to Resistance* (New York: Routledge, 2010), 49-100.

24. For a succinct overview of the PKK-Turkey conflict, see Spyridon A. Plakoudas, "The PKK and the Guerrilla Tradition of the Turkey's Kurds," *Rubin Center*, February 22, 2015, http://www.rubincenter.org/2015/02/the-pkk-and-the-guerrilla-tradition-of-turkeys-kurds/ (accessed January 21, 2017).

25. Erik J. Zürcher, *Turkey: A Modern History*, 3rd ed. (London: I. B. Tauris, 2004), 319-23; and Güneş, *Kurdish National Movement*, 101-76.

26. Konrad Hirschler, "Defining the Nation: Kurdish Historiography in Turkey in the 1990s," *Middle Eastern Studies* 37, no. 3 (July 2001): 145-66.

27. Hafez al-Asad was the father of Bashar al-Asad, the current president of Syria.

28. For a brief update on recent events, Jonathan Steele, "Turkey and the Kurds: A Chance for Peace?" *New York Review of Books*, April 20, 2017, 20, 22, 24; review of *The Kurds of Turkey: National, Religious and Economic Identities*, by Cuma Çiçek (London: I. B. Tauris, 2017), http://www.nybooks.com/articles/2017/04/20/turkey-and-the-kurds-a-chance-for-peace/ (accessed April 21, 2018).

REFERENCES

Atatürk'ün Söylev ve Demeçleri. 3 vols. Ankara: Atatürk Araştırma Merkezi. 2006.

Bayir, Derya. *Minorities and Nationalism in Turkish Law*. New York: Routledge, 2016.

Berkes, Niyazi. *The Development of Secularism in Turkey*. Montreal: McGill University Press, 1964.

Çağaptay, Soner. "Race, Assimilation and Kemalism: Turkish Nationalism and the Minorities in the 1930s." *Middle Eastern Studies* 40, no. 3 (May 2004): 86-101.

Davison, Roderic H. *Reform in the Ottoman Empire, 1856-1876*. 2nd ed. New York: Gordian Press, 1973.

Devereux, Robert. *The First Ottoman Constitutional Period: A Study of the Midhat Constitution and Parliament*. Baltimore: Johns Hopkins University Press, 1963.

Earle, Edward Meade. "The New Constitution of Turkey." *Political Science Quarterly* 40, no. 1 (March 1925): 73-100.

Eissenstat, Howard. "Modernization, Imperial Nationalism, and the Ethnicization of Confessional Identity in the Late Ottoman Empire." In *Nationalizing Empires*, edited by Alexei Miller and Stefan Berger, 429-59. Budapest: Central European University Press, 2015.

Findley, Carter V. *Bureaucratic Reform in the Ottoman Empire: The Sublime Porte, 1789-1922*. Princeton, NJ: Princeton University Press, 1980.

Gawrych, George W. *The Crescent and the Eagle: Ottoman Rule, Islam and the Albanians, 1874-1913*. London: I. B. Tauris, 2006.

Güneş, Cengiz. *The Kurdish National Movement in Turkey: From Protest to Resistance*. New York: Routledge, 2012.

Hanioğlu, M. Şükrü. *Atatürk: An Intellectual Biography*. Princeton, NJ: Princeton University Press, 2011.

Heper, Metin. *The State and the Kurds in Turkey: The Question of Assimilation*. New York: Palgrave, 2007.

Hirschler, Konrad. "Defining the Nation: Kurdish Historiography in Turkey in the 1990s." *Middle Eastern Studies* 37, no. 3 (July 2001): 145-66.

Karpat, Kemal H. *The Politicization of Islam: Reconstructing Identity, State, Faith, and Community in the Late Ottoman Empire*. Oxford: Oxford University Press, 2001.

Lewis, Bernard. *The Emergence of Modern Turkey*. 3rd ed. Oxford: Oxford University Press, 2002.

Mango, Andrew. *Atatürk: The Biography of the Founder of Modern Turkey*. Woodstock, NY: Overlook Press, 2000.

Mutlu, Servet. "Ethnic Kurds in Turkey: A Demographic Study," *International Journal of Middle Eastern Studies* 28, no. 4 (November 1996): 517-41.

Plakoudas, Spyridon A. "The PKK and the Guerrilla Tradition of the Turkey's Kurds." *Rubin Center*. February 22, 2015. http://www.rubincenter.org/2015/02/the-pkk-and-the-guerrilla-tradition-of-turkeys-kurds/ (accessed January 21, 2017).

Shaw, Stanford J., and Ezel Kural Shaw. *History of the Ottoman Empire and Modern Turkey*. Vol. 2. *Reform, Revolution, and Republic, the Rise of Modern Turkey, 1808-1975*. Cambridge: Cambridge University Press, 1977.

Steele, Jonathan. "Turkey and the Kurds: A Chance for Peace?" *New York Review of Books*, April 20, 2017, 20, 22, 24; Review of *The Kurds of Turkey: National, Religious and Economic Identities*, by Cuma Çiçek. London: I. B. Tauris, 2017. http://www.nybooks.com/articles/2017/04/20/turkey-and-the-kurds-a-chance-for-peace/ (accessed April 21, 2018).

Tarih IV: *Türkiye Cumhuriyeti*. İstanbul: Devlet Matbaası, 1931.

Üngör, Uğur Ümit. *The Making of Modern Turkey: Nation and State in Eastern Anatolia, 1913-1950*. Oxford: Oxford University Press, 2011.

Zürcher, Erik J. *Turkey: A Modern History*. 3rd ed. London: I. B. Tauris, 2004.

Chapter 3

The Social Practice of (In) equality in Nazi Germany

David S. Frey

> The women and children and everyone were shot down ... there were a lot of fellows who took a delight in it.
>
> —PFC Müller, *Wehrmacht.*[1]

This essay challenges assumptions about equality as a positive principle tied to rights and freedoms. By applying the theory of social practice to the concept of equality, it will demonstrate how the oppression, denial of freedoms, and even murder enable privileged groups and individuals to develop and accept defective notions about the nature of equality. The construction of the Nazi racial state provides us with a disturbing example of how actions and practices can allow for a visceral and profoundly unequal sense of equality to germinate. By specifically concentrating on the behavior of German women and soldiers on the Eastern Front in the German Army, the *Wehrmacht*, during the early phases of World War II, I will make the case that Nazi Germany only came to know and experience equality through the destruction of the Jews. First, however, it will be necessary to describe the social apparatus to which the *Wehrmacht* itself belonged and on which it relied.

SOCIAL PRACTICE THEORY AND THE NAZI *VOLKSGEMEINSCHAFT*

In contrast to legal, philosophical, or sociological constructions of equality and inequality, social practice theory looks at the web of relationships involving people, their knowledge and actions, their forms of comprehension, and their institutions. A practice is "a routinized type of behavior which consists of several elements, interconnected to one other: forms of bodily activities, forms of mental activities, 'things' and their use, a background knowledge in the form of understanding, know-how, states of emotion and motivational knowledge."[2] Most theorists of social practice believe that there is a recursive association between activity and the social systems which shape them, meaning that activities are not only influenced by systems, but they change those systems as well.[3] In short, social "practice is a temporally and spatially dispersed nexus of doings and sayings."[4] Social practice theory thus provides ways of understanding power, norms, subjectivity, and change in social life.

In order to investigate the social practice of equality among Germans during the Nazi era, I will scrutinize the dynamic and reciprocal relationship between equality and inequality. My argument, inspired by the work of David Schoenbaum from nearly fifty years ago, is that the Nazi concepts of equality demanded the establishment of extreme forms of inequality. Schoenbaum brilliantly wrote that "Nazi social theory denied equality while at the same time asserting it."[5] Without that inequality, which in its most radical manifestation involved the extermination of Jews, Roma, Sinti, and various Slavic groups, and even asocial or disabled "Aryans," the Nazi project of creating an egalitarian racial state would have failed. My intent in offering this analysis is that this troubling case study forces readers to think deeply about whether the establishment of equality for some, not as an ideal or simply as a law but in practice, requires some degree of mistreatment, suppression, or subordination of others. In other words, do people only experience equality when they realize advantages, privileges, rights, and opportunities which others do not enjoy? In order for equality to be made legible or comprehensible to the common person, must groups devise mentalities of inequality, unequal bodies, discriminatory institutions, and symbols of difference and exclusion?

Scholars have generally described the Nazi racial project as one of the historical archetypes of inequality. This is, of course, true. Nazi ideology was based on a global vision of racial hierarchy, where culture-producing "races" such as Aryans stood at the top, and races unable to produce culture, such as various African races, as well as "parasitic" non-races such as Jews, languished at the bottom.[6] Yet the Nazi vision also included an expansive sense of equality for those in the correct racial category. The core principles behind the Nazi efforts to socially re-engineer Germany were the concepts of the *Volk*, a people (understood as racially defined) and the Volksgemeinschaft, the people's community (described below). Most scholars describe the *Volksgemeinschaft* as the Nazi answer to the divisive and disruptive nature of modernity. Race, the Nazis believed, not class, was what should unify societies. A state based on race, a *Volksstaat*, would eliminate social barriers, resulting in what historian Dan Stone calls "the fantasy of a life in common."[7] According to the Nazis, modern capitalism and its offshoots, cosmopolitanism and Communism, had corrupted the natural order of things, and the *Volksgemeinschaft* was the only antidote. Historian Michael Wildt defines the *Volksgemeinschaft* as "the promise of a meta-modern order of racial inequality in which the Volk, producing and protecting its homogeneity, experiences itself as sovereign."[8] Others, such as Ian Kershaw, designate the *Volksgemeinschaft* as a product of the Great War, born of the trenches. Nearly all scholars agree that the *Volksgemeinschaft* valorized racial community and comradeship above all else, promising a utopian condition of equality of opportunity and privilege for all within its confines.

While the Nazis may not have invented the idea of the *Volksgemeinschaft,* they took it, in the words of Peter Fritzsche, to its "most radical conclusion."[9] The concept permeated all Nazi organizations. The Nazis, through propaganda, teaching, ritual, and service, cultivated love of *Volk* and commitment to the *Volksgemeinschaft* in schools, universities, youth programs, civil society organizations, family education seminars, and even in marriage counseling. "Young men learned the principles for building a manly community in the Hitler Youth camps, in preparation for service in the *Wehrmacht* and the SS. Even commerce and businesses were to cease being a battleground for competing interests, and to conform to the community ideal by being promoted to a united 'business community.'"[10] Over the course of the 1930s, the Nazis naturalized the *Volk,* convincing the majority of the population that race constituted the natural, biological unit of humanity. This concept was critical to rationalizing Jewish exclusion. Alfons Heck, a young German boy who became a Hitler Youth leader, noted that this broad effort to popularize, publicize, teach, and institutionalize the *Volk* and its "other," the Jew, led him to accept the idea of the Jewish menace and thus the idea that Jewish deportation was just.[11]

Segregation of Jews and other undesirables from the *Volksgemeinschaft* necessitated a raft of changes which broke down and reassembled the social fabric of Germany. Legislation designed to reverse the emancipation of these lesser groups, Jews in particular, was critical. The Nazis enacted a series of laws which stripped Jews and other "suspect groups" of legal equality. This deprivation of rights included, for example:

- The Laws for the Restoration of the Professional Civil Service (April 1933), which expelled Jews from civil service positions, including teachers, doctors, and university students, as well as government bureaucrats;
- The Nuremberg Laws, which defined Jews by blood, restricted the rights of Jews and those of "mixed blood" [*Mischlinge*] to marry or to have sexual relations with "persons of German blood," deprived Jews of the right to vote, and eventually expanded these restrictions to other non-Aryan groups;

- The Law for the Protection of the Hereditary Health of the German People (October 18, 1935) which required "alien" races and racially "less valuable" individuals to be registered and thus excluded from the national community;
- Other laws which limited Jewish involvement in a large range of free professions, culminating with the *Berufsverbot* [Job prohibition] of 1938;
- Laws which limited Jewish use of public facilities, parks, beaches, etc.; forbade Jews from hunting (February 5, 1937) and owning carrier pigeons (November 29, 1938); and even forbade Jews from being tour guides;
- Laws which limited and then banned Jewish ownership of businesses and employment of Aryans. These culminated with the Decree for the Exclusion of Jews from German Economic Life (November 1938), which forced Jews to sell their businesses at a fraction of their worth, and its follow-on decrees which required Jews to sell bonds, shares, jewelry, art, and other valuables only to the Nazi state;
- Laws which determined where Jews could live, what middle names they could have, and required that they publicly identify themselves with marked passports and by sewing stars of David on their clothing.[12]

Nazi construction of a racial state also involved creation of institutions and practices that simultaneously produced cohesion and exclusion. The Nazis organized boycotts of Jewish businesses, arranged public festivals in which they burned books written by Jewish authors, and awarded prizes to holiday floats which denigrated Jews (fig. 3.1). As the 1930s progressed, Nazi authorities further divided society, becoming increasingly draconian in punishing those who sought to maintain ties with Jews. Crimes of miscegenation were subject to arbitrary continued internment in concentration camps after one served one's prison sentence, in effect making miscegenation a capital offense.[13] The Nazis and their supporters hung signs and banners proclaiming hatred for Jews everywhere, above houses, on welcome signs for towns and cities, even on planes, boats, and cars (figs. 3.2-3.3). These signs declared "Jews are unwanted here," "Jews are a menace," or "The Jews are our misfortune." The state and Nazi Party tolerated, if not encouraged, public denigration of Jews, through name-calling, rock-throwing, bullying, and shunning of Jews on playgrounds, in schools, at bathhouses, in the street and in stores, and at sporting events.[14] Mockery and public humiliation, according to historian Alon Confino, were "central to German anti-Jewish violence: they were essential in order to overcome a sense of discomfort at the violation of an intimacy."[15] Put another way, these steps were necessary to reconfigure German comprehension of equality.

The Nazis further institutionalized racial inequality through "synchronization of the Party and State" [*Gleichschaltung*]. State agencies, educational institutions, scientific associations such as the German Society for Racial

Figure 3.1 The Jew Devourer, displayed during a Shrove Tuesday festival. Courtesy of The United States Holocaust Memorial Museum.

Figure 3.2 Private plane emblazoned with "The Jews are our misfortune." Courtesy of the Stadtarchiv Nürnberg.

Hygiene, and university research organizations eliminated Jews from jobs and positions of influence. To insure the health of the *Volk,* the Nazis established Racial Hygiene boards of doctors, nurses and social workers; created Hereditary Health Courts; built offices such as the "Racial-Hygienic and Hereditary

Figure 3.3 "Whoever buys from Jews steals the property of the people." Alon Confino, A World without Jews: The Nazi Imagination from Persecution to Genocide (New Haven, CT: Yale University Press, 2014), 90.

Research Center" in the Reich's Health Office; and founded a Department of Jewish Affairs in the Security Office of the *Schutzstaffel* [Protective Squadrons, more commonly known as the SS]. All of these efforts were designed to categorize and separate the population, to create a bureaucratic and scientific infrastructure for differentiating and separating peoples. They ultimately led to an initiative, known as the T-4 program, which legitimized the euthanizing of some 70,000 congenitally or physically disadvantaged individuals who were declared "unworthy of life" by panels of scientists, psychiatrists, and physicians.[16] As the war began and the Nazi state expanded eastward, the Nazis created organizations such as the Office of the Reich Commissioner for the Strengthening of Germandom which categorized peoples across Europe, determining those who qualified as *Volksdeutsch* [German/Aryan] and who were the alien races to be excluded from German society.

Such were the processes and organizations created by the Nazis during the period leading up to and at the start of World War II in order to determine who could belong to the *Volkgemeinschaft.* For those who qualified there were significant benefits to share as well as obligations of citizenship. Millions of youths and adults wore uniforms signifying their belonging, such as those of the League of German Women or the Nazi militia, the *Sturmabteilung* [Assault Detachments, or SA, commonly referred to as Storm Troopers]. Perhaps more importantly, these uniforms suppressed visible signs of class difference and created an appearance of equality. Laws provided benefits to members of the *Volk,* such as marriage loans, maternity benefits, family and child tax credits, home furnishings, child education allowances, public transportation subsidies, and access to exclusive types of welfare such as *Winterhilfe* [Winter Welfare]. The *Nationalsozialistische Volkswohlfahrt* [National Socialist People's Welfare], a *de facto* method of wealth equalization, became the largest civic organization in the Reich, incorporating over 10 percent of the German population.[17] Fritz Reinhardt, deputy finance minister under the Nazis from 1933-1945, introduced "countless tax breaks" for the lower and middle classes of German society, narrowed pension gaps between white and blue collar workers, and lowered standards of entrance into civil service professions.[18] All of these efforts had the effect of flattening German society, making it in essence more equal, if not egalitarian. The Nazis purposely propagated new celebrations of heroes and holidays, such as *Gedenktag für die Gefällenen der Bewegung* [Memorial Day for the Fallen Heroes of the Nazi Movement] and Hitler's Birthday. Eventually these public festivals morphed into mandatory events. Nazi songs such as the *Horst Wessel* replaced or supplemented the national anthem. The Nazi flag, of course, became a household accoutrement, flown by all except by Jews, who were legally forbidden to do so. The German sociologist Franz Janka points to these various programs, symbols, and staged events—the flags, parades, holidays, Motherhood awards, uniforms, and party rallies—as manifestations of the *Volksgemeinschaft,* proposing that Nazi society relied on these elements because it was a society based not on reason but on an "emotional" convergence.[19]

The Nazis thus instituted public practices as well as "material incentives in both public and private spheres" in order to enhance support for the regime, spread acceptance of the *Volksgemeinschaft,* and shore up the belief that the *Volkstaat* [People's State] promoted equality.[20] Indeed, the Nazis not only promised but also managed to deliver to Germans greater social mobility and relative equality than they had enjoyed "during either the Wilhelmine (E) mpire or the Weimar Republic."[21] In the first six years of Nazi rule, people were twice as likely to experience upward mobility as compared to the 1927-1933 period of the Weimar Republic.[22] Unemployment disappeared for "Aryans." For those *Volksgenossen* [national comrades], there was greater security and order. Life measurably improved. The Nazis pressured employers to improve work conditions, and the Nazis themselves built public housing, recreation facilities, etc., for the benefit of the *Volk.*[23] Further, the Nazis devised programs that heightened the impression of material gain. For example, one-third of all German workers received benefits of the *Kraft durch Freude* [Strength through Joy] program, which provided state-subsidized vacations and allowed many, for the first time, to travel.[24] As a result, it "promoted both a greater sense of social equality among Germans and an abiding sense of entitlement as *Volksgenossen.*"[25] The state provided reduced price theater and movie tickets, cheap radios [*Volksempfänger*] and even sought (but failed) to create inexpensive, mass-produced cars [*Volkswagen*].[26] This new consumerism, tied to the rise of the *Volksgemeinschaft*, led to "prosperity … improvements in living standards … the dissolution of old traditions and affiliations … and equality."[27] After the annexation of Austria, even outright appropriation of Jewish assets (such as apartments and businesses) and their redistribution to Germans, either by individuals who felt empowered to steal or through state systems, helped further entrench Nazi concepts of equality.[28] Overall, this broad variety of tangible improvements forged a "material, psychological, and social integration of the majority."[29] By using material incentives to, in essence, bribe the *Volksgenossen* to buy into the Party's racial project while simultaneously excluding others from these same benefits, the Nazis effected a fundamental reordering of social values and a reconfiguration of thinking about the concept of equality. This social practice was critical for the Nazis. It allowed the regime to gain legitimacy, if not support, from the majority of Germans.[30]

Membership in the *Volk* also entailed responsibilities, which likewise had a leveling effect. Young boys and girls were obliged to join the *Hitler Jugend* [Hitler Youth] and the *Bund deutscher Mädel* [League of German Girls] or BDM. For men, military service became mandatory after 1935. Labor service also became a requirement for men and in due course also for women through the institution of the *Reichsarbeitsdienst* [Reich Labor Service] and the *Reichsarbeitsdienst—weibliche Jugend* [Reich Labor Service, female youth]. These communal organizations, where shared labor, uniforms, and egalitarian forms of address served to build unity among Germans and cement the concept of *Volksgemeinschaft*, while further separating privileged Germans from those outside the *Volk*. Götz Aly, in his provocative study, *Hitler's Beneficiaries*, argues that "for millions of Germans … appeal lay in the promise of real equality within the ethnic community…. For many people, the regime's aim of leveling out class distinctions was realized" by participation in all of the above mentioned organizations, plus the *Wehrmacht*.[31] In sum, although inequality was the fundamental basis of Nazi society, social practice did produce a sense of equality among those lucky enough to be part of the in-group, the German *Volk*.

CREATING EQUALITY THROUGH THE PRACTICE OF INEQUALITY

Over the last twenty years, scholars have come to recognize this inverse relationship between empowering the *Volk* and disenfranchising, persecuting, and eventually eliminating Jews. Holocaust historian Peter Longerich has written that "de-Jewification" was the tool the Nazis used to win widespread acceptance of and commitment to the *Volk*.[32] Alon Confino has demonstrated that the "improving quality of life for most Germans simultaneously meant discrimination of Jews … [and that] by the mid-1930s, this discrimination had become a way of life."[33] What I propose, however, is that this system of isolating, dispossessing, excluding, and eliminating Jews and other "undesirables"—this system of inequality—was not merely empowering for those deemed to be members of the *Volk,* but it was *the method* for creating a new sense of equality within the *Volk.*

The war, maintains Götz Aly, accelerated the obliteration of class barriers. Social status and income did not affect whether one qualified for state services under the Reich. In that sense, all national comrades were treated equally. Egalitarian rationing policies bolstered Nazi popularity, a fact observed by Social Democrats in Berlin, who secretly reported on morale throughout Germany. They noted that "the working classes thoroughly welcome the fact that 'the better off' have, in practical terms, ceased to be that."[34] Yet these were just some of the practices of equality under the Nazis. The everyday German understood equality, I contend, not only through the lens of inequality, but also through the *practice* of it. I will illustrate this by examining the behavior of two groups during the early years of World War II: Nazi women and soldiers in the *Wehrmacht.* I will demonstrate that, through persecution and savagery on the Eastern and Southern fronts, German women and men came to experience and comprehend equality.

During the 1930s, participation in a much greater range of social services allowed German women to "feel part of a larger whole."[35] Sibylle Hübner-Funk, in her book *Loyalität und Verblendung* [*Loyalty and blindness*], writes that the Nazi state was particularly successful in radically transforming "female socialization," which integrated women into the "higher" duties of the state. This, Hübner-Funk noted, produced the feeling of "being needed." This gave women a new, more equal, communal sense of value which transcended the individual.[36]

This notion of feeling needed, of a gain in status, and a sense of freedom and equality was summed up by Renate Finckh, a leader of the BDM. Finckh wrote: "I sang about freedom with a 'shining heart' and felt free while doing it; free from oppression by the father I feared, free from the constraints of old-fashioned methods for raising daughters, free from the pressure to get good grades from 'politically unreliable' teachers, free from the imposition of having to think about people with different political opinions.... That's how I could feel free and still be willing to obey every order."[37] With the outbreak of war, German girls and women found even greater autonomy and opportunity, even while living in what scholars agree was a state that did not practice gender equality. Wartime mobilization gave women the opportunity to find "honor, and an increase in status" in the new positions for which they found themselves eligible.[38]

Prior to the war, women were increasingly incorporated into the labor force through the Year of Duty and the *Reichsarbeitsdienst—weibliche Jugend*, as well as through racial hygiene programs, which included forced sterilization and euthanasia. Women eventually became conscripted into the war effort as well. In 1941, the Nazi state mandated Auxiliary War Service (6 month labor service), which mainly brought women into armaments industries. During the war, women entered the workforce in millions, took part in conflict as *Wehrmacht* auxiliaries, nurses, and in direct support of armed forces.[39] They moved to occupied lands and the front, either in military support positions, as part of the Germanization programs in the East, or in the employ of private companies. Women and girls built anti-tank fortifications and contributed to the construction of the *Westwall.* In diaries, these individuals speak of pride in their achievements, social advancement, an improvement in status, and a feeling of participatory equality.[40] They also experienced new forms of equality in social practice: participation in violent expulsions and plundering of Jews and Poles. "Young women and teenage girls," writes Gudrun Schwartz, "took an active part in this ethnic cleansing."[41]

The practice of sharing the spoils of war and the expropriation of Jewish property certainly appealed to German women who chose to travel eastward to conquered or newly incorporated lands. "Furniture, rugs, clothes, household items, and even houses that belonged to deported Jews became available to deserving *Volksgenossen*, and furthermore, personal belongings could be bought at dirt-cheap prices at the *Judenmärkte* [Jew markets] in major cities, or were distributed by the *Winterhilfe* [Winter Welfare], often without the original tags having been removed."[42] These goods helped raise the standard of living of those in the lower and middle classes. For some, the new bed, the fur coat, the set of dinnerware, offered a lifestyle improvement that otherwise could not be attained, along with an unprecedented sense of material equality.

Melita Maschmann, writing about her experience in the BDM, claimed "No slogan fascinated me so much as the *Volksgemeinschaft*.... What bound me to this fantastical ideal was the hope that it could bring about a state of affairs in which people of all strata could live like brothers and sisters."[43] It was this promise of equality and empowerment that compelled her to work in the occupied East. As the head of the Women's Labor Service camp, she oversaw operations to force Poles from their homes and confiscate their assets and houses. When she interacted with starving, begging Poles she was not only unmoved, but "it also gave her an almost enthusiastic feeling of superiority. She was even unmoved during her travels through the Lodz and Kutno ghettos."[44] She and the over 25,000 BDM girls who participated in the Eastern Action in 1941-1942 came to better understand the equality of membership in the *Volksgemeinschaft* through the privileges it gave them.[45] Suppression of the Jewish and non-Jewish Poles became a matter of course, became normal daily life, "privileges of the German occupiers ... [who] took advantage of the opportunity of participation that Hitler's state offered and enjoyed the fact that Nazi racist practices secured (for them) a higher" status than that of any male member of an "inferior" ethnic group.[46]

It is this social practice of inequality that gave German women in the East the palpable sense of equality as national comrades [*Volksgenossen*]. For many of the hundreds of thousands of women who joined, service in the East was the most "interesting," "wonderful," and liberating job they had ever had.[47] By war's end, the *Wehrmacht's* women's auxiliary corps alone employed over one-half million, and over 350,000 women were involved in the German Red Cross. Some were directly "involved in the crimes committed by the *Wehrmacht* and the SS in various ways." Nearly all "lived and worked in an atmosphere of murder and crime, were bystanders, and, as such, witnesses. Many were profiteers, some became accomplices, and still others became perpetrators themselves."[48] Because these "German women mimicked men doing the dirty work of the regime—the work that was necessary to the future existence of the Reich—they (believed they) were racial equals."[49]

Historian Wendy Lower, whose work *Hitler's Furies* analyzes women perpetrators, agrees that empowerment, opportunity, and the ability to transcend gender inequities were critical incentives for women who joined the killing frenzy and the "intoxication of the East" (*Ostrausch*). Among others, she examines spouses of concentration camp supervisors and women who directly participated in extermination and horrific medical experimentation. These volunteers "saw these mass-murder sites as places of employment and opportunity. The uniform was impressive, the pay was good, and the prospect of wielding power was appealing."[50] Some female concentration camp guards, according to Hilde Zimmermann, "'flirted with acting like men' by torturing inmates, wishing to demonstrate what kind of tough guys they were."[51] Others, such as SS spouse Erna Petri, explained how shooting Jews was for her an expression of equality. "I did not want to stand behind the SS men. I wanted to show them that I, as a woman, could conduct myself like a man. So I shot 4 Jews and 6 Jewish children. I wanted to prove myself to the men."[52]

For many of the millions of men in the *Wehrmacht*, SS, *Ordnungspolizei* [Order Police] and other Nazi organs under arms, the practices of abuse and mass murder were also empowering, equalizing, and community constructing. Similar to those of German women, the motives which German men had for participation in and perpetration of genocide varied. Psychologists, sociologists, historians, political scientists, philosophers, and a host of other scholars have tried to identify the multiplicity of causes and dynamics that permit individuals to choose to commit genocide. A non-exhaustive sampling of explanations includes:[53]

(1) Internal/hardwired human proclivities, such as:
   (a) Innate fear of difference or hatred that manifests in enthnocentrism or xenophobia;
   (b) Innate willingness to obey orders;

   (c) Innate "authoritarian personality";
   (d) Need to fulfill basic human needs, including security, effectiveness and control, autonomy, and understanding one's place in the world;
   (e) Innate desire to perform well;
   (f) Innate evil/criminality; and
   (g) Boredom.
(2) Developmental tendencies, such as:
   (a) Learned behaviors influenced by family upbringing, societal/cultural norms and traditions, education, etc.;
   (b) Age cohort;
   (c) Learned hatreds; and
   (d) Deindividuation resulting from group membership.
(3) Situational dynamics, such as:
   (a) Chaotic or wartime situations where there is an absence of restraint, where "normal" rules and ethics are not enforced;
   (b) Tightly-knit groups where the incentives of peer pressure and the penalties for opposition are strong;
   (c) Performances, celebrations, festivities, rituals, or group initiation rites, such as hazing, group sexual violence, etc.;
   (d) An expression of social dominance or affirmation of superiority;
   (e) Relative diversity or lack of diversity in society;
   (f) Historical time period and place; and
   (g) Escalating commitments, i.e. a situational process of increasing radicalization of conduct.
(4) Idealism, such as:
   (a) Belief in an ideology or mission that transcends self;
   (b) Belief that correctness of cause justifies any means necessary; and
   (c) Cognitive simplicity, a willingness to think primarily in us vs. them dichotomies.
(5) Self-interest, such as:
   (a) Career advancement;
   (b) Self-enrichment;
   (c) Self-preservation; and
   (d) Opportunity for "unpunished inhumanity."
(6) Self-deception, such as:
   (a) The diffusion of responsibility/group absolution (a.k.a. the Banality of Evil argument: I was a mere cog in the machine);
   (b) Repression of conscience; and
   (c) Legal absolution from punishment.

Yet what has not been fully examined is how the acts of mass killing contributed to the ways in which German soldiers, police, and militia members experienced a broadened notion of equality and opportunity as members of the *Volksgemeinschaft.* Many scholars have begun to scratch at the surface, paying particular attention to the role that plunder played in stimulating support for the Nazis' genocidal campaign. Historian Omer Bartov, for example, proposed that the Nazi war machine brought a process of "festive enrichment and socioeconomic improvement" with it through Eastern Europe, and he describes genocide as "a mechanism for social mobility."[54] Historians Christian Gerlach, Frank Bajohr, and Götz Aly have reached similar conclusions.[55] Gerlach documents the widespread looting practiced by German soldiers, primarily as an official function, noting specifically that this forced redistribution was not merely confined to the Nazi elite.[56] Bajohr indicts the *Wehrmacht,* police, and occupation apparatus for their involvement in the plunder of Jews and others and the corrupt system for the distribution of stolen goods. This corruption further caused radicalization of policy and action because it encouraged a "growing circle of beneficiaries with a strong personal interest in never becoming liable to recourse" to kill to cover their tracks. In other words, corruption, plunder, and killing created an equality of opportunity and an equality of guilt.[57]

A recent study of secret recordings of German prisoners of war provides the most compelling evidence for my contention regarding *equality through social practice.* In their book, *Soldaten,* Sönke Neitzel and Harald Welzer note that entering the *Wehrmacht* or the SS marked a fundamental transition for individuals, one in which men lost "control over the enactment of their own identities." These institutions, which they describe as "total institutions," "establish(ed) a specific form of socialization in which group norms and responsibilities have far more influence on individuals than under normal social conditions."[58] Yet it was more than small group dynamics and institutional culture that changed behaviors. "Integration proceeded by maintaining difference," they maintain.

> Once the theory (of the master race) was cast in laws and regulations, even the lowest unskilled laborer could feel superior to a Jewish writer, actor, or businessman.... The resulting boost to the self-esteem of member of the *Volk* was reinforced by a reduced sense of social anxiety. It was a new and unfamiliar feeling to belong, inalienably and by law, to an exclusive racial elite.... The National Socialist project did not just promise a gloriously envisioned future. It offered concrete advantages in the present such as better career opportunities in all areas, including in the *Wehrmacht.*[59]

Superiority, I propose, was socially constructed through the active mistreatment of "inferiors": Jews, Slavs, Roma, Sinti, etc. The acts perpetrated against these groups created cohesion among the privileged Germans, binding them together, creating a sense of equality among the perpetrators. "At the beginning everybody was happy to be a soldier. They felt like members of the master race. 'I'm a soldier. Nobody can do anything to me!' And so on. Whenever soldiers were on leave, they strutted around as if they were terribly important."[60] This was, however, a qualitatively different sense of importance than they had experienced in peacetime. They were now empowered by an equality grounded on the social practice of impunity.

In war, social ties and a shared feeling of duty are a major influence on the behavior of fighting men.[61] For members of the *Wehrmacht*, camaraderie, or esprit de corps, served as a powerful bond that provided security, dependability, support, and recognition.[62] However, such power can easily become destructive. The camaraderie and obedience experienced by the soldiers and killers of the *Wehrmacht* and SS did not cause them to forfeit all agency. In fact, they retained a "small measure of freedom of action."[63] They did not just follow orders. They used this freedom, an equality defined by impunity, to practice excessive, savage violence.

Impunity was not simply the effect of years of propaganda and internalization of the idea of the *Volksgemeinschaft*. It was sanctioned by German leaders who lifted legal and moral restraints through a series of directives and orders. When the *Wehrmacht* was in the midst of its final preparations for the invasion of the Soviet Union in May 1941, Field Marshal Wilhelm Keitel issued what became known as the Barbarossa Decree. Based on guidance from Adolf Hitler delivered months before, this decree made it clear that military courts would not have jurisdiction for assassinations, and that summary judgment by all members of the Armed Forces against enemies—defined as combatants or partisans—was permissible. In other words, crimes against humanity committed by soldiers against Red Army soldiers, Soviet citizens, and prisoners of war were to be exempted from prosecution.[64] The Armed Forces High Command [*Oberkommando des Wehrmacht*] also issued "Directives for the Behavior of the Troops in Russia." Known as the Commissar Order, dated May 19, 1941, its second point was both forthright and harsh: "This struggle requires ruthless and energetic action against Bolshevik agitators, guerillas, saboteurs, and Jews, and the total elimination of all active or passive resistance."[65] The blanket directive to end all forms of resistance, coupled with incendiary language directed at all "Asiatic soldiers of the Red Army," essentially gave German soldiers free rein. An order issued on May 2 by General Hoeppner, commander of the 4th Panzer Group, stated unequivocally that "this war must have as its goal the destruction of today's Russia and for this reason it must be conducted with unheard-of harshness. Every clash must, in its conception and execution, be guided by the iron will to completely and mercilessly annihilate the enemy."[66]

On August 10, 1941, two months after the invasion of the USSR, 6th Army Commander Walther von Reichenau issued an order which declared that the

The Reichenau Order, 10 October 1941

RE: Conduct of the troops in the East

In many instances, confusion still prevails regarding the conduct of the troops in their dealings with the Bolshevist system. The primary goal of the campaign against the Jewish-Bolshevist system is the absolute destruction of the means of power and the eradication of Asian influence in the European cultural sphere. As a result, tasks arise for the troops that transcend traditional one-dimensional soldiership.

The soldier in the East is not only a fighter according to the rules of the art of waging war, but also the bearer of the inexorable *völkische* concept and the avenger of all the bestialities that were visited on the Germans…Therefore, the soldier must fully understand the necessity for severe but just atonement by the Jewish subhumanity. This has the further goal of nipping in the bud uprisings to the rear of the *Wehrmacht*, which, as experience shows, are always instigated by Jews…

The soldier has two tasks to fulfill, far removed from all political considerations about the future:

1) Utter destruction of Bolshevist heresy, of the Soviet state and its war machine;

2) The merciless extermination of foreign cunning and cruelty, thereby securing the life of the German *Wehrmacht* in Russia. This is the only way we can live up to our historic task of liberating the German people once and for all from the Asiatic-Jewish peril.

Figure 3.4 "The Reichenau Order, approved by Hitler." Translation courtesy of the United States Holocaust Memorial Museum, Levine Institute for Holocaust Education.

"necessary execution of criminal, Bolshevist, and mainly Jewish elements would have to be carried out."[67] 11th Army Commander Erich von Manstein and 17th Army Commander Karl-Heinrich von Stülpnagel both issued similar orders justifying deadly attacks on Jews and Communists. Not to be outdone, Reichenau issued a more forceful order in October which Hitler immediately decided should be circulated throughout the Army (fig. 3.4):

For soldiers fighting in the East, these official directives both authorized and encouraged atrocity. Distinguishing between combatants and the innocent is a time-honored ethical principle of warfare, but the German Army's authorized disregard for any norms, laws, and traditions of war made the eastward expansion both illegal and immoral. To be identified as "racially inferior," "primitive," "treacherous," and "inhuman hordes" excluded Jews and Slavs from any form of sympathetic or humane consideration. Yet exclusion and integration were two sides of the same coin, and thus the Nazi denigration of Jews and Slavs, whether combatants or not, became psychologically appealing and emotionally attractive to many German soldiers, binding them together.[68] In his study of how Germans became Nazis, Peter Fritzsche found that "many Wehrmacht soldiers felt drawn to the killing operations … standing around as spectators, taking photographs, and volunteering to be shooters."[69] The result was that soldiers and officers of varied ranks took part in executions.[70] Those who participated, regardless of rank, drank together, dined together, and mixed in a way that erased socioeconomic difference, producing a profound and unprecedented sense of equality.[71] Leaders of the *Wehrmacht* realized this, and even before the invasion of Russia, they created environments and issued orders purposely designed to inflame killing passions and encourage further separation between Germans and others. Soldiers reported that in Poland they were excused from duty so they could attend SS organized public executions. Neitzel and Welzer conclude that these allowances were regular practice, and that "the executions were accompanied by a ritual of humiliation designed especially for the occasion."[72] They based these inferences on hundreds of examples, including the remarks of a *Wehrmacht* officer named Wehner who casually remarked, "When I meet a Jew I could shoot him out of hand. The number of Jews we killed in Poland. We did them in mercilessly."[73] Soldiers justified killing simply because they perceived their victims to be "cheeky" or because they walked on the wrong side of the street or had materials a soldier coveted.[74] In a shared impunity, they discovered a form of equality they had never before imagined: the power to decide between life and death.

Marcel Reich-Ranicki, a German Jew deported to Poland, witnessed how this power was exercised by

> German soldiers robbing, humiliating, and murdering Jews—and having fun "hunting down the Jews.... Any German who wore a uniform and had a weapon could do whatever he wished with a Jew in Warsaw. He could compel him to sing or to dance or to shit in his trousers, or go down on his knees and beg for his life. He could suddenly shoot him dead or kill him in a slower, more torturous manner. He could order a Jewish woman to undress, to clean the street with her underwear and then, in front of everybody, to urinate. There was no one to spoil the fun of those German troops, no one to stop them from maltreating Jews."[75]

This maltreatment included exploiting forced laborers, particularly Jews, as sex slaves. Numerous Ukrainians interviewed by Father Patrick Desbois attest to this. Anna Dychkant of Busk, Ukraine, reported that beautiful girls "weren't killed straight away. (One named) Silva had to live with the German commander. The other girls waited on the other soldiers. When the girls got pregnant, they were killed."[76] Neitzel and Welzer cite a recorded prison camp conversation between two German POWs, Helmut Hartlelt, a 23 year-old mechanic, and Horst Minnieur, a 21 year-old sailor, in which both assume they and other soldiers had the right to have their sexual desires satisfied by forced laborers, and acknowledge there was a practice of shooting Jewish women after sex. It was, for the soldiers, "as though some sort of higher power had preordained that select people ...—*had* to become victims."[77]

According to Lower, Army Commanders in Ukraine during 1941 played a major role in overseeing the killing of Jews, forced labor, and the appropriation of Jewish property.[78] Actions taken by the *Wehrmacht* occupation authority included:

- Use of troops to mark Jewish property;[79]
- Army involvement in mass killing operations, ostensibly as retaliation.[80] 300,000 Jews were murdered during the *Wehrmacht* administration of Ukraine. Wehrmacht propaganda units "broadcast anti-Semitic declarations and turned some executions into public spectacles";[81]
- *Wehrmacht* registration of Jews, marking and expropriation of Jewish property, and collection of arbitrary taxes;
- *Wehrmacht* allowance for "Ukrainian and *Volksdeutsche* auxiliaries, German railroad workers, postal employees, construction foremen, foresters, and other local recruits" to be involved in "genocidal hunts for Jews" which became "a bloodthirsty sport."[82]

Neither was atrocious mistreatment and murder reserved solely for Jews. The *Wehrmacht* encouraged its men to kill surrendering Soviet soldiers on the spot. "Wehrmacht leadership had practically given those detailed to guard the Soviet prisoners *carte blanche* to use their weapons at will."[83] If they were not shot in the act of surrendering, these men (and some women) were likely to perish in the makeshift POW camps to which they were sent, where Soviet prisoners died by the millions through shootings, exposure, and starvation.[84]

The *Wehrmacht's* treatment of its "enemies" in the East, be they Poles, Jews, or Soviet POWs, tells us much about how Nazi soldiers experienced equality. While certainly there were stories of large numbers of German soldiers and officers repulsed by the business of mass killing, the *Wehrmacht* and many of its soldiers were clearly invested in a war of annihilation and expropriation. Antisemitism was widespread within the German army, from draftees to general officers, although it was not universal.[85] Stephen Fritz and Omer Bartov, as well as other scholars, fundamentally agree that the "mentality of Germany's military elite … hardly varied from that of the Führer" on issues of expansion and the need for a "war of annihilation, within which the destruction of the Jews played a key role."[86] Historian Peter Longerich has established that in the East there existed a very

> high degree of cooperation between the Wehrmacht on the one hand and the Police and the SS on the other … units of the Wehrmacht supported mass shootings by the Police and the SS in a variety of ways, such as providing transport and munitions, for example. Members of the Wehrmacht took part directly in these "operations," either sealing off the areas in which they took place or joining the firing squads themselves.[87]

Eventually, the very fact of widespread voluntary assistance by *Wehrmacht* soldiers became a concern for some commanders. That they issued numerous orders to stop such volunteering is evidence that the Army's involvement in mass killings had become a norm, part of the "everyday reality of war."[88] The secret recordings of German POWs show that soldiers and officers through the rank of general were not afraid to boast of their inhumanity to others. Further, these atrocities rarely evoked outrage or criticism, suggesting that "such stories and not the humane ones, reflected the normal everyday reality of World War II."[89]

This appalling episode in human history teaches us to avoid superficial assumptions about the nature of equality. It teaches us to confront what potentially lies beyond laws and philosophical theories when the concept of equality is applied to policy and becomes palpable in lived experience. There is no guarantee that equality, taken as an ideal to be translated into social practice, will be preserved and not distorted, or even perverted. Thanks to the Nazi regime's program that upheld a racial interpretation of *Volksgemeinschaft*, the very idea of equality became sinister and murderous. For many Germans, especially women and soldiers, the Nazi notion of equality offered unprecedented opportunity for enrichment, advancement, status, and power. For these Germans, equality depended for its realization on inequality, on the marginalization, mistreatment, theft, and disenfranchisement of both Jews and other "suspect" races within Germany. With the onset of war, the concept of equality assumed a pernicious new form. Social mobility by means of plunder now became possible for millions of *true* Germans. Equality among the *Volk* brought with it an unquestioned entitlement to superiority, which thus permitted the torture, rape, and murder of those declared to be inferior. And worst of all, when equality was experienced as conferring impunity, the concept metastasized into the ghastly freedom to commit genocide.

NOTES

1. PFC Müller, *Wehrmacht*, quoted in Sönke Neitzel and Harald Welzer, *Soldaten: On Fighting, Killing and Dying, The Secret WWII Transcripts of German POWs*, trans. Jefferson Chase (New York: Alfred A. Knopf, 2012), 81.

2. Andreas Reckwitz, "Towards a Theory of Social Practices: A Development in Culturalist Theorizing," *European Journal of Social Theory* 5, no. 2 (2002): 249.

3. Elizabeth Shove, Mika Pantzar, and Matt Watson, *The Dynamics of Social Practice: Everyday Life and How It Changes* (London: Sage, 2012), 3.

4. Theodore R. Schatzki, *Social Practices: A Wittgensteinian Approach to Human Activity and the Social* (Cambridge: Cambridge University Press, 1996), 89.

5. David Schoenbaum, *Hitler's Social Revolution: Class and Status in Nazi Germany, 1933-1939* (1966; New York: W. W. Norton, 1980), 55. Schoenbaum continued "[The Nazi] campaign for egalitarianism intended not so much to change class relations, a function of profession and education, as to change status, self-image, the state of mind."

6. Timothy Snyder, *Black Earth: The Holocaust as History and Warning* (New York: Tim Duggan Books, 2015), 4-5. Snyder claims that Hitler thought of Jews as a non-race, an unnatural group who resisted the laws of nature and who sought to conquer through corrupting the behaviors of races, causing degeneracy.

7. Dan Stone, *Histories of the Holocaust* (Oxford: Oxford University Press, 2010), 263.

8. *Michael Wildt,* Hitler's Volksgemeinschaft and the Dynamics of Racial Exclusion: Violence against Jews in Provincial Germany, 1919–1939 (New York: Berghahn Books; Jerusalem: Yad Vashem, 2012), 272.

9. Peter Fritzsche, *Life and Death in the Third Reich* (Cambridge, MA: Harvard University Press, 2009), 39.

10. Frank Bajohr, "Mass Murder and Community Building," *German History* 30, no. 1 (2012): 122.

11. Alfons Heck, quoted in Christopher J. Powell, "Genocidal Moralities: A Critique," in *New Directions in Genocide Research*, ed. Adam Jones (London and New York: Routledge, 2012), 46.

12. See, for example, Michael Burleigh and Wolfgang Wippermann, *The Racial State: Germany, 1933-1945* (1991; Cambridge: Cambridge University Press, 2003), 44-51, 80-96; Peter Longerich, *The Holocaust: Nazi Persecution and Murder of the Jews* (New York: Oxford University Press, 2010), 52-93; and Peter Hays, *Why? Explaining the Holocaust* (New York: W. W. Norton, 2017), 81.

13. Burleigh and Wippermann, *Racial State*, 84.

14. Wendy Lower, *Hitler's Furies: German Women in the Nazi Killing Fields* (Boston and New York: Houghton Mifflin Harcourt, 2015), 27.

15. Alon Confino, *A World Without Jews: The Nazi Imagination from Persecution to Genocide* (New Haven, CT: Yale University Press, 2014), 110.

16. Burleigh and Wippermann, *Racial State*, 51-59.

17. Fritzsche, *Life and Death in the Third Reich*, 51.

18. Götz Aly, *Hitler's Beneficiaries: Plunder, Racial War, and the Nazi Welfare State*, trans. Jefferson S. Chase (New York: Metropolitan Books, 2006), 26.

19. Franz Janka, *Die braune Gesellschaft: Ein Volk wird formatiert* [*The Brown Society: A People Is Created*] (Stuttgart: Quell, 1997), 360-64, cited in Stone, *Histories of the Holocaust*, 263-64.

20. Raul Caruso, "Identity and Incentives: An Economic Interpretation of the Holocaust," in *Economic Aspects of Genocides, Other Mass Atrocities, and Their Prevention*, ed. Charles H. Anderton and Jurgen Brauer (Oxford: Oxford University Press, 2016), 319.

21. Aly, *Hitler's Beneficiaries*, 13. Christian Gerlach echoes this claim in *The Extermination of the European Jews* (Cambridge: Cambridge University Press, 2016), 350.

22. Hans Dieter Schäfer, *Das gespaltene Bewusstsein: Vom Dritten Reich bis zu den langen fünfziger Jahren* [*The Divided Consciousness: From the Third Reich to the Long Fifties*] (Gottingen: Wallstein, 2009), 18.

23. Schoenbaum, *Hitler's Social Revolution*, 111; Helga Schmidt, "There Was Never Any Particular Sympathy for the Jews," in *What We Knew: Terror, Mass*

Murder, and Everyday Life in Nazi Germany, An Oral History, ed. Eric A. Johnson and Karl-Heinz Reuband, (Cambridge, MA: Basic Books, 2005), 177.

24. Neitzel and Welzer, *Soldaten*, 33.

25. Fritzsche, *Life and Death in the Third Reich*, 61.

26. David Welch, "Nazi Propaganda and the *Volksgemeinschaft:* Constructing a People's Community," *Journal of Contemporary History* 39, no. 2 (April 2004): 219.

27. Birthe Kundrus, "Greasing the Palm of the *Volksgemeinschaft?* Consumption under National Socialism," in *Visions of Community in Nazi Germany: Social Engineering and Private Lives*, ed. Martha Steber and Bernhard Gotto (Oxford: Oxford University Press, 2014), 157.

28. Gerlach, *Extermination of the European Jews*, 269ff. Gerlach also points out that Hitler bragged on multiple occasions that his program had provided social mobility by forcing Jews to vacate "hundreds of thousands of jobs" which meant that an equal number of "children of proletarians and farmers will be able to rise into these positions" (ibid., 281).

29. Neitzel and Welzer, *Soldaten*, 33.

30. Fritzsche, *Life and Death in the Third Reich*, 64. David Cesarani further explains how asset appropriation fed this process. "As the pace of Aryanization accelerated, even Germans who had looked askance at the violation of property rights felt compelled to join the gold rush or see rivals prosper" (*Final Solution: The Fate of the Jews 1933-1949* [New York: St. Martin's Press, 2016], 135).

31. Aly, *Hitler's Beneficiaries*, 30. The Nazis saw shared work projects as critical elements of creating *Verkameradschaftung* [comradeship] and *Volkwerdung* [building the people].

32. Peter Longerich, *Politik der Vernichtung: Eine Gesamtdarstellung der nationalsozialistischen Judenverfolgung* [*The Politics of Annihilation: An Overview of National Socialist Persecution of the Jews*] (Munich: Piper Verlag, 1998), 578, quoted in *Soldaten*, by Neitzel and Welzer, 30-31; see also Longerich, *Holocaust*.

33. Confino, *World without Jews*, 99.

34. Social Democrats, quoted in Aly, *Hitler's Beneficiaries*, 322n19.

35. Gudrun Schwartz, "'During Total War, We Girls Want to be Where We Can Really Accomplish Something': What Women Do in Wartime," in *Crimes of War: Guilt and Denial in the Twentieth Century*, ed. Omer Bartov, Anita Grossmann, and Mary Nolan (New York: New Press, 2002), 124.

36. Ibid., 124-25.

37. Ibid., 125. This sort of sense of belonging, empowerment, camaraderie, and even civic involvement was also felt by women who joined the Ku Klux Klan. See Kathleen M. Blee, *Women of the Klan: Racism and Gender in the 1920s* (Berkeley: University of California Press, 2009), 24-25, 36, 118-23, 128.

38. Schwartz, "During Total War," 125.

39. Ibid., 125-26.

40. Ibid., 126-27; Lower, *Hitler's Furies*, 55.

41. Schwartz, "During Total War," 128.

42. Saul Friedländer, "The Wehrmacht, German Society, and the Knowledge of Mass Extermination of the Jews," in *Crimes of War: Guilt and Denial in the*

Twentieth Century, ed. Omer Bartov, Anita Grossmann, and Mary Nolan (New York: New Press, 2002), 27-28.

43. Melita Maschmann, *Fazit: Mein Weg in der Hitler-Jugend* [*Upshot: My Journey in the Hitler Youth*] (Munich: Deutscher Taschenbuch-Verlag, 1981), cited in Stone, *Histories of the Holocaust*, 263.

44. Schwartz, "During Total War," 128.

45. Ibid.

46. Ibid., 128-29.

47. Ibid., 129.

48. Ibid., 131; see also Jill Stephenson, *Women in Nazi Germany* (London and New York: Routledge, 2013), 112, 128; Lower, *Hitler's Furies*, 166.

49. Lower, *Hitler's Furies*, 62.

50. Ibid., 22.

51. Thomas Kühne, *Belonging and Genocide: Hitler's Community, 1918-1945* (New Haven, CT: Yale University Press, 2010), 148.

52. Erna Petri, quoted in Lower, *Hitler's Furies*, 155.

53. This list was assembled from a range of readings and discussions. Some fundamental and useful texts on the psychology of perpetration, particularly German perpetration, include: Erik Erikson, "Hitler's Imagery and German Youth," *Psychiatry* 5, no. 4 (1942): 475-93; Stanley Milgram, *Obedience to Authority* (New York: Harper and Row, 1974); Christopher R. Browning, *Ordinary Men: Reserve Police Battalion 101 and the Final Solution in Poland* (New York: Harper Perennial, 1998); George C. Browder, "Perpetrator Character and Motivation: An Emerging Consensus?" *Holocaust and Genocide Studies* 17, no. 3 (Winter 2003): 480-97; James Waller, *Becoming Evil: How Ordinary People Commit Genocide and Mass Killing*, 2nd ed. (Oxford: Oxford University Press, 2007); Daniel Chirot and Clark McCauley, *Why Not Kill Them All? The Logic and Prevention of Mass Political Murder* (Princeton, NJ: Princeton University Press, 2006); Harald Welzer, "On Killing and Morality: How Normal People Become Mass Murderers," in *Ordinary People as Mass Murderers: Perpetrators in Comparative Perspective*, ed. Olaf Jensen and Claus-Christian W. Szejnmann (Basingstoke: Palgrave, 2008), 165-81; Dave Grossman, *On Killing: The Psychological Cost of Learning to Kill in War and Society*. rev. ed. (New York: Back Bay Books, 2009); Ervin Staub, *Overcoming Evil: Genocide, Violent Conflict, and Terrorism* (Oxford: Oxford University Press, 2011); Richard Overy, "'Ordinary Men,' Extraordinary Circumstances: Historians, Social Psychology, and the Holocaust," *Journal of Social Issues* 70, no. 3 (2014): 515-30; and Albert Bandura, *Moral Disengagement: How People Do Harm and Live with Themselves* (New York: Worth, 2016).

54. Omer Bartov, "Eastern Europe as the Site of Genocide," *Journal of Modern History* 80, no. 3 (September 2008): 576.

55. Frank Bajohr, "The Holocaust and Corruption," in *Networks of Nazi Persecution: Bureaucracy, Business, and the Organization of the Holocaust*, ed. Gerald D. Feldman and Wolfgang Seibel (New York: Berghahn Books, 2006), 127; In his introduction, Aly notes "The Nazi leadership established a framework for directly sharing the spoils of its military victories with the majority of Germans—the profits derived

from crippling the economies of occupied and dependent countries, the exploitation of work performed by forced laborers, the confiscated property of murdered Jews, and the deliberate starvation of millions of people, most notably in the Soviet Union. Those benefits, in turn, made the recipients amenable to Nazi propaganda and gave them a vested interest in the Third Reich" (Aly, *Hitler's Beneficiaries*, 4).

56. Gerlach, *Extermination of the European Jews*, 276ff.

57. Bajohr, "Holocaust and Corruption," 125. Bajohr gives the example of how *Wehrmacht* occupation authorities in Serbia seized and sold off confiscated goods "at dumping prices to Wehrmacht members, who in part used this opportunity to literally make bulk purchases" which they sent home to family and friends (ibid., 130).

58. Neitzel and Welzer, *Soldaten*, 16.

59. Ibid., 29, 32.

60. Erwin Hammel, "They Felt Like Members of the Master Race," in *What We Knew: Terror, Mass Murder, and Everyday Life in Nazi Germany, An Oral History*, ed. Eric A. Johnson and Karl-Heinz Reuband, (Cambridge, MA: Basic Books, 2005), 166.

61. Neitzel and Welzer, *Soldaten*, 21.

62. Ibid., 22.

63. Ibid., 20.

64. Jürgen Förster, "The Wehrmacht and the War of Extermination against the Soviet Union," *Yad Vashem Studies* 14 (1987): 402-519, https://www.yadvashem.org /untoldstories/documents/studies/Jurgen_Forster.pdf (14).

65. Translation of original document provided to author by United States Holocaust Memorial Museum.

66. Translation of original document provided to author by United States Holocaust Memorial Museum.

67. Quoted in Longerich, *Holocaust*, 242.

68. Neitzel and Welzer, *Soldaten*, 32-33.

69. Fritzsche, *Life and Death in the Third Reich*, 200.

70. Neitzel and Welzer, *Soldaten*, 136.

71. Dr. Edward Westermann, discussion with author, West Point, New York, March 8, 2017.

72. Neitzel and Welzer, *Soldaten*, 81.

73. Ibid., 229.

74. Peter Longerich, "From Mass Murder to the 'Final Solution': The Shooting of Jewish Civilians during the First Months of the Eastern Campaign within the Context of the Nazi Jewish Genocide," in *The Holocaust. A Reader*, ed. Simone Gigliotti and Berel Lang (Malden, MA: Blackwell Publishing, 2005), 206; and the story of Gerhard M. in *Amateur Photographer* (2004), dir. Irina Gedrovich, pro. Efim Reznikov and Olesya Buryachenko (Granat Studio Cinematography Service, Russian Ministry of Culture).

75. Marcel Reich-Ranicki, quoted in Kühne, *Belonging and Genocide*, 102.

76. Anna Dychkant, quoted in Father Patrick Desbois, *The Holocaust by Bullets* (New York: Palgrave Macmillan, 2008), 126.

77. Neitzel and Welzer, *Soldaten*, 118; emphasis in the original. For more on involvement of the *Wehrmacht* in raping, pillaging, and plundering, see *Nazi Policy on the Eastern Front, 1941: Total War, Genocide, and Radicalization*, ed. Alex J. Kay, Jeff Rutherford, and David Stahel (New York: University of Rochester Press, 2012), 246-52.

78. Wendy Lower, "The 'Reibungslose' Holocaust? The German Military and Civilian Implementation of the 'Final Solution' in Ukraine, 1941-1944," in *Networks of Nazi Persecution: Bureaucracy, Business, and the Organization of the Holocaust*, ed. Gerald D. Feldman and Wolfgang Seibel (New York: Berghahn Books, 2006), 237.

79. Ibid., 238.

80. Ibid., 239.

81. Ibid., 245. See also Daniel Uziel, *The Propaganda Warriors: The Wehrmacht and the Consolidation of the German Home Front* (Oxford: Peter Lang, 2008), 108; and Daniel Utzig, "Wehrmacht Propaganda Troops and the Jews," trans. William Templer, *Yad Vashem Studies* 29 (2001): 29-65, http://www.yadvashem.org/odot_pdf/microsoft%20word%20-%202021.pdf, 11.

82. Lower, "'Reibungslose' Holocaust?" 249.

83. Longerich, *Holocaust*, 249.

84. Ibid., 248.

85. Jeremy Black, *The Holocaust. History & Memory* (Bloomington: Indiana University Press, 2016), 50.

86. Stephen G. Fritz, *Ostkrieg: Hitler's War of Extermination in the East* (Lexington: University of Kentucky Press, 2011), 70; Omer Bartov, "Savage War: German Warfare and Moral Choices in World War II," in *The Holocaust: A Reader*, ed. Simone Gigliotti and Berel Lang (Malden, MA: Blackwell Publishing, 2005), 222.

87. Longerich, *Holocaust*, 243.

88. Ibid., 243.

89. Neitzel and Welzer, *Soldaten*, 95, 143. The authors write "…it was very unusual for soldiers to feel repulsed (by mass executions) out of *principle*. Even more rare [*sic*] were instances in which first- or secondhand knowledge of brutality prompted soldiers to reflect on the moral character of the war" (ibid., 143).

Chapter 4

Social Inequality and the United States Army

The (Un)lucky Seven

Morten G. Ender and Betsy Lucal

On any given day, print, broadcast and social media feature news items related to social inequality and diversity. More often than not, they touch on seven significant inequalities in US society: (1) race and ethnicity, (2) sex and gender, (3) socio-economic class, (4) sexuality, (5) physical ability, (6) age, and (7) religious affiliation. Consider some possible examples: the *New York Times* reports on the latest US Census data about income, wealth, and poverty; a *Wall Street Journal* editorial focuses on same-sex marriage; MSNBC's scrolling news feed includes a Supreme Court decision on affirmative action; the *Huffington Post* headlines new legislation that affects senior citizens; *Mother Jones* highlights the "first woman" to accomplish some extraordinary feat; National Public Radio covers the latest terrorist bombings by religious fundamentalists; FOX News does an exposé on the plights faced by disabled travelers seeking accessible airline seats; and *Duffelblog* satirizes the Pentagon's response to Generation Z. These seven issues permeate the local and national news media cycle. The same issues are prevalent in the US Army.[1]

In 1877, seventy-five years after the establishment of West Point, Henry O. Flipper became the first African American to graduate from the United States Military Academy. Rejected by his fellow white cadets, which included being silenced for his entire four years, Flipper endured and became one of the first African American officers to command US troops.[2] Despite progress, racial inequality and institutional racism persists in the US Army, specifically with regard to promotion rates and access to veterans' care.[3] Hateful examples exist as well. In May 2016, sixteen African American, female West Point cadets posed for a celebratory pregraduation photograph, and the images—one showing fists raised—went viral. Significant online comments praised their accomplishments. An equal number demanded their expulsion, many accompanied with extreme racist, sexist, vile, and vitriolic commentary.[4]

As the US Congress and the larger society debated the role of women in combat, Leigh Ann Hester, a Sergeant in the Kentucky National Guard serving in Iraq, became the first US woman since World War II to earn a Silver Star for gallantry in combat, the nation's third-highest medal for valor in the face of the enemy. US Army Specialist Monica Lin Brown, who served in Afghanistan in 2007, also received this medal.[5] In fact, thousands of US women have served in Iraq and Afghanistan, hundreds of them wounded or killed. The first Female Engagement Teams deployed in April 2010 in Afghanistan. These comprised four- and five-member units who teamed with all-male patrols in order to engage Afghani women, who are culturally off limits to men, especially to foreign men.[6] On January 24, 2013, US Army policy began to allow women to serve alongside male counterparts in combat arms units below brigade levels. A cluster of women have now graduated from the rigorous and previously all-male Army Ranger School at Fort Benning, Georgia.

Hope Unseen tells the story of Captain Scott Smiley, the US Army's first blind active-duty officer.[7] Since serving in Iraq, where he lost his eyesight in a suicide bombing, Captain Smiley earned an MBA at Duke University, taught at West Point, and served as the Army's first blind Company Commander.[8] Similarly, in the spring of 2003 in Iraq, an antitank mine blew off Major David Rozelle's foot and part of his leg. MAJ Rozelle became one of the first officers with an artificial leg and foot to rejoin his unit, resume command, and return to combat.[9] Thus, advanced prosthetics, determination, and sheer will, along with steady institutional and social support, have enabled both CPT Smiley, MAJ Rozelle, and other US military personnel with physical impairments to stay in uniform, return to active duty, and maintain quality of life in their chosen profession.

In September 1862, Charles "Charley" King became (and remains) the youngest US soldier to die in combat. He was twelve years old and served as a drummer boy in the Battle of Antietam.[10] Today, eighteen years of age is the youngest age for enlistment, although those aged seventeen years can join any branch of the US military with parental consent. Notably, the voting age for young adults was lowered from twenty-one to eighteen years of age in 1971, the impetus being that young men were drafted to serve in Vietnam at eighteen years old but were prohibited to vote on matters affecting their destiny until they reached twenty-one years of age. At the other end of the spectrum, the US Army increased the age of first enlistment from forty to forty-two years of age in 2006. Lieutenant General Robert L. Caslen, Jr., born in 1953, continued to serve nobly through his retirement 2018 and even made the short list as President Trump's National Security Advisor.[11]

Although religious freedom and tolerance are held aloft as ideal in US society, expressions of religious intolerance are not uncommon in its history, though much less so in the US Army. Muslim Americans have a rich tradition of serving the country, and many volunteered to fight after the terrorists' attack on 9/11.[12] The US military now recognizes more than eighty different denominations and sects and allows for thirty-nine different grave markers, headstones, and memorial plaques. The most recent addition followed a nine-year court case that was filed by the family members of a Wiccan service member killed in Iraq; they were seeking a federally provided Wiccan faith headstone for the soldier.[13]

What about social class? With the creation of an all-volunteer force in 1973, which replaced the policy of educational deferments available during the Vietnam War, the working class has disproportionately served in the US armed forces. During the 1990s, a significant concern grew that members of the US population, especially the upper-middle socio-economic class and elites would continue to avoid service in significant numbers. Some noted that fewer members of the US Congress had military experience, making them less cautious about putting US service member in harm's way. Popular press in the 2000s continued to argue that higher social classes and elites avoided service.[14] While elites seem historically to avoid military service, the US military however appears fairly representative of the social class distribution of the United States. For example, US service member fatalities in Iraq appear to correspond to the social class and other demographic distributions of the US population.[15] Of special note, three of the four candidates in 2008 for President or Vice President had children in the military who were serving in Iraq or Afghanistan (former Vice President Joseph Biden, Senator John McCain, and former Alaska Governor Sarah Palin—the Obama children were under 18 at the time). Further, Harvard University and other Ivy League schools are restoring ROTC on their campuses following the repeal of Don't Ask, Don't Tell (DADT) policy on September 20, 2011, a discriminatory policy prohibiting gays, lesbians, and bisexuals from serving openly in the military. Vietnam War protests in 1969 had provided the impetus for closing Harvard's ROTC program.[16]

Former West Point cadet Katie Miller is perhaps the face of the repeal of DADT. Miller self-identified publically as a lesbian while a sophomore at West Point in 2010. While others have come out either during or after their military service, Miller uncharacteristically appeared in uniform as an openly homosexual cadet in contravention of DADT.[17] She subsequently resigned her appointment to the US Military Academy despite having compiled a highly successful record, which placed her in the top one percent of her class. She appeared on the MSNBC television news program the *Rachel Maddow Show* in August 2010 and in early September attended the MTV Video Music

Awards as a guest of Lady Gaga. On December 22, 2010, President Barack Obama signed into law the *Don't Ask, Don't Tell Repeal Act of 2010*.[18] The law, instituted on September 20, 2011, established a process for repealing the original *Don't Ask, Don't Tell* directive which had been signed December 21, 1993 by President Bill Clinton.[19] The policy had been intended as a compromise to protect closeted homosexuals from harassment and involuntary discharge. However, the effect was to create *de facto* inequality between open heterosexuals and closeted gay, lesbian, and bisexual service members. The repeal of DADT allowed LGB service members to serve openly (but did not include a "T" for transgender military members).

The most recent change in policy occurred during the Obama administration when the ban against transgender service members was lifted. The new policy allows transgender service members as of October 1, 2016 to remain in the military and serve openly, with transgender military enlistments scheduled to begin July 1, 2017. However, at this writing and the change of administrations, the policy is liquid. Many months have passed since the initial change in policy,[20] and the US Secretary of Defense had granted a six-month extension for a review of the latter component.[21] The United States could join eighteen other nations that allow open transgender service members to serve their country.[22] As of June 2014, the United States had ranked 37th of 102 nations, behind Romania and Chile, in terms of comparative LGBT policies in their militaries.[23] Should accessions be allowed, the United States is sure to increase its ranking when the index is updated, possibly even reaching the top ten. Yet the topic remains contested terrain, especially under the current Trump administration. Not unlike racial minorities with fifty years of integration behind them, women, LGB and transgender troops can expect an uphill battle for full inclusion.

Because of US military "manpower" needs, the social movements in the military of the seven social groups described above reflect the ongoing citizenship revolution in Western industrialized nations.[24] David Segal has called this one of the major social trends in the United States, a development "reflected both in the growth of industrial democracy and in the extension of citizenship rights to new sectors of the population."[25] These "sectors" are sociodemographic groups specifically associated with the (un)lucky seven. The right to bear arms and to place oneself in harm's way in service to one's newly adopted nation is both a real and symbolic manifestation of loyalty to country and a rite of passage to full citizenship. Segal argues that this connection between the military and citizenship emerged out of the US and French Revolutions and continues down to the present day as traditionally excluded groups seek full citizenship and legitimacy in the eyes of the state.[26] Historically, whites, men, Christians, the young and fit, the upper and middle classes (in command positions), and heterosexuals comprised the "luckiest" of the seven in the military. In the course of US history, non-whites, women, non-Christians, the aged and the young, disabled, underclasses, and sexual and gender minorities—the relatively unlucky counterparts of the seven—have sought full recognition through military service. The military has followed or led US society in creating non-discrimination policies protecting these "sectors." As a result, the US military has become one of the most diverse organizations in US society, which raises the question: How *inclusive* is the new military, relative to this diversity?

UNDERSTANDING INEQUALITY AND THE (UN)LUCKY SEVEN: KEY TERMS

Certain fundamental concepts associated with social inequality, and with diversity more generally, will help sharpen the previous examples of the (un) lucky seven within the US Army. To begin, *social differentiation* refers to the fact that individuals have distinct qualities and characteristics; they differ in social status, the positions they hold in society. This fact is the source of *social diversity*, which can be defined as the variety created in a society by the existence of groups distinguished by differences in social position, point of view, and how they make sense of the world. People see and experience the world differently, at least in part, because they have varied spatio-temporal relations to it. We have no control over where we are born, or in what era. Our birth places us on the luck continuum. You might ask yourself: Which social characteristics are you (un)lucky enough to possess, either individually or combined, and how does it impact your social status?

Attention to diversity or *multiculturalism* is an attempt to recognize, value, understand, and even celebrate differences without elevating one location or point of view above another. When differences are used for the purposes of ranking one individual or group below another, usually in terms of negative *attitudes* toward them, then we have *prejudice*. When unfair social actions directed toward them are based on prejudice, then we have *discrimination*. In contrast, *inclusion* is the result of fair social action. It implies not only bestowing dignity, respect, and inherent worth on people from varied backgrounds but also, pragmatically, leveraging their form of diversity without concentrating exclusively on it (e.g., by the creation of Female Engagement Teams). In this way, diverse people become involved, empowered, promoted, and included in all facets of social life rather than becoming indiscernible—for example, invisible in an "inclusive" organization.[27]

One would hope that folks know that the real culture of the US is not the ideal culture. We strive to be the shining beacon on the hill, but we are not quite there yet. If our national story ended with merely recognizing social differentiation, there would be little more to say. But, for certain social characteristics, these differences are only the beginning. Differences allow us to place people into categories, into boxes.[28] These categories help us make sense of the world. They provide us with ways of organizing information and making decisions about how we act. We could not survive socially without them, as we would be faced constantly with random bits of information and no schema for figuring out how to respond to oceans of information. We interact with people and treat them in particular ways based on the categories in which we think they belong. By placing people into categories based on selected characteristics, we can begin to attach meaning to those characteristics and categories.

It is important to remember that categories are social constructions. In other words, though we often use physical characteristics for deciding which category someone belongs to, the categories themselves are not naturally occurring. We devised them, and then we use them because we believe they are there; they are shared social constructions. Placing people into categories emphasizes commonalities and leads us to overlook any differences among the people within a category. We become aware of this when we encounter cases where a dominant paradigm is subverted: autistic Rhodes Scholar; female high-school footballer; Muslim American soldier; Black female mathematicians; African American First Lady; gay rapper; blond haired, blue-eyed Muslim; elderly marathon runner; Asian male lead in a film with no martial arts; or a female Admiral.

Differences between people can be visible or invisible. When a particular category has been assigned high importance, we are willing to go to great lengths to figure out what grouping to which someone belongs. Physical differences such as skin color are easily discerned, at least in the majority of cases. Other physical differences, such as male versus female genitals, are made visible by other signals and markers, such as the way most women and men dress. But other differences are invisible most of the time. Religious and sexual orientation typically lack markers, they cannot be determined simply by looking. In some cases, age can be deceptive, especially where legal constraints are at work. For example, what features distinguish getting "carded" when purchasing alcohol? In practice it seems, many establishments sidestep the challenge by deciding to obtain age identification verification from everyone asking to be served alcohol. In today's world, social class is by and large not visible, although most US citizens lack class consciousness anyway. Talk shows and reality television are most often about race, gender, and sexuality, and rarely about social class.

Some categories have a particular kind of importance, one in which the members are valued over those in other categories. In other words, the issue here is not diversity itself but rather that some differences have significant kinds of meaning attached to them. This prompts the question: To what degree is a category—social economic class, race or ethnicity, gender, sexuality, religion, (dis)ability, and age—more or less significant?[29] The answer is inevitably complicated, because studying social inequality, diversity, and inclusion requires trying to understand how different forms of inequality relate to one another. After all, no one is *just* a man or *just* Latina/o or *just* heterosexual—all of us experience these seven social categories in a variety of combinations.

For more than two decades scholars have sought to determine the best way to conceptualize and understand these relationships. Are they best viewed as "multiple jeopardy" or as "intersecting oppressions" that exist in a "matrix of domination?"[30] Should we think about them in terms of "doing difference?"[31] How do individuals actually experience these relationships on a day-to-day basis? How do various categories combine with each other to influence peoples' experiences?

Thinking about social inequalities in the context of the areas of social life where they occur can help us make sense of complex relationships. These areas include institutions such as the family, workplace, politics, the mass media, medicine, law, education, and the military. Institutions have a past, present, and future. Language and popular culture force inequality upon us as well. Basically, these (un)lucky seven categories permeate our lives.

But why these seven? First, the (un)lucky seven categories exist because a critical mass of research has documented that these groups do suffer social injustices in US society and, in many cases, around the globe. And, society's military is influenced by the larger society in which it is embedded. While the US military is influenced by the larger society, however, it is not a mirror image of the larger society. Second, social categories are created from differences which come to be evaluated in hierarchical terms. They become categories whose members are ranked and evaluated unequally, creating *social inequality*. When differences are turned into unequal categories, the people in the favored categories end up having unequal access to valuable resources, including material goods, positions, opportunities, and experiences, while some individuals gain disproportionate amounts of wealth, power, and prestige. Groups at the top of the hierarchy get more stuff; they are privileged and advantaged. Groups at the bottom have access to fewer resources; they are socially disadvantaged and often oppressed by those above them. The social structure does not benefit them. Accordingly, those lucky to have been born with the historical and prevailing social characteristics that are privileged—male, white, Christian, fit, youthful, middle-class, and straight—may typically possess advantages unavailable to a Muslim with a disability who is Black, poor, elderly, and lesbian. However, difference by itself is not the problem; it is how we interpret difference that matters in terms of inequality.

In terms of difference, *disadvantaged groups* are defined as "different from" the *advantaged group*. In these contexts, the *privileged group* provides the standard by which other groups are judged. Other groups, sometimes referred to as *Others*, are considered deviant and deficient in comparison with the more powerful group. For example, the old standard on the US Census specified four racial categories, plus the further category of "Some Other Race," but allowed only one category to be picked[32] Today, the post-2000 questionnaire lists six categories, including "Some Other Race"—but, significantly, allows more than one category to be chosen. We see that the government finally "got it," at least partially, when it comes to race and to ethnicity. Within the (un)lucky seven of race and ethnicity, people experienced enough difference to demand multiple categories. In essence, "multiracials" are now no longer "Others." Seeing "them" as different from "us" allows us to justify treating them differently—usually poorly. It allows us to assume that we cannot understand them, and/or that we have nothing in common with them. This attitude, again, is often the basis for *stereotypes*, which are overgeneralizations, often negative, about an individual or group in another category. The generalization captures some characteristics and may have some utility. However, overgeneralization reflects the assumption that *all* members of a group share certain characteristics. Similarly, people are often split up into dichotomous, mutually exclusive groups that are considered as opposites. This process can be seen even when we recognize more than two groups. For example, we are well aware of the existence of many religious groups in the United States. Yet for many people the only meaningful distinction is between Christians and non-Christians—two groups assumed to be extremely different from one another, and where the differences are considered all-important.

The (un)lucky seven social categories provide individuals a basis for understanding our most important *identities*, the ways we see ourselves in relationship to the social world. These categories not only provide other people with clues about how to interact with us and how to expect us to act, they also provide us with a sense of what kind of people we might want to become and to be, and how we are expected to act.

Individuals sometimes lack a strong sense of identity based on these categories; and the salience of their identities often varies across situations. For example, because they are surrounded by men and are serving in units defined as being for men, US Army women serving in Female Engagement Teams are probably much more aware of themselves as women than as a person of a particular social class when they are forward deployed. Similarly, a Jewish soldier may be much more aware of his religion when he hears daily Muslim prayers coming from outside his Forward Operating Base on Fridays as well as Christian services at the base's chapel on Sundays. United States citizens who have travelled outside the United States gain a better appreciation of what it means to be a US citizen, even though they would usually find it difficult to recapture that sense of what "being American" means when they are at home. Experiencing other cultures often provides us with a window through which to see into our own society. We get to view the United States as others see us (and as a minority).

CLOSED AND LOCKED DOORS WITH NO KEYS: SYSTEMATIC INEQUALITY

The *relational model of inequality* prescribes that, for every *privileged* group, there is a corresponding *oppressed* group, and that privilege can exist only where oppression exists (and conversely). It also reminds us that privileged people and groups enjoy advantages only because other people and groups are subordinated and, in many cases, are oppressed.

A *system of oppression and privilege* can be defined as a set of attitudes, behaviors, and social arrangements by which members of one group are excluded and subordinated while others are granted advantages.[33] Structurally, oppression comprises a web of interrelated barriers, boundaries, and limitations, "an enclosing structure of forces and barriers which tend to the immobilization and reduction of a group or category of people."[34] For privileged groups, the social structure is empowering, freeing, and enabling; it provides them with resources for getting things done socially.[35]

For individuals, being located in a privileged position can lead to feelings of *entitlement*, the sense that they deserve the good things they get. Because they do not experience the barriers faced by the oppressed, privileged people may have a difficult time believing such barriers even exist. For individuals located in an oppressed position, the result can be to have feelings of being undeserving or even of futility. Given that the cards are stacked against you, why bother to make the effort to succeed? Negative experiences of this sort can result in a *psychological reactance*, a desire to change the self or to change the structure that is oppressive. Extreme cases of resistance are hate crimes and terrorism. But a healthier collective reaction aims to realize some form of civil justice, and justice for all rather than for a few. Groups advocating on behalf of the (un)lucky seven include Leaders of a Beautiful Struggle (race and ethnicity); Women's Sports Foundation (sex and gender); the Gray Panthers (elderly); SPART*A (LGBT); K9s for Warriors (disabled); Kiva (socio-economic class); and Families Against Cult Teachings (religious affiliation).[36]

Imagine the obstacles confronting oppressed groups as a series of doors that lead toward resources and opportunities. Each time such a person arrives at a door and wants to pass through, what happens next? The door might open easily, but just as easily it might remain firmly closed. The person may not receive any key, yet cannot force it open. Some people might actively block the door. Failure to negotiate one door in the series may make the goal of reaching what lies beyond other doors hopeless. Doors represent choices, often choices to be made alone. Some oppressed people are shown a door but never guided through it or helped to overcome the fear of the unknown on the other side; some are never shown any door at all.

Conversely, members of a privileged group find doors already open, or are handed the keys to get through them. They are likely to have escorts and mentors to guide them, as well as others on the far side ready to welcome them. Some doors may be exceptionally wide, and privileged groups may also have a wide choice of doors. There may not even be a door—simply an archway. Entry is expected and rewarded. Such ease of passage can make it difficult for privileged persons to understand why "others" are not simply making their way forward with all of the resources and opportunities available. After all, US society prides itself on liberty, social mobility, justice, individualism, and its claims that there is equality of opportunity to open the doors. However, not everyone has an equal opportunity to open and pass through doors. This is a fact related not to individual deficiencies or to lack of talents but to structural and real social inequality.

How is social inequality constructed and maintained? We often think of race, gender, and sexuality in terms of individuals with these characteristics: an African American lesbian, for example, or a Latino heterosexual man. Social inequality operates no less at the institutional level. It is built into the structure of society. Ideologies and social institutions tend to maintain the *status quo*, the existing order, which has the effect of preserving social inequality. One of the reasons why social inequality is so pervasive and pernicious is that it is both psychological and sociological: it exists both in our heads, in the form of self-identity, and outside of us in the form of institutions and ideologies.

We find both diversity and inequality operating in all of our social institutions—the family, politics, the economy, education, work, sports, medicine, and the military. In some cases, institutions have explicit policies that both prohibit specific groups and also attempt to be inclusive of others. The US military's DADT was an explicit organizational policy that restricted members of the group from openly revealing their sexual orientation in an institutional context.[37] Other institutions have no explicit policies in place but have cultural practices embedded in them. For example, the aged in US culture can lose their high social status in their own families and become dependent on their children.[38] Even our so-called blind justice system benefits the wealthy.[39] Some claim that the US legal system is becoming a wealth-based criminal justice system because legal resources for the poor have consistently declined while tough-on-crime politicians have promoted increased spending on policing and prisons. In contrast, a college or university may have a diversity policy that is inclusive of diverse people rather than exclusive. Many of these have explicit inclusion statements and practices built into their strategic plans.[40] Likewise, print journalists are attempting to be more inclusive in the coverage of human events and concern for their readership.[41]

An *ideology* is a set of ideas about how the world operates, or should operate. It provides us with a world view, a set of beliefs, even a myth-system. *Hegemonic* or *ruling ideologies* function to legitimate the *status quo*. They provide reasons why the world should remain as it is. Ruling ideologies support the existing power structure, providing benefits for the privileged. The appeal of hegemonic ideologies is enhanced when most people accept their beliefs as common sense, as defining an unquestioned perspective about how the world operates. In contrast, *Counterhegemonic* or *resistant ideologies* provide alternatives to the existing structure, offering reasons that the *status quo* should be changed. Resistant ideologies are a key part of social change. If people can imagine an alternative to the existing system they can then act upon it to achieve change.

Families, religion, government and politics, mass media, education, criminal justice—and yes, the military—are often sources of hegemonic ideologies, but they do not necessarily have to be. *We can be the change we imagine*. Indeed, the US military has responded dramatically in the past six years with three significant changes in policy: the elimination of DADT for gay, lesbian, and bisexual service members (2011); approval of women undertaking combat roles (2013); and transitioning towards the enlistment of transgender service members (2016).

NOW WHAT?

This essay is a primer on the nature of social inequality with an emphasis on the US Army. The social characteristics that most differentiate social inequities, to restate, are the (un)lucky seven: race and ethnicity, sex and gender, social class, religious affiliation, ability, sexual orientation, and age. Although such a primer could similarly be applied to educational or sports and leisure institutions in US society, the military is an instructive choice. Not only is the military an important social institution comprising of millions of people, its own history helps counteract a feeling of hopelessness that the *status quo* can never change.

In terms of race and ethnicity, the US military was the first major social institution to be broadly desegregated, in 1948[42], well before the US Supreme Court's decision in *Brown v. Board of Education of Topeka* in 1954 that the maintenance of separate public schools for black and white students was unconstitutional.[43] Granted, in 1947, a singular person—former US Army lieutenant Jackie Robinson signed with the Brooklyn Dodgers, breaking the color line in professional baseball, but during this period churches, the criminal justice system, politics, the economy, neighborhoods, the work world, mass media, marriage, and health care all remained relatively segregated in the US. Another notable military first, Colonel Clotilde Bowen was the first African American female physician in the armed forces. She graduated from medical school in 1947 and began her medical career in the military in 1955.[44] Today, racial and ethnic minorities are highly represented in the US military and daily exercise leadership at all levels of the organization. Even so, inclusion is not complete.[45]

In the public sector, significant social changes have allowed women to pursue athletic careers in sports. The number of girls and women playing sports exploded with the passing of Title IX in 1972, which required increased athletic opportunities for women. Young women can now grow up dreaming of playing professional basketball and soccer when, not too long ago, they had to leave the country to pursue such a dream. In 1948, the *Women's Armed Services Integration Act* provided women with a more regular but still slightly segregated status in the US military. Thirty years later, in 1978, the Women's Army Corp (WAC) was abolished, providing women with relative full integration into the military. The first women graduated from West Point in 1980. Women deployed to Panama in 1989, the Persian Gulf in 1990, Somalia in 1992, and their participation in nontraditional and counterinsurgency military roles in Afghanistan and Iraq began in 2001, though not formally included in direct combat arms units (although many experienced direct combat and some died). With combat exclusion of women lifted in 2013, the first women graduated from the rigorous Ranger School in 2015. Achieving their proportional representation at all levels in the military, however, will be an ongoing effort.

The US Army Wounded Warriors Project (AW2) project is an official US Army program that identifies service members with severe physical, mental and emotional wounds, illnesses, and injuries.[46] The AW2 appears to be progressing along a path aligned with the *Americans with Disabilities Act* (ADA) of 1990. Unprecedented in US history, "disabled" service members are staying on active duty in unprecedented numbers. They are fulfilling assignments reserved for "able" bodied service members, not because of their injuries but in spite of them. Nevertheless, people with designated pre-existing physical, mental, and emotional disabilities continue to be prohibited from first term enlistment and commissioning.

The age of first enlistment had increased to forty-two years old at the height of the Iraq War but subsequently receded with the meeting of enough quality accessions under thirty-five years of age. It could conceivably return as US health, nutrition, and physical fitness create opportunities for an aging population. Religious tolerance in the US military began under the *Armed Forces Integration Act of 1948* and stretches to protect new spiritual orientations. As noted above, social class representation expanded recently as ROTC returned to some elite campuses such as Harvard University.[47] Age at first enlistment is likely never to be under seventeen years old unless there is a major demographic shift in the United States. Yet the Junior Reserve Officer Training Corps (JROTC) and US military boarding schools remain pervasive and active for US high school age adolescents. The repeal of DADT and transgender prohibitions will allow gay, lesbian, bisexual, and transgender soldiers to feel respected and be legally protected as full citizens in the US military.[48]

What will happen when once we have identified the constituent groups in the on-going citizenship revolution and the issues that in effect constitute locked doors? Will all these groups seek even further full recognition? First, diversity and successful inclusion are not equivalent to an absence of problems. There is a need to constantly and consistently monitor diversity and inclusion against the values that the organization recognizes as salient. The US Army cherishes seven core values: *loyalty*, *integrity*, *duty*, *honor*, *personal courage*, *respect*, and *selfless service*.[49] In addition, there are common variables needed for success in military-related mission accomplishment: among them are *physical and mental readiness*, *skills acquisition*, *privacy*, *morale*, and both *task* and *social cohesion* along the chain-of-command. These values and variables need to be operationalized and measured in order to fully understand the US military's commitment to diversity and inclusion.

Looking to the broader society, which are the next groups on the horizon seeking full citizenship in the US Army? Federal civilian employees? Government contractors? Felons? Political activists? Foreign nationals? Undocumented immigrants? This would expand the debate from the (un)lucky seven to thirteen? Consider, for example, the situation of undocumented immigrants. The DREAM Act failed to receive enough votes in the US Congress despite the support it had from President Barack Obama. The DREAM Act legislation called for allowing adults who spent their formative years culturally and structurally in the United States, but who were not born here, to gain a path to US citizenship via a college degree or through military service.[50] Currently, the US military enlists and commissions US citizens or legal residents. A legal resident is defined as someone who was born elsewhere but has become a legal permanent resident of the United States.[51] However, individuals from particular countries are banned from serving; and, once in the service, individuals from some countries are prohibited from entering the officer ranks and from assignment to jobs that require certain types of security clearance.

An estimated 65,000 children were brought to the US illegally who have graduated from US high schools but who lack a legal residency status. Many seek full citizenship through military service. A recent study showed that some 54 percent of US citizens would approve granting legal status to children brought to the US illegally if they attend college or join the military.[52] Here then might well be the next group seeking full citizenship status. Who will come after that? Can the US military eliminate all discrimination based on social characteristics and allow everyone to serve based on standards of merit or of need? If task and skill are the keys in a meritocracy, how might the military further open doors easier and wider. How might they create new doors? Evidence shows that diversity seems to make us smarter and better.[53] Clearly, the citizenship revolution in the United States continues.

NOTES

1. For a more in-depth background and discussion of the US military, diversity, and inclusion relative to the (un)lucky seven see the book *Inclusion in the American Military: A Force for Diversity*, ed. David E. Rohall, Morten G. Ender, and Michael D. Matthews (Lanham, MD: Lexington Books, 2017).

2. See Henry Ossian Flipper, *The Colored Cadet at West Point: Autobiography of Lieutenant Henry Ossian Flipper, U.S.A., First Graduate of Color from the U.S. Military Academy (Blacks in the American West)* (Lincoln: University of Nebraska Press, 1998). COL Ty Seidule provides a revealing overview of the treatment of black cadets at West Point in "From Slavery to Black Power: Racial Intolerance at West Point, 1778-2015," in *Intolerance: Political Animals and Their Prey*, ed. Bruce Chilton and Robert E. Tully (Lanham, MD: Hamilton Books, 2017).

3. James Burk and Evelyn Espinoza, "Race Relations within the US Military," *Annual Review of Sociology* 38, no. 1 (2012): 401-22.

4. Tom Lombardo, "West Point: Cadet Photo was Inappropriate, but Not Political," *Army Times*, May 10, 2016, https://www.armytimes.com/story/military/2016/05/10/west-point-cadet-photo-inappropriate-but-not-political/84196326/ (accessed November 23, 2016).

5. Eric Schmitt, "Female M. P. Wins Silver Star for Bravery in Iraq Firefight," *New York Times*, June 17, 2005, http://www.nytimes.com/2005/06/17/national/17medal.html (accessed October 1, 2016). Four US Army nurses were awarded the Silver Medal in World War II.

6. Elisabeth Bumiller, "Letting Women Reach Women in Afghan War," *New York Times*, March 6, 2010, http://www.nytimes.com/2010/03/07/world/asia/07women.html (accessed March 9, 2011).

7. CPT Scotty Smiley, with Doug Crandall, *Hope Unseen: The Story of the U.S. Army's First Blind Active-Duty Officer* (Brentwood, TN: Howard Books, 2010).

8. Information about laws pertaining to people with disabilities is available at U. S. House, *Americans with Disabilities Act* (ADA). Public Law 101-336, 104 Stat. 327. July 26, 1990. 101st cong., 2nd sess. https://www.ada.gov/ada_intro.htm (accessed October 9, 2017).

9. Patrick O'Driscoll, "Losing a Limb Doesn't Mean Losing Your Job," *USA Today*, May 5, 2004, http://www.usatoday.com/news/nation/2004-05-05-cover-fit-to-serve_x.htm (accessed March 10, 2011).

10. Pennsylvania Civil War 150, "Charles "Charley" King: Great Sacrifices Were Made at the Battle of Antietam, And One Very Small One," 2011, http://pacivilwar150.com/people/children/Story.aspx?id=4 (accessed March 8, 2011).

11. Peter Baker and Maggie Haberman, "Trump to Interview 4 Candidates for National Security Adviser," *New York Times*, February 18, 2017, https://www.nytimes.com/2017/02/18/us/politics/trump-candidates-national-security-adviser.html?_r=0 (accessed June 5, 2017).

12. Michelle Sandhoff, *Service in a Time of Suspicion: Experiences of Muslims Serving in the US Military Post-9/11* (Iowa City: University of Iowa Press, 2017).

13. Charlotte Hunter and Lyman Smith, *Military Leadership and Education & Religion's Role in the U.S. Military Mission* (Patrick Air Force Base, Cocoa Beach, FL: Defense Equal Opportunity Management Instituted Research Directorate, Technical Report Number 01-10, 2010), http://www.deomi.org/EOEEOResources/documents/Training_for_Religious_Awareness_Hunter_and_Smith.pdf (accessed March 9, 2011).

14. Jonathan D. Glater, "Blue Collars in Olive Drab," *New York Times,* May 22, 2005, http://www.nytimes.com/2005/05/22/national/class/MILITARY-FINAL.html (accessed March 9, 2011). See also, Kathy Roth-Douquet and Frank Schaeffer, *AWOL: The Unexcused Absence of America's Upper Classes from Military Service and How it Hurts Our Country* (New York: Harper, 2006).

15. Morten G. Ender, *American Soldiers in Iraq: McSoldiers or Innovative Professionals?* (London and New York: Routledge, 2009), 147.

16. See James Dao, "Ban Lifted, R.O.T.C. to Return to Harvard's Campus," *New York Times,* March 21, 2012, http://www.nytimes.com/2012/03/22/us/ban-lifted-rotc-to-return-to-harvards-campus.html (accessed June 5, 2017).

17. See John Wetenhall, "Top Ranked Lesbian Cadet Leaves West Point," *ABC News.com,* August 13, 2010, https://abcnews.go.com/US/lesbian-west-point-cadet-resigns/story?id=11395858 (accessed July 4, 2018).

18. U.S. Congress. House. *Don't Ask, Don't Tell Repeal Act of 2010.* H.R. 2965, 111th cong., 2nd sess., December 15, 2010. https://www.congress.gov/bill/111th-congress/house-bill/2965 (accessed July 4, 2018).

19. U.S. Department of Defense, *Don't Ask, Don't Tell*, Directive Number 1304.26. December 21, 1993, President William J. Clinton.

20. Morten G. Ender, Diane M. Ryan, Danielle A. Nuszkowski, Emma Sarah Spell, and Charles B. Atkins, "Dinner and a Conversation: Transgender Integration at West Point and Beyond." Special issue, *Social Sciences* 6, no. 1 (2017): 27; doi:10.3390/socsci6010027, http://www.mdpi.com/journal/socsci/special_issues/focusing_on_the_T_in_LGBT_studies (accessed March 20, 2018).

21. Lolita C. Baldor, "Mattis Delays New Transgender Policy for US Military," *Military Times,* June 30, 2017, http://www.militarytimes.com/articles/mattis-delays-transgender-policy-by-six-months (accessed July 3, 2017).

22. M. Joycelyn Elders, George R. Brown, Eli Coleman, Thomas A. Kolditz, and Alan M. Steinman, "Medical Aspects of Transgender Military Service," *Armed Forces & Society* 41, no. 2 (2014): 199-220.

23. Joshua Polchar, Tim Sweijs, Philipp Marten, and Jan Hendrik Galdiga, *LGBT Military Index* (The Hague: The Hague Centre for Strategic Studies, 2014), http://projects.hcss.nl/monitor/88/ (accessed October 16, 2016).

24. For additional "firsts" and examples of diversity and inclusion in the US Army, see the U.S. Army, Diversity Office (ADO), "Army Diversity: Strength in Diversity," http://www.armydiversity.army.mil/ (accessed on April 25, 2011).

25. David R. Segal, *Recruiting for Uncle Sam: Citizenship and Military Manpower Policy* (Lawrence: University of Kansas Press, 1989), 2.

26. Segal, *Recruiting for Uncle Sam*, 10.

27. Vincenza Priola, Diego Lasio, Silvia De Simone, and Francesco Serri, "The Sound of Silence: Lesbian, Gay, Bisexual and Transgender Discrimination in 'Inclusive Organizations,'" *British Journal of Management* 25, no. 3 (2014): 488-502.

28. For a more informed and interesting discussion of using categories as tools, visit sociologist Max Weber's notion of an *ideal type*—"an analytical construct that serves the investigator as a measuring rod to ascertain similarities as well as deviations in concrete cases" (Dead Sociologists' Society, "Max Weber," n.d., http://media.pfeiffer.edu/lridener/DSS/DEADSOC.HTML [accessed on July 4, 2018]).

29. Certainly there are other areas of diversity and inequality that exist, including citizens versus non-citizens, rural versus urban versus suburban, working versus not-working, information rich versus information poor, and First, Second, and Third World nations. These are certainly emerging categories that you'll want to monitor and may come to extend the (un)lucky seven to the (un)lucky 13!

30. Patricia Hill Collins, "Toward a New Vision: Race, Class, and Gender as Categories of Analysis and Connection," *Race, Sex, & Class* 1, no. 1 (1993): 25-45.

31. Candace West and Sarah Fenstermaker, "Doing Difference," *Gender & Society* 9, no. 1 (1995): 8-37.

32. See the U.S. Census Bureau, *Race*, n.d. https://www.census.gov/topics/population/race/about.html (accessed July 4, 2018).

33. Susanne Bohmer and Joyce L. Briggs, "Teaching Privileged Students about Gender, Race, and Class Oppression," *Teaching Sociology* 19, no. 2 (1991): 154-63.

34. Marilyn Frye, *The Politics of Reality: Essays in Feminist Theory* (Freedom, CA: Crossing Press, 1983), 10-11.

35. Anthony Giddens, *The Constitution of Society* (Berkeley: University of California Press, 1984).

36. Background information for these organizations are available online: Leaders of a Beautiful Struggle, http://lbsbaltimore.com/about-us/; Women's Sports Foundation, https://www.womenssportsfoundation.org/; the Gray Panthers, http://www.graypanthersnyc.org/; SPART*A, http://www.spartapride.org/; K9s for Warriors, http://www.k9sforwarriors.org/; Kiva, https://www.kiva.org/; and Families Against

Cult Teachings, https://www.familiesagainstcultteachings.org/ (all accessed August 30, 2017).

37. Aaron Belkin, "Don't Ask, Don't Tell: Is the Gay Ban Based on Military Necessity," *Parameters* 33, no. 2 (Summer 2003): 108-19.

38. Hani Fakhouri, "Growing Old in an Arab American Family," in *Age through Ethnic Lenses: Caring for the Elderly in a Multicultural Society*, ed. Laura Katz Olson (Lanham, MD: Rowman and Littlefield, 2001), 160-69.

39. Economist, "Too Poor to be Defended: The Right of Indigent Criminal Defendants to a Lawyer Is Increasingly in Jeopardy," *Economist* 346, no. 8063 (1998): 21-22.

40. For example, see Pennsylvania State University's website dealing with workforce diversity, cultural inclusiveness, and employment equity, http://ohr.psu.edu/diversity-and-inclusion (accessed June 5, 2017).

41. Herbert J. Gans, "Toward a New Journalism," *Chronicle of Higher Education* 49, no. 21 (2003): 16-17.

42. Harry S. Truman's Executive Order 9981 began the process of desegregation by declaring that "equality of treatment and opportunity for all persons in the armed services with regard to race, color, religion, or national origin." See Harry S. Truman Library & Museum, *Desegregation of the Armed Forces*, 2011, http://www.trumanlibrary.org/whistlestop/study_collections/desegregation/large/index.php?action=chronology (accessed June 5, 2017).

43. U.S. Supreme Court, *Oliver Brown, et al. v. Board of Education of Topeka, et al.* 347 U.S. 483 (May 17, 1954).

44. Judith Bellafaire and Mercedes Herrera Graf, *Women Doctors in War* (College Station: Texas A&M University Press, 2009), 134.

45. Burk and Espinoza, "Race Relations," 401-22.

46. See the U.S. Army Wounded Warrior Program (AW2), http://myarmybenefits.us.army.mil/Home/Benefit_Library/Federal_Benefits_Page/Army_Wounded_Warrior_Program_(AW2).html (accessed June 5, 2017).

47. Notably, faculty at Columbia University raised new (un)lucky seven concerns regarding the return of ROTC to campus. In particular, they referenced physical disability and age as discriminatory practices that need to be addressed by the US military. See Jacques Barzun, "Columbia University's ROTC Shame," *Wall Street Journal*, March 10, 2011, http://online.wsj.com/article/SB10001424052748704132204576190482383897922.html (accessed June 5, 2017).

48. U.S. Department of Defense, *Support to the DoD Comprehensive Review Working Group Analyzing the Impact of Repealing 'Don't Ask, Don't Tell' Volume 1: Findings From the Surveys* (Washington, DC: Pentagon, November 2010), http://archive.defense.gov/home/features/2010/0610_dadt/ (accessed June 5, 2017).

49. See U.S. Army, *Army Values*, August 15, 2013, https://www.army.mil/standto/archive_2013-08-15 (accessed July 12, 2018).

50. See the Dream Act Portal 218/60, "Welcome to the DREAM Act Portal," n.d., http://dreamact.info/ (accessed June 5, 2017).

51. For background on immigrants in the US military see Jeanne Batalova, *Immigrants in the US Armed Forces*, Migration Policy Institute, 2008, http://www.migr

ationinformation.org/USfocus/print.cfm?ID=683 (accessed June 5, 2017). See also Margaret D. Stock, "Essential to the Fight: Immigrants in the Military, Five Years After 9/11," *Immigration Policy in Focus* 5 (2006):1-7; and Amy Lutz, "Who Joins the Military?: A Look at Race, Class, and Immigration Status," *Journal of Political and Military Sociology* 36, no. 2 (2008): 167-88.

52. See Jeffrey M. Jones, "Slim Majority of Americans Would Vote for DREAM Act Law," *GALLUP*, December 19, 2010, http://www.gallup.com/poll/145136/Slim-Majority-Americans-Vote-DREAM-Act-Law.aspx (accessed June 5, 2017).

53. Katherine W. Phillips, "How Diversity Makes Us Smarter," *Scientific American*, October 1, 2014, https://www.scientificamerican.com/article/how-diversity-makes-us-smarter/ (accessed June 5, 2017).

REFERENCES

Baker, Peter, and Maggie Haberman. "Trump to Interview 4 Candidates for National Security Adviser." *New York Times*, February 18, 2017. https://www.nytimes.com/2017/02/18/us/politics/trump-candidates-national-security-adviser.html?_r=0 (accessed June 5, 2017).

Baldor, Lolita C. "Mattis Delays New Transgender Policy for US Military." *Military Times,* June 30, 2017. http://www.militarytimes.com/articles/mattis-delays-transgender-policy-by-six-months (accessed July 3, 2017).

Barzun, Jacques. "Columbia University's ROTC Shame." *Wall Street Journal*, March 10, 2011. http://online.wsj.com/article/SB10001424052748704132204576190482383897922.html (accessed June 5, 2017).

Batalova, Jeanne. *Immigrants in the US Armed Forces*. Migration Policy Institute. 2008. http://www.migrationinformation.org/USfocus/print.cfm?ID=683 (accessed June 5, 2017).

Belkin, Aaron. "Don't Ask, Don't Tell: Is the Gay Ban Based on Military Necessity." *Parameters* 33, no. 2 (Summer 2003): 108-19.

Bellafaire, Judith, and Mercedes Herrera Graf. *Women Doctors in War*. College Station: Texas A&M University Press, 2009.

Bohmer, Susanne, and Joyce L. Briggs. "Teaching Privileged Students about Gender, Race, and Class Oppression." *Teaching Sociology* 19, no. 2 (1991): 154-63.

Bumiller, Elisabeth. "Letting Women Reach Women in Afghan War." *New York Times*, March 6, 2010. http://www.nytimes.com/2010/03/07/world/asia/07women.html (accessed March 9, 2011).

Burk, James, and Evelyn Espinoza. "Race Relations within the US Military." *Annual Review of Sociology* 38, no. 1 (2012): 401-22.

Collins, Patricia Hill. "Toward a New Vision: Race, Class, and Gender as Categories of Analysis and Connection." *Race, Sex, & Class* 1, no. 1 (1993): 25-45.

Dao, James. "Ban Lifted, R.O.T.C. to Return to Harvard's Campus." *New York Times,* March 21, 2012. http://www.nytimes.com/2012/03/22/us/ban-lifted-rotc-to-return-to-harvards-campus.html (accessed June 5, 2017).

Dead Sociologists' Society. "Max Weber." N.d. http://media.pfeiffer.edu/lridener/DSS/DEADSOC.HTML (accessed on July 4, 2018).

Dream Act Portal 218/60. "Welcome to the DREAM Act Portal." n.d. http://dreamact.info/ (accessed June 5, 2017).

Economist. "Too Poor to be Defended: The Right of Indigent Criminal Defendants to a Lawyer Is Increasingly in Jeopardy." *Economist* 346, no. 8063 (1998): 21-22.

Elders, M. Joycelyn, George R. Brown, Eli Coleman, Thomas A. Kolditz, and Alan M. Steinman, "Medical Aspects of Transgender Military Service." *Armed Forces & Society* 41, no. 2 (2014): 199-220.

Ender, Morten G. *American Soldiers in Iraq: McSoldiers or Innovative Professionals?* London and New York: Routledge, 2009.

Ender, Morten G., Diane M. Ryan, Danielle A. Nuszkowski, Emma Sarah Spell, and Charles B. Atkins. "Dinner and a Conversation: Transgender Integration at West Point and Beyond." Special issue. *Social Sciences* 6, no. 1 (2017): 27. doi:10.3390/socsci6010027. http://www.mdpi.com/journal/socsci/special_issues/focusing_on_the_T_in_LGBT_studies (accessed March 20, 2018).

Fakhouri, Hani. "Growing Old in an Arab American Family." In *Age through Ethnic Lenses: Caring for the Elderly in a Multicultural Society*, edited by Laura Katz Olson, 160-69. Lanham, MD: Rowman and Littlefield, 2001.

Flipper, Henry Ossian. *The Colored Cadet at West Point: Autobiography of Lieutenant Henry Ossian Flipper, U.S.A., First Graduate of Color from the U.S. Military Academy (Blacks in the American West).* Lincoln: University of Nebraska Press, 1998.

Frye, Marilyn. *The Politics of Reality: Essays in Feminist Theory*. Freedom, CA: Crossing Press, 1983.

Gans, Herbert J. "Toward a New Journalism." *Chronicle of Higher Education* 49, no. 21 (2003): 16-17.

Giddens, Anthony. *The Constitution of Society*. Berkeley: University of California Press, 1984.

Glater, Jonathan D. "Blue Collars in Olive Drab." *New York Times,* May 22, 2005. http://www.nytimes.com/2005/05/22/national/class/MILITARY-FINAL.html (accessed March 9, 2011).

Harry S. Truman Library & Museum. *Desegregation of the Armed Forces*. 2011. http://www.trumanlibrary.org/whistlestop/study_collections/desegregation/large/index.php?action=chronology (accessed June 5, 2017).

Hunter, Charlotte, and Lyman Smith. *Military Leadership and Education & Religion's Role in the U.S. Military Mission*. Patrick Air Force Base. Cocoa Beach, FL: Defense Equal Opportunity Management Instituted Research Directorate, Technical Report Number 01-10, 2010. http://www.deomi.org/EOEEOResources/documents/Training_for_Religious_Awareness_Hunter_and_Smith.pdf (accessed March 9, 2011).

Jones, Jeffrey M. "Slim Majority of Americans Would Vote for DREAM Act Law." *GALLUP*, December 19, 2010. http://www.gallup.com/poll/145136/Slim-Majority-Americans-Vote-DREAM-Act-Law.aspx (accessed June 5, 2017).

Lombardo, Tom. "West Point: Cadet Photo was Inappropriate, but Not Political." *Army Times*, May 10, 2016, https://www.armytimes.com/story/military/2016/05/10/west-point-cadet-photo-inappropriate-but-not-political/84196326/ (accessed November 23, 2016).

Lutz, Amy. "Who Joins the Military?: A Look at Race, Class, and Immigration Status." *Journal of Political and Military Sociology* 36, no. 2 (2008): 167-88.

O'Driscoll, Patrick. "Losing a Limb Doesn't Mean Losing Your Job." *USA Today*. May 5, 2004. http://www.usatoday.com/news/nation/2004-05-05-cover-fit-to-serve_x.htm (accessed March 10, 2011).

Pennsylvania Civil War 150. "Charles "Charley" King: Great Sacrifices Were Made at the Battle of Antietam, And One Very Small One." 2011. http://pacivilwar150.com/people/children/Story.aspx?id=4 (accessed March 8, 2011).

Phillips, Katherine W. "How Diversity Makes Us Smarter." *Scientific American*, October 1, 2014. https://www.scientificamerican.com/article/how-diversity-makes-us-smarter/ (accessed June 5, 2017).

Polchar, Joshua, Tim Sweijs, Philipp Marten, and Jan Hendrik Galdiga. *LGBT Military Index*. The Hague: The Hague Centre for Strategic Studies, 2014. http://projects.hcss.nl/monitor/88/ (accessed October 16, 2016).

Priola, Vincenza, Diego Lasio, Silvia De Simone, and Francesco Serri. "The Sound of Silence: Lesbian, Gay, Bisexual and Transgender Discrimination in 'Inclusive Organizations.'" *British Journal of Management* 25, no. 3 (2014): 488-502.

Rohall, David E., Morten G. Ender, and Michael D. Matthews, eds. *Inclusion in the American Military: A Force for Diversity*. Lanham, MD: Lexington Books, 2017.

Roth-Douquet, Kathy, and Frank Schaeffer. *AWOL: The Unexcused Absence of America's Upper Classes from Military Service and How it Hurts Our Country*. New York: Harper, 2006.

Sandhoff, Michelle. *Service in a Time of Suspicion: Experiences of Muslims Serving in the US Military Post-9/11*. Iowa City: University of Iowa Press, 2017.

Schmitt, Eric. "Female M. P. Wins Silver Star for Bravery in Iraq Firefight." *New York Times*, June 17, 2005. http://www.nytimes.com/2005/06/17/national/17medal.html (accessed October 1, 2016).

Segal, David R. *Recruiting for Uncle Sam: Citizenship and Military Manpower Policy*. Lawrence: University of Kansas Press, 1989.

Seidule, COL Ty. "From Slavery to Black Power: Racial Intolerance at West Point, 1778-2015." In *Intolerance: Political Animals and Their Prey*, edited by Bruce Chilton and Robert E. Tully, 69-88. Lanham, MD: Hamilton Books, 2017.

Smiley, CPT Scotty, with Doug Crandall. *Hope Unseen: The Story of the U.S. Army's First Blind Active-Duty Officer*. Brentwood, TN: Howard Books, 2010.

Stock, Margaret D. "Essential to the Fight: Immigrants in the Military, Five Years After 9/11." *Immigration Policy in Focus* 5 (2006):1-7.

U.S. Army. *Army Values,* August 15, 2013, https://www.army.mil/standto/archive_2013-08-15 (accessed July 12, 2018).

———. Diversity Office (ADO). "Army Diversity: Strength in Diversity." http://www.armydiversity.army.mil/ (accessed on April 25, 2011).

———. Wounded Warrior Program (AW2). http://myarmybenefits.us.army.mil/Home/Benefit_Library/Federal_Benefits_Page/Army_Wounded_Warrior_Program_(AW2).html (accessed June 5, 2017

U.S. Census Bureau. *Race*. https://www.census.gov/topics/population/race/about.html, n.d. (accessed July 4, 2018).

U.S. Department of Defense. *Support to the DoD Comprehensive Review Working Group Analyzing the Impact of Repealing 'Don't Ask, Don't Tell' Volume 1: Findings From the Surveys.* Washington, DC: Pentagon, November 2010. http://archive.defense.gov/home/features/2010/0610_dadt/ (accessed June 5, 2017).

———. *Don't Ask, Don't Tell.* Directive Number 1304.26. December 21, 1993. President William J. Clinton.

U. S. House. *Americans with Disabilities Act* (ADA). Public Law 101-336, 104 Stat. 327. July 26, 1990. 101st cong., 2nd sess. https://www.ada.gov/ada_intro.htm (accessed October 9, 2017).

———. *Don't Ask, Don't Tell Repeal Act of 2010.* H.R. 2965. 111th cong., 2nd sess., December 15, 2010. https://www.congress.gov/bill/111th-congress/house-bill/2965 (accessed July 4, 2018).

U.S. Supreme Court. *Oliver Brown, et al. v. Board of Education of Topeka, et al.* 347 U.S. 483 (May 17, 1954).

West, Candace, and Sarah Fenstermaker. "Doing Difference." *Gender & Society* 9, no. 1 (1995): 8-37.

Wetenhall, John. "Top Ranked Lesbian Cadet Leaves West Point," *ABC News.com,* August 13, 2010. https://abcnews.go.com/US/lesbian-west-point-cadet-resigns/story?id=11395858 (accessed July 4, 2018).

Chapter 5

Civil War Pension Policy

The Politics of Policy Subsystems

Brandon Jason Archuleta

> When Gertrude Janeway died in 2003, she was still getting a monthly cheque for $70 from the Veterans Administration—for a military pension earned by her late husband, John, on the Union side of the American civil war that ended in 1865. The pair had married in 1927, when he was 81 and she was 18. The amount may have been modest but the entitlement spanned three centuries, illustrating just how long pension commitments can last.
>
> —*The Economist*, April 7, 2011[1]

Military pensions have a long and, at times, controversial history in American political development.[2] This excerpt from the *Economist* highlights just how important, and neglected, military pension policies have become over time. Who would have thought the U.S. government still paid Civil War pensions? In fact, as recently as 2012, the United States Department of Veterans' Affairs acknowledged it still provided pension benefits for elderly relatives of two Civil War veterans.[3] Indeed, to appreciate the political development of military pension policies over the course of U.S. history, one must understand that these redistributive policies reside at the intersection of America social, economic, and defense policy with a powerful policy subsystem in control.

Political scientist Harold Lasswell poignantly noted that politics boils down to one essential question: "who gets what, when, and how?"[4] It follows, then, that politics determines who wins and who loses through the distribution of benefits and burdens in society. By distributing these benefits and burdens, policymakers can both alleviate and exacerbate inequality in society. Such was the case with Civil War pension policy. In an effort to alleviate poverty among Union veterans with generous service pensions in the aftermath of the war, legislators, lobbyists, bureaucrats, and even presidents inadvertently exacerbated socioeconomic inequality between the North and South as ex-Confederates were denied access to—and thus burdened by—the same pension system that benefited Union veterans. While this essay does not specifically explore the impact of that socioeconomic and regional inequality in the post-Civil War era, it does examine how the politics of the public policymaking process contribute to inequality in society. This important lesson is broad and generalizable across an array of socioeconomic issues plaguing the U.S. today, including veterans' policy.

After more than a decade of war in Iraq and Afghanistan, research on the American political development of veterans' benefits, particularly military pensions, is necessary for both scholars and policymakers alike as the Departments of Defense and Veterans' Affairs collaborate to care for a new generation of veterans separating from the military. This essay helps in part to meet this need, starting with a brief review of prior works in the field.

PRECURSORS

Scholars of American political development have written extensively about veterans' pensions in the context of U.S. social policy. Henry Glasson, whose research spanned nearly twenty years, was the first to chronicle the intellectual history and political development of American military pensions, finding a "sharp distinction" between pre- and post-Civil War pension policies.[5] He argues that by the early twentieth century, the U.S. pension system had become "more generous—even lavish—than that of any other nation in the history of the world."[6] Looking beyond government generosity, Richard Bensel examined the growth in veterans' pensions through the lens of American sectional tensions. He notes that because "pension recipients allied themselves with the core industrial elite and thus formed a coalition large enough to successfully defend a high tariff as a part of the national political economy, the redistribution of this tariff revenue through the Civil War pension system became a major element in the political strategy of development."[7] However, sectionalism is only one aspect of the pension story and cannot adequately explain how veterans' pensions persisted in the years since Reconstruction.

Theda Skocpol argued that the federal government played a central role in expanding social benefits to "worthy" citizens throughout the late nineteenth century, particularly to soldiers and mothers. "Over several decades," she writes, "Civil War pensions evolved from a restricted program to compensate disabled veterans and the dependents of those killed or injured in military service into an open-ended system of disability, old-age, and survivors' benefits for anyone who could claim minimal service time on the northern side of the Civil War."[8] Skocpol credits "political forces of late-nineteenth century American patronage democracy" for driving the expansion of various social benefits and establishing the foundation of the American welfare state. Like sectionalism, however, patronage politics alone cannot explain the pension policy story in its entirety. Offering a different perspective, Laura Jensen claims that the roots of American social policy are actually as old as the Republic itself: "national legislative bodies selectively entitled groups of Americans to social benefits from the very beginning of the nation's existence."[9]

But the scholarship on veterans' pensions is not so much wrong as it is woefully incomplete. A new approach is necessary—one that shows how all parts of the complicated phenomenon of pension policy came to fit together and how they evolved. The focus of this essay is on the political development of veterans' pension policy in the wake of the Civil War through the "Billion Dollar Congress" of 1889-1891.

A SUBSYSTEM APPROACH TO CIVIL WAR PENSION POLICY

Following the Civil War, a complex and dynamic political system emerged whose concern was the creation of pension policy for veterans. This system comprised what is known as a "policy subsystem." It had six distinct components. First, *congressional committees* with jurisdiction on Civil War pensions evolved and came to effectively wield power. Second, the *Pension Bureau* dedicated itself to delivering veterans' pensions in the name of political patronage and partisan politics. Third, *private interests* of dubious scruple, such as pension attorneys and claim agents, actively lobbied the U.S. Congress for new pension legislation and in turn solicited veterans for their business. Fourth, powerful *veterans' service organizations* like the Grand Army of the Republic rallied veterans and families in the name of sacrifice and became a force to be reckoned with in Congress. Fifth, attentive and unflattering *media coverage* of the pension system contributed to a national conversation on the merits of veterans' pension policy. Finally, several *U.S. presidents*—the most elite policy entrepreneurs—weighed into pension politics at various points attempting to influence policymaking. The functional parts of this policy subsystem—the people who kept it thriving—strove for decades, sometimes in harmony, sometimes with internal friction, to shape pension policies for a specific target population: veterans, widows, mothers, and orphans (see fig. 5.1).

The most common though often misapplied term for a policy subsystem is *iron triangle*. An iron triangle is a "relatively closed policy arena emphasizing stable relations among a limited number of participants (i.e., Congress,

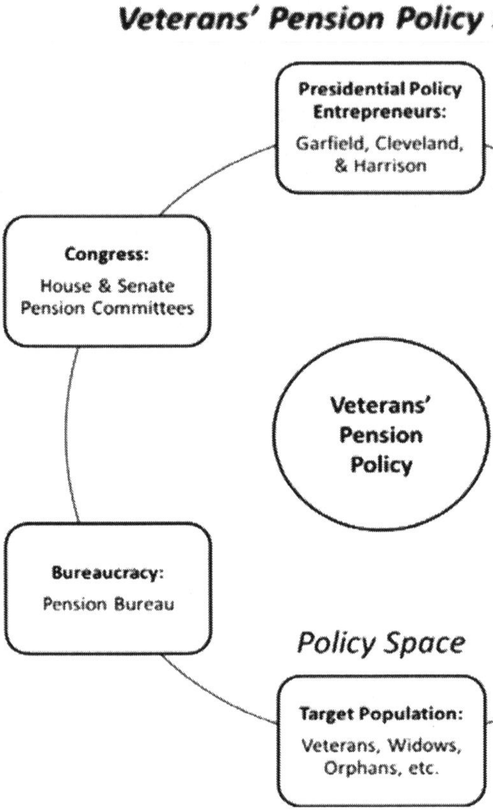

Figure 5.1 Post-Civil War Veterans' Pension Policy Subsystem. Chart design by Brandon Jason Archuleta.

bureaucracies, and interest groups)."[10] This shows an iron triangle to be quite narrow in scope, whereas a policy subsystem is broader and much more inclusive. A policy subsystem is best defined as "a coalition of policy-influencing and policy-making entities that work together via one or more identifiable strategies in response to conflict or potential conflict over policy."[11] Imagine a dynamic network of various institutional and individual experts who push and pull policies towards preferred ends, using any and all means necessary. As such, subsystems aim to maintain stability by retaining control of the issues in question, thereby limiting access and potential threats from the external policymaking environment. Therefore, the self-interested subsystem keeps a tight grip on both institutional structure and issue definition for the sake of maintaining its primacy in the policymaking process.[12] Institutional arrangements among familiar actors and agencies help perpetuate the subsystem's formulation of particular policies, thereby enabling it to maintain its control.

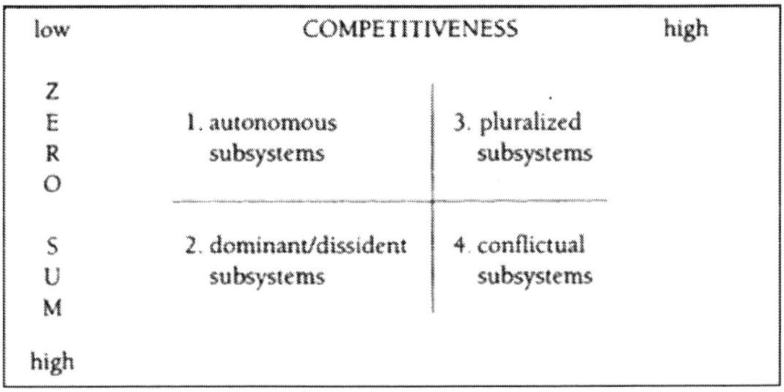

Figure 5.2 Two-by-Two Model, Subsystem Typology. Daniel McCool, "The Subsystem Family of Concepts: A Critique and a Proposal," *Political Research Quarterly* 51, no. 2 (1998): 562.

Subsystems also have territorial, functional, and substantive dimensions involving researchers, advocacy groups, and journalists dedicated to an issue with some level of expertise.[13] All of these features are certainly present in the case of the veterans' policy subsystem.

Policy scholars have gone to great lengths to develop typologies based on the level of conflict within the subsystem.[14] Daniel McCool, for instance, has devised a two-by-two model of autonomous, dominant/dissident, pluralized, and conflictual subsystems (fig. 5.2).

McCool uses two measures to determine the level of conflict in a given subsystem: *competitiveness* and *zero-sum largess*, which he describes in these words: "Subsystem competitiveness is determined by the relative political resources of competing coalitions, such as financial resources, expertise, intensity of commitment, and ability to utilize information to generate public support." Zero-sum largess "refers to the perceived extent and relative availability of resources that can be used to cover outcome costs and benefits. Low zero-sum indicates an allocation of outcome costs/benefits that is perceived as not creating a direct loss to others."[15] An autonomous policy subsystem, McCool writes, "virtually controls policy, due to overwhelming political power in the face of weak opposition. They have a great deal of autonomy from other political forces, and use their strategic overhead to maintain their competitive advantage."[16] Interestingly, he cites veterans' policy as the "best example today" of an autonomous policy subsystem in view of "considerable government largess even in times of budgetary stringency."[17] However, McCool misses the long historical arc of veterans' pension policy and its chaotic political development over the course of U.S. history. Veterans' policy, especially with regard to disability and service pensions, only evolved into an autonomous policy subsystem through the latter half of the twentieth century, following World War II. Given McCool's own typology, veterans' policy in the post-Civil War era and beyond is better thought of in terms of a dominant policy subsystem. Veterans' pension policy was once an issue that pervaded American life and saw new actors and institutions fluidly enter and exit the fray in the years following the Civil War. Veterans' pensions were so much a part of the public psyche that no subsystem could possibly have controlled the issue with complete autonomy.

CIVIL WAR AND THE RISE OF THE VETERANS' PENSION POLICY SUBSYSTEM

An historical precedent having been set during the American Revolution and affirmed following the War of 1812, Union lawmakers considered military pension policy once again as the nation found itself torn asunder by a gruesome Civil War.[18] On July 22, 1861, Congress authorized President Lincoln to raise 500,000 soldiers for the Union cause against the Confederacy. Buried in section six of "An Act to Authorize the Employment of Volunteers to Aid in Enforcing the Laws and Protecting Public Property," was a one-time provision of $100 to any volunteer (their widow or living relative) who would be wounded or disabled in the service of his country, in addition to overdue pay, allowances, and disability benefits.[19] Rather than simply rely on patriotism to recruit an army, Union lawmakers looked to pensions as an effective policy instrument for wartime recruitment and retention. No doubt, reluctant patriots were comforted by the fact that should the unthinkable happen, their families would be financially cared for. In addition to legislation providing for wounded veterans, Union lawmakers also authorized voluntary retirements for Army and Marine Corps officers with forty consecutive years of military service.[20] Like their wounded comrades in arms, voluntary retirees would also be eligible for retirement pay and benefits.

The following year, Congress went even further with the *General Law Pension Act of 1862*. This was the most generous disability pension law to date as it expanded eligibility beyond benefits for veterans, widows, and orphans, and extended them to mothers and sisters as well.[21] Further, the pension act that President Lincoln signed into law on July 14, 1862 created an open-ended clause for which any service member wounded in the service of his nation since March 4, 1861 would be entitled to disability benefits. Additionally, the statute did not specify "volunteer," thus leaving an opening for conscripts to claim their benefits as well. Notably, Union loyalty was required of any beneficiary.[22]

While much of the floor debate in the U.S. House of Representatives on May 13, 1862 focused on bureaucratic implementation of the proposed pension policy, a second-term Congressman from Indiana, William Holman, raised serious objections to the bill's details whose provisions did not go far enough, he argued. Although his efforts failed to win support, his inclination towards *pension equity*—a recurring theme in future pension debates—was quite clear. Holman largely agreed that rank-based salaries were necessary to recruit and retain talented soldiers for the Union cause, but regarded similarly structured pension policies as discriminatory because they ought to be "an expression of gratitude and a provision against want."[23] Even before the bloodiest battles of the Civil War, politicians openly debated and framed salaries and pensions as instruments to recruit, retain, and reward.

Despite little controversy in Congress, the *Pension Act of 1862* raised concerns about burdening the public purse. The U.S. Pension Bureau received some 4,411 applications from wounded veterans by November 15, 1862,[24] and predicted that an annual appropriation of $7 million would be sufficient to cover Civil War pensions in any given year.[25] However, by 1865, annual payments exceeded $8.5 million.[26] Despite Pension Bureau Commissioner Joseph Barrett's rosy prediction, early "apprehensions in some quarters of an extravagant, if not unsupportable, annual burden resulting from the law" proved to be warranted.[27] The focus on disability pensions followed an established pattern. Since the American Revolution, Congress authorized disability pensions at the outset or soon after the end of conflict, growing more generous over time; whereas, generous service pensions tended to come years, even decades, after the end of war.[28] This was true of the *Pension Act of 1818* for veterans of the American Revolution, the *Pension Act of 1871* for veterans of the War of 1812, and the *Dependent Pension Act of 1890* for *Union* veterans of the Civil War. With the exception of half-pay service pensions during the Revolution, Congress established disability benefits well before ever granting service pensions to survivors in their old age.

THE SUBSYSTEM FORMS

The fight to pass the *Arrears Act of 1879* not only exacerbated pension disparities and raised regional tensions, it more importantly marked the rise of the dominant veterans' pension policy subsystem. This legislation held that those Civil War veterans or their survivors who never filed for a service or a disability pension were still entitled to do so, with a retroactive start date at the time of the soldier's discharge.[29] In some instances, new applicants would be entitled to a lump sum upwards of $1,000 for back pay in addition to monthly benefits.[30] Pension costs to the federal government actually started a slow and steady decline from 1873 to 1878. After years of strong support from organizations like the Grand Army of the Republic, business interests such as private claim agents and pension attorneys, and of course the target population of veterans' themselves, passage of the *Arrears Act* seemed inevitable.

Indeed, mounting political pressure from state legislatures before U.S. Senate reelections might have pushed some senators to ultimately support the bill. Glasson cites Senator Ingalls, chairman of the Senate Committee on Pensions, as having been politically "attacked" by strong pension interests in his state with circular letters opposing his reelection. In fear of losing his seat, "Senator Ingalls brought the bill before the Senate and championed its passage on January 16, 1879, not long before balloting began in the Kansas Legislature."[31] The Senate went on to pass the U.S. House version of the bill, forty-four to four. President Hays signed the bill into law on January 25, 1879. Although a triumph for pension interests and veterans, the media would later call the *Arrears Act* a "raid on the treasury."[32]

Signs of an independent and fluid veterans' pension policy subsystem emerged in the 1880s. Pension Bureau bureaucrats processed pension claims with an eye toward earning the Republican Party's political favor. Private interests like veterans' service organizations and pension claim agents frequently lobbied for revisions to existing pension legislation and for enactment of new pension bills to maintain political relevance and draw members and clients to the issue. Politicians happily sponsored, revised, and passed pension legislation into law hoping to curry constituent votes. Interested national and local media covered the process as it unfolded. During this time, the strongest opposition to the emerging pension policy subsystem came from Democrats, President Grover Cleveland especially, who opposed using pensions to curry political favor and redistribute wealth.

Pension Committees

The two congressional committees at the center of the veterans' pension policy subsystem were the U.S. House Committee on Invalid Pensions and the U.S. Senate Committee on Pensions. The House charged its Committee on Invalid Pensions with reviewing individual Civil War pension claims and drafting general and special pension legislation. Accordingly, the Committee on Invalid Pensions wielded a great deal of jurisdictional oversight of the U.S. Pension Bureau, its executives, and was a key component to the policy subsystem that would arise in the wake of the Civil War. One other House committee of note was the U.S. Committee on Pensions (1880-1946). Created in 1880, its jurisdiction included all other war related pension matters, leaving the Civil War to the Committee on Invalid Pensions. The Senate Committee on Pensions (1816-1946) enjoyed primary jurisdiction and oversight on war related pension matters throughout its existence. While the U.S. Senate Committee on Military Affairs and Finance would occasionally take up pension issues, the Senate Committee on Pensions remained the most important venue for veterans' pension issues in the upper chamber.[33] Throughout their existence, the House and Senate pension committees worked diligently to process individual pension claims and offer pension legislation to aid America's ailing and indigent veterans.

When Pension Bureau correspondence to the Congress increased in the 1880s, the pension committees institutionalized a claims review process on Friday evenings, dubbed "pension nights."[34] However, this diligent work was hardly altruistic, as members of Congress often treated veterans' pension policy as a partisan issue and paid little attention to details before voting to approve applications. Glasson notes, "On 'pension day' there is commonly no quorum present" as the few members present pass bills reported by the committee "in a perfunctory manner and with remarkable speed."[35]

Pension Bureau

In 1881, some sixteen years after the war between North and South had ended, President James Garfield appointed W. W. Dudley, a former Union colonel, to head the Pension Bureau. When he assumed office (Dudley would later testify) the Pension Bureau had between "seven hundred and eight hundred" employees. When he left office in 1884, the Pension Bureau had grown to "between sixteen hundred and seventeen hundred" employees. In fact, as of June 30, 1884, there were 1,552 pension employees with another 150 special examiners to be added to the rolls.[36] This explosion in pension bureaucrats might simply be attributed to the growth in pension claims requiring adjudication and the need for special examiners to investigate such claims in the field. However, there was a far more political reason—Republican Party politics.

After assuming office, Commissioner Dudley issued a pamphlet titled, "General Instructions to Special Examiners," which outlined duties for those Pension Bureau employees charged with investigating pension claims in the field. The eighty-five-paragraph guide covered material on claims processing, witness interviews, fraud, widows, minors, and "colored claimants, among other topics," and that the directives contained in the document:

> are intended to allow Special Examiners a greater discretion than has formerly been permitted in the examination of claims before this Office, and their duties call for the most vigorous efforts and soundest judgment... It is the duty of the Government to ascertain who are entitled to receive pensions as provided by existing law, and Examiners are expected and required to obtain whatever facts are necessary to prevent the payment of improper pensions, and to assist in bringing to punishment those who are knowingly guilty of violating the provisions of the pension law.[37]

While fairness and equity were the goals, implementation of the guidance was wanting. In fact, Dudley used his position as commissioner to dole out and expedite pension claims to veterans in battleground states like Indiana to garner electoral favor for the Republican Party. An 1886 Democratic Party campaign book describes a wide-ranging Republican Party agenda in the Pension Bureau using internal documents as evidence. For example, in a letter dated September 9, 1880 from Fort Wayne, Indiana, Colonel Richard Burke requests the Commissioner of Pensions to place three names on the "special list [to] receive the most prompt attention of his office."[38] In a follow-up note two days later, S. W. Dorsey, referring to Burke's letter, requests the Chair of the Republican National Committee, Marshall Jewell, to "induce, if possible, the Commissioner of Pensions to report to each one of these men that their cases are made special [as] it will help us [win] hundreds of votes in Ft. Wayne." As the Democratic Party notes in its own analysis, "us," in this case refers to the Republican Party's effort to garner votes through bureaucratic favors.

Politicizing the pension system left an enduring partisan legacy by mobilizing veterans into the Republican Party's fold. Heywood T. Sanders observes that the Party "had established, in the case of ex-soldiers, a national political machine—a formal organization which provided specific material inducements to a mass of voters."[39] Morton Keller concurs: "The Bureau of Pensions was the most uncompromisingly political branch of the late nineteenth century federal bureaucracy."[40]

Despite the reality of the Pension Bureau's partisanship, Commissioner Dudley maintained a public stance of objectivity during the 1884 election season. He also urged the Special Examiners to remain apolitical during the upcoming election season. Yet he paid scant heed to his own guidance. On September 20, 1884, Dudley tendered his resignation as Commissioner of Pensions—effective November 10, 1884—to lead the Republican campaign effort in Ohio.[41] From the Garfield administration's perspective, a large Pension Bureau responsive to the needs of veterans who vote their pocket books was a huge political asset leading up to the 1884 campaign. But the Democratic members of Congress in particular were not fooled and they pursued the matter. Dudley returned to Washington from his home in Indiana throughout 1885 and testified on multiple occasions before the U.S. House Select Committee on Payment of Pensions, Bounty, and Back Pay, an *ad hoc* investigatory panel. In one such hearing on February 25, 1885, the *New York Times* reports:

> [The] witness's attention was called to the allegation that claims from Ohio and Indiana had been pushed ahead of those of other states for political reasons. In reply, [Commissioner Dudley] … declared that no class or section had been

unduly favored by his order or with his knowledge, and that had any favoritism been shown by any subordinate the man would have lost his place.[42]

Later that year, the Committee Chairman, A. J. Warner of Marietta, Ohio, further pressed Commissioner Dudley on his political influence in the Pension Bureau.

WARNER: You would doubtless admit (I know you would) that if a man has a right to a pension, it is because of disabilities incurred in the service and not because of politics?

DUDLEY: I shall agree with you fully on that proposition.

WARNER: And that politics ought not to enter into the question of a settlement of claims?

DUDLEY: They certainly ought not.

WARNER: Would you not think it quite as objectionable and as grave an offense for a man holding a judicial position [such as yourself] to allow politics to affect cases, as for a judge on the bench to let it be known, or have it understood, that the political opinions of a man would affect his rights in court?

DUDLEY: Yes, and if anything more so.

WARNER: You have spoken about an order which you issued forbidding special examiners to engage in politics.

COMMISSIONER DUDLEY: Yes, sir.

WARNER: When you left the office of Pensions, where did you leave it to go?

DUDLEY: To go on leave of absence.

WARNER: Where?

DUDLEY: I went to Ohio.

WARNER: What to do?

DUDLEY: I went there for the purpose of assisting my party.

WARNER: You went there to conduct a political campaign?

DUDLEY: I do not assume that I conducted it. I went to render such assistance as I could.

WARNER: Did you not virtually take charge of the campaign under the direction of the Republican central committee of the State?

DUDLEY: That is a matter personal to myself. I do not regard it as a proper subject of inquiry for this committee. I regard it as a matter personal to myself, and not a matter subject to be inquired into by the committee; and I decline to answer the question. I state, very frankly, that I went there and did what I could to help my party.[43]

This contentious exchange between the chairman and the witness illustrates an emerging policy subsystem at work. The members of Congress, clearly prepared, knew the answers to their questions beforehand and pushed Commissioner Dudley to admit certain facts about his undue political influence on the claims process. In so doing, Congress asserted its legislative oversight functions of an executive agency by holding its leaders accountable, on occasion even earning public attention from one of the prominent newspapers in the country on matters of veterans' pension policy.

Attorneys and Claim Agents

Enterprising pension attorneys and professional claim agents used pension legislation, especially the new *Arrears Act of 1879*, to expand their business and build wealth by advertising their services in newspapers, journals, and magazines in order to raise awareness and to attract eligible clients. Their efforts throughout the 1880s helped facilitate the enormous growth of applications to the Pension Bureau and thereby the cost to taxpayers.

Claims attorneys Gardner and Burgess, for instance, published a guide intended for pension claim agents and veterans. Their pamphlet, *A Manual of Instructions for the Preparation of Government Claims for Bounty and Back Pay, Pensions, Prize Money, Navy Pay, and for Horses Lost in Battle*, outlines order and eligibility for pension entitlement (soldier, widow, children, mother, and sister) and the rules for presenting evidence of disability, dependence, or loss of property during military service (including horses under an 1849 law). Their pamphlet even includes pre-filled application forms and sample statements of dependence to assist applicants. The bottom of one form reads: "Please remit or deliver the Certificate or Warrant payable on and under my Claim for value… herewith attached, to my duly authorized Attorneys, *Gardner & Burgess***,** of *Washington City, D.C.***,** who are fully authorized by me to receive and conduct all correspondence in the claim and to receive and receipt the Certificate when issued."[44]

Thanks to a simple form, veterans and dependents could easily apply for a pension claim while simultaneously becoming clients of Gardner and Burgess, without so much as ever meeting these attorneys-at-law. The information processing role played by such private interests was vital in helping veterans navigate a cumbersome albeit often politically motivated bureaucracy.

As authorized under the *Pension Act of 1862*, pension attorneys and claim agents earned a fixed $5 fee for every application filed on a veteran's behalf, with an extra $1.50 for any necessary sworn statements testifying to the veteran's disabilities. For them, write two disability scholars, it was a "volume business."[45] "Never before in American History had advocates been involved in activities of such grand and social and political scale, in efforts to help veterans pursue monetary gain, public acceptance and recognition."[46] But for veterans, employing a pension attorney or claim agent did not come without the risk of exploitation, and there is evidence that unscrupulous claim agents and pension attorneys looked for ways to profit from the pension system at the expense of their veteran clients. Historian Herbert Agar writes, "As a result [of generous Union pensions], claim agents traveled the country looking for ex-soldiers who had something the matter with them and persuading them to blame it on the war."[47]

Grand Army of the Republic

Beyond the private interests of claim agents and pension attorneys, powerful soldier advocacy groups like the Grand Army of the Republic (GAR) actively lobbied the Congress on behalf of the veterans' community. On March 8, 1884, the Senate Committee on Pensions heard testimony from representatives of the GAR who claimed to represent some 220,000 veteran soldiers and sailors of the Civil War.[48] In fact, the GAR formed its own Committee on Pensions to mirror the committee in the U.S. Senate. GAR representative, General Louis Wagner described "its pension committee as a breakwater between Congress and those [veterans] who demanded pensions."[49] This organizational innovation effectively raised the political clout of the GAR, signaling that in order for the Congress to revise or consider new pension policies, the Senate Committee on Pensions could only proceed with the concurrence of its GAR counterpart.

Without robust congressional staffs to assist members with preparation, committee hearings served as a most powerful venue for the effective and efficient exchange of information. Senators and witnesses discussed everything from rank-based pension eligibility to fraudulent claims. The 1884 Senate Committee hearing and question period provided an opportunity to exchange information, signal policy preferences, raise concerns, and clarify positions. Aside from brief prepared statements from the committee chairman and GAR representatives, the most substantive exchanges occurred during the candid question-and-answer period when the GAR laid the groundwork for what would become most extensive expansion of military pension policy in American history—the *Dependent Pension Act of 1890*. Arguing in favor of pensions for widows, General George S. Merrill, representing the GAR, declared "in regard to the continuance of a soldier's pension to his widow … if a soldier having a pension today for a cause, is killed in a railroad accident, or dies from any cause not directly traceable to the disability which gives him the pension, then his pension is wiped out, and the widow gets no pension. That seems to us to be very unjust."[50] The question of extending pensions to poor widows soon led to the following exchange between General Merrill and Senator Henry Blair of New Hampshire:

BLAIR: If a man who rendered service in any war, and there is no war later than that of the rebellion, is actually disabled, or pecuniarily dependent—

MERRILL: I would leave out the dependent part in all bills. I do not like the idea of making paupers of our soldiers.

BLAIR: But you do make paupers of the mothers. I do not like the idea that poverty is dishonorable, whether it is on the pension list or elsewhere.

MERRILL: [A] mother who at the time of the death of her son was in comfortable circumstances, and therefore not entitled to a pension, may be the reverses of business or fortune have become a candidate for the almshouse. Yet she cannot get today a pension because she was not dependent upon the son at the time of the son's death. We think that is wrong, and that if she became dependent since, that at the time and during the continuance of the dependence a pension should be granted.[51]

In a dynamic policy subsystem, ideas and information that permeate and flow from one institution to another provide the necessary frame of reference for future legislation. Whether GAR believed the political mood in Washington was ready for pension expansion in 1884 is unclear. However, what is clear is that GAR representatives believed in their mission to represent veterans and would use information and anecdotes to frame their arguments for new pension policies.

The GAR's Committee on Pensions pursued pension expansion again two years later. On January 19, 1886, the Senate Committee on Pensions held another hearing for GAR to present its position. In his opening statement before the committee, General Merrill asserts, "We come to you today with precisely the same recommendations without change, except in the form in which they are here given, as we presented to your committee two years ago." He further claims GAR membership had grown to some 300,000 veterans and that the organization's Committee on Pensions was the designated "mouthpiece" for its members "in all matters of pension legislation."[52] In a circular presented to the Senate committee, GAR once again laid out its policy preferences in terms of pension expansion to widows, minor children, and mothers under various circumstances of a veteran's death. In addition, GAR recommended specific dollar amounts for pensions to disabled veterans—for instance, $100 a month "for men who lost both eyes, or arms, or legs, or an arm and a leg, or disability equivalent thereto." By specifying payments for varying degrees of disability, the GAR Committee on Pensions demonstrated its close study and intimate understanding of the challenges facing disabled veterans as they attempted to make a living and support their families.

General Merrill declared the GAR to be "the only great organization that represents everybody, that has no possible connections with political questions, and takes in all parties and all organizations."[53] He restated the GAR's proposal to give pensions to widows whose husbands died from disease or causes unrelated to wartime disabilities as well as to the parents of veterans who became impoverished since their son's death. He also took a rather generous position on issues such as pension eligibility and lackluster fraud prevention. "If 100 men are standing in line and 5 of them are not really entitled, I would say give it to the 5 rather than denying the 95 who are deserving,"[54] he said. Merrill's statement, bold though it was, elicited no response from the Senate committee.

Presidents, Politics, and Pensions

In 1881, a former Union general and rising Republican star, Benjamin Harrison, was elected to the U.S. Senate by the Indiana State Legislature. As a colonel in General Sherman's army, Harrison had commanded a brigade during the Atlanta campaign and garnered significant praise from his superiors for displaying valor at the battle of Peachtree Creek in 1864.[55] In 1865, just months before leaving the service for Indiana, Harrison earned his final promotion to Brigadier General, solidifying his reputation as a warrior, patriot, and leader. Not surprisingly, Senator Harrison was a champion of Civil War service pensions. His position and consistent advocacy for generous pension benefits stood in stark contrast to that of the Democrat occupying the Oval Office from 1885 to 1889—President Grover Cleveland.

President Cleveland was ever suspicious of growing pension rolls and frustrated with the Congress that happily contributed to the pension bloat. As Agar notes, "By 1885, 325,000 pensioners were on the roll. The pension authorities were lax and the list was growing rapidly; but the authorities were not lax enough to satisfy the more sentimental or the more vote-hungry Congressmen."[56] Senator Henry Blair of New Hampshire, an old soldier himself and an ally of the GAR, had pushed House Bill 10457 through Congress.[57] The "Blair Bill," as it was known, bore the official title: "An act for the relief of dependent parents and honorably discharged soldiers and sailors who are now disabled and dependent upon their own labor for support." The bill called for anyone (including surviving parents) with three months of honorable service to the Union during the war—whether engaged in combat or not—to be awarded a pension for "any form of disability, no matter how or when acquired, including the disability of old age."[58] Needless to say, President Cleveland opposed the legislation.

On February 11, 1887, President Cleveland vetoed the Blair Bill, contributing to his long list of first term vetoes numbering in the hundreds. In his 4,193-word veto message to Congress, Cleveland cited growing pension statistics, the nation's prior experience with military pensions, and pointed to historical trends which grant old age pensions to veterans nearly four decades after war, not for the mere twenty-two years which the Blair Bill proposed. Moreover, President Cleveland also framed his veto in terms of a public tax burden and federal revenue:

> Under [Civil War pension] statutes 561,571 pensions have been granted from the year 1861 to June 30, 1886, and more than 2,600 pensioners have been added to the rolls by private acts passed to meet cases, many of them of questionable merit, which the general laws did not cover.... If this bill should become a law, with its tremendous addition to our pension obligation, I am thoroughly convinced that further efforts to reduce the Federal revenue and restore some part of it to our people will, and perhaps should, be seriously questioned.... I am not willing to approve a measure presenting the objections to which this bill is subject, and which, moreover, will have the effect of disappointing the expectation of the people and their desire and hope for relief from war taxation in time of peace.[59]

Aside from the tax burden, the reality of party politics throughout this period suggests that Cleveland had little to gain politically by backing pension legislation. Cleveland only won the election of 1884 by carrying his home state of New York by 1,149 votes. Ardently opposed to party patronage, Cleveland ran for the White House on an anti-corruption platform and, at the time, the Pension Bureau and pension system were already bastions of political corruption and patronage. As president, Cleveland vetoed some 300 individual pension bills, earning himself the ire of both Civil War veterans and, not surprisingly, the Grand Army of the Republic.[60] Cleveland's opposition to veterans' pensions represented the single most powerful threat to the rising policy subsystem. As the nation's most visible policy entrepreneur with constitutional veto powers at his disposal, Cleveland's efforts to break up the subsystem's policy monopoly were quite successful. However, his success undoubtedly contributed to the downfall of his reelection campaign in 1888.

Against the background of presidential vetoes, not least Cleveland's of the Blair Bill, Benjamin Harrison found himself seeking the Republican Party's nomination for president just seven years after his election to the U.S. Senate. The following excerpt from the 1888 Republican Party platform summarizes the argument in favor of veterans' pensions and shows how the Republicans wished to be the favorite in the eyes of veterans when compared with the Democrats and President Cleveland:

> The gratitude of the Nation to the defenders of the Union cannot be measured by laws. The legislation of Congress should conform to the pledges made by a loyal people and be so enlarged and extended as to provide against the possibility that any man who honorably wore the Federal uniform shall become the inmate of an almshouse, or dependent upon private charity. In the presence of an overflowing treasury it would be a public scandal to do less for those whose valorous service

> preserved the government. We denounce the hostile spirit shown by President Cleveland in his numerous vetoes of measures for pension relief, and the action of the Democratic House of Representatives in refusing even a consideration of general pension legislation.[61]

In September 1888, Harrison accepted the Republican nomination for the presidency, responding warmly to the party's position: "It can hardly be necessary for me to say," he writes, "that I am heartily in sympathy with the declaration of the convention upon the subject of pensions to our soldiers and sailors.... I may add that measures in behalf of the surviving veterans of the war and of the families of their dead comrades should be conceived and executed in a spirit of justice and of the most grateful liberality."[62] Harrison's support of spending measures favorable to the veterans' cause would exacerbate sectionalism and help usher in the era of the "Billion Dollar Congress" in 1890.

Tariff receipts in the 1880s had yielded a significant and rising budget surplus (alluded to as the "outflowing treasury" in the Republican Party's platform), and thereby created the decade's "most pressing fiscal problem."[63] As Democrats saw it, tariffs placed an undue tax burden on the South and the West. Republicans viewed tariffs, and the redistributive social policies that they facilitated, as the glue that held their party's electoral coalitions together. During the Harrison presidency, the Pension Bureau "reopened old cases, rerated existing pensions upward, and generally rewarded political allies and supporters" to meet political ends.[64]

Moreover, the *Union only* policy that persisted well beyond the close of the Civil War left few Southern residents eligible for pension benefits. Regional tensions grew from the reality that the South was still being largely punished for waging war against the North. Historian Walter Prescott Webb estimates that some $7 billion in pension benefits went to residents in the North whereas only $1 billion went to residents in the South and the West.[65] This lopsided redistribution of wealth and the remaining budget surplus led Democrats to favor cutting tariffs by lowering foreign trade barriers, while Republicans preferred to maintain tariffs and simply increase federal spending.[66] Northern Republicans and southern Democrats alike knew that any expansion of Civil War pensions would largely favor the northeast and mid-west, excluding the democratic South, leaving it farther and farther behind. This expectation no doubt contributed to President Cleveland's veto of the Blair Bill.[67] Taken together, this episode in U.S. history evinces the role partisan politics can play in exacerbating, not alleviating, socioeconomic inequality.

Watchdog Media and Growing Public Concern

After winning the 1888 presidential election largely by linking tariffs to veterans, the "soldier-president" Benjamin Harrison moved to consolidate his victory by placing service pensions at the top of his political agenda. The importance of the policy subsystem is also apparent in President Harrison's second Pension Commissioner, former Illinois Congressman and IRS Commissioner, Green B. Raum. Following the short and disastrous tenure of his first pension commissioner, the *Nation* magazine declared that the "nominal executive," President Harrison, "does not dare appoint any man ... before he has procured the endorsement of Gen. R.A. Alger, Commander-in-Chief of the Grand Army of the Republic.... The situation is without precedent."[68]

Media involvement in policy matters like this is a staple of the policy subsystem. Following Raum's appointment (with the GAR's support), both Republican and Democratic printed journals that praised the new commissioner for his executive leadership, Civil War service, and objectivity. Despite the initial accolades, however, Raum proved to be just as liberal in his favorable interpretation of pension laws for applicants as was his predecessor.[69]

In addition to media attention, veterans' pension policy pervaded public debate during this period. On June 1, 1890, Edward H. Hall preached a sermon at the First Parish Church in Cambridge, Massachusetts, titled, "An Indignity to Our Citizen Soldiers." With a passionate rhetoric, Hall recounts the history of Civil War pension policy for his congregation, detailing the initial enthusiasm to care for the new generation of veterans; the number of pension claims filed since 1861; the dollar amount dispersed from the treasury; and—not least—the growth of private interests surrounding veterans' pensions and its corrupting effect:

> Unfortunately, it was not the soldiers alone who thought themselves concerned in the matter. The making out of so many thousand claims and the expenditure of so many millions of dollars proved so lucrative a business, and the possibility of extending these claims in various directions proved so strong a temptation, that a great and thriving trade sprang up, based upon the soldier's needs. Plenty of honest men there were, no doubt, among these pension agents, but outside this lesser circle was formed a far larger ring, whose sole thought was to awaken discontent among the recipients of pensions and bring to bear upon Congress a pressure, apparently for the people themselves, for an increase of the nation's liberal gratuities. The country was flooded with circulars and appeals, military societies were led on step by step to countenance these friendly efforts in their behalf, public sentiment was quietly and successfully played upon to sympathize with the soldier's sufferings and to forget that anything had yet been done to relieve him, politicians were reminded of the rich party capital to be secured by coming forward as the soldier's friends,—until an entirely new era of pension legislation, unknown to the period of war itself, began.[70]

Hall returns to the theme of financial excess:

> We find ourselves in the extraordinary and even grotesque position to-day of paying, in pensions to our former soldiers, more than any European nation pays for its standing army, and yet at this moment, two bills are passing back and forth between the United States Senate and House, which, if adopted, will add 200,000 or 380,000 new names to the pension roll, and increase the annual expenditure by $40,000,000 to $80,000,000, or if certain pending amendments are adopted, by $470,000,000.[71]

The $40-$80 million range mentioned by Hall was in line with the $50 million initial estimate of arrears made by Dudley's predecessor at the Pension Bureau, J. A. Bentley.[72] Passage of new legislation in 1890 undoubtedly inspired a sense of excess spending among Americans. Defying initial estimates, spending on arrears for pensions alone had ballooned to $118 million in 1891 and to nearly $140 million by the end of the decade.[73]

Fulfilling his campaign promises and ensuring that his administration was "liberal with the boys," veterans' pensions exploded under the Harrison presidency and the "Billion-Dollar Congress" of 1889-1891, just as Hall predicted.[74] This is mostly due to the loose interpretation of laws already on the books and enactment of the *Dependent Pension Act of 1890*, which passed the Senate with thirty-one Republicans and three Democrats in favor over eighteen Democrats in opposition.[75] The *Dependent Pension Act of 1890* also passed the House. This new legislation relaxed eligibility restrictions more than any pension policy had before and now includes:

> all persons who served ninety days or more in the military or naval service of the United States during the late war of Rebellion and who have been honorably discharged therefrom, and who are now or who may hereafter be suffering from a mental or physical disability of a permanent character, not the result of their own vicious habits, which incapacitates them from the performance of manual labor.[76]

In his second State of the Union address on December 1, 1890, President Harrison acknowledged the new pension legislation and justified its burden: "There is no economy to the Government in delay, while there is much hardship and injustice to the soldier. The anticipated expenditure, while very large, will not, it is believed, be in excess of the estimates made before the enactment of the law."[77] Harrison deeply believed that veterans deserved society's benefits, for he thought they had already borne a lifetime of hardship and injustice in many cases. The soldier president thus stood by the expanded benefits, as he promised he would, presenting the policy as moral and ethical.

Once codified into law, U.S. pension liabilities ballooned between 1891 and 1900 as budget surpluses fell. By 1893, an astounding 41.5 percent of federal income went to veterans' benefits. Dedicating two-fifths of federal revenue to pension spending is politically irresponsible, especially considering that Americans did not share these benefits equally.[78] Indeed, the policy subsystem that dominated veterans' pensions throughout the late nineteenth century disproportionally favored the North at the expense of the South. Southern states like Virginia,[79] Texas, and Georgia[80] were left to their own devices as veterans of the Confederacy were cut out of the federal government's largess. This political exclusion undoubtedly contributed to regional disparities and socioeconomic inequality in the late nineteenth and early twentieth centuries.

Long the Republican champion of veterans' interests, Harrison was nevertheless wrong about managing the costs. He lost his bid for reelection in 1892 to his predecessor in the White House, Democrat Grover Cleveland. Never before and never since has an incumbent president lost reelection to his predecessor. No doubt, government largess and public debt played an important role in the acrimonious presidential campaign of 1892 and its outcome.

CONCLUSION

But the veterans' pension story does not end there. On the contrary, the policy subsystem of the late nineteenth century would leave a lasting mark on future veterans' pension policy debates as subsystem institutions evolved and transformed through two world wars and beyond, thereby revealing a consistent pattern: First, policymakers rely on military pensions to recruit and to retain service members in the midst of a wartime emergency. Next, in the wake of war, prominent veterans' service organizations form to foster camaraderie and to provide policy advocacy within that veterans' community, including more generous pension benefits for their service and sacrifice. As time passes, one generation of veterans gives way to a new generation of veterans. Similarly, the language that framed pensions as a tool to recruit and to retain young troops gives way to language framing pensions as rewards and as social provisions for aging soldiers. Finally, with each new war, the federal government restructures and transforms its bureaucratic institutions to keep pace with the evolution of veterans' benefits. This pattern of pension policy repeats itself over the course of American history, not least in the aftermath of the recent wars in Iraq and Afghanistan. And, all the while, the media keenly observes and comments on developments.

The challenge for contemporary policymakers charged with advocating, legislating, and implementing military pension policies in the future is to ensure that these social provisions against want alleviate—not exacerbate—socioeconomic inequality. Thus, military pensions should serve as policy instruments to recruit and retain the nation's best and brightest young people in uniform. And when their service is complete, these same policy instruments should provide sufficient means for these veterans to separate from the military and transition to a comfortable civilian life, one commensurate with their years of national service and personal sacrifice.

NOTES

1. Economist, "Falling Short," *Economist.* April 7, 2011, http://www.economist.com/node/18502013 (accessed April 22, 2018).

2. This essay is adapted from a chapter of my dissertation, "The Military Pension Promise: Autonomous Policy Subsystems, Blue Ribbon Defense Commissions, and the Twenty-First Century All-Volunteer Force" (PhD diss., University of Texas at Austin, 2015).

3. Mike Baker, "Costs of U.S. Wars Linger for over 100 Year," *Associated Press*, March 19, 2013, https://tippingpointnorthsouth.org/2013/06/05/costs-of-u-s-wars-linger-for-over-100-years/ (accessed April 23, 2018).

4. Harold D. Lasswell, *Politics: Who Gets What, When, How* (New York: Whittlesey House, 1936), i.

5. Henry Glasson, *Federal Military Pensions in the United States*, ed. David Kinley (New York: Oxford University Press, Carnegie Endowment for International Peace, 1918), 4.

6. Ibid., 2.

7. Richard Franklin Bensel, *Sectionalism and American Political Development: 1880-1980* (Madison: University of Wisconsin Press, 1984), 60.

8. Theda Skocpol, *Protecting Soldiers and Mothers: The Political Origins of Social Policy in the United States* (Cambridge, MA: Harvard University Press, 1992), 102.

9. Laura Jensen, *Patriots, Settlers, and the Origins of American Social Policy* (Cambridge: Cambridge University Press, 2003), 9.

10. James Thurber, "Dynamics of Policy Subsystems in American Politics," in *Interest Group Politics*, 3rd ed., ed. Allen J. Cigler and Burdett A. Loomis (Washington, DC: Congressional Quarterly Press, 1991), 323.

11. Daniel McCool, "The Subsystem Family of Concepts: A Critique and a Proposal," *Political Research Quarterly* 51, no. 2 (1998): 558.

12. Frank R. Baumgartner and Bryan D. Jones, *Agendas and Instability in American Politics*, 2nd ed. (Chicago: University of Chicago Press, 2009).

13. Paul A. Sabatier and Christopher Weible, "The Advocacy Coalition Framework: Innovations and Clarification," in *Theories of the Policy Process,* 2nd ed., edited by Paul A.. Sabatier (Boulder, CO: Westview Press, 2007), 189-222; Matthew Zafonte and Paul Sabatier, "Shared Beliefs and Imposed Interdependencies as Determinants of Ally Networks in Overlapping Subsystems," *Journal of Theoretical Politics* 10, no. 4, (1998): 473-505.

14. Jeffrey Worsham, *Other People's Money: Policy Change, Congress, and Bank Regulation.* (Boulder, CO: Westview Press, 1997); McCool, "Subsystem Family of Concepts," 551-70.

15. McCool, "Subsystem Family of Concepts," 561.

16. Ibid., 562.

17. Ibid., 563.

18. Glasson, *Federal Military Pensions.*

19. U.S. Statutes at Large, "An Act to Authorize the Employment of Volunteers to Aid in Enforcing the Laws and Protecting Public Property," 37th cong., 1st sess., chaps. 9, July 22, 1861, 270, https://www.loc.gov/law/help/statutes-at-large/37th-congress/session.../c37s1ch9.pdf (accessed April 23, 2018).

20. U.S. Statutes at Large, "An Act Providing for the Better Organization of the Military Establishment," 37th cong., 1st sess., chap. 42, sec. 15, August 3, 1861, 287-91, at 289.

21. Skocpol, *Protecting Soldiers*; Jensen, *Patriots, Settlers.*

22. U.S. Statutes at Large, "An Act to Grant Pensions," 37th cong., 2nd sess., Chap 166, July 14, 1862, 566-69, https://www.loc.gov/law/help/statutes-at-large/37th-congress/session-2/c37s2ch166.pdf (accessed April 23, 2018).

23. William Holman, "Remarks on the House Floor," *Congressional Globe.* 37th cong., 2nd sess., May 13, 1862, part 3.

24. "Pension Bureau; Abstract of the Annual Report of Hon. Joseph H. Barrett, Commission of Pensions," *New York Times*, December 3, 1862, 2. https://www.nytimes.com/1862/12/03/archives/the-pension-bureau-abstract-of-the-annual-report-of-hon-joseph-h.html (accessed April 22, 2018).

25. Glasson, *Federal Military Pensions.* 129.

26. "Pension Bureau, Report of Commissioner Barrett," *New York Times*, December 9, 1865, 3, https://www.nytimes.com/1865/12/09/archives/the-pension-bureau-report-of-commissioner-barrett.html (accessed April 22, 2018).

27. Glasson, *Federal Military Pensions.* 128.

28. Jensen, *Patriots, Settlers*, 207-10.

29. U.S. Statutes at Large, "An Act to Provide That All Pensions on Account of Death, or Wounds Received, or Disease Contracted in the Service of the United States," 45th cong., 3rd sess., chap. 23, January 25, 1879, 265, https://www.loc.gov/law/help/statutes-at-large/45th-congress/session-3/c45s3ch23.pdf (access April 23, 2018).

30. Glasson, *Federal Military Pensions.* 151.

31. Ibid., 161.

32. "Military Pensions." *New York Times*, July 17, 1921, 26, https://timesmachine.nytimes.com/timesmachine/1921/07/17/109813379.html?pageNumber=26 (accessed June 6, 2018).

33. National Archives, Senate Records, Group 46, https://www.archives.gov/research/african-americans/record-groups/rg-046-senate.html (accessed April 23, 2018).

34. Skocpol, *Protecting Soldiers*, 122.

35. Glasson, *Federal Military Pensions*, 277.

36. W. W. Dudley, "Testimony before the House Committee on Payment of Pensions, Bounty, and Back Pay," in *Hearings on Administration of the Pension Office*, 48th cong., 2nd sess., HR 2683, November 26, 1885, 242.

37. W. W. Dudley, "General Instructions to Special Examiners of the United States Pension Bureau," *U.S. Pension Bureau* (Washington, DC: Government Printing Office, 1881), 7.

38. U. S. Democratic Congressional Committee, "Republican Abuses in the Pension Bureau," in *The Campaign Book of the Democratic Party, 1886*, 6-8, 33-35, at 8 (Washington, DC: R. O. Polkinhorn, 1886), https://babel.hathitrust.org/cgi/pt?id=wu.89073007403 (accessed April 23, 2018).

39. Heywood T. Sanders, "Paying for the Bloody Shirt: The Politics of Civil War Pensions," in *Political Benefits: Empirical Studies of American Public Programs*, ed. Barry S. Rundquist (Lexington, MA: Lexington Books, 1980), 138.

40. Morton Keller, *Affairs of State: Public Life in Late Nineteenth Century America* (Cambridge, MA: Harvard University Press, 1977), 311.

41. W. W. Dudley, "Letter to Special Examiners," September 20, 1884; repr. U.S. Democratic Congressional Committee, "Republican Abuses in the Pension Bureau," in *The Campaign Book of the Democratic Party, 1886*, 6-8, 33-35 (Washington, DC: R. O. Polkinhorn, 1886), 77, https://babel.hathitrust.org/cgi/pt?id=wu.89073007403 (accessed April 22, 2018).

42. "Mr. Dudley and the Pension Office Abuses," *New York Times*, February 25, 1885, 3, https://www.nytimes.com/1885/02/26/archives/mr-dudley-and-the-pension-office-abuses-the-excommissioner.html (accessed April 23, 2018).

43. U.S. Congress, House, "Testimony Taken by the Committee on Payment of Pensions, Bounty, and Back Pay Relating to the Administration of the Pension Office" (Washington: Government Printing Office, 1885), 259. The titles preceding the two participants' names of "CHAIRMAN" and "COMMISSIONER" are not included in this excerpt.

44. Gardner and Burgess, *A Manual of Instructions for the Preparation of Government Claims for Bounty and Back Pay, Pensions, Prize Money, Navy Pay, and for Horses Lost in Battle* (Washington, DC: Gibson Brothers, 1864), 27; emphasis in the original.

45. Peter Blanck and Chen Song, "Civil War Pension Attorneys and Disability Politics," *University of Michigan Journal of Law Reform* 35, nos. 1-2 (Fall 2001-Winter 2002): 12, https://pdfs.semanticscholar.org/8aa8/28f3e3def87147c05b52d9bdae7f3fbd2a45.pdf (accessed April 23, 2018).

46. Ibid., 5.

47. Herbert Agar, *The Price of Union* (Boston: Houghton Mifflin Company, 1950), 582.

48. George S. Merrill, "Statement before the Committee on Pensions of the United States Senate," *Hearings on the Grand Army of the Republic Committee on Pensions*. 48th cong., 1st sess., March 8, 1884, transcript, Sen 48A-E16, 1.

49. Louis Wagner, "Testimony before the Committee on Pensions of the United States Senate," *Hearings on the Grand Army of the Republic Committee on Pensions*, 48th cong., 1st sess., March 8, 1884, transcript, Sen 48A-E16, 5.

50. Merrill, "Statement before the Committee on Pensions" (1884), 3.

51. Merrill, "Statement before the Committee on Pensions" (1884); and Henry W. Blair, "Statement before the Committee on Pensions of the United States Senate," *Hearings on the Grand Army of the Republic Committee on Pensions*, 48th cong., 1st sess., March 8, 1884, transcript, Sen 48A-E16, 4-5. The titles preceding the two participants' names, "MR." and "GENERAL," are not included in this excerpt.

52. George S. Merrill, "Statement before the Committee on Pensions of the United States Senate." *Hearings on the Grand Army of the Republic Committee on Pensions,* 49th cong., 2nd sess., January 19, 1886. Transcript. UB373.A3.1886, 1.

53. Ibid., 2.

54. Ibid., 7.

55. Charles W. Calhoun, *Benjamin Harrison* (New York: Times Books, 2005), 24.

56. Agar, *Price of Union*, 582.

57. Agar notes that Blair was a "Republican Senator with a gallant war record [who] claimed that every Union soldier should be pensioned, [because] every soldier came out of the war weaker than he went into it" (ibid.).

58. Ibid., 582-83.

59. Grover Cleveland, "Veto Message." *American Presidency Project, UCSB*, February 11, 1887. http://www.presidency.ucsb.edu/ws/index.php?pid=71488&st=Veto+Message&st1= (accessed April 23, 2018).

60. Roland Hugins, *Grover Cleveland: A Study in Political Courage* (Washington, DC: Anchor-Lee, 1922), 2830.

61. "Republican Party Platform of 1888," *American Presidency Project, UCSB*, http://www.presidency.ucsb.edu/ws/index.php?pid=29627 (accessed April 23, 2018).

62. Benjamin Harrison, "Letter Accepting the Presidential Nomination," September 11, 1888, *American Presidency Project, UCSB*, http://www.presidency.ucsb.edu/ws/?pid=76068 (accessed April 22, 2018).

63. Keller, *Affairs of State*, 381.

64. Bensel, *Sectionalism,* 66.

65. Agar, *Price of Union*, 583.

66. Peter Trubowitz, *Defining the National Interest: Conflict and Change in American Foreign Policy* (Chicago: University of Chicago Press, 1998), 50.

67. Skocpol, *Protecting Soldiers and Mothers,* 124-26. Skocpol writes that Cleveland claimed the pension legislation was vaguely worded and therefore vetoed it. However, this interpretation misses the larger point that, in Cleveland's view, the pension rolls had become burdensome and would only exacerbate future budgets if the Blair bill passed.

68. "The Week," *Nation* 1266, October 3, 1889, 261-63, http://www.unz.org/Pub/Nation-1889oct03-00261?View=PDFPages (accessed April 23, 2018).

69. William Barlow, "US Pension Commissioner Green B. Raum of Illinois," *Journal of the Illinois State Historical Society* 60, no. 3 (1967): 299-300.

70. Edward H. Hall, *An Indignity to Our Citizen Soldiers: A Sermon* (Cambridge, MA: John Wilson, 1890), 5-6.

71. Ibid., 7.

72. Glasson, *Federal Military Pensions*, 163.

73. Ibid., 203.

74. Barlow, "US Pension Commissioner Green B. Raum," 297.

75. U.S. Congress, Senate, "Vote 192," 51st cong., 2nd sess., June 23, 1890. https://www.govtrack.us/congress/votes/51-1/s192 (accessed June 13, 2018).

76. U.S. Statutes at Large, "An Act Granting Pensions to Soldiers and Sailors," 51st cong., 1st sess., June 27, 1890, chap. 634, 182-83 at 182, https://www.loc.gov/

law/help/statutes-at-large/51st-congress/session-1/c51s1ch634.pdf (accessed April 23, 2018).

77. Benjamin Harrison, "Second Annual Message," December 1, 1890, *American Presidency Project, UCSB*, http://www.presidency.ucsb.edu/ws/index.php?pid=29531 (accessed April 22, 2018).

78. Bernard Rostker, *Providing for the Casualties of War: The American Experience Through World War II* (Santa Monica, CA: RAND, 2013), 261.

79. Mark E. Rodgers, *Tracing the Civil War Veteran Pension System in the State of Virginia: Entitlement or Privilege* (Lewiston, NY: Edwin Mellon Press, 1999).

80. Mary L. Wilson, "The Confederate Pension Systems in Texas, Georgia, and Virginia: The Programs and the People" (PhD. diss., University of North Texas, 2004).

REFERENCES

Agar, Herbert. *The Price of Union.* Boston: Houghton Mifflin Company, 1950.

Archuleta, Brandon Jason. "The Military Pension Promise: Autonomous Policy Subsystems, Blue Ribbon Defense Commissions, and the Twenty-First Century All-Volunteer Force." PhD diss., University of Texas at Austin, 2015.

Baker, Mike. "Costs of U.S. Wars Linger for over 100 Year." *Associated Press.* March 19, 2013. https://tippingpointnorthsouth.org/2013/06/05/costs-of-u-s-wars-linger-for-over-100-years/ (accessed April 23, 2018).

Barlow, William. "US Pension Commissioner Green B. Raum of Illinois." *Journal of the Illinois State Historical Society* 60, no. 3 (1967): 297-312.

Baumgartner, Frank R., and Bryan D. Jones. *Agendas and Instability in American Politics.* 2nd ed. Chicago: University of Chicago Press, 2009.

Bensel, Richard Franklin. *Sectionalism and American Political Development: 1880-1980.* Madison: University of Wisconsin Press, 1984.

Blair, Henry W. "Statement before the Committee on Pensions of the United States Senate." *Hearings on the Grand Army of the Republic Committee on Pensions.* 48th cong., 1st sess., March 8, 1884. Transcript. Sen 48A-E16, 33p.

Blanck, Peter, and Chen Song, "Civil War Pension Attorneys and Disability Politics." *University of Michigan Journal of Law Reform* 35, nos. 1-2 (Fall 2001-Winter 2002): 1-81. https://pdfs.semanticscholar.org/8aa8/28f3e3def87147c05b52d9bdae7f3fbd2a45.pdf (accessed April 23, 2018).

Calhoun, Charles W. *Benjamin Harrison.* New York: Times Books, 2005.

Cleveland, Grover. "Veto Message." *American Presidency Project, UCSB.* February 11, 1887. http://www.presidency.ucsb.edu/ws/index.php?pid=71488&st=Veto+Message&st1= (accessed April 23, 2018).

Dudley, W. W. "General Instructions to Special Examiners of the United States Pension Bureau." *U.S. Pension Bureau.* Washington, DC: Government Printing Office, 1881.

———. "Letter to Special Examiners." September 20, 1884. Reprint. U.S. Democratic Congressional Committee. "Republican Abuses in the Pension Bureau." In *The Campaign Book of the Democratic Party, 1886*, 6-8, 33-35, 77. Washington,

DC: R. O. Polkinhorn, 1886. https://babel.hathitrust.org/cgi/pt?id=wu.89073007403 (accessed April 22, 2018).

———. "Testimony before the House Committee on Payment of Pensions, Bounty, and Back Pay." In *Hearings on Administration of the Pension Office*. 48th cong., 2nd sess., HR 2683, November 26, 1885, 242-260.

Economist. "Falling Short." *Economist*. April 7, 2011. http://www.economist.com/node/18502013 (accessed April 22, 2018).

Gardner and Burgess, esq. *A Manual of Instructions for the Preparation of Government Claims for Bounty and Back Pay, Pensions, Prize Money, Navy Pay, and for Horses Lost in Battle*. Washington, DC: Gibson Brothers, 1864.

Glasson, Henry. *Federal Military Pensions in the United States*. Edited by David Kinley. New York: Oxford University Press, Carnegie Endowment for International Peace, 1918.

Hall, Edward H. *An Indignity to Our Citizen Soldiers: A Sermon*. Cambridge, MA: John Wilson, 1890.

Harrison, Benjamin. "Letter Accepting the Presidential Nomination." September 11, 1888. *American Presidency Project, UCSB*. http://www.presidency.ucsb.edu/ws/?pid=76068 (accessed April 22, 2018).

———. "Second Annual Message." December 1, 1890. *American Presidency Project, UCSB*. http://www.presidency.ucsb.edu/ws/index.php?pid=29531 (accessed April 22, 2018).

Holman, William. "Remarks on the House Floor." *Congressional Globe*. 37th cong., 2nd sess. May 13, 1862. Part 3.

Hugins, Roland. *Grover Cleveland: A Study in Political Courage*. Washington, DC: Anchor-Lee, 1922.

Jensen, Laura. *Patriots, Settlers, and the Origins of American Social Policy*. Cambridge: Cambridge University Press, 2003.

Keller, Morton. *Affairs of State: Public Life in Late Nineteenth Century America*. Cambridge, MA: Harvard University Press, 1977.

Lasswell, Harold D. *Politics: Who Gets What, When, How*. New York: Whittlesey House, 1936.

McCool, Daniel. "The Subsystem Family of Concepts: A Critique and a Proposal." *Political Research Quarterly* 51, no. 2 (1998): 551-70.

Merrill, George S. "Statement before the Committee on Pensions of the United States Senate." *Hearings on the Grand Army of the Republic Committee on Pensions*. 48th cong., 1st sess., March 8, 1884. Transcript. Sen 48A-E16, 33 p.

———. "Statement before the Committee on Pensions of the United States Senate." *Hearings on the Grand Army of the Republic Committee on Pensions*, 49th cong., 2nd sess., January 19, 1886. Transcript. UB373.A3.1886, 1 p.

"Military Pensions." *New York Times*, July 17, 1921, 26. https://timesmachine.nytimes.com/timesmachine/1921/07/17/109813379.html?pageNumber=26 (June 6, 2018).

"Mr. Dudley and the Pension Office Abuses." *New York Times*, February 25, 1885, 3. https://www.nytimes.com/1885/02/26/archives/mr-dudley-and-the-pension-office-abuses-the-excommissioner.html (accessed April 23, 2018).

National Archives. Senate Records, Group 46. https://www.archives.gov/research/african-americans/record-groups/rg-046-senate.html (accessed April 23, 2018).

"Pension Bureau; Abstract of the Annual Report of Hon. Joseph H. Barrett, Commission of Pensions." *New York Times*, December 3, 1862, 2. https://www.nytimes.com/1862/12/03/archives/the-pension-bureau-abstract-of-the-annual-report-of-hon-joseph-h.html (accessed April 22, 2018).

"Pension Bureau, Report of Commissioner Barrett." *New York Times*, December 9, 1865, 3. https://www.nytimes.com/1865/12/09/archives/the-pension-bureau-report-of-commissioner-barrett.html (accessed April 22, 2018).

"Republican Party Platform of 1888." *American Presidency Project, UCSB*. http://www.presidency.ucsb.edu/ws/index.php?pid=29627 (accessed April 23, 2018).

Rodgers, Mark E. *Tracing the Civil War Veteran Pension System in the State of Virginia: Entitlement or Privilege.* Lewiston, NY: Edwin Mellon Press, 1999.

Rostker, Bernard. *Providing for the Casualties of War: The American Experience Through World War II.* Santa Monica, CA: RAND, 2013.

Sabatier, Paul A, and Christopher Weible. "The Advocacy Coalition Framework: Innovations and Clarification." In *Theories of the Policy Process,* 2nd ed., edited by Paul A. Sabatier, 189-222. Boulder, CO: Westview Press, 2007.

Sanders, Heywood T. "Paying for the Bloody Shirt: The Politics of Civil War Pensions." In *Political Benefits: Empirical Studies of American Public Programs*, edited by Barry S. Rundquist, 137-159. Lexington, MA: Lexington Books, 1980.

Skocpol, Theda. *Protecting Soldiers and Mothers: The Political Origins of Social Policy in the United States.* Cambridge, MA: Harvard University Press, 1992.

Thurber, James. "Dynamics of Policy Subsystems in American Politics." In *Interest Group Politics*, 3rd ed., edited by Allen J. Cigler and Burdett A. Loomis. Washington, DC: Congressional Quarterly Press, 1991.

Trubowitz, Peter. *Defining the National Interest: Conflict and Change in American Foreign Policy.* Chicago: University of Chicago Press, 1998.

U.S. Congress. House. "Testimony Taken by the Committee on Payment of Pensions, Bounty, and Back Pay Relating to the Administration of the Pension Office." Washington: Government Printing Office, 1885.

———. Senate. "Vote 192." 51st cong., 2nd sess., June 23, 1890, http://www.govtrack.us/Congress/votes/51-1/s192 (accessed June 13, 2018).

U. S. Democratic Congressional Committee. "Republican Abuses in the Pension Bureau." In *The Campaign Book of the Democratic Party, 1886*, 6-8, 33-35. Washington, DC: R. O. Polkinhorn, 1886. https://babel.hathitrust.org/cgi/pt?id=wu.89073007403 (accessed April 23, 2018).

U.S. Statutes at Large. "An Act to Authorize the Employment of Volunteers to Aid in Enforcing the Laws and Protecting Public Property." 37th cong., 1st sess., Chap. 9, July 22, 1861, 269-71. https://www.loc.gov/law/help/statutes-at-large/37th-congress/session.../c37s1ch9.pdf (accessed April 23, 2018).

———. "An Act Providing for the Better Organization of the Military Establishment." 37th cong., 1st sess. Chap. 42, sec. 15, August 3, 1861, 287-91, at 289, https://www.loc.gov/law/help/statutes-at-large/37th-congress/session-1/c37s1ch42.pdf (accessed April 23, 2018).

———. "An Act to Grant Pensions." 37th cong., 2nd sess. Chap 166. July 14, 1862, 566-69. https://www.loc.gov/law/help/statutes-at-large/37th-congress/session-2/c37s2ch166.pdf (accessed April 23, 2018).

———. "An Act to Provide That All Pensions on Account of Death, or Wounds Received, or Disease Contracted in the Service of the United States." 45th cong., 3rd sess., Chap. 23. January 25, 1879, 265. https://www.loc.gov/law/help/statutes-at-large/45th-congress/session-3/c45s3ch23.pdf (access April 23, 2018).

———. "An Act Granting Pensions to Soldiers and Sailors." 51st cong., 1st sess., June 27, 1890. Chap. 634, 182-83. https://www.loc.gov/law/help/statutes-at-large/51st-congress/session-1/c51s1ch634.pdf (accessed April 23, 2018).

"The Week." *Nation* 1266, October 3, 1889, 261-63. http://www.unz.org/Pub/Nation-1889oct03-00261?View=PDFPages (accessed April 23, 2018).

Wagner, Louis. "Testimony before the Committee on Pensions of the United States Senate." *Hearings on the Grand Army of the Republic Committee on Pensions*, 48th cong., 1st sess., March 8, 1884. Transcript. Sen 48A-E16, 33p.

Wilson, Mary L. "The Confederate Pension Systems in Texas, Georgia, and Virginia: The Programs and the People." PhD. diss., University of North Texas, 2004.

Worsham, Jeffrey. *Other People's Money: Policy Change, Congress, and Bank Regulation.* Boulder, CO: Westview Press, 1997.

Zafonte, Matthew, and Paul Sabatier. "Shared Beliefs and Imposed Interdependencies as Determinants of Ally Networks in Overlapping Subsystems." *Journal of Theoretical Politics* 10, no. 4, (1998): 473-505.

Chapter 6

Selecting a Military Court-Martial Panel

A Study in Inequality

LTC Christopher Jacobs

The right to a jury trial in criminal cases is a bedrock principle of the United States of America's criminal justice system. Highlighted by police-involved fatalities in Ferguson, Missouri; Staten Island, New York; and Baltimore, Maryland, the power and appeal of a jury in a criminal trial transcends the courtroom.[1] Americans instinctively desire outcomes in criminal cases that have been tested by the fire of the adversarial process—a process that demands the participation of impartial juries. Despite the unique nature of the military justice system, the same respect for the role of the jury (known as panel "members"[2] in military parlance) exists in the military. Unfortunately, as a matter of constitutional interpretation and statutory development, the military panel is vastly inferior to its civilian counterpart. This essay will explain why such differences currently exist and will argue that these differences are an anachronism which perpetuates inequality in the criminal justice system for those serving in the military.

CONVENING A COURT-MARTIAL

The military court-martial traces its lineage directly to Article I, Section 8, Clause 14 of the U.S. Constitution, which gives Congress the power "to make Rules for the Government and Regulation of the land and naval Forces."[3] In furtherance of that duty, Congress created the Uniform Code of Military Justice (UCMJ).[4] The Manual for Court-Martial, a product of the executive branch, builds upon the statutory authority of the UCMJ by filling out the details for creating and conducting courts-martial.[5] "Unlike civilian courts which exercise continuing jurisdiction, military courts are authorized to hear only those cases which have been referred to it [*sic*] by the key figure in this process [namely], the convening authority."[6] The convening authority is a military commander of sufficient rank to create or "convene" a given court-martial.[7] In essence, the convening authority determines whether or not to proceed with a court-martial, the level of court-martial to which the case will be referred, the charges to be leveled against an accused (known as the 'defendant' in the civilian criminal justice system), and which officers and enlisted Soldiers of his command will serve as members of the court-martial panel (the jury).[8]

Created by statute, the modern court-martial markedly differs from its historical antecedent in the Articles of War:

> The modern court-martial has been extensively civilianized and, in more ways than not, closely resembles trial in federal district court. A military judge presides over the court-martial, rules on evidentiary matters and instructs the panel. The court-martial is an adversarial proceeding in which a trial counsel prosecutes the government's case, and the accused [the defendant] is represented either by appointed military defense counsel, a civilian defense counsel, or a combination of the two.... Although there are many functional differences between a court-martial panel and a jury, both perform the similar fact-finding role of listening to the evidence and determining guilt or innocence beyond a reasonable doubt.[9]

Despite these similarities, a major structural anomaly differentiates military panels from their civilian counterparts: the authority possessed by the convening authority to personally select the members of the panel. This key distinction has been the source of much animus, academic literature, and judicial decision-making. "There are no voter-registration or driver's license lists, no venire panels or jury wheels, and no random selection of a representative cross-section of the community,"[10] such as are used in the civilian world. Instead, the convening authority selects members who, "in his opinion, are best qualified for the duty by reason of age, education, training, experience, length of service, and judicial temperament."[11] Because the same person who controls the charges also personally decides who will sit in judgment of the accused, the military panel is, in both practice and perception, inferior to an impartial civilian jury. "The subjective nature of this statutory mandate to select court members according to the personal judgment of the convening authority is, in the words of a former Chief Judge of the United States Court of Appeals for the Armed Forces (CAAF), 'the most vulnerable aspect of the court-martial system; the easiest for critics to attack.'"[12] In essence, the absence of an impartial panel subjects the military accused to an inferior system of justice; at the very least, it readily gives that impression.

HISTORICAL DEVELOPMENT OF MILITARY JUSTICE

Even though the authority of Congress to regulate the Army and the Navy flows directly from the Constitution, the first set of rules governing the American military actually pre-date the Constitution. "On June 14, 1775, before it had even appointed a Commander in Chief for the Army, Congress appointed a committee to prepare rules and regulations for the government of the Army."[13] Sixteen days later, Congress adopted the committee's proposed Articles.[14] Not fully satisfied with the 1775 Articles of War, George Washington asked Congress to revise them—a task that was taken up by John Adams and Thomas Jefferson and approved by Congress in September 1776.[15] Similar to those in the British Articles of War, there were provisions requiring the personal involvement of the convening authority in the court-martial process.[16] The revised Articles of War were later adopted by the new Congress in 1789.[17]

Over the course of the next one-and-a-half centuries, the Articles of War changed numerous times, most notably in 1806 when Congress included "a clause barring double jeopardy, a two-year statute of limitations, a provision allowing the accused to challenge a member of the court, and a provision that a prisoner standing mute would be presumed to plead innocent."[18] In 1874, Congress delineated the class of officers granted the authority to serve as general court-martial convening authorities.[19] Congress also included provisions "allowing for the appointment of a judge advocate to any court-martial" and "allowing for continuances."[20]

The modest changes to the Articles of War throughout the nineteenth century were followed by "revolutionary"[21] changes in the twentieth century.[22] In 1916, Congress began the process of grafting even more fundamental principles of justice and individual rights onto the military justice system. In addition to creating the three types of court-martial that exist to this day (summary court-martial[23], special court-martial[24], and general court-martial[25]), the 1916 Articles of War added provisions that substantially increased fundamental due process protections for an accused. These include: the addition of a judge advocate to serve as a member of general and special courts-martial and to rule on the admissibility of evidence (a significant change, since there were no military judges at this point)[26]; the ability of the accused to be represented by counsel at general and special courts-martial;[27] the right of the accused not to be forced to incriminate himself;[28] the right to at least five days of preparation for trial at a general court-martial following the serving of charges[29]; and the right to be served charges within eight days of arrest, and to trial within ten days of being served.[30]

After World War I, it became increasingly clear that the Articles of War would require even more extensive revision. "The 1916 revisions did not wholly stand the testing fires of … World War I. Troops, officers, and soldiers alike returned with bitter complaints about military justice."[31] These complaints spurred Congress into action and, "in 1920 the Congress enacted a new set of 121 articles of war."[32] The revisions provided an accused even more due process protections. For example, the accused now had the right to a defense counsel, a thorough pretrial investigation at which the accused "was to be given full opportunity for cross-examination and to present matters in defense or mitigation;" and a board of review.[33] While such changes were noble in intent, the military justice system was still deficient in structure. "Notwithstanding these changes, which most agreed represented a fair effort to improve military due process, a troublesome aspect remained. A single commander could prefer charges, convene the court, select the members and counsel, and review the case."[34]

The Articles of War as they existed after the 1920 revisions are, with minor exceptions, the Articles that shepherded military justice through World War II.[35] Just as had occurred in the aftermath of World War I, the conclusion of World War II spurred Congress to conduct a further overhaul of the military justice system. This time, the revisions were not simply grafted onto the existing Articles of War. Rather, the review led to extensive substantive and procedural changes. In fact, "concerns about sentence disparity, harsh treatment, and unlawful command influence over the court-martial system produced a strong reform movement that eventually resulted in the Uniform Code of Military Justice."[36] By serving their country honorably in wartime, the men and (at this point) the women of the military earned the right to a better, more just, legal system. The countless voices of citizens who took part in the war could not be ignored.

> Congress would not have enacted the UCMJ in 1950 if not for the near-universal military service of eligible male citizens during World War II. The shared experience of millions of citizens who were then returning to civilian life served to identify the weaknesses of military justice and motivated Congress to modernize—or "civilianize"—those practices.[37]

The result was the promulgation of the UCMJ as a wholesale replacement of the Articles of War and a compromise between two competing principles, namely, justice and discipline.[38] "Congress struggled to balance the need for the commander to maintain discipline within the ranks against the belief that the military justice system could be made [more fair], to protect the rights of servicemembers against arbitrary actions of commanders."[39]

Indeed, the rights now accorded an accused under the UCMJ are extensive. "At trial, the accused is entitled to virtually the same procedural protections he would have in a state or federal criminal court—largely because Article 36(a) requires that the rules of procedure for military courts parallel the procedures used in federal courts."[40] A non-exhaustive list of these trial rights includes: a speedy trial; pretrial discovery; examination and testing of the government's evidence; witness production (including expert witnesses); witness confrontation; assistance from experts at government expense; election of trial by judge alone or by military members; *voir dire*; and the filing of pretrial motions.[41] In addition to these pretrial and trial rights, there are comprehensive appellate rights, including the right to seek review by the respective service Court of Criminal Appeals, the U.S. Court of Appeals for the Armed Forces (CAAF), and the United States Supreme Court.[42] With all the rights now built into the military justice system, it is markedly different from the Articles of War from which it originated. Yet, one crucial component remains. The commander is still intimately involved in the process, deciding which cases go to trial, the nature of the charges that will be brought, the level of court-martial to which the cases will be referred, and, most importantly, which members of the command will sit in judgment of the accused.[43]

What started as a mechanism to maintain discipline within the military has evolved into a system whose purpose is to promote justice. "In examining the military criminal justice system, the terms 'justice' and 'discipline' are often used to describe the two competing ideals or values which inform the system ... [and which] frame the military justice conundrum."[44] The UCMJ does not provide an answer as to which of the two ideals should be given priority.[45] Fortunately, the Manual for Courts Martial (MCM) fills the gap. According to its Preamble, "the purpose of military law is to promote justice, to assist in maintaining good order and discipline in the armed forces, to promote efficiency and effectiveness in the military establishment, and thereby to strengthen the national security of the United States."[46] By virtue of being listed first, justice is given primacy over discipline. This placement is not mere happenstance; it is a reflection of the freedom that has been purchased by the countless sacrifices of the men and women of the military.

Unfortunately, the transformation of military justice into a system designed to promote the ends of justice (a system that could be viewed as a mirror image of Article III courts)[47]is not complete. "Under the [UCMJ] military personnel are denied the right to grand jury indictment, trial by impartial jury, and bail ...There is no doubt that military personnel enjoy less constitutional rights than their civilian counterparts."[48]

THE RIGHT TO TRIAL BY AN IMPARTIAL JURY

To the casual reader, especially someone familiar with the processes of civilian law, the Sixth Amendment to the Constitution is clear and reassuringly forthright:

> In all criminal prosecutions, the accused shall enjoy the right to a speedy and public trial, by an impartial jury of the State and district wherein the crime shall have been committed, which district shall have been previously ascertained by law, and to be informed of the nature and cause of the accusation; to be confronted with the witnesses against him; to have compulsory process for obtaining witnesses in his favor, and to have the Assistance of Counsel for his defense.[49]

But in the military justice system there remains a notable exception to these rights—the right to an impartial jury. How is it that Congress could provide service members all the remaining protections of the Sixth Amendment, save this one?

According to the United States Supreme Court, the answer lies in the Sixth Amendment's immediate predecessor, the Fifth Amendment. The Fifth Amendment states, in pertinent part, that "No person shall be held to answer for a capital, or otherwise infamous crime, unless on a presentment or indictment of a Grand Jury, *except in cases arising in the land or naval forces, or in the Militia, when in actual service in time of War or public danger*[.][50] Thanks to the Court's decision regarding a petition brought by Lambdin P. Milligan, these two amendments have been forever linked. As a result, Congress has Supreme Court sanction for denying the right of an impartial jury to servicemembers accused of crime.

On May 10, 1865, barely a month after Lee's surrender at Appomattox, Virginia, Lambdin P. Milligan submitted a *habeas corpus* petition seeking release from confinement.[51] At the time, he was in jail awaiting capital punishment pursuant to conviction by a military commission that had convened in Indianapolis, Indiana. Because Milligan had been tried and convicted by military commission, the same person who approved the charges (the convening authority) also determined the composition of the military panel. In his *habeas* petition, Milligan insisted that he was a citizen of the United States, that he had lived in Indiana for twenty years, and that he had never served in the Army or Navy of either the United States or the Confederate States of America. Accordingly, he claimed the military commission had no jurisdiction to try him and requested release from confinement.[52] Publishing the order of the court, Justice Davis agreed with Milligan, writing, "on the facts stated in said petition and exhibits, the military commission mentioned therein had no jurisdiction legally to try and sentence said Milligan in the manner and form as in said petition and exhibits are stated."[53] In other words, Milligan could not be tried before a military commission because he was a civilian, not a combatant, and the civilian courts remained in operation.

Unfortunately, in the course of his opinion, Justice Davis included the following dicta regarding the interplay of the Fifth and Sixth Amendments:

> Another guarantee of freedom was broken when Milligan was denied a trial by jury. The great minds of the country have differed on the correct interpretation to be given to various provisions of the Federal Constitution; and judicial decision has been often invoked to settle their true meaning; but until recently no one ever doubted that the right of trial by jury was fortified in the organic law against the power of attack. It is now assailed; but if ideas can be expressed in words, and language has any meaning, this right—one of the most valuable in a free country—is preserved to every one accused of crime who is not attached to the army, or navy, or militia in actual service. The sixth amendment affirms that "in all criminal prosecutions that accused shall enjoy the right to a speedy and public trial by an impartial jury," language broad enough to embrace all persons and cases; but the fifth, "excepts cases arising in the land or naval forces, or in the militia, when in actual service, in time of war or public danger;" *and the framers of the Constitution, doubtless, meant to limit the right of trial by jury, in the sixth amendment, to those persons who were subject to indictment or presentment in the fifth.*[54]

The last clause of the last sentence had absolutely nothing to do with the issue at hand. After all, the entire point of Milligan's petition was that he had never been a member of the United States or Confederate Army or Navy. Consequently, there was no need for Justice Davis to address the applicability of the Fifth and Sixth Amendments to members of the military.

Unfortunately, since the opinion's issuance his pronouncement has consistently been used by the Court to deny servicemembers the right to an impartial jury. Seventy-six years after *Milligan*, in *Ex parte Quirin*, the Supreme Court reiterated, and thereby reinforced, the *Milligan* Court's unfortunate and unnecessary dicta.[55] Citing *Milligan*, the *Quirin* court noted, "the fact that 'cases arising in the land or naval forces' are excepted from the operation of the Amendments does not militate against th[e] conclusion [that individuals tried by military commission do not have the right to demand a trial by jury]. Such cases are expressly excepted from the Fifth Amendment and are deemed excepted by implication from the Sixth."[56] Given the entrenchment of this principle, Congress has not felt obliged to untie the knot binding the Fifth and Sixth Amendments—a knot that deprives servicemembers of their constitutional right to be tried by an impartial jury.

ANALYSIS OF THE OPERATIVE LANGUAGE

The terse text of the Fifth and Sixth Amendments does not support Justice Davis's infamous linkage of the two clauses. First and foremost, there is no clear language that links the Fifth Amendment phrase "except in cases arising in the land or naval forces, or in the Militia, when in actual service in time of war or public danger" to the Sixth Amendment. Granted, the two amendments do share certain words, such as: "crime," "criminal," "law," and "jury." Rather than linking the two Amendments, however, one of these shared words serves to highlight a key separation between them. The "jury" mentioned in the Fifth Amendment is specifically identified as a "Grand Jury," whereas the "jury" specified in the Sixth Amendment is a trial jury. The grand jury and the trial jury are two distinct entities that serve distinct roles. Grand juries are typically much larger than trial juries and they operate in secret. More importantly, the grand jury is a function of the prosecutorial arm of criminal justice. By virtue of their authority to decide not to return an indictment, "grand jurors ... share half the power of nonprosecutorial discretion."[57] By contrast, the trial jury, an entity that does not meet in secret, is more closely associated with the role of the judge than with the prosecution. Both the trial jury and the judge share the ability to acquit the accused, after the issuance of an indictment, for any reason whatsoever.[58]

The separation of pre-indictment and post-indictment responsibilities largely holds when comparing the general purposes of the Fifth and Sixth Amendments. The Fifth Amendment focuses on matters best characterized as conditions precedent to a trial: no person can be tried for a capital or infamous crime unless and until a grand jury issues an indictment; no person can be twice placed in jeopardy for the same offense (a fact which affects a prosecutor's initial charging decision); no person can be compelled to be a witness against himself (which affects pretrial evidence collection); and, finally, no person can be deprived of life, liberty, or property without due process of law (which highlights the fact that pretrial stages of a trial can be just as important to due process as those that take place after indictment). The Sixth Amendment, however, speaks more to what must take place after a person has been charged. For example, the accused has a right to a speedy and public trial; the right to a jury composed of people from the general area where the alleged crime was committed (or, in the military context, from the relevant military command to which the accused belonged); the right to confront the witnesses against him (there is no confrontation right at the grand jury because the defendant is not present); the right to compulsory process for securing the presence of witnesses at trial; and the right to legal representation at trial. Though not perfect, there is enough of a "before trial" versus "during trial" distinction between the two amendments to preclude an implication that the founding fathers intended the two to operate in tandem, much less to forever bar servicemembers from the right to trial by an impartial jury.

There is another textual clue that countermands Justice Davis's marriage of the two amendments. The Sixth Amendment explicitly ties "all criminal prosecutions" to "the accused", the two phrases being separated by nothing more than a comma. The latter phrase constitutes a term of art in military justice practice. In the UCMJ, it is the sole expression used to identify any servicemember who is believed to have committed a particular offense. After the word "Defendant," the Index to the MCM states, "*See* Accused."[59] In fact, other than this reference in the index, the UCMJ does not use the word "defendant" at all. Even in the non-criminal realm of adverse administrative actions in the military (for example, expelling a person from the Army for being a poor, albeit non-criminal, Soldier), the unfortunate Soldier is referred to as a "respondent" not a "defendant." Anyone acquainted with the system of military criminal justice will immediately take note of the Sixth Amendment's use of the words, "the accused"—a usage which strongly suggests that in *all* criminal prosecutions, including military prosecutions, the "accused" has a right to an impartial jury.[60] For the military justice practitioner, the use of this term is a beacon in the dark, illuminating a right to which servicemembers are just as entitled as anyone else to whom the Constitution applies. The framers of the Constitution, having been tested by the fires of the Revolutionary War, would likely have been sensitive to the delicate balance between military discipline and military justice. The plain language of the Fifth and Sixth Amendments accounts for this balance without depriving servicemembers of a valuable constitutional protection.

Some writers have attempted to link the Fifth and Sixth Amendments by citing an initial House draft of the Tenth Amendment,

> Tenth. The trial of all crimes (except in cases of impeachment, and in cases arising in the land and naval forces, or in the militia when in actual service in time of war or public danger) shall be by an impartial Jury of the vicinage, with the requisite of unanimity for conviction, the right of challenge, and other accustomed requisites; and no person shall be held to answer for a capital, or otherways [*sic*] crime, unless on a presentment or indictment by a Grand Jury; but if a crime be committed in a place in possession of an enemy, or in which an insurrection may prevail, the indictment and trial may by law be authorized in some other place within the State.[61]

By including both the grand jury and the trial jury rights within a listing of privileges excepted from application to cases arising in the land and naval forces, the House signaled an intent to deny both rights to servicemembers, or so the argument contends. However, "the Senate objected to the House version. Initially, the Senate stripped the House's Tenth Article of its petit jury guarantee and, a few days later, combined the grand jury provision (including the military exclusion) with another proposed amendment ... [that] became our present Fifth Amendment."[62] Far from supporting a claim that the military exception should apply to both forms of jury, the drafting history reinforces the opposite conclusion. The drafters had a clear opportunity to link the two rights to the military exception clause, and affirmatively chose to break them apart. This affirmative act is much more telling of the Founders' intent than Justice Davis's bald assertion that "the framers of the Constitution, doubtless, meant to limit the right of trial by jury."[63]

In sum, the last sentence of Justice Davis's paragraph does not make sense within the plain reading of the document. Had the framers intended that the Sixth Amendment should not apply to servicemembers, they could have qualified the Sixth Amendment as easily as they had the Fifth. Or, easier still, they could have added a phrase such as "nor shall the accused in all criminal prosecutions be denied the right to an impartial jury of the State and district wherein the crime shall have been committed" immediately before the words, "except in cases arising in the land or naval forces" within the body of the Fifth Amendment. Either method would have left no doubt as to their intention. As it is, servicemembers have been denied a right that is "fortified in the organic law" and "one of the most valuable in a free country" by virtue of a judicial interpretation—and a dubious one at best.[64] One would hope the denial of such an important right would have more basis in the plain language of the text.

Adding insult to injury, subsequent Supreme Court caselaw repeated and solidified Justice Davis's unfortunate dicta. As a result, the Fifth and Sixth Amendments have become inextricably linked. For example, in *Johnson v. Sayre*, the Court expanded Justice Davis's foundation and interpreted the "time of war" provision in the Fifth Amendment to refer only to cases arising in the militia, not the land or naval forces.[65] This interpretation meant that servicemembers could not avail themselves of the protections of the Fifth and Sixth Amendments at all, even during peacetime. In his dissenting opinion in *Solorio v. United States*, Justice Marshall took exception to this interpretation, noting:

> The language of this exception could be understood to mean that "cases arising in the land or naval forces," as well as in the militia, are only excepted from the requirement of grand jury indictment or presentment "in actual service in time of war or public danger." This Court, however, has interpreted the "time of war" provision as referring only to cases arising in the militia, not the land or naval forces.... I am not convinced this reading of the Fifth Amendment is correct, but need not rely on a different interpretation here.[66]

It is unfortunate that Justice Marshall was not compelled to answer that particular issue in deciding the matter at hand. If Justice Davis had exercised the same degree of restraint, this issue would be moot, and servicemembers might have retained a fundamental right available to their civilian counterparts—the right to be judged by an impartial jury.

THE SUPREME COURT'S ATTEMPT TO LIMIT THE DAMAGE CAUSED BY *MILLIGAN*

In 1969, the Supreme Court held in *O'Callahan v. Parker* that "in order for a court-martial convened pursuant to the [UCMJ] to have jurisdiction to try a member of the Armed Forces, the offenses with which the soldier was charged had to be 'service connected.'"[67] By creating this "service connection" test, the Court attempted to limit the types of offenses for which a servicemember could be court-martialed. In effect, the Court sought to use the "arising in" phrase of the Fifth Amendment to narrow the scope of cases amenable to courts-martial. The Court's rationale for developing the service connection test was quite telling. Essentially, the Court was concerned with the disparity (inequality) between the constitutional rights available to a military accused as compared to those available to a civilian defendant. The Court declared:

> We find nothing in the history or constitutional treatment of military tribunals which entitles them to rank along with Article III courts as adjudicators of the guilt or innocence of people charged with offenses for which they can be deprived of their life, liberty, or property. Unlike courts, it is the primary business of armies and navies to fight or be ready to fight wars should the occasion arise. But trial of soldiers to maintain discipline is merely incidental to an army's primary fighting function. To the extent that those responsible for performance of this primary function are diverted from it by the necessity of trying cases, the basic fighting purpose of armies is not served. *And conceding to military personnel that high degree of honesty and sense of justice which nearly all of them undoubtedly have, it still remains true that military tribunals have not been and probably never can be constituted in such way that they can have the same kind of qualifications that the Constitution has deemed essential to fair trials of civilians in federal courts.*[68]

In other words, to protect servicemembers from being too often subjected to the diminished constitutional protections inherent in their own system of justice, the *O'Callahan* Court created the "service connection" test to narrow the aperture and thereby limit the reach of the UCMJ.

The chief concerns for the *O'Callahan* Court were the purpose, structure, and function of military panels:

> There is great difference between trial by jury and trial by selected members of the military forces. It is true that military personnel because of their training and experience may be especially competent to try soldiers for infractions of military rules. Such training is no doubt particularly important where an offense charged against a soldier is purely military, such as disobedience of an order, leaving post, etc. But whether right or wrong, the premise underlying the

> constitutional method for determining guilt or innocence in federal courts is that laymen are better than specialists to perform this task. This idea is inherent in the institution of trial by jury.[69]

This passage offers insight into the Court's thinking. It suggests that the criteria set out in Article 25 of the UCMJ which the Convening Authority must consider in selecting panel members—namely age, education, training, experience, length of service, and judicial temperament—are pertinent only to selecting members to vote on purely military offenses, since only those offenses require some particularized knowledge or understanding of military life. Conversely, for offenses with no military connection, it is preferable to have laymen sit in judgment. Unfortunately, the UCMJ does not make this distinction. Panels selected by the convening authority are selected for all offenses. In fact, a military charge sheet does not distinguish between offenses that are "military" in character (violation of a lawful order, missing a movement, disrespect) and offenses that might be viewed as more "civilian" in nature, especially when the victim happens to be a civilian (assault, rape, drunk driving, failure to pay a just debt). A violation of any of the punitive articles of the UCMJ is a violation of military "law"—period.

After identifying several structural differences between panels and juries, the *O'Callahan* Court identified the danger posed by a system that relies upon a convening authority to personally select the members of the panel:

> the suggestion of the possibility of influence on the actions of the court-martial by the officer who convenes it, selects its members and the counsel on both sides, and who usually has direct command authority over its members is a pervasive one in military law, despite strenuous efforts to eliminate the danger.[70]

The Court's concerns over the shortcomings of the military justice system buttressed its decision to devise a wholesale alteration to the jurisdictional scheme for courts-martial. The Court articulated its concern in these words: "there are dangers lurking in military trials which were sought to be avoided by the Bill of Rights and Article III of our Constitution. Free countries of the world have tried to restrict military tribunals to the narrowest jurisdiction deemed absolutely essential to maintaining discipline."[71]

THE INHERENT DANGERS OF THE COURT-MARTIAL PANEL SELECTION PROCESS

For their part, the military courts have also identified the dangers inherent in the power of the convening authority (CA) to select the members of the panel.

In 2001, the Court of Appeals for the Armed Forces (CAAF) identified the following premise in *U.S. v. Wiesen*:

> As a matter of due process, an accused has a constitutional right, as well as a regulatory right, to a fair and impartial panel. Indeed, "impartial court-members are a *sine qua non* for a fair court-martial." That is not to say that an accused has a right to the panel of his choice, just to a fair and impartial panel.[72]

The UCMJ clearly establishes that the CA must personally select the members of the panel. This does not entail that the CA cannot have help in accomplishing this task. Given the CA's numerous responsibilities, it may "rely upon [its] staff to nominate court members."[73] In other words, the CA can turn to subordinate commanders and its Staff Judge Advocate for assistance, although the danger remains that such individuals might have a partisan interest in the case at hand.

Nevertheless, in the process of compiling the list of panel members from which the CA makes the final selection, certain practices are presumptively invalid. In *U.S. v. Dowty* (2004), CAAF listed the following examples of improper screening practices: devising a list of nominees based solely on the basis of rank; excluding potentially qualified members below a given rank; deliberately stacking the pool of potential members; submitting nominees who were supporters of a command policy of hard discipline; and excluding more junior officers and enlisted members in an attempt to prevent light sentences.[74] By virtue of being explicitly noted by the court, each of these practices had actually been attempted. Accordingly, all participants in the court-martial process must be especially vigilant to their presence. But this need only emphasizes the defective foundation of the military panel, because it is extremely difficult, if not impossible, for the defense counsel to ensure that such screening practices scrupulously comply with the letter and spirit of Article 25 of the UCMJ.[75] As a result, the CA may unwittingly apply the Article 25 selection criteria to an improperly nominated pool of candidates, thus rendering the final selection inherently flawed and leaving the vaunted Article 25 criteria utterly powerless to protect the rights of the accused.[76]

The Article 25 criteria together serve more as a palliative than a protection. How, for example, can attorneys and judges determine whether a CA has properly applied the criteria in selecting a particular panel? In other words, how is it possible to systemically test whether the CA has, in fact, complied with the express language of Article 25, that "the convening authority shall detail as members thereof such members of the armed forces as, in his opinion, are best qualified for the duty by reason of age, education, training, experience, length of service, and judicial temperament."[77] Do these criteria carry equal weight or are some more important by virtue of their placement on the list? For example, should the criterion "age" be afforded more importance because it is listed first? And which way does the "age" criterion cut? Should the CA select panel members who are more likely to be closer in age to the accused (hence making younger members preferable)? Or should the CA select members who are older and more experienced? This latter interpretation, however, highlights a potentially internal inconsistency within the criteria themselves. Both "age" and "experience" are separately listed criteria and in different numerical order. If the intent of Article 25 is to select members who are older and more experienced, then two of the listed criteria are merely redundant. Interpreted in this manner, the two criteria would lose any individual meaning. But if the criteria do not carry any individual significance, why are they listed separately in the first place?

While the criteria seem intended to guide a CA's decision-making process, in reality they could also serve as a *post hoc* justification for any selections a CA might make. Consider the second criterion: education. What exactly does this mean and how should it be applied? Does it mean that a panel member must have received only some level of education in order to be eligible for consideration? Or is it meant as an evaluative criterion, implying that higher levels of education are more preferable? Since the CA is charged with selecting only the "best qualified," does their *level* of education or the *quality* of their educational institution matter more? For example, should the CA consult college-ranking services to determine which of the nominees received a "better" education? If so, what ranking service should be consulted? Where should the service academies fall in this ranking system? What about college majors? Should an engineering major be given more weight than a humanities major, or *vice versa*? And what is the difference between "education" and "training" (the third criterion)? Does the nature of the training matter? For example, should the CA prefer individuals with training in military justice or training in airborne operations? Should the defense counsel be allowed to question a CA to find out why a senior officer with a degree from a prestigious university was not selected to serve on a particular court-martial panel over other selectees with seemingly lesser qualifications?—These questions illustrate how difficult (quite possibly impossible) it is for the attorneys and judges involved in courts-martial to ensure that the Article 25 criteria have been followed and that the criteria are being applied consistently by different CAs.[78]

Finally, is the CA allowed to consider factors beyond those listed in Article 25? Assume that a CA believes that after strictly applying the Article 25 criteria, the First Brigade commander is the absolute "best qualified" individual to sit on the court-martial panel. However, the CA also knows that over the course of the next six months First Brigade is scheduled for extensive training in preparation for a potential upcoming deployment. Can the CA take this additional information into consideration in order to bypass the otherwise "best qualified" individual within the command? Or should the CA comply with Article 25, select the officer to sit on the panel, and then invoke the authority set forth in Article 25(e) to excuse this particular officer from sitting on a given court-martial when doing so would conflict with scheduled training?[79] This may seem like a distinction without a difference. There is, however, a very good reason for selecting the latter course of action: it establishes a record. The Defense Counsel would be able to see the trail of excusals and then decide if that trail merited further inquiry. How can participants in the court-martial process know whether the CA elected option one or option two? Lacking such knowledge, who can say that the panel is truly "best qualified"?

Once the panel is seated in the court-martial, other dangers might arise. Chief among these is the concern that the panel is not truly impartial. "The UCMJ and common law incorporate a number of methods to validate this right, including *voir dire*, the challenge for cause, and the peremptory challenge."[80] The trial counsel (prosecutor) and the defense counsel use these tools to identify potential bias which can then be used to challenge a given panel member for cause, not unlike what obtains in federal criminal law practice. In military practice, there are two forms of bias: actual and implied. "The test for actual bias is whether any bias 'is such that it will not yield to the evidence presented and the judge's instructions.'"[81] The key difference between actual bias and implied bias is in the eye of the beholder. "While actual bias is reviewed through the eyes of the military judge or the court members, implied bias is reviewed under an objective standard, viewed through the eyes of the public ... the focus 'is on the perception or appearance of fairness of the military justice system.'"[82] In *U.S. v. Wiesen*, the implied bias at issue was the fact that the senior member of the panel held a supervisory position over six other members. These seven votes constituted a two-thirds majority sufficient to obtain a conviction. In a case such as this, the court noted, "we are placing an intolerable strain on public perception of the military justice system."[83]

In *Wiesen*, the implied bias sufficient to overturn the decision was identified by the defense counsel and developed during *voir dire*. The same method is used in federal courts to challenge potential jurors for cause. In contrast, the Article 25 court-martial panel selection criteria merely set the range of potential panel members available for selection by the CA but are inadequate for ensuring an impartial panel. Yet, if the CA begins with a list of proposed panel members who have been improperly screened, the members ultimately selected by the CA will comprise a flawed panel, which the selection criteria can do nothing to prevent. Why does the military adhere to this process? Why not simply select a random pool of officers and enlisted personnel from a given command to be on-call for court-martial panel duty for a predetermined amount of time (say, six months) and permit this panel to be tested and winnowed through *voir dire*? From the randomly selected initial pool (prior to *voir dire*), the command should apply the available qualification standards listed in Rules for Court-Martial (R.C.M.) to excuse unqualified panel members[84]. Utilizing this procedure, the CA would not exercise any discretion in selecting the members of the panel, although the panel members would still have to meet certain qualification tests (for example, the requirement that members should normally be senior in rank to the accused).[85] Though the resulting panel could not in all fairness be labelled "best qualified," its members would each be "qualified" and the panel itself would be free of any taint—intentional, unintentional, or perceived—occasioned by the CA's personal involvement. This procedural change would be a significant improvement and an encouraging step to ensure that servicemembers, like the civilians they serve and protect, also enjoy the right to be tried by an impartial jury.

However, without a change of heart by the Supreme Court or intervention by Congress, this revision will not occur. The reason lies in the inherent power of the convening authority—a power the military services assiduously protect. Before broaching this matter, however, it is necessary to give further consideration to the service connection test by which the Supreme Court in 1969 sought to limit the types of offense over which courts-martial would have jurisdiction.

THE SERVICE CONNECTION TEST: REVISITED

The *O'Callahan* "service connection" test lasted a mere eighteen years. In 1987, the Court overruled *O'Callahan* in *Solorio v. United States*. Delivering the opinion of the Court, Chief Justice Rehnquist wrote:

> In 1969, the Court in *O'Callahan v. Parker* departed from the military status test and announced the 'new constitutional principle' that a military tribunal may not try a serviceman charged with a crime that has no service connection . . . On reexamination of *O'Callahan*, we have decided that the service connection test announced in that decision should be abandoned.[86]

In its opinion, the majority disagreed with the historical evidence relied upon by the *O'Callahan* Court. The *Solorio* Court's re-examination of history dovetailed with its support for the doctrine of judicial deference to Congress on matters concerning the regulation of the military:

> Decisions of this Court after *O'Callahan* have ... emphasized that Congress has primary responsibility for the delicate task of balancing the rights of servicemen against the needs of the military. As we recently reiterated, "judicial deference

> ... is at its apogee when legislative action under the congressional authority to raise and support armies and make rules and regulations for their governance is challenged."[87]

With the overruling of the service connection test, the military only had to show that a servicemember was "a member of the Armed Services at the time of the offense charged" in order to establish court-martial jurisdiction.[88]

While the majority did not speculate about the effects this expansion of jurisdiction would have on the constitutional rights of the accused, the question did not escape the attention, or ire, of those members of the court who dissented. Writing for this group, Justice Marshall began by noting the effect the majority's ruling would have on servicemembers' Fifth and Sixth Amendment rights:

> Less than 20 years ago, this Court held in *O'Callahan v. Parker* ... that, to be subject to trial by court-martial, a criminal offense charged against a member of the Armed Forces had to be "service connected," lest the phrase "cases arising in the land or naval forces" in the Fifth Amendment "be expanded to deprive every member of the armed services of the benefits of an indictment by the grand jury and a trial by a jury of his peers." Today the court overrules *O'Callahan.* In doing so, it disregards constitutional language and principles of *stare decisis* in its singleminded determination to subject members of our Armed Forces to the unrestrained control of the military in the area of criminal justice.[89]

Despite painting the military justice system in a rather bad light, the dissent correctly notes that servicemembers stand to lose precious constitutional rights under the majority's decision. Justice Marshall observed:

> The protections afforded individuals by the Fifth and Sixth Amendments are central to our constitutional scheme of justice. The right to trial by jury, in particular, "ranks very high in our catalogue of constitutional safeguards." *United States ex. rel. Toth v. Quarles*, 350 U.S. at 16. These protections should not be lightly abrogated. Consequently, the exception in the Fifth Amendment for cases arising in the Armed Forces must be strictly construed.[90]

Rather than being strictly construed, the exception language in the Fifth Amendment continues to be the basis for denying servicemembers the right to an impartial jury under the Sixth Amendment. The denial is not occasioned by the text of the Constitution. As Justice Davis explained in his original dicta, the denial is based upon implication—a linkage, if you will—between the Fifth Amendment's grand jury and the Sixth Amendment's impartial trial jury, because of the burden that the right to an impartial jury would place on the military's need to instill discipline.

Herein lies the rub. Since 1920, the UCMJ and its predecessor, the Articles of War, have mandated an alternative to the grand jury. While this alternative does not provide the same level of constitutional protection as the grand jury,[91] it does establish a process that can be rather burdensome to the command. This alternative process is known as the Article 32 Preliminary Hearing (or simply as an "Article 32" in military jargon).[92] Pursuant to this article:

(1) No charge or specification may be referred to a general court-martial for trial until completion of a preliminary hearing, unless such hearing is waived by the accused.
(2) The purpose of the preliminary hearing shall be limited to the following:
  (A) Determining whether there is probable cause to believe an offense has been committed and the accused committed the offense.
  (B) Determining whether the convening authority has court-martial jurisdiction over the accused.
  (C) Considering the form of the charges.
  (D) Recommending the disposition that should be made of the case.[93]

Granted, the recommendations made by the Preliminary Hearing Officer (PHO) at the conclusion of the hearing do not bind the Convening Authority, who may pursue charges against an accused contrary to the recommendation of the PHO.[94] However, Article 32 provides numerous due process advantages that a grand jury does not. Most importantly, the preliminary hearing is not conducted in secret. In fact, Article 32 guarantees the accused the following procedural rights: to be advised of the charges; to be represented by either military defense counsel or civilian counsel at the hearing; to cross-examine the witnesses against him; to present evidence in defense and mitigation; and to request additional witnesses favorable to his or her cause.[95] All of this testimony is taken under oath and can used by the parties at trial (for example, to impeach a witness on the basis of a prior inconsistent statement).

In the notorious *Milligan* decision, Justice Davis famously proclaimed that servicemembers are not entitled to the right to an impartial jury under the Sixth Amendment because, by implication, they are excepted from the right to a grand jury in the Fifth Amendment. Put another way, servicemembers are not entitled to a trial by an impartial jury because they are not entitled to a grand jury. However, servicemembers (through Article 32) are afforded a procedurally burdensome alternative to a grand jury. The myriad rights enshrined in this process were created by a Congress that was well aware of the impact these requirements would have on a CA's ability to move a case to trial.[96] With this in mind, what prevents Congress from affording servicemembers a functional equivalent to an impartial jury? The next section will focus on possible reasons for its reluctance to lessen the authority of the convening authority.

CONGRESSIONAL RELUCTANCE

Like any bureaucracy, the United States military is not immune to politics. Unfortunately, military justice is not immune to such considerations either. Much of the literature defending the right of the CA to personally select members of a court-martial panel focuses on the responsibility of the CA (as commander) to maintain discipline within the command. Professor Schlueter has contended that, "from the beginnings of the United States' military justice system, courts and most commentators agreed that the system was designed to protect and promote military discipline."[97] In support of this argument, he quotes an 1879 letter from General William Tecumseh Sherman to General W. S. Hancock:

> The object of the civil law is to secure to every human being in a community all the liberty, security, and happiness possible, consistent with the safety of all. The object of military law is to govern armies composed of strong men, so as to be capable of exercising the largest measure of force at the will of the nation.[98]

However, there is a competing theory which holds that although the military justice system originated as a system to maintain discipline, it has evolved over the course of United States history into a system whose purpose is to promote justice. In other words, the system that exists today is different in both function and purpose from the one created by the Founding Fathers. In today's military, it is justice that ensures discipline, not the iron fist of the commander:

> Insofar as our fundamental goal is concerned, it is clear that military criminal law in the United States is justice-based. This is not, however, incompatible with discipline. Congress has, at least implicitly, determined that discipline within the American fighting force requires that personnel believe that justice will be done. In short, the United States uses a justice-oriented system to ensure discipline; in our case, justice is essential to discipline.[99]

Carrying the justice-based theme one step further, the Judge Advocate General of the Air Force drew a direct connection between the Air Force's ability to promote justice and its ability to recruit new Airmen to fill its ranks:

> America's mothers and fathers send their sons and daughters to us to join our all-volunteer force because they believe their children will be fairly treated.

> They believe and expect that we will adhere to due process in judging their children, should they violate our code; otherwise, they would not have sent them to us. As a result, when we adhere to due process, we send a message to those parents, parents of other prospective Airmen and all Airmen everywhere that they can trust the Air Force to treat its Airmen fairly and to protect and promote justice within our service. By protecting our recruiting and retention pipelines, due process safeguards our combat effectiveness.[100]

This passage calls attention to the fact that servicemembers are not extraneous actors. They belong to "We the People": they represent the United States in all its diversity. However different as "we" may be, we are united by one Constitution. Accordingly, in their pre- and post-military lives, servicemembers are accorded all the protections of the United States Constitution. Why would people volunteer to serve and protect their fellow citizens knowing that doing so would entitle them to fewer rights than they would otherwise possess? The answer is intuitively simple. People understand there may be occasions when individual rights must bend to security. For example, in time of war people understand and readily accept the need for certain restrictions on the freedom of speech, such as prohibitions on publishing the departure schedules of troop transport ships.

However, comparable restrictions need not exist within the domain of military justice. Our military does not operate as it did in 1776. In today's world, courts-martial regularly take place in combat zones. When a case is too complex to be tried in a combat zone, it is transferred to a secure military installation in the United States. The fundamental point is this: given the historical development of military justice and the manner in which it is currently employed, there is no overriding military necessity for today's servicemembers to sacrifice rights to which they would otherwise be entitled, especially when the right at issue is the fundamental right to be tried by an impartial jury.

Nevertheless, current events demonstrate that the pendulum may be swinging back in the direction of favoring military discipline over military justice. This change is epitomized by the military services' reaction to the scourge of sexual harassment within the ranks. The film, *The Invisible War*,[101] brought the issue out of the shadows and placed it squarely before the public—and Congress. In the aftermath of the film's release, United States Senator Kirsten Gillibrand (D-N.Y.) led the charge to change the culture of the military on reporting and responding to allegations of sexual assault. Unsatisfied with the military's efforts to remedy this issue on its own, Senator Gillibrand proposed legislation that would have removed sexual assault cases from the ambit of the CA and placed them within the realm of a District Attorney-analogue, to be established at each military installation. In effect, Senator Gillibrand proposed "civilianizing" this particular category of criminal offense, thereby drastically limiting the influence of the CA. After months of intense debate, Senator Gillibrand's proposal failed by the narrowest of margins, falling "just five votes short of the [sixty] she needed to overcome a filibuster."[102] Intense lobbying efforts by the military services and their allies on Capitol Hill succeeded. Their rallying cry was elegant in its simplicity: Senator Gillibrand's proposal was an attack on the core authority of the convening authority and would diminish the ability of commanders to maintain good order and discipline in their units, most especially in the area of sexual assault.

In order to improve its understanding of the military's efforts to prevent and respond to allegations of sexual assault, Congress created a panel known as the Response Systems Panel, or RSP.[103] The mission of the RSP was to visit military installations; to meet with convening authorities, Judge Advocates, medical providers, and others involved in the prevention and response to sexual assaults; and to report its findings and recommendations back to Congress.[104] In addition to its informational role, the RSP also spurred intimate discussion between Staff Judge Advocates (the CA's Legal Advisor) and their respective CAs on the various roles that CAs play in military justice. Not surprisingly, what emerged was a consensus among CAs that they had to continue to play an omnipresent role in military justice in order to lead their units (and their services as a whole) properly. What also emerged, however, were frank discussions whether CAs needed to retain all of their various military justice authorities. The door was thus opened to the possibility of disaggregating some of the CA's current military justice functions, such as the power to personally select the members of military panels. Unfortunately, those who were willing to entertain the notion of disaggregation were effectively silenced when Senator Gillibrand's proposal failed, and when Congress as a whole passed the 2014 National Defense Authorization Act (NDAA).[105]

The 2014 NDAA not only slammed the door on rethinking the need for CAs to exercise their role in selecting the membership of panels, it also enacted measures that rolled back some of the procedural protections that had been mainstays in military justice practice. A case in point is the changes the NDAA made to Article 32. Practically, the changes reinforced the CA's ability to maintain good order and discipline at the expense of due process protections for the accused (especially when the charges include allegations of sexual assault).

NECESSITY OF SUPREME COURT INTERVENTION

The United States Supreme Court should lead the way in recognizing the right of servicemembers to be tried by an impartial jury. The Court should undertake this endeavor for several reasons. First, it was the Court that created the problem. Thanks to the knot tied by Justice Davis, the Fifth Amendment grand jury military exception has been inseparably bound to the Sixth Amendment right to a trial by an impartial jury. As a result, the progressive improvements in military justice from the Articles of War through the UCMJ—changes that saw military justice begin the transition from a system focused on discipline to a system devoted to justice—have conveniently sidestepped the issue of the CA's ability to personally select the members of the court-martial panel.

With the Supreme Court sanction in place, Congress has not been compelled to reconsider the fairness and impartiality of military panels. Even more worrisome are recent efforts by Congress to roll back some military justice procedural due process protections in an effort to make it easier for CAs to pursue courts-martial in sexual assault cases. By favoring exigency over due process, Congress has demonstrated that it is unwilling to consider making a change to the UCMJ that could be perceived as detracting from the power of a CA to maintain discipline. Therefore, if such a change is ever to happen, it must be instigated by the Supreme Court. By untying the knot binding the two amendments, the Court would ensure that the Sixth Amendment right to an impartial jury applies to all Americans.

NOTES

1. On November 24, 2014, a grand jury in Ferguson, Missouri made the decision not to issue an indictment in the shooting death of Michael Brown by a police officer. Mr. Brown was not armed at the time of the shooting. As a result of the grand jury's decision, rioting broke out in Ferguson, and in other major metropolitan cities throughout the United States. See CBS Interactive and Associated Press, "Ferguson Grand Jury Decision Sparks Protests Nationwide," *CBS News*, November 24, 2014, http://www.cbsnews.com/news/ferguson-grand-jury-decision-sparks-protests-nationwide/ (accessed July 5, 2017).

2. Manual for Courts-Martial, United States pt. II, R.C.M 501-03 (2012 Edition) (hereafter cited MCM). References and endnotes in this chapter will follow the style of *The Bluebook: A Uniform System of Citation*, 17th ed. (Cambridge, MA: Harvard Law Review Association, 2000).

3. U.S. Const. art. I, § 8, cl. 14.

4. MCM, *supra* note 2, pt. 1, ¶ 3.

5. MCM, *supra* note 2, pt. 1, ¶ 4. "The [MCM] shall consist of [a] Preamble, the Rules for Courts-Martial [R.C.M.], the Military Rules of Evidence [M.R.E.], the Punitive Articles, and Nonjudicial Punishment Procedures (Part I-V)." *Id.*

6. David A. Schlueter, Military Criminal Justice – Practice and Procedure 178 (3d ed. 1992).

7. MCM, *supra* note 2, R.C.M. 504. There are three types of courts-martial: summary court-martial, special court-martial, and general court-martial, in ascending order. The rank and position of the commander determine the type of court-martial to which the case may be referred. For example, a Division Commander in the rank of Major General may refer a case to any of the three types of court-martial, as appropriate. The highest level of court-martial, the general court-martial, is empowered to adjudge any sentence authorized by law. The other two forms of court-martial are restricted in the types of cases they may hear and the amount of punishment they may deliver.

8. *Id.*, R.C.M. 503.

9. MAJ Christopher W. Behan, *Don't Tug on Superman's Cape: In Defense of Convening Authority Selection and Appointment of Court-Martial Panel Members*, 176 MIL. L. REV. 190, 192 (2003).

10. *Id.* at 193.

11. UNIFORM CODE OF MILITARY JUSTICE, art. 25(d)(2) (2012).

12. Behan, *supra*, note 10, at 193 (citing *United States v. Smith*, 27 M.J. 242 (C.M.A. 1988) (Cox, J., concurring) (hereafter cited UCMJ).

13. *Id.* at 208 (citing Gordon D. Henderson, *Courts-Martial and the Constitution: The Original Understanding*, 71 HARV. L. REV. 293, 298 n.41 (1957)).

14. Behan, *supra* note 10, at 209 (citing WILLIAM WINTHROP, MILITARY LAW AND PRECEDENTS 47 (2d ed. 1920 reprint)).

15. *Id.*, also citing 5 JOURNALS OF THE CONTINENTAL CONGRESS, 1774-1789, at 670-71 n.2.

16. Behan, *supra* note 10, at 209-11.

17. Behan, *supra* note 10, at 214-15. "Following ratification of the Constitution in 1789, the First Congress ... expressly adopted the Articles of War that were already in force to govern the Army." *Id.*

18. SCHLUETER, *supra* note 7, at 27.

19. SCHLUETER, *supra* note 7, at 29.

20. SCHLUETER, *supra* note 7, at 30. A "judge advocate" is the title used to denote an officer in the Judge Advocate General's (JAG) Corps of each of the respective branches of the military. In order to become a member of the JAG Corps, the officer must be an attorney. A "continuance" refers to a delay that is granted in a given proceeding.

21. SCHLUETER, *supra* note 7, at 31.

22. *Id.*

23. UCMJ art. 20 (2012). A summary court-martial may "adjudge any punishment not forbidden by this chapter except death, dismissal, dishonorable discharge, confinement for more than one month, hard labor without confinement for more than 45 days, restriction to specified limits for more than two months, or forfeiture of more than two-thirds of one month's pay." *Id.*

24. UCMJ art. 19 (2012). A special court-martial may "adjudge any punishment not forbidden by this chapter except death, dismissal, dishonorable discharge, confinement for more than one year, hard labor without confinement for more than three months, forfeiture of pay exceeding two-thirds pay per month, or forfeiture of pay for more than one year." *Id.*

25. UCMJ art. 18 (2012). A general court-martial may "adjudge any punishment not forbidden by this chapter, including the penalty of death when specifically authorized by this chapter." *Id.*

26. Schlueter, *supra* note 7, at 31, citing 39 Stat. L. 619, Art. 11, 650 (1916).

27. *Id.*, Article 17.

28. *Id.*, Article 24.

29. *Id.*, Article 70.

30. Schlueter, *supra* note 7, at 31, n. 60.

31. Schlueter, *supra* note 7, at 31.

32. *Id.* at 32.

33. *Id.*

34. *Id.*

35. *Id.*

36. Behan, *supra* note 10, at 220. "During World War II, the armed services conducted nearly two million courts-martial. There had been over one hundred executions, and at war's end, some forty-five thousand service members were still incarcerated." *Id.*

37. Diane H. Mazur, *Rehnquist's Vietnam: Constitutional Separatism and the Stealth Advance of Martial Law*, 77 Ind. L.J. 701, 744-45 (2002) (footnotes omitted).

38. David A. Schlueter, *The Military Justice Conundrum: Justice or Discipline?*, 215 Mil. L. Rev. 1, 4 (2013).

39. *Id.*

40. *Id.* at 10.

41. *Id.* at 10-11. "Voir dire" is the process whereby the counsel involved in a case ask questions of potential panel members (jurors) to determine their suitability to sit on the panel (jury).

42. *Id.* at 12 (citing UCMJ arts. 66-67a (2012)). "In certain cases, a servicemember may seek *certiorari* review by the Supreme Court of a decision by the CAAF." *Id.*

43. In addition, the CA also decides whether to accept the findings and recommendations of the Preliminary Hearing Officer; whether to grant defense requests for expert witnesses and/or assistance; and whether to enter into pretrial agreements (plea deals). The CA also serves as the Senior Rater for the Staff Judge Advocate (the officer in charge of the prosecution team) and, quite often, the most senior members of the panel (jury). Because of the inherent conflict of interest this might create, a separate Army Regulation governing Officer Evaluation Reports was compelled to state that "Duty as a member of a court-martial or an HQDA-convened selection board will not be considered in preparing an evaluation report." *See* U.S. Dep't of Army, Reg 623-3, Evaluation Reporting System 55 (Nov. 4, 2015) (hereafter cited AR 623-3).

44. Schlueter, *supra* note 38, at 15.

45. *Id.*

46. MCM, *supra* note 2, pmbl.

47. U.S. Const. art. III. Given the Constitution's structural attempt to separate power among three distinct branches of the federal government, Article III refers to the judicial branch. Military courts-martial are not Article III courts.

48. Michael I. Spak, *Military Justice: The Oxymoron of the 1980s*, 20 CAL. W. L. REV. 436, 437-38 (1984) (footnotes omitted).

49. U.S. CONST. amend. VI.

50. U.S. CONST. amend. V; emphasis added.

51. Ex Parte Milligan, 71 U.S. (4 Wall.) 2, 18 L. Ed. 281 (1866). *Habeas Corpus* refers to a procedure that individuals in confinement or detention can use to seek judicial review of their confinement.

52. *Milligan*, 71 U.S. at 108.

53. *Milligan*, 71 U.S. at 108.

54. *Milligan*, 71 U.S. at 123 (emphasis added).

55. Ex parte Quirin, 317 U.S. 1, 63 S. Ct. 2, 87 L. Ed. 3, (1942).

56. *Quirin*, 317 U.S. at 40, citing *Milligan*, 71 U.S. at 123.

57. AKHIL REED AMAR, AMERICA'S UNWRITTEN CONSTITUTION: THE PRECEDENTS AND PRINCIPLES WE LIVE BY 430 (2012). "[I]f a president decides to enforce a *criminal* statute, he must persuade members of a truly independent agency—namely, a grand jury composed of ordinary citizens whom he did not pick and cannot remove. These citizens have every right and power to just say no to any proposed prosecution on the simple ground that they believe that prosecution would be unwise or unjust, even if technically lawful. Thanks to the explicit wording of the Fifth Amendment, if these citizen-jurors stand on conscience and just say no, no prosecution for serious federal (nonmilitary) crime can ever be brought." (emphasis in original) *Id.*

58. *Id.* at 431.

59. MCM, *supra* note 2, index, at 15.

60. The only reference to the term "accused" in the American Articles of War of 1776 (enacted Sep. 20, 1776) occurs in Section X, art. 1: "Whenever any officer or soldier shall be *accused* of a capital crime, or of having used violence, or committed any offense against the persons or property of the good people of any of the United American States...the commanding officer...to which the person or persons so *accused* shall belong, are required...to deliver over such *accused* person or persons to the civil magistrate." (emphasis added) WILLIAM WINTHROP, MILITARY LAW AND PRECEDENTS 964 (2d ed. 1920 reprint). A United States Military Academy textbook on military law and the procedures of courts-martial published in 1907, traced the development of military law in the United States up to the time it was published:

> The original American Articles of War were adopted from the British Articles and the laws governing the British army at that time, by resolution of the Continental Congress, June 30, 1775. A new code was substituted September 20, 1776, which was amended in 1786. [*sic*] and by the act of September 29, 1789, those rules previously established were recognized and continued in force under the Constitution. These Articles were rearranged, modified and promulgated by Act of Congress of April 10, 1806, and continued in force with a few modifications until the Act of June 22, 1874, and were later included as Sec. 1342 of the Revised Statutes of the United States of 1878. Various amendments have been made, but there has been no complete revision thereof, and, as amended from time to time, these Articles are still (1906) in force.

EDGAR S. DUDLEY, MILITARY LAW AND THE PROCEDURE OF COURTS-MARTIAL 6 (1907). Colonel Edgar S. Dudley, then Professor of Law at the United States Military

Academy, referred to the officer or Soldier pending a court-martial as "the accused" consistently throughout the book. For example, a paragraph concerning the duties of the judge advocate for the court-martial states that "[t]he judge-advocate having received the order convening the court and appointing him judge-advocate thereof… should furnish the accused with a copy of the charges." *Id.* at 77.

61. Behan, *supra* note 10, at 252.

62. *Id.*

63. *Milligan*, 71 U.S. at 123.

64. *Milligan*, 71 U.S. at 123. For an excellent discussion of the textual weakness of the linkage of the military exception language of the Fifth Amendment to the Sixth Amendment right to a trial by jury, *See* Major Guy P. Glazier, *He Called for His Pipe, and He Called for His Bowl, and He Called for His Members Three—Selection of Military Juries by the Sovereign: Impediment to Military Justice*, 157, MIL. L. REV. 1, 14 (1998).

65. *Johnson v. Sayre*, 158 U.S. 109, 114 (1895).

66. *Solorio v. United States*, 483 U.S. 435, 107 S. Ct. 2924, 97 L. Ed. 2d 364, 380 note 2 (1987) (Dissent).

67. *O'Callahan v. Parker,* 395 U.S. 258 (1969).

68. *O'Callahan*, 395 U.S. at 263. (emphasis added).

69. *O'Callahan*, 395 U.S. at 263.

70. *O'Callahan*, 395 U.S. at 264. The Court supported this position with a footnote that stated, "See, *e.g.*, the cases listed in Hearings on Constitutional Rights of Military Personnel before the Subcommittee on Constitutional Rights of the Senate Committee on the Judiciary pursuant to S. Res. No. 260, 87th Cong., 2d Sess., 780-781 (1962), in each of which the Court of Military Appeals [now called the Court of Appeals of the Armed Forces] reversed court-martial convictions on the ground of excessive command influence." *O'Callahan*, 395 U.S. at n. 5.

71. *O'Callahan*, 395 U.S. at 265.

72. *United States v. Wiesen*, 56 M.J. 172, 174 (2001) (internal citations omitted).

73. *United States v. Dowty*, 60 M.J. 163, 170 (2004).

74. *Dowty,* 60 M.J. at 170.

75. In the military justice system, the prosecutor is called a Trial Counsel and the military defense attorney is called a Defense Counsel. The Trial Counsel works directly for the Staff Judge Advocate and the Staff Judge Advocate is the personal legal advisor to the Convening Authority. The Defense Counsel, however, does not. In the U.S. Army, for example, all military Defense Counsel belong to a separate organization within the Judge Advocate General's Corps known as the Trial Defense Service.

76. The following concerns were inspired by Major Stephen Lamb's critique of the guidance (or the lack thereof) given to CAs by Article 25 and the courts which have been called upon to interpret Article 25. Major Stephen A. Lamb, *The Court-Martial Panel Selection Process: A Critical Analysis*, 137 Mil. L. Rev. 103, 152-154 (1992).

77. UCMJ art. 25 (2012).

78. As noted by Major James Hill, "The standard method of panel selection provides [accused servicemembers] no way of verifying their CAs are complying with the provisions of Article 25(d)(2)." Major James T. Hill, *Achieving Transparency In*

the Military Panel Selection Process With the Preselection Method, 205 Mil. L. Rev. 117, 122 (2010).

79. UCMJ art. 25(e) (2012).

80. *Wiesen*, 56 M.J. at 174.

81. *Wiesen*, 56 M.J. at 174.

82. *Wiesen*, 56 M.J. at 174 (internal citations omitted).

83. *Wiesen*, 56 M.J. at 175.f .

84. Specifically, R.C.M. 912(f)(1)(C) through (L), *supra* note 2. This recommendation for a random selection of panel from among the officers and enlisted members present at a given military installation or deployed location differs from the model proposed by Major Guy P. Glazier, *supra* note 64. Unlike the system proposed by Maj. Glazier, the convening authority would retain some responsibilities with regard to the selection of panel members. This involvement, however, would be largely administrative in nature as the convening authority would no longer exercise any independent discretion in the selection process.

85. MCM, *supra* note 2, R.C.M. 912(f)(1)(K).

86. *Solorio v. United States*, 483 U.S. 435, 440-441 (1987).

87. *Solorio*, 483 U.S. at 447 (footnotes omitted).

88. *Solorio*, 483 U.S. at 451.

89. *Solorio*, 483 U.S. at 452 (Marshall, J., dissenting). *Stare decisis* is a legal doctrine whereby courts will comply with or follow the precedents established by previously-decided cases.

90. *Solorio*, 483 U.S. at 456 (Marshall, J., dissenting).

91. The Preliminary Hearing Officer (PHO) makes findings and recommendations to the convening authority that are not binding. The convening authority is free to refer the case to general court-martial against the recommendation of the PHO. This differs from the power of the civilian grand jury to refuse to issue an indictment, thereby preventing the prosecution from moving forward with the case. For a more detailed explanation of the role of the PHO, *See* U.S. Dep't of Army, Pam. 27-17, Procedural Guide for Article 32 Preliminary hearing Officer (June 18, 2015) (hereafter cited DA Pam. 27-17).

92. UCMJ art. 32 (2012).

93. UCMJ art. 32(a) (2012).

94. Unlike the decision of a civilian grand jury not to return an indictment, which is binding upon the prosecutor.

95. UCMJ art. 32(b) (2012).

96. Because the preliminary hearing officer's recommendation is not binding upon the CA, the Article 32 offers less protection to the Accused than a Grand Jury offers to a civilian defendant.

97. Schlueter, *supra* note 7, at 19-20.

98. Schlueter, *supra* note 7, at 21, *citing* Letter to General W. S. Hancock, President of Military Serv. Inst., from W. T. Sherman (Dec. 9, 1879), *reprinted in* General William T. Sherman, Military Law 130 (1880) (reprinted from The Journal of the Military Service Institution of the United States).

99. Schlueter, *supra* note 7, at 24, *citing* 1 Francis A Gilligan & Fredric Lederer, Court Martial Procedure § 1-20.00, at 2 (1991).

100. Schlueter, *supra* note 7, at 25, *citing* LTG Richard C. Harding, *A Revival in Military Justice*, Reporter, Summer 2010, at 4.

101. The Invisible War (Chain Camera Pictures, 2012).

102. Associated Press, *Tumult Over Military Sexual Assaults Far from Over* (Mar. 12, 2014). Notably, "[Senator Gillibrand] garnered support from [eleven] Republicans, including conservative Sen[ators] Ted Cruz of Texas, Rand Paul of Kentucky and David Vitter of Louisiana." *Id.*

103. The full title of this panel was the Response Systems to Adult Sexual Assault Crimes Panel (RSP) and it consisted of several subcommittees: the Comparative Systems Subcommittee, the Victims Services Subcommittee, and the Role of the Commander (Convening Authority) Subcommittee.

104. *National Defense Authorization Act* (NDAA), § 576(d)(1) (FY 2013). "The Secretary of Defense shall establish a panel to conduct an independent review and assessment of judicial proceedings conducted under the UCMJ involving adult sexual assault and related offenses since the H.R. 4310-128 amendments made to the UCMJ." *Id.*

105. The 2014 NDAA was signed into law by President Obama on December 26, 2013.

REFERENCES

Amar, Akhil Reed. America's Unwritten Constitution: The Precedents and Principles We Live By 430 (2012).

Associated Press. *Tumult Over Military Sexual Assaults Far from Over* (Mar. 12, 2014).

Behan, MAJ Christopher W. *Don't Tug on Superman's Cape: In Defense of Convening Authority Selection and Appointment of Court-Martial Panel Members*, 176 Mil. L. Rev. 190, 192 (2003).

CBS Interactive and Associated Press. "Ferguson Grand Jury Decision Sparks Protests Nationwide." *CBS News*. November 24, 2014. http://www.cbsnews.com/news/ferguson-grand-jury-decision-sparks-protests-nationwide/ (accessed July 5, 2017).

Dudley, Edgar S. Military Law and the Procedure of Courts-Martial 6 (1907 Edition).

Ex Parte Milligan. 71 U.S. (4 Wall.) 2, 18 L. Ed. 281 (1866).

Ex parte Quirin. 317 U.S. 1, 63 S. Ct. 2, 87 L. Ed. 3, (1942).

Gilligan, Francis A, & Fredric Lederer. Court Martial Procedure § 1-20.00, at 2 (1991).

Glazier, MAJ Guy P. *He Called for His Pipe, and He Called for His Bowl, and He Called for His Members Three—Selection of Military Juries by the Sovereign: Impediment to Military Justice*, 157, Mil. L. Rev. 1, 14 (1998).

Harding, LTG Richard C. *A Revival in Military Justice*, Reporter, Summer 2010, 4.

Henderson, Gordon D. *Courts-Martial and the Constitution: The Original Understanding*, 71 Harv. L. Rev. 293, 298 n.41 (1957).

Hill, MAJ James T. *Achieving Transparency In the Military Panel Selection Process With the Preselection Method*, 205 Mil. L. Rev. 117, 122 (2010).

The Invisible War (Chain Camera Pictures, 2012).

Johnson v. Sayre, 158 U.S. 109, 114 (1895).

Journals Of The Continental Congress, 1774-1789.

Lamb, MAJ Stephen A. *The Court-Martial Panel Selection Process: A Critical Analysis*, 137 Mil. L. Rev. 103, 152-154 (1992).

Mazur, Diane H. *Rehnquist's Vietnam: Constitutional Separatism and the Stealth Advance of Martial Law*, 77 Ind. L.J. 701, 744-45 (2002).

National Defense Authorization Act (NDAA), § 576(d)(1) (FY 2013).

O'Callahan v. Parker, 395 U.S. 258 (1969).

Schlueter, David A. Military Criminal Justice – Practice and Procedure 178 (3d ed. 1992).

Schlueter, David A. *The Military Justice Conundrum: Justice or Discipline?*, 215 Mil. L. Rev. 1, 4 (2013).

Sherman, General William T. Military Law 130 (1880).

Solorio v. United States, 483 U.S. 435, 107 S. Ct. 2924, 97 L. Ed. 2d (1987).

Solorio v. United States, 483 U.S. 435, 440-441 (1987).

Spak, Michael I. *Military Justice: The Oxymoron of the 1980s*, 20 Cal. W. L. Rev. 436, 437-38 (1984).

U.S. Const (U.S. Constitution).

U.S. Dep't of Army, Pam. 27-17 (DA Pam), Procedural Guide for Article 32 Preliminary hearing Officer (June 18, 2015).

U.S. Dep't of Army, Reg 623-3 (AR), Evaluation Reporting System 55 (Nov. 4, 2015).

United States. Manual for Courts-Martial (MCM) (2012 Edition).

United States. Uniform Code of Military Justice (UCMJ) (2012 Edition).

United States v. Dowty, 60 M.J. 163, 170 (2004).

United States v. Smith, 27 M.J. 242 (C.M.A. 1988).

United States v. Wiesen, 56 M.J. 172, 174 (2001).

Winthrop, William. Military Law and Precedents. (2d ed. 1920 reprint).

Chapter 7

United Nations Peace Missions and Protection of Civilians

Equality versus Efficiency?

Darya Pushkina

The continuing violence in the Democratic Republic of Congo and in Central African Republic, the threats to peacekeepers in Mali and elsewhere, the steadily deteriorating situation in Syria—not to mention the humanitarian tragedies created by these and other violent conflicts throughout the world—have led policy-makers, scholars and the public to speculate about the nature of contemporary international peace and security. These discussions reflect the common concern to understand what the international community's responsibility should be in regard to conflict-situations previously considered as exclusively internal affairs.[1]

The United Nations (UN) has been the main global actor in the matters of international peace and security since its formation in 1945, and UN peacekeeping operations remain one of the most important tools at the disposal of global organizations determined to meet the challenges of peace and security. However, since UN peace missions have become more complex, robust, and oriented towards protecting the civilian population, its peace commitments have put the organization at risk of being seriously overstretched. The problem is particularly evident where the UN has formed partnerships with regional organizations in order to ensure the protection of civilians. But implementing the peacekeeping principle known as Protection of Civilians (POC) requires a clear definition of who should be counted as civilians in civil wars without uniforms: that is, how to distinguish the civilians who need to be protected.

This essay argues that the UN lacks a clear definition of what constitutes a successful peacekeeping operation and that this is one of the reasons why the attempt to balance efficiency and equality, especially in the area of protecting civilians, has not always delivered satisfactory results. Peacekeeping missions should be evaluated not only on the performance of peacekeepers on the ground, but also on whether violence was limited, human suffering reduced, conflict spread prevented, and progress made towards positive peace.

EVALUATION OF UN PEACEKEEPING

The continuing violence in the Democratic Republic of Congo, the failing state in Central African Republic, the controversial situation in Syria, as well as the humanitarian tragedies created by these and other internal violent conflicts have led policy-makers, scholars, and the public to make many speculations about the nature of contemporary international peace and security. Many are also concerned with the nature of responsibility that the international community has with regard to the situations previously considered as exclusively internal affairs. The UN has been the main global actor in the matters of international peace and security since its formation in 1945 and UN peacekeeping operations remain one of the most important tools at the disposal of global organization in order to meet the challenges of peace and security.[2]

According to the UN New Horizon Progress Reports, "peacekeeping appears to be entering a period of consolidation."[3] Current UN focus is on global partnerships—including other UN bodies, European Union (EU), North Atlantic Treaty Organization (NATO), African Union (AU), as well as host countries; robust peacekeeping, protection of civilians, nexus between peacekeeping and peace-building; and more effective initiatives toward peacekeeping such as deterrence, use of force, and operational readiness. In addition to evaluation of mandate implementation, this paper argues that the UN should create a broader definition of success to include general criteria such as limiting violence, reducing human suffering, preventing conflict spread and recurrence after departure, and contributing to progress made toward positive peace. This more developed definition of success should be shared with the regional organizations which in turn would help the UN to have more productive partnerships, particularly with the EU and AU. Consequently, this should contribute to better implementation of the POC principle and an improved balance between efficiency and equality in civilian protection by peacekeeping missions.

While many UN documents stress the importance of peacekeepers' contribution to peace-building, not solely in keeping peace, the tendency to evaluate the missions in policy-making circles is mostly based on mandate fulfillment. Nonetheless, it is important to broaden the criteria for evaluation peacekeeping contribution to the larger goals of international peace and security. Peacekeeping missions should be evaluated not only on the performance of peacekeepers on the ground (mandate evaluation), but also on whether violence was limited, human suffering reduced, conflict spread prevented, and progress was made toward positive peace (PPP) made. These measures will also help to evaluate more wholesome results of protection civilian population at large. While these are high standards, only by employing them can one reasonably evaluate whether UN peace operations are in fact mitigating threats to international peace and security.[4]

Based on this broader definition of success, for example, the UN's evaluation does not correspond to the above-mentioned definition in several important cases. The United Nations Transitional Administration in East Timor (UNTAET) and the United Nations Mission to Support in East Timor (UNMISET) in Timor-Leste are widely considered by the UN to be the examples of what its peacekeeping can do right. Mandates were largely implemented, a new country was formed, UN patronage existed for several years without major breaks. At the same time, a more attentive look into progress toward positive peace measures calls to attention the violent outbreaks of 2006 and the extremely fragile strength of the state with much local dissatisfaction, not only because of the situation within the country, but also because of the UN actions labeled as "neo-colonial" by some and "benevolent directorship" by others.[5] The more in-depth analysis demonstrates that the lack of attention to the local channels of power and the application of Kosovo's approach of treating Timor-Leste as *terra nulla* [nobody's land], created much more controversial outcomes for the UN missions than were generally acknowledged.

Similar differences in the UN and some observers' evaluations can be found in the case of UN missions in Croatia. If evaluated according to the broader criteria, United Nations Protection Force/Force de Protection des Nations Unies (UNPROFOR) in Croatia and *United* Nations Confidence Restoration Operation (UNCRO) missions largely failed, as opposed to the UN's classification of them as partially successful. UNPROFOR/UNCRO achieved a peaceful withdrawal of the Yugoslav People's Army (JNA), and partially succeeded in demilitarizing the United Nations Protected Areas (UNPAs), yet the missions did not prevent the warring parties from participating in the Bosnian conflict as well as failing to prevent ethnic cleansing and large-scale Serbian refugee flows. In addition, the mission failed to assist the return of several displaced Croats. The UN peacekeepers managed to sustain cease-fires for some time, but failed to prevent several major cease-fire violations, including the final Croatian military attacks that ended the hopes for a negotiated settlement of the conflict. A follow-up mission, United Nations Transitional Administration for Eastern Slavonia, Baranja and Western Sirmium (UNTAES), was successful by all measurements. Large-scale violence did not follow and the most acute problem remained the destiny of the Serbian minority in Eastern Slavonia. UNTAES was deployed in the area to assist the situation there. UNTAES has mostly fulfilled its mandate with more success in demilitarization and less in refugee resettlement. In terms of the overall situation in the area, the mission was largely successful in sustaining cease-fire and preventing armed clashes; there were virtually no conflict-related casualties during the mission's deployment, and the war did not recur after the mission left.

When applying the broader criteria for success to the universe of post-cold war peacekeeping operations conducted by the UN, one is faced with the approximately evenly distributed successes, partial successes, and failures. A variation of success was demonstrated in limiting violence, preventing violent deaths, refugee and internally displaced peoples' resettlement, and preventing outflows. UN missions, however, have been rather successful in preventing the spread of the conflict into regional instability. Although somewhat unexpectedly, UN missions have also been successful in conflict resolution contribution, measured in this project as preventing a return to war within two years after departure, and, somewhat less successful in the contribution to the PPP measure.[6,]UN peacekeeping has been particularly unsuccessful in preventing genocide and/or civilian massacres, which significantly undermines one of its major current goals—the protection of civilians.

PROTECTION OF CIVILIANS (POC)

The POC principle directly stems from "Responsibility to Protect" idea.[7] Based on the outcome document of the 2005 World Summit, a 2009 report by the Secretary-General outlined three pillars of the responsibility to protect:

(1) The State carries the primary responsibility for protecting populations from genocide, war crimes, crimes against humanity and ethnic cleansing, and their incitement;
(2) The international community has a responsibility to encourage and assist States in fulfilling this responsibility;
(3) The international community has a responsibility to use appropriate diplomatic, humanitarian and other means to protect populations from these crimes. If a State is manifestly failing to protect its populations, the international community must be prepared to take collective action to protect populations, in accordance with the UN Charter.[8]

Putting an end to humanitarian atrocities is categorized at a level of extreme importance for the United Nations and is as threatening as preventing interstate/civil war. Ramesh Thakur, examing the transformation of UN operations, analyzes its ever-changing roles, relationships, and structure. Thakur is constantly asking how, when, and why force may be used in any given situation, in any given location, and strongly argues that the growing divide between legality and legitimacy is evidence of a crippling international community with outstanding inequality. He acknowledges tensions between the United States as a super power and forceful entity, as well as the United Nations, as it stands tall as an international law enforcement system. Thakur's work covers the international peace and security policy agenda as it identifies the responsibility to protect in the broader context of international and UN policy, and as it examines to what extent do we carry out a duty and are held responsible to protect those that do not live within our own societies.[9]

The definition of protection of civilians in the context of United Nations Peacekeeping Operations (PKOs) is composed of three interpretations and approaches of protection: (1) rights-based approach, (2) stabilization and peace building as durable forms of protection, and (3) physical protection from harm. This means that the protection of civilians is not only physical protection in the context of UN peacekeeping operations, but also includes the protection of individual rights in accordance with international human rights law, humanitarian law and refugee law, as well as the creation of a secure and peaceful environment for civilians in which to live.[10] Therefore, it is particularly important to have a holistic approach to peacekeeping operations' evaluation.

In 2015, The Kigali Principles on the Protection of Civilians were introduced. The Kigali Principles are a set of eighteen pledges for the effective implementation of the protection of civilians in UN peacekeeping. The principles came out of the high level International Conference on the Protection of Civilians held in Rwanda on the May 28-29, 2015. The principles address the following aspects of peacekeeping: assessment and planning, force generation, training and equipping personnel, performance, and accountability. While they are framed around the protection of civilians, the principles address broader deficiencies that undermine the effectiveness of peacekeeping operations conducted in volatile situations, including peacekeeper abuse.[11]

A UN trend, beginning in the early twenty-first century, focused on the issues of civilian protection using methods such as robust peacekeeping, exhibited by troop numbers and their capacities. At the same time, many issues remain unclear, namely what robust peacekeeping means in conceptual and operational terms, what kind of capabilities the UN needs to implement it effectively, what "effectively" means in this context, what are the potential risks of robust peacekeeping, and so on. One of the potential risks of robust peacekeeping with the mandate to protect civilians can be the dilemma of how to mitigate the harm done to civilians during operations that require force.[12]

To a significant degree these challenges stem from an unclear definition of the protection of civilians and the different interpretations of what it means by various actors. A detailed study described significant differences in concepts and in practical implementation during the UN's Mission in the Democratic Republic of Congo (MONUC) deployment in the Democratic Republic of Congo (DRC) within the mission, as well as between the mission and the UN headquarters. For example, operations between the MONUC and the Armed Forces of the Democratic Republic of the Congo (FARDC), as the FARDC had a consistent record of abuse against civilians, especially when it was moving into areas held by rebel groups. This is precisely what the MONUC was supposed to assist the FARDC to do. The report underlined that "responses revealed multiple understandings of the concept of 'protection of civilians' in the context of a UN peacekeeping operation."[13]

Doubts about the UN's capacity and will for the protection of civilians in peace operations as well as the UN's resources to implement this principle were reinforced in 2012 by the extreme challenges UN operations faced in Côte d'Ivoire, the DRC and South Sudan.[14] It is very important to understand "the capacity gap" that the world organization faces. The UN routinely lacks the necessary material resources to perform complex state-building and POC tasks. For example, there are many unfulfilled vacancies in peacekeeping operations. The UN simply has not been able to fill all the positions for civilian experts that it needs in state-building operations. There are not enough civilian experts applying to PKOs, with the most glaring and current example of the United Nations Organization Stabilization Mission in the Democratic Republic of the Congo (MONUSCO), where a large part of vacancies in the civilian component are not filled. That problem is particularly clear in the context of civil wars—where states are often weak, fragile, or even failed, and the UN attempts to (re)build collapsed state institutions and help a state's civilian population. The introduction of Unmanned Arial Vehicles (UVAs) and other technologies can partially ameliorate the "capacity gap." During meetings of the heads of PKOs in Africa, the heads of the UN missions have stated that the warring parties have often been using extremely sophisticated weapons, moving quickly from area to area, and that the missions could seriously improve their performance if they are provided with the necessary equipment, particularly helicopters and UVAs.[15] UVAs, on the other hand, also directly contribute to the dilemmas of equality versus efficiency, especially in the context of POC populations.[16]

PARTNERSHIPS FOR PROTECTION OF CIVILIANS

There have been many speculations in the beginning of the twenty-first century where regional organizations can fit in. Given the UN's attention to partnerships, it is interesting to evaluate how regional organizations might be able to fill in successes in those tasks where the UN has come short of full success, particularly with the protection of civilians. Over the last twenty years, several regional organizations broadly understood and participated in peace operations alongside the UN or with UN authorization.

The importance of coordination—horizontally with the other regional organizations—has been stressed in the "A New Partnership Agenda."[17] Some recent examples of cooperation with other organizations include the UN's work with NATO in Afghanistan and Kosovo, the AU in Darfur, and with the EU in Chad and Kosovo. In the light of the UN's goal of protection of civilians, the United Nations Security Council (UNSC) authorized several other organizations' missions with this task: the Interim Emergency Multinational Force in Bunia, Operation Artemis in the DRC; Operation Licorne in Côte d'Ivoire; Economic Community of West African States (ECOWAS) in Côte d'Ivoire (ECOMICI); the African Union Mission in Sudan (AMIS) in Dafur; Eufor R. D.Congo in DRC; and the 2007 European Union Force (EUFOR) in Chad. These partnerships, however, present various cooperation challenges and limitations.

One of the most profound examples of UN/AU partnerships with regard to the protection of civilians has been the African Union/United Nations Hybrid Operation in Darfur (UNAMID). Among UNAMID staff and leaders, POC was regularly cited as the core aim of the peacekeeping operation with reference to the mandate. Senior uniformed personnel commented that "POC gives us our legal mandate to exist. Take that out and we go home." In the same vein, a senior mission leader said, "The ability to fulfil that [POC] role will be the yardstick against which success will be judged, right now by the people and by history." These were representative views among senior mission staff. When pressed, however, UNAMID personnel and leaders could not provide a mission-wide description of what its plans were to protect civilians either "under imminent threat" or more broadly.[18]

One of the reasons for the lack of a cohesive mission description can be that the UN and AU have different approaches to peacekeeping. The UN believes that the three main principles should be followed (consent particularly on the side of the host government, impartiality, and non-use of force), and that four conditions should be present for success: (1) cease-fire and other indicators that parties are committed to peace; (2) positive regional engagement; (3) SC members should be unified in their approach; and (4) clear mandates with resources backing. The AU believes that in some places like Somalia, these conditions can now hamper the potential for success and peace should be created first before being kept.[19] The AU did adhere, at least constitutionally, to the Responsibility to Protect (R2P) principle, although the willingness to implement this principle in practice, as well as the AU's rather limited capacities (during one of its most successful operations in Burundi the

AU relied largely on external donors financial support)[20] would not make the AU the main candidate for POC implementation.

In general, one can observe that operationalization of the POC and the related principle of R2P remains undetermined as of today and there are problems not only with regard to the UN-AU partnership in the POC, but also in the UN-EU relationship in peace operations. It is particularly challenging for European governments to decide on intervention based on these principles outside of the region. The difficulty of serving alongside each other in the matters of international peace yet in a blurry situation of civil war was exemplified in EUFOR's Chad/ north-eastern Central African Republic (CAR) mission and EU-UN collaboration in eastern DRC.

In Chad/CAR, for example, EUFOR intervened in the context of an ongoing conflict and created conditions for the UN to take over. While there were some notable successes, overall, EUFOR Chad/CAR mission's performance was largely determined by the EU's limited military capacities. In Chad the EU military, the UN police training forces, and the Chadian police were meant to implement POC; however, the mission did not fully succeed in the POC. The EU seems more prepared for short-term military stabilizing missions than for long-lasting complex situations,[21] yet protection of civilians is more required in the latter. It can be argued that since the EU is stronger in its civilian component, the EU can supplement the UN's mission with qualified civilians assigning the POC rather than with militarized force.

At the same time the EU has deployed twenty-five security operations since 2003, and most of them have been in the country with a UN mission presence. In the DRC in 2003 and 2006, the EU deployed military troops (Operation Artemis), as well as civilian missions. At the same time during the 2008-2009 crisis in eastern DRC, the EU decision-making process was too state-dependent and EU action never materialized, despite UN Secretary-General's pleas. While the EU-UN relationship is rather institutionalized and the specific partnership was built for eastern DRC (EU battle groups), the partnership did not manage to overcome difference in their interests.[22] Finnish Foreign Minister Alexander Stubb was then asking, "if we don't send them to Congo where do we send them?"[23] Yet, the EU failed to send rapid reaction force in response to the 2008 DRC crisis.[24]

Overall, while the EU has improved its conflict management potential, going from failures in Croatia, Bosnia, and Kosovo to a largely successful operation Concordia in Macedonia, it is doubtful that the organization would demonstrate the same level of success outside of the region in terms of both political will and capabilities.[25] Although the EU has established Battle Groups, it has no military headquarters. It is politically difficult for democratic European governments to decisively intervene outside of the region. In addition, the EU and UN have not developed the same definitions of peace operations effectiveness related to R2P and POC principles, thus the

EU's active participation in the implementation of those principles outside of Europe, even when acting as a UN partner, remains limited.

It is important to also note that in UN peacekeeping operations, different contributions of developed and developing world countries to peacekeeping operations where the developed world contributes resources and developing personnel,[26] also pertains to the issues of equality and efficiency. There is a need to implement a new, more advanced training system; one that has centers in the countries that are contributing personnel to these missions in order for them to be trained from the beginning.

THE MISSION IS POSSIBLE

Within the UN peacekeeping discussions, there seem to be three major questions that arise regularly. The first: whether or not the UN/UN peacekeeping missions have the right to intervene with the domestic politics, treatment of civilians, etc. of a given host country, against this country's decisions. The second, whether or not it is appropriate for UN peacekeeping operations to use force in defense of the POC mandate. And, the third is the need to plan extraction measures of UN peacekeepers themselves post mission.

During UN peacekeeping meetings, many speakers and representatives express their support for civilian protection; yet some participants believe that the concept of the POC must be more clearly and carefully defined before action is taken and should never be used as a pretense for intrusion into domestic affairs of a state. The matter is further complicated by the fact that there is no agreement on how to evaluate UN peacekeeping missions, especially in the context of the POC.

The UN's cooperation with regional organizations in general and especially in the protection of civilians still seems to be *ad hoc*. It is unlikely that regional organizations will participate on a large scale in keeping peace outside of their region and the trend for the EU, for example, seems to be increasing participation in UN operations rather than sending EU forces while the AU might be the most eager participant yet with the most limited abilities so far. It remains to be seen how willing and successful the UN and regional organizations would be to implement POC principles. Given the previous peacekeeping record, the lack of common understanding of POC, and the lack of a clear definition of successful peace operations that target larger values than just mandates' implementation, the focus on the POC principle remains more an ad hoc implementation than a steady principle. Yet the record of peace operation successes gives us a more optimistic outlook that, given certain conditions, UN peace operations, including those with Protection of Civilians mandate, are still missions that are possible.

NOTES

1. Dr. Pushkina thanks Kayla Goldstein, Syracuse University, in 2016-2017 academic year on Bard-Smolny exchange at St. Petersburg State University's Faculty of Liberal Arts and Sciences, for research assistance, editing, additions, and collaboration on written material.

2. Peacekeeping has been one of the main tools for the United Nations to manage complex crises. However, it is not mentioned in the UN Charter. We owe the *de facto* name for UN peacekeeping operations—"Chapter 6 and a Half"—to former Secretary-General Dag Hammarskjold. Peacekeeping originated as simply the interposition of lightly-armed international forces between warring parties to maintain cease-fires and to prevent a resurgence of hostilities as well as to create more secure conditions while diplomatic solutions to the underlying causes of the conflict were sought. Post-Cold war peacekeeping operations attempt to address military, political and economic problems. Although the three main principles of peacekeeping (neutrality, consent of the host state and use of force only in self-defense) remain largely intact, in some cases peacekeeping troops are granted an enforcement mandate under Chapter 7 of the "Charter of the United Nations," October 24, 1945, http://www.un.org/en/charter-united-nations/ (accessed April 23, 2018). The beginning of the twenty-first century saw a rise in frequency of strong peacekeeping missions with robust enforcement mandates—more extensive and more expensive missions directed toward overall stability in the conflict zones. To date the UN has conducted seventy-one peacekeeping operations, currently fourteen still underway. The UN deploys 95,301 personnel from 128 troop-contributing countries (http://www.un.org/en/peacekeeping/resources/statistics/factsheet.shtml [accessed July 7, 2017]).

3. United Nations, Department of Peacekeeping Operations and Department of Field Support, "New Horizon Initiative: Progress Report No. 1," October 2010, New York, http://www.un.org/en/peacekeeping/documents/newhorizon_update01.pdf (accessed July 13, 2017).

4. For elaboration of this argument see Darya Pushkina, "A Recipe for Success? Ingredients of a Successful Peacekeeping Mission." *International Peacekeeping* 13, no. 2 (Summer 2006): 133-149.

5. Darya Pushkina and Philipp Maier, "United Nations Peacekeeping in Timor-Leste," in *External Interventions in Civil Wars: The Role and Impact of Regional and International Organizations*, ed. Stefan Wolff and Oya Dursun-Özkanca (London and New York: Routledge, Taylor & Francis, 2014), 28-47.

6. Darya Pushkina, "United Nations Peace Operations: Mission Possible" (forthcoming 2018).

7. For an excellent analysis of "Responsibility to Protect," please, refer to *Theorising Responsibility to Protect*, ed. Ramesh Thakur and William Maley (Cambridge: Cambridge University Press, 2015).

8. United Nations, Outreach Programme on the Rwanda Genocide, "Background Information on the Responsibility to Protect" (New York: Department of Public Information, March 2014), http://www.un.org/en/preventgenocide/rwanda/about/bgresponsibility.shtml (accessed June 22, 2017).

9. Ramesh Thakur, *The United Nations, Peace and Security*, 2nd ed. (Cambridge: Cambridge University Press, 2016).

10. United Nations, Cabinet Office, "The United Nations Peacekeeping Operations and Protection of Civilians: @PKO Now!" by Tomoko Matsuzawa, Program Adviser, August 23, 2013, http://www.pko.go.jp/pko_e/organization/researcher/atpkonow/article056.html (accessed June 22, 2017).

11. Global Centre for the Responsibility to Protect, "The Kigali Principles on the Protection of Civilians," May 29, 2015, http://www.globalr2p.org/resources/985 (accessed June 22, 2017).

12. The first UN mission with the protection of civilians mandate was UNAMSIL in Sierra Leone, currently there are ten missions with such mandate although formulated differently on case-to-case basis.

13. Independent study jointly commissioned by the United Nations, Department of Peacekeeping Operations and the Office for the Coordination of Humanitarian Affairs, "Protecting Civilians in the Context of UN Peacekeeping Operations: Successes, Setbacks and Remaining Challenges," by V. Holt and G. Taylor (New York: United Nations, 2009), 167.

14. Stockholm International Peace Research Institute (SIPRI), "SIPRI Yearbook 2013," July 2013, Oxford University Press for SIPRI, http://www.sipri.org/yearbook/2013/02 (accessed August 13, 2013).

15. See, for example, June 26, 2013 meeting of the heads of PKOs in Africa with the United Nations, Security Council, "Peace and Security in Africa: Secretary-General's Special Envoy," SC/11049, https://www.un.org/press/en/2013/sc11049.doc.htm (accessed April 23, 2018).

16. For more information of various aspects of Unmanned Arial Vehicles (UVAs), consult the Center for the Study of the Drone, at Bard College, 2018, http://dronecenter.bard.edu/ (accessed April 24, 2018).

17. United Nations, "A New Partnership Agenda: Charting a New Horizon for UN Peacekeeping, Department of Peacekeeping Operations and Department of Field Support," 16, New York, July 2009, http://www.un.org/en/peacekeeping/documents/newhorizon.pdf/ (accessed August 22, 2013).

18. United Nations, "Protecting Civilians, " 165.

19. Arthur Boutellis and Paul D. Williams, "Peace Operations, the African Union and the United Nations: Towards a More Effective Partnerships," *International Peace Institute* (April 1, 2013): 1-28, at 7.

20. Anne-Marie Penn Rodt, *The European Union and Military Conflict Management* (London: Routledge, 2014).

21. Malte Brosig, "The Multi-actor Game of Peacekeeping in Africa," *International Peacekeeping* 17, no. 3 (2010): 327-42, at 338.

22. Richard Gowan, "From Rapid Reaction to Depayed Inaction? Congo, the UN and the EU," *International Peacekeeping* 18, no. 5 (2011): 593-611.

23. Ibid, 594

24. Ibid, 607.

25. Anne-Marie Penn Rodt and Stefan Wolff, "European Union Conflict Management in the Western Balkans," *Civil Wars* 14, no. 3 (September 2012): 414-30.

26. United Nations. "Peacekeeping," N.d., http://www.un.org/en/peacekeeping/resources/statistics/contributors (accessed July 13, 2017).

REFERENCES

Boutellis, Arthur, and Paul D. Williams. "Peace Operations, the African Union and the United Nations: Towards a More Effective Partnerships." *International Peace Institute* (April 1, 2013): 1-28.

Brosig, Malte. "The Multi-actor Game of Peacekeeping in Africa." *International Peacekeeping* 17, no. 3 (2010): 327-42.

Center for the Study of the Drone, at Bard College. 2018. http://dronecenter.bard.edu/ (accessed April 24, 2018).

Global Centre for the Responsibility to Protect. "The Kigali Principles on the Protection of Civilians." May 29, 2015. http://www.globalr2p.org/resources/985 (accessed June 22, 2017).

Gowan, Richard. "From Rapid Reaction to Depayed Inaction? Congo, the UN and the EU." *International Peacekeeping* 18, no. 5 (2011): 593-611.

Pushkina, Darya. "A Recipe for Success? Ingredients of a Successful Peacekeeping Mission." *International Peacekeeping* 13, no. 2 (Summer 2006): 133-49.

———. "United Nations Peace Operations: Mission Possible" (forthcoming 2018).

Pushkina, Darya, and Philipp Maier, "United Nations Peacekeeping in Timor-Leste." In *External Interventions in Civil Wars: The Role and Impact of Regional and International Organizations*, edited by Stefan Wolff and Oya Dursun-Özkanca, 28-47. London and New York: Routledge, Taylor & Francis, 2014.

Rodt, Anne-Marie Penn. *The European Union and Military Conflict Management*. London: Routledge, 2014.

Rodt, Anne-Marie Penn, and Stefan Wolff, "European Union Conflict Management in the Western Balkans." *Civil Wars* 14, no. 3 (September 2012): 414-30.

Stockholm International Peace Research Institute (SIPRI). "SIPRI Yearbook 2013." July 2013. Oxford University Press for SIPRI. http://www.sipri.org/yearbook/2013/02 (accessed August 13, 2013).

Thakur, Ramesh. *The United Nations, Peace and Security*. 2nd ed. Cambridge: Cambridge University Press, 2016.

Thakur, Ramesh, and William Maley. *Theorising Responsibility to Protect*. Cambridge: Cambridge University Press, 2015.

United Nations. "Charter of the United Nations." October 24, 1945. http://www.un.org/en/charter-united-nations/(accessed April 23, 2018).

———. "Peacekeeping." N.d. http://www.un.org/en/peacekeeping/resources/statistics/contributors (accessed July 13, 2017).

United Nations. Cabinet Office. "The United Nations Peacekeeping Operations and Protection of Civilians: @PKO Now!" by Tomoko Matsuzawa, Program Adviser, August 23, 2013. http://www.pko.go.jp/pko_e/organization/researcher/atpkonow/article056.html (accessed June 22, 2017).

United Nations. Department of Peacekeeping Operations and Department of Field Support. "New Horizon Initiative: Progress Report No. 1." October 2010. New York. http://www.un.org/en/peacekeeping/documents/newhorizon_update01.pdf (accessed July 13, 2017).

———. "A New Partnership Agenda: Charting a New Horizon for UN Peacekeeping, Department of Peacekeeping Operations and Department of Field Support," New York, July 2009, http://www.un.org/en/peacekeeping/documents/newhorizon.pdf/ (accessed August 22, 2013).

United Nations. Department of Peacekeeping Operations, Office for the Coordination of Humanitarian Affairs. "Protecting Civilians in the Context of UN Peacekeeping Operations: Successes, Setbacks and Remaining Challenges." by V. Holt and G. Taylor. New York: United Nations, 2009.

United Nations. Outreach Programme on the Rwanda Genocide. "Background Information on the Responsibility to Protect." New York: Department of Public Information, March 2014. http://www.un.org/en/preventgenocide/rwanda/about/bgresponsibility.shtml (accessed June 22, 2017).

United Nations. Security Council. "Peace and Security in Africa: Secretary-General's Special Envoy." June 26, 2013. SC/11049. https://www.un.org/press/en/2013/sc11049.doc.htm (accessed April 23, 2018).

Part II

THEOLOGICAL PERSPECTIVES

Chapter 8

Ultimately Equal and Relatively Complicated

Questions about Equality in Teaching Buddhist Studies

Dominique Townsend

As part of a collaborative conference organized by West Point and Bard College titled "Equality—More or Less" in April 2017, this essay reflects on the topic of equality in Tibetan Buddhism from a pedagogical perspective. I consider some common challenges that arise when teaching about Buddhism and equality in a liberal arts classroom, and reflect on ways to address those challenges.

As background, it is important to note that undergraduate students frequently arrive in Buddhist studies courses thirsting for a system that will exemplify peace, equanimity, simplicity, and goodness. In class, they encounter a diverse and complicated array of systems that have been constructed by human beings over time. As a subject of study, Buddhism demonstrates its very own array of social ills and historical failings, alongside its many merits and virtues. In this essay, I consider how best to reckon with student expectations, and disappointments, about the complex status of equality in Tibetan Buddhist texts and institutions, which have been shaped but not defined by Indian Buddhism. In the first part of the essay I present two examples of apparent inequality—related to gender dynamics and intellectual hierarchies—drawn from the Buddhist texts that I assign to students. In the latter part of the essay I introduce an influential Mahāyāna Buddhist interpretive framework, commonly known as "The Two Truths," and argue this hermeneutic tool can help students meaningfully engage with apparent inconsistencies in Buddhism, without falling into the potential extremes of romanticizing or rejecting Buddhist traditions. Since my focus here is pedagogical, I draw exclusively from texts that I assign in my undergraduate courses.

Ideals of equality, for instance between the interests of self and of other, are critically important in Tibetan Buddhist philosophy and practice. At the same time, there are also striking examples of inequality, most notably in regard to gender, which students in Buddhist studies courses duly notice and critique. Such questioning can be extremely productively since it develops students' critical thinking skills and builds their tolerance for complexity. Yet such questioning also entails the risk that students might preemptively dismiss Buddhist perspectives as inconsistent, contradictory, or hypocritical if what they find in Buddhist sources is not in keeping with their preconceptions about Buddhism. From a pedagogical perspective, this is a problem since it is a missed opportunity for learning, not only about Buddhist studies, but also about how to grapple with other complex and ambiguous topics. In some cases students hold their preconceptions about Buddhism quite dear, which causes them to react strongly when challenged by course materials. My responsibility as a teacher is in part to help students discern and appreciate complexity, without making knee-jerk assessments. By practicing these critical cognitive skills in a Buddhist studies course (as in any other course) students can develop tools for encountering multilayered and ambivalent histories, narratives, and topics more broadly.

To begin to approach the Buddhist studies material, I will begin with an anecdote. During a recent class session, students discussed the historical Buddha's purported refusal to allow the first group of women who sought to become ordained as nuns or *bhikṣuṇī* (the male counterpart is monks or *bhikṣu*) into the Buddhist community. Hearing that Buddha turned the women away from following in his footsteps, one student remarked, "That's so unenlightened. It just doesn't seem … Buddhist!"

As the students went on to discuss, the story, set in India during the fifth century BCE, tells us that Buddha eventually conceded, swayed by the persuasion of his stepmother Maha Prajapati Gautamī and his cousin Ānanda. Among his closest and most accomplished disciples, Gautamī and Ānanda pleaded with Buddha to allow women as well as men to follow in his footsteps and join the ordained Buddhist community or *sangha*, citing Buddha's previous assertion that women have the same ability to achieve awakening as men. This exchange led to the formation of the four-fold *sangha*, including laywomen, laymen, nuns, and monks.[1] This came as good news in class, but to the student's further dismay, the canonical texts go on to tell us that when Buddha consented for women to be ordained, he is said to have imposed what are called the "eight heavy rules" (*garudharma*) on nuns, laying the foundation for systemic gender inequality that persists to the present.[2] Moreover, Buddha is said to have prophesied that Buddhism's duration as an institution would be cut short due to women's involvement.[3]

Buddhist thinkers today debate and contest the veracity and correct interpretation of this story. It might prove impossible to determine whether Buddha really laid out these guidelines himself, or whether his institutional successors over time portrayed him this way in a projection of their own qualms about the correct place of women in the Buddhist tradition. Regardless, the attitudes conveyed by this narrative of resistance within the early Indian Buddhist community to women's ordination continue to impact women's opportunities in Buddhist institutions across Asia and globally.

This story about my student's disappointment with Buddhism as he encountered it in class demonstrates the broader dynamic around questions of equality that I examine in this essay, particularly around gender and intellectual status. As cases in point, I present two examples that arise in Buddhist studies courses. The first, just alluded to, involves women's status in Tibetan Buddhist institutions and literature. The second example I explore involves a common Indian and Tibetan system of categorizing Buddhist practitioners' intellectual capacities (i.e., higher, middling, and lower), which is employed widely in literature and oral instructions. These intellectual categories correspond to important epistemological hierarchies that are used to organize the material of Buddhist learning. The rubric arguably, or at least rhetorically, restricts the "highest" and most efficacious teachings to the "highest caliber" students and practitioners. In the undergraduate classroom, this feature of Buddhist education and epistemology often strikes students as another instance of inequality, since it appears to limit some Buddhist practitioners' access to the most beneficial teachings. Once again, this just does not "seem Buddhist" to many students, who sense unfairness in a system that limits access to the most purportedly valuable Buddhist learning.

After presenting these two cases in more detail, I turn to a third important topic of study within Buddhist studies courses—the Buddhist interpretive framework of the Two Truths. For students, this doctrine can help make sense of inconsistencies and ambivalence, modeling as it does critical thinking without adherence to a rigid position. However, it can also seem to explain away apparent inequalities too smoothly, as I discuss below. This doctrine is interpreted differently by the three major Buddhist traditions of *Theravāda* [the Way of the Elders], *Mahāyāna* [the Great Vehicle], and *Vajrayāna* [Esoteric Buddhism]. From the Tibetan Buddhist perspective, it offers a means for making sense of the relationship between the *ultimate* truth of how things really are and the *relative* truth of how things appear. The Two Truths doctrine is directly connected to a system of Buddhist hermeneutics used to create hierarchies of texts and sources of textual authority in Buddhism, based on the distinction between provisional versus ultimate levels of meaning. According to this system, the only texts that are not provisional are those that uphold the ultimate relativity or emptiness of all things.[4] This is an expression of a non-dualist interpretation of the Two Truths.

Before turning to the examples of gender inequality and intellectual hierarchies, I should say that these cases seem to me to be radically different in nature, and therefore difficult to compare. Indeed, Indian and Tibetan Buddhist sources also treat the topics of gender and intellectual hierarchies in completely different ways. In regard to the status of women, throughout Buddhism's long and diverse history, Buddhists have argued about, problematized, theorized, and contradicted each other in both productive and stymying exchanges, debating the relevance and significance of gender, and female gender in particular. Conversely the view that the most sophisticated and potentially transformative teachings are appropriate only for prepared students, when taught by a qualified teacher in the correct context, is foundational to Tibetan Buddhist hermeneutics. Pedagogically this makes sense to me, since it resonates with an approach that personalizes material to fit the needs, goals, and abilities of the individual student. Many Buddhist teachers and scholars are deeply committed to the view that certain interpretations of Buddhist thought are appropriate only for those who have progressed to a level of sophistication and readiness (through careful training in this life, and through karma from past lives). By this estimation, a student who is unready for the highest level of Buddhist interpretation might fall into nihilism or unethical behavior, if she or he lacks the capacity to fully integrate teachings on the ultimate nature of reality. There are many instances of reform intended to avoid intellectual elitism, especially in East Asian Buddhism, but the system of intellectual hierarchies and the usefulness of the Two Truths as an interpretive tool appears to be generally accepted in the Tibetan context. For the purposes of this essay, what connects these examples is that they prompt a similar response from students in regard to the question of equality.

THE ROOTS OF STUDENT PRECONCEPTIONS

College students are not alone in their expectations for Buddhism to be egalitarian. Beyond the classroom, there exists a widely held preconception that Buddhists hold hierarchies as anathema and that all Buddhist traditions espouse radical equality. Interpretations of Buddhism in contemporary global culture frequently are based on a limiting perspective that expects all Buddhists to be enlightened, pacifist, vegetarian, humanist meditators who have fully integrated the ideal of ultimate equality into their way of being.[5] Mass media portrayals, unexamined stereotypes, and projections of the Buddhist as an exotic other, for instance through the problematic Shangri-la image of Tibet, all contribute to this tendency to expect Buddhism to provide perfect balance and equality.[6] Widespread preconceptions about Buddhism and equality are not solely Orientalist projections based on fantasies about the East, although that is part of the problem.

More constructively, the idea that Buddhism purely espouses social and personal equality has a genuine basis in Buddhist teaching and practice. Buddhist notions of equality stem from centrally important and deeply influential Buddhist claims that all beings have the potential for enlightenment, and the related ethical mandate that all beings can and should cultivate enlightenment, for the sake of all. According to the Buddha's foundational insight, as expressed through the Four Noble Truths, all unenlightened beings suffer due to ignorance about the nature of reality. The Mahāyāna Buddhist worldview that originated in India and that is aspired to today in East Asia, Vietnam, Tibet, and the broader Himalayan region is likewise profoundly egalitarian in this same sense. This Mahāyāna worldview centers on the crucial claim that anyone (regardless of gender or intellect among innumerable other factors) can wake up to the nature of reality and become free from dissatisfaction and suffering.

Equally important for students considering the topic of equality in Buddhist contexts are Buddhist claims that all sentient beings are equal in their basic wish to be happy and to avoid suffering, and related practices designed to diminish preferential treatment for any particular sentient beings over others. In this very important regard, all beings, regardless of gender or capacity, *are* equal in a specific and essential way, namely their need for liberation from ignorance and suffering. Likewise, related meditation practices familiar to practitioners across Buddhist cultures are designed to diminish preferential treatment for any particular sentient beings over others. To accomplish the aims of such practices demands recognizing all beings as equal.

These profound ideals about the equal needs of all living beings—and the responsibility for Buddhists to cultivate equal compassion for all of them—have shaped the thinking and being of countless remarkably enlightened persons, throughout the history of Buddhism, in the many diverse cultures where it has taken root. Nevertheless, the power of such teachings and teachers apparently does not engender perfect social equality, for instance because of the threats of misogyny and elitism that exist everywhere. Against this backdrop, potent pedagogical opportunities arise around the dissonance students experience when they encounter instances of social inequality in Buddhist contexts.

Concerns about Buddhism and social equality are not only historical but also have sharp contemporary ramifications. Today, social, religious, economic, and political authority is instantiated through hierarchies based on claims about gender and intellectual capacity. Again, it is not only college students who are concerned with perceived inequalities. Practitioners of

Tibetan Buddhism also take issue with inconsistencies and the gender problems in particular are debated heatedly across the Buddhist world, in Asia and globally. An instance in point is the ongoing debate about full ordination for women in the Tibetan Buddhist tradition, discussed below. In the classroom, it is crucial to introduce students to historical and contemporary Buddhist social movements that seek to address gender inequality, as well as to canonical texts that either defend it based on sociological or historical grounds, or refute it based on philosophical grounds.

WOMEN AS "LOW BORN"

The expectation for Buddhist traditions to espouse social equality, and the disappointment students experience when they sometimes fail to do so, arises most sharply around women's status in Buddhist institutions and societies, and the presence of patriarchy, androcentrism, and misogyny in some influential Buddhist texts.[7]

To illustrate, consider a very common word for "woman" in the Tibetan language. Classical Tibetan was formalized in the seventh century specifically in order to translate and import Buddhist texts from India, at a time when Tibetan rulers were eagerly embracing Buddhism. The most common word for "woman" in Tibetan language is translatable literally as "low-birth" (Tibetan: *skye dman*). This term seems to have been coined during the period when Classical Tibetan was being influenced by Indian Buddhism, and the term "low-birth" reflects and supports a widely held view among many Buddhists that women have lesser access to enlightenment than do men. It can be argued that this is because women's lives are seen as more difficult, but this is not a full explanation, and the suggestion of misogyny should not be taken lightly or disregarded.[8]

At the same time, some authoritative Indian and Tibetan Buddhist texts assert that women can become enlightened just as men can, and such texts tend to claim that gender is "non-dual" and without inherent existence or significance. In keeping with Indian and Tibetan interpretations of the Two Truths, this can be understood to mean that the differences between men and women are performances that are fluid and changing, not fixed, permanent, or "real" in the sense of being lasting or essential. Many Buddhist texts claim that all beings, regardless of sex or gender, have the potential for enlightenment.[9] These claims seem to be in direct contradiction to other canonical assertions that a woman must be reborn as a man in order to achieve enlightenment. This has long been a vibrant arena of Buddhist discourse, and today it is a focus of activism and institutional change in some parts of the Tibetan Buddhist community.

For students in my undergraduate courses, the Buddhist interpretive framework of the Two Truths provides a potential theoretical framework for grappling with the complex array of data on the status of women in Tibetan Buddhist texts and institutions. Regardless of whether students are "convinced" of the efficacy of the framework, testing out the Buddhist hermeneutical tool on the topic of gender is a meaningful exercise. To explain, influential Indian and Tibetan Buddhist texts of the Mahāyāna tradition address the problem of conventional gender inequality within the philosophical framework of ultimate truth. A famous example is from the *Vimalakīrti Nirdeśa Sūtra* [The Holy Teaching of Vimalakīrti: A Mahāyāna Scripture], likely composed around the first century in India. According to the text, Śāriputra, a close disciple of the Buddha, addresses a fully enlightened goddess on the troubled subject of her supposedly inferior sex. Within this particular story Śāriputra represents a flawed Buddhist perspective (here polemically associated with early Buddhist views as opposed to the later Mahāyāna views the text espouses). He is impressed by the goddess's brilliance, but he cannot fathom that a female could have such realization, even though she is no ordinary woman but a goddess. In the text, the character of Śāriputra represents the prominent view that only males can achieve enlightenment. In expressing this view he is made out within the narrative to be a buffoon. The exchange, which often elicits the most vibrant class discussions of my introductory Buddhism course, unfolds as follows:

Śāriputra: Goddess, what prevents you from transforming yourself out of your female state?

Goddess: Although I have sought my "female state" for these twelve years, I have not yet found it. Reverend Śāriputra, if a magician were to incarnate a woman by magic, would you ask her, "What prevents you from transforming yourself out of your female state?"

Śāriputra: No! Such a woman would not really exist, so what would there be to transform?

Goddess: Just so, reverend Śāriputra, all things do not really exist. Now, would you think, "What prevents one whose nature is that of a magical incarnation from transforming herself out of her female state?"

> Thereupon, the goddess employed her magical power to cause the elder Śāriputra to appear in her form and to cause herself to appear in his form. Then the goddess, transformed into Śāriputra, said to Śāriputra, transformed into a goddess, "Reverend Śāriputra, what prevents you from transforming yourself out of your female state?"
>
> And Śāriputra, transformed into the goddess, replied, "I no longer appear in the form of a male! My body has changed into the body of a woman! I do not know what to transform!

> The goddess continued, "If the elder could again change out of the female state, then all women could also change out of their female states. All women appear in the form of women in just the same way as the elder appears in the form of a woman. While they are not women in reality, they appear in the form of women. With this in mind, the Buddha said, "In all things, there is neither male nor female."[10]

As radical as this might seem, the tale is not at all marginal within Buddhist authoritative literature. It is a famous and often quoted episode in one of the most influential and widely translated Indian Mahāyāna sutras, beloved and revered across the Buddhist world. As we can see, there are certainly Buddhist sources that provide a ringing critique of gender inequality—the challenge for students is that such texts coexist in Buddhist literature with other much more misogynist materials.

Moreover, this is not the only Buddhist narrative that demonstrates the ultimate relativity of gender. A similar episode of transformation takes place in the *Lotus Sutra*, a text which is extremely influential in East Asian Buddhism. (This text is not as prominent in the Tibetan context, but it is relevant here since I assign it to students, and questions about equality inevitably arise.) In the *Lotus Sutra* an eight-year old dragon princess similarly transforms herself out of her female state in order to demonstrate her enlightenment, again to the poor blundering Śāriputra.

> At that time Śāriputra said to the dragon girl, "You suppose that in this short time you have been able to attain the unsurpassed way. But this is difficult to believe. Why? Because a woman's body is soiled and defiled, not a vessel for the Law. How could you attain the unsurpassed bodhi [awakening]? The road to Buddhahood is long and far-reaching. Only after one has spent immeasurable kalpas [aeons] pursuing austerities, accumulating deeds, practicing all kinds of paramitas [perfections], can one finally achieve success. Moreover, a woman is subject to the five obstacles. First, she cannot become a Brahma heavenly king. Second, she cannot become the king Shakra. Third, she cannot become a devil king. Fourth, she cannot become a wheel-turning sage king. Fifth, she cannot become a Buddha. How then could a woman like you be able to attain Buddhahood so quickly?"
>
> At that time the dragon girl had a precious jewel worth as much as the thousand-million-fold world which she presented to the Buddha. The Buddha immediately excepted [*sic*] it. The dragon girl said to Bodhisattva Wisdom Accumulated and to the venerable one, Śāriputra, "I presented the precious jewel and the World-Honored One accepted it—was that not quickly done?"
>
> They replied, "Very quickly!"
>
> The girls said, "employ your supernatural powers and watch me attain Buddhahood. It shall be even quicker than that!"

> At that time the members of the assembly all saw the dragon girl in the space of an instant change into a man and carry out all the practices of a bodhisattva [someone on the Mahāyāna path to awakening], immediately proceeding to the Spotless World of the south, taking a seat on a jeweled lotus, and attaining impartial and correct enlightenment. With the thirty-two features and the eighty characteristics, he expounded the wonderful Law for all living beings everywhere in the ten directions.[11]

When reading both of these Buddhist canonical texts in class, students are quick to note quite appropriately that these episodes are not about actual women but about magical goddesses or dragon princesses. Further, in both stories there is a strong polemical thrust from the Mahāyāna perspective against the earlier Buddhist tradition generally referred to as Theravāda, in which Śāriputra occupies one of the most venerated and saintly positions. These points raise rich interpretive questions, which lead to sharp thinking and analysis, in part thanks to being open-ended and unsolvable. For instance, to what extent are these stories more about critiquing the views of intellectual adversaries than they are about the status of women?

Alongside such complex narratives, students new to Buddhist studies also contend with explicitly androcentric and misogynist expressions. A prominent treatment of female imagery in authoritative Buddhist texts composed primarily for ordained male readers highlights the female body as the dangerous object of potential desire, which from a Buddhist perspective is rooted in ignorance.[12] A classic example is found in *A Guide to the Bodhisattva's Way of Life*, an ethical manual that is said to encompass the full scope of Mahāyāna teachings and which is extremely important in Tibetan Buddhism. The great Indian Buddhist master Śāntideva composed this masterpiece of ethical and philosophical thinking in the eighth century. When addressed in classroom discussions, passages such as the following excerpt raise concerns about misogyny:

> These unclean female bodies
> Are not found without a price:
> In order to obtain them I exhaust myself
> And in future will be injured in the hells.[13]

There is an abundance of similar statements in this and many other authoritative Buddhist sources, from all the major traditions. Students are challenged to navigate the diversity of Buddhist voices, sexist and anti-sexist. Buddhist communities in Tibet and elsewhere have already developed sophisticated interpretive tools for thinking about these apparent inconsistencies, just as present-day Buddhists advocating gender equality have addressed sexism in practice through a variety of means. Students ask, what does this mean for the power structures in Buddhist institutions made up of living, breathing Buddhists of diverse genders and various levels of perceived intelligence? What is the relationship between the "ultimate" philosophical reality of non-dual gender equality and the "relative" social reality of gender inequality? Tibetan theories on the Two Truths provide a framework in which to begin to think through these questions without rigidly adhering to one prescribed point of view.

Conventional inequalities are especially pronounced around institutional and systemic differences between Tibetan Buddhist monks and nuns. As mentioned above, this includes access to resources, including material support from the lay community as well as intellectual resources in the form of education and training. Along with these instances of resource inequality, and perhaps underlying it, is the long standing but highly problematized and widely contradicted claim, by Buddhists as well as scholars of Buddhism, that women cannot attain enlightenment, but must first attain positive karma to be reborn in a male body, at which time enlightenment becomes feasible. Across the diverse Buddhist traditions we find the view that fully ordained monks have the clearest access to enlightenment since they are the least encumbered by worldly activities such as parenting, earning a living, and more. The practical impacts of this claim, although it is debated in canonical sources perhaps just as often and as vehemently as it is supported, have for centuries shaped hierarchies and the subjectivities of Tibetan Buddhist women and men.

When I explore these topics with students, this often leads us to the real-world debate around whether contemporary Tibetan Buddhist nuns should have the opportunity to be fully ordained, despite there not being a preexisting, unbroken tradition of full ordination for nuns in Tibet. There are three ordination systems across the Buddhist world, and certain features are held in common.[14] To be fully ordained as a monastic in any Buddhist tradition generally requires a quorum of ordained monks for new monks, and a larger quorum of monks plus nuns to ordain new nuns. With rare exceptions, in order for the ordination to be valid, all the monks and nuns must be from the same ordination tradition as those being ordained. The reason for this is that Buddhist traditions maintain a strong focus on uninterrupted lineages which can be traced back to India (at least in principle), and whether fictionally or realistically, back to the historical Buddha as the originator of Buddhist ordination. However, this requirement of uninterrupted lineage results in institutional and conceptual problems where women's ordination is concerned. For instance, in the case of Tibet, the lineage of ordination for woman was either never established or was broken in about the tenth century.[15]

That said, many Tibetan Buddhist women lead lives of committed Buddhist practice in community with other novice nuns, or *anis* as they are called in Tibetan. They are not, however, fully ordained. In important ways, this, in combination with the "eight heavy rules" (described above) that instantiate ordained women's inferior status, means that even the most learned, accomplished, and wise Tibetan Buddhist *anis*, as permanent novices, hold less authority than do their male counterparts. This perpetuates a structure of entrenched disparity in regard to institutional authority as well as perceived access to enlightenment. Since, again, ordination is believed to set up the best circumstances for achieving Buddhist awakening. On the socioeconomic front, the ramifications are grave since Buddhist lay people tend to donate to communities of monks, who are perceived as more fully embodying Buddha's teachings. Therefore historically nuns' communities have been impoverished relative to monks' communities.[16]

Today some Tibetan women are seeking full ordination. Tibetan Buddhists across the world heatedly debate the question of full ordination for women, especially visibly now that Buddhism has a global presence and is under the scrutiny of thinkers raised in a feminist climate. The Dalai Lama has expressed support for Tibetan women interested in full ordination, but at the same time he has resisted breaking with tradition and forcing the broader Tibetan Buddhist community to accept a new ordination for women.[17] Possible solutions include starting a new ordination for women, or importing one from another tradition, as was done in other Buddhist cultures, such as Sri Lanka, where ordination was not available to women for many years but has been reestablished successfully.[18] Reflecting the same diversity of perspectives on the female gender that we find in Buddhist texts, Tibetan Buddhists hold widely varying positions on the question of full ordination for women. There is a significant conservative, patriarchal contingent among Tibetan monastic authorities that stands against the possibility of new ordination as a break with history and tradition. There are also many more individual and subtle arguments against a change, from women and men alike.

Recently, a group of Tibetan nuns began the process of receiving full ordination, under the guidance of the current seventeenth Karmapa Lama, a leading hierarch within Tibetan Buddhism. The Karmapa has taken radical action and begun the process of establishing a new ordination lineage for women in his Kagyu School, establishing original iconographic and ritual practices to support the new ordination event.[19] By inviting fully ordained Taiwanese nuns to perform the necessary rituals, in cooperation with others supporting this effort, he established a quorum to begin the years long three-part full ordination process for a group of nineteen nuns in Bodhgaya, India, in early 2017.[20] This process takes time and is in its early stages, so it is unpredictable whether the lineage will flourish. In teaching about the contemporary situation, the new ordination is important in part because it demonstrates flexibility on the part of the Tibetan Buddhist tradition that is in keeping with the Tibetan philosophical assertion that gender norms are not fixed nor permanent.

INTELLECTUAL HIERARCHIES

A second area of apparent inequality that prompts discussion among liberal arts students concerns traditional Buddhist divisions of students and practitioners into categories of high, middle, and low capacity. Especially in the esoteric context of Tibetan Buddhism, teachings and instructions for ritual and meditative practice are organized to suit the needs and propensities of each of these hypothetical groups, and from a certain perspective one could argue only the "best" students have access to the highest teachings. This is first and foremost a means for categorizing different types of knowledge, and it is hard to calculate how it maps onto lived experience of Buddhists seeking teachings. Crucially, a practitioner's chances of achieving enlightenment are shaped in part by the type of teachings they receive and practice. Therefore there are soteriological implications since this rubric suggests that Buddhist practitioners of middling and of lower capacity do not have opportunities equal to students with the highest capacity.

Mahāyāna and Vajrayāna teachings rest on the basic Buddhist hermeneutical and pedagogical assertion that Buddha taught different levels of truth to suit the needs of students with varying capacities or levels of intelligence and readiness to learn. The claim that Buddha presented different views of reality to suit the needs of different students in different contexts also shapes Tibetan Buddhist monastic curricula, which are structured around the premise that different types of students should be instructed differently, sometimes employing methods that seem contradictory to one another. Likewise, the premise that some people are ready for teachings (such as the ultimate emptiness of all phenomena expressed in the non-dualist view of the Two Truths) that other people are not ready for, justifies the restriction of advanced esoteric teachings. An important source for undergraduate students on this topic is *The Life of Milarepa*, which recounts the life story of a Tibetan who endures a grueling and transformative quest for a teacher who would guide him on the path of esoteric Buddhist practice.[21] Again, this culture of restricted access can strike liberal arts college students in Buddhism courses as unjust or as elitist and hypocritical.

Some of the problems that arise for students new to this material are complicated by the effects of contemporary global culture and the internet, for example around the issue of access to esoteric texts now widely available in translation. According to the principles of esoteric Buddhism, these texts should be "protected" by secrecy and by rules of transmission that reserve the highest teachings for students of the highest caliber, who are well prepared to read and to practice such texts. Now that many esoteric texts are available on the internet, and even studied in Buddhism classes, the longstanding structures that protected the intellectual hierarchy are being reevaluated by Tibetan Buddhist teachers, practitioners, translators, and publishers.

Students ask, who makes the decision about what teachings should be engaged with by a particular practitioner? The primary sources we read in class tell us: ideally a teacher who knows a student well and personally. It is a fundamental element in all Buddhist pedagogies that different people have different capacities and therefore require different methods of training and different materials to learn, governing who should learn what, and when. From a widely held Tibetan Buddhist perspective, his undergirds distinctions between the major philosophical traditions of Buddhism, as well as serving as the basis for the protection of certain esoteric teachings as being appropriate for only the highest caliber students. This is an altogether distinct question from gender norms, but this categorization is likewise colored by thinking about ultimate and conventional truths, and what is at stake for Tibetan Buddhists (at least rhetorically) is nothing short of access to enlightenment. In teaching college students, this opens up a rich area of dialogue, for example around the ideals of liberal arts education, intellectual elitism, open access, and personalized learning.

THE "TWO TRUTHS" OF ULTIMATE AND CONVENTIONAL LEVELS OF REALITY

Keeping in mind these two examples of apparent inequality that are discernible in Indian and Tibetan Buddhist texts by college students studying Buddhism, the hermeneutical framework of the "Two Truths" can help students grapple with what Buddhist texts contain and to reconcile contradictory claims about ultimate equality and conventional hierarchies. The Two Truths doctrine is an influential and widely held philosophical framework that is important to all three major traditions of Buddhism (Theravāda, Mahāyāna, and Vajrayāna) although it is interpreted differently in each tradition. The Tibetan tradition is known primarily for its Vajrayāna practices, but encompasses elements of all three traditions.

From a well-established Tibetan Buddhist perspective, the ultimate truth (also called the absolute truth) is how things really are—impermanent and without a fixed self or essence. This level of reality is how enlightened people like the Buddha experience phenomena. The conventional truth (also called the relative truth) is how things seem to be according to the perspective of unenlightened people (the vast majority of humanity over the course of time). We see things as ultimately fixed and real, when they are actually relative and ever changing. Buddhist philosophical schools debate about exactly how this teaching should be interpreted, but they agree that there is no other (third or forth or so on) truth besides the ultimate and conventional levels.[22]

Debates about how the Two Truths doctrine should be interpreted have been central to defining various philosophical approaches in Tibetan Buddhism. The second-century Indian Buddhist philosopher Nāgārjuna, founder of the important Middle Way School, which has been extremely influential in Tibet, wrote:

> Without a foundation in the conventional truth,
> The significance of the ultimate cannot be taught.
> Without understanding the significance of the ultimate,
> Liberation is not achieved.[23]

Ultimate truth is the nature of things as they really are, as opposed to how we perceive and experience them conventionally, and yet we rely on the conventional to recognize and express the ultimate nature of things. An analogy is often made between this type of Buddhist perspective on reality and quantum physics, which gives us insights into the ways the world works that are contrary to our experience. Buddhist practitioners claim that one can practice and cultivate a way of perceiving and experiencing the world that is perfectly in keeping with ultimate truth. They call that "awakening" or "enlightenment." This is hard to do by any estimation, but it is a central Buddhist claim that it is possible. Relative or conventional truth corresponds to the way reality appears to us, and how we experience the world in our unenlightened state.

The trick comes with the claim, central to Tibetan Buddhist philosophies, and either frustrating or delightful to college students, that ultimate and relative truths are "non-dual." In other words, *the only thing that is ultimately true is that everything is relative.* According to this view, all phenomena and the sense of self we experience to be so real are posited to be empty of inherent, lasting existence (ultimately) and we experience them as "real" only because they exist relative to other phenomena and selves. From this perspective reality and truth comprise a web of interrelated, mutually defining relationships that give rise to the impression that things are ultimately real. The ultimate truth is that everything is relative, conditioned by our conventional experiences, which are valid, but interdependent and not permanent, as they seem to be from our unenlightened perspective.

What does this have to do with equality? There are many ways to explore this question but for the purposes of this essay on teaching Buddhist studies,

I have focused on two types of hierarchy—in particular, gender and intellectual hierarchies. These hierarchies govern Buddhist experience on the level of worldly influence, resources, and authority, as well as on the level of the highest Buddhist soteriological aim of enlightenment.

CONCLUSION

Khandro Rinpoche, a contemporary Tibetan Buddhist teacher, has been quoted as saying, "If being a woman is an inspiration, use it. If it is an obstacle, try not to be bothered by it."[24] This pragmatic advice, directed at Buddhist practitioners rather than at students in a Buddhist Studies course, might be productively applied to the examples mentioned earlier.

First encounters with Buddhist views can be off-putting. I am struck by the disappointment shown by my students, as well as by others new to Buddhist doctrines, when they discover examples of apparent social inequality. Their expectation and hope are that Buddhism represents a perfectly enlightened, humanist system, not just normatively but in its lived practices across the globe. In thinking about how most effectively to teach students experiencing this disappointment, first and foremost we need to examine our cultural preconceptions and treat Buddhist materials, like all texts, within their historical and cultural contexts. Secondly, we need to examine why we expect Buddhist texts and people to be enlightened rather than interested in enlightenment. There is a big difference.

As we navigate those pitfalls, we might shift our attention to include the question that drives this essay, can introducing liberal arts students to the Buddhist interpretive framework of the Two Truths, as a hermeneutic tool, help them understand Buddhism more fully while also allowing them an opportunity to develop critical thinking and tolerance for complex topics more broadly? I deeply admire and appreciate the poetic and philosophical elegance of non-dualist thinking about the Two Truths. I also recognize a potential misuse—to brush off instances of inequality as *merely* relative (not ultimately real) and therefore not worthy of attention. I critique this potential application, whether by students new to the framework or by Buddhist thinkers. In this regard, it is worth posing two possible pitfalls: (1) Might this Buddhist interpretive framework in fact perpetuate social inequality within the Tibetan Buddhist context? And, (2) Might applying this Buddhist interpretive tool settle student doubts about social inequality too facilely and preclude thinking critically about Buddhism? These are genuine possibilities that can only be combatted by vigilant self-reflection and critical thinking. Most importantly, the Buddhist materials continually remind us that insight into complex topics must always be tempered by compassion, and vice versa.

When teaching about Buddhism I cannot in good conscience explain away examples of inequality in Buddhist thinking and practice. On the contrary these tend to be very fruitful areas of inquiry and allow students, and I would argue Buddhist practitioners, to learn more about how Buddhist thinkers in diverse times and places have grappled with complexity, including but not limited to gaps between ideals and social realities. These were and are very important questions for Buddhist authors and practitioners, just as they are for monks and nuns, or students in a liberal arts classroom today. Taking a Tibetan Buddhist interpretation of the Two Truths as a model can help students as they develop critical analysis of complex topics, within and beyond Buddhist studies.

NOTES

1. The ideal is for the laity to support the ordained nuns and monks materially by making offerings, and for the ordained community to support the laity ritually and "spiritually" by dedicating their lives to practicing the Buddha's teachings.

2. Rita Gross, *Buddhism After Patriarchy: A Feminist History, Analysis, and Reconstruction of Buddhism* (Albany: SUNY Press, 1992). Gross glosses the eight heavy or "special" rules for nuns in this way: nuns, however senior, must honor and bow to a monk, however junior; nuns must spend the yearly rainy season retreat in a place supervised by monks; monks would determine the bi-yearly dates for confessional meetings; monks would interrogate nuns accused of breaking rules (but not vice versa); monks would determine nuns' punishment for infractions (but not vice versa); monks would participate in nuns' ordination (but not vice versa); nuns could not criticize a monk (but not vice versa); nuns could not admonish a monk (but not vice versa) (ibid., 36).

3. See Diana Y. Paul, with Frances Wilson, *Women in Buddhism: Images of the Feminine in Mahāyāna Tradition*, 2nd ed. (Berkeley: University of California Press, 1985); and Gross, *Buddhism After Patriarchy.*

4. *Buddhist Hermeneutics*, ed. Donald S. Lopez Jr. (Honolulu : University of Hawaii Press, 1988).

5. Dzongsar Jamyang Khyentse, *What Makes You Not a Buddhist* (Boston: Shambhala, 2007).

6. See Donald S. Lopez, Jr., *Prisoners of Shangri-La: Tibetan Buddhism and the West* (Chicago: University of Chicago Press, 1998). Also, for an excellent summary of related misconceptions about Buddhism and their historical context, see Robert E. Buswell Jr. and Donald S. Lopez Jr., "Ten Misconceptions About Buddhism," *UCLA Newsroom*, http://newsroom.ucla.edu/stories/ten-misconceptions-about-buddhism-249449 (accessed November 2017).

7. See Alan Sponberg, "Attitudes Toward Women and the Feminine in Early Buddhism," in *Buddhism, Sexuality, and Gender*, ed. José Ignacio Cabezón. (Albany: SUNY Press 1992), 3-33. Sponberg provides an extremely useful overview of what

he terms "soteriological inclusiveness," "institutional androcentrism," "ascetic misogyny," and "soteriological androgyny" as a way to make sense of the complex and contradictory treatments of the feminine in Buddhist literature (ibid., 8).

8. See Dan Martin, "The Woman Illusion? Research Into the Lives of Spiritually Accomplished Women Leaders of the 11th and 12th Centuries," in *Women in Tibet*, ed. Janet Gyatso and Hannah Havnevik (New York: Columbia University Press, 2005), 49-82.

9. Paul, *Women in Buddhism*, 80-94.

10. *The Holy Teachings of Vimalakīrti: A Mahāyāna Scripture*, trans. Robert A. F. Thurman (University Park: Pennsylvania State University Press, 1976), 62-63.

11. *The Lotus Sutra*, trans. Burton Watson, http://www.english.fgs2.ca/sites/default/files/pdf/The%20Lotus%20Sutra.pdf (accessed October 2017).

12. See Liz Wilson, *Charming Cadavers: Horrific Figurations of the Feminine in Indian Buddhist Hagiographic Literature* (Chicago: University of Chicago Press, 1996).

13. *A Guide to the Bodhisattva's Way of Life*, trans. Stephen Batchelor (Dharamasala, India: Library of Tibetan Works and Archives, 1993), 114.

14. For an array of perspectives on Buddhist ordination, see *Dignity and Discipline: Reviving Full Ordination for Buddhist Nuns*, ed. Thea Mohr and Jampa Tsedroen (Boston: Wisdom, 2010).

15. See Hildegard Diemberger, *When a Woman Becomes a Religious Dynasty: The Samding Dorje Phagmo of Tibet* (New York: Columbia University Press, 2007).

16. See Gregory Schopen, *Buddhist Nuns, Monks, and Other Worldly Matters: Recent Papers on Monastic Buddhism in India* (Honolulu: University of Hawaii Press, 2014).

17. See *Dignity and Discipline*, ed. Mohr and Tsedroen.

18. Janet Gyatso, "Female Ordination in Buddhism: Looking into a Crystal Ball, Making a Future," in *Dignity and Discipline: Reviving Full Ordination for Buddhist Nuns*, ed. Thea Mohr and Jampa Tsedroen (Boston: Wisdom, 2010), 1-22.

19. Janet Gyatso, "Recently, Under the Bodhi Tree: New Female Ordination in Tibetan Buddhism," lecture delivered at Bard College, Annandale-on-Hudson, New York, September 28, 2017.

20. On the ordination ceremony, see http://kagyuoffice.org/history-in-the-making-the-first-step-toward-full-ordination-for-tibetan-buddhist-nuns/ (accessed November 2017).

21. Tsangnyon Heruka, *The Life of Milarepa*, trans. Andrew Quintman (New York: Penguin Classics, 2010).

22. See Guy Newland, *The Two Truths in the Madhyamika Philosophy of the Geluk-ba Order of Tibetan Buddhism* (Ithaca, NY: Snow Lion, 1992).

23. Jay L. Garfield, *The Fundamental Wisdom of the Middle Way: Nagarjuna's Mulamadhyamakakarika* (New York: Oxford University Press, 1995), xxii.

24. Khandro Rinpoche, http://www.dakinipower.com/jetsun-khandro-rinpoche/ (accessed June 2018).

Chapter 9

The Rabbinic Meritocracy and Its Discontents

Shai Secunda

Aristotle's principle of equality famously requires that like cases be treated as like.[1] In such a scheme, resolving social inequality means living up to this ideal when it has been breached. Alternatively, it entails reordering the relationships between unequal people so that they are now deemed equal and hence worthy of the same treatment. Both missions are commendable, though the latter form of "equalizing" does come with certain dangers. When old inequalities are dismantled, new ones often grow in their place and become further entrenched, obscured by the proud claim that equality has finally been achieved.

In this essay, I follow one such dynamic at a foundational moment in the history of Judaism, when late antique rabbis replaced priestly hierarchies by democratizing access to the tradition, yet in the process established harder-to-detect inequalities. At the same time, rabbinic texts show that the rabbis did not entirely ignore the problems inherent in the establishment of this knowledge meritocracy, as they enacted and subvert these dynamics in striking ways.

One of the driving forces in the invention of normative Judaism, the form of the religion that grew out of late antique rabbinic Judaism and which has dominated since the Middle Ages, was a gradual movement towards equality[2]—at least as far as free-born Jewish males were concerned.[3] Ancient Judaism was a textually and legally fixated religion. Thus, at the core of this project was the opening-up of access to the study, interpretation, and application of Jewish texts. This was a major development. In Second Temple times, access to Scripture and scriptural law had been dominated by a heredity class of Levitical priests who enjoyed considerable economic and political power in Jewish society. Although there certainly were rival groups of Jewish scholars and interpreters, the priests were well-established leaders with biblical precedent. One passage from Deuteronomy asserts that the ultimate site of authority, backed by capital punishment, was an elevated spot of God's choosing understood to be the priestly-run, Jerusalem Temple:

> If a case is too baffling for you to decide, be it a controversy over homicide, civil law, or assault—matters of dispute in yours courts—you shall promptly go up to the place that the Lord your God will have chosen, and appear before the Levitical priests, or the magistrate in charge at the time, and present your problem. When they have announced to you the verdict in the case you shall carry out the verdict that is announced to you from that place that the Lord chose, observing scrupulously all their instructions to you. You shall act in accordance with the instructions given you and the ruling handed down to you; you must not deviate from the verdict that they announce to you either to the right or to the left. Should a man act presumptuously and disregard the priest charged with serving there the Lord your God, or the magistrate, that man shall die. Thus you will sweep out evil from Israel. All the people will hear and be afraid and will not act presumptuously again. (Deuteronomy 17:8-13)[4]

In the years following the Roman destruction of Jerusalem and its Temple in 70 CE and the Second Jewish Revolt in the early 130s CE, a group of biblical and legal interpreters based in the Galilee, bearing the prestigious title rabbi (literally, "my master"), but emphatically claiming no special collective lineage, began to flourish. Their rulings, interpretations, and lore were compiled in major rabbinic works, first in the foundational legal compilation known as the Mishnah compiled around 200 CE.[5] Subsequently, this material was intensely studied in two rabbinic centers, in the Galilee and the Mesopotamia. The result was the creation of the Palestinian Talmud and the far more significant Babylonian Talmud between the fifth and sixth centuries, which ultimately shaped the basic contours of Judaism as we recognize them today.[6]

In consolidating their power, the rabbinic movement had to demote the priests from their authoritative perch and replace them with non-priestly scholars—read, the rabbis. They accomplished this discursively, by virtually omitting any mention of priests when recounting the origins of their authority, and via that distinctly rabbinic mode of biblical interpretation known as Midrash. Thus, the opening passage of the mishnaic tractate Ethics of the Fathers (Avot) charts the transmission of the Torah from Moses to Joshua and down to the elders and sages, cuts out non-rabbinic priests almost entirely and mentions only one rabbinicized High Priest.[7] Likewise, an early third-century Midrash on Deuteronomy thoroughly rereads the above cited passage from Deuteronomy as a rabbinic curriculum of learning no longer centered in Jerusalem, rather in Yavneh—the coastal town where the rabbinic movement constituted itself after the Second Jewish Revolt.[8]

The extent to which the rabbis fully abandoned the old, pre-meritocratic trappings of wealth and family prestige can been debated.[9] However, a clear trend of open access to learning in rabbinic Judaism is undeniable and is manifest in the establishment in Yavneh of what looks like a democratic, intellectual society.[10] This is apparent in the rise of novel theologies that asserted that regardless of natural aptitude, everyone was welcome to take part in rabbinic scholarship—"one who accomplished much [in his learning] and one who accomplished little are equal, as long as they direct their heart towards heaven."[11] Finally, as with the American Dream, we find the construction of new rags-to-riches heroes, perhaps the most famous being the legendary sage Rabbi Akiva, who began Torah study as a poor, middle-aged ignoramus, and with the support of a beautiful wife who always believed in him, was able to ascend to the heights of rabbinic society.[12]

* * *

The efforts of late ancient rabbis to wrest sacred texts away from the exclusive control of priests towards the broader public certainly sounds like a positive development. There is no doubt that the popular conception of the Protestant Reformation and its resulting revolutions have something to do with this appreciation. Still closer to home, the work ethic powering the American Dream promises that doors of all kind, including gateways to knowledge and to understanding, are open to anyone willing to invest the time and energy in their pursuit. This is particularly apparent in the history of education in the United States, where the removal of racial and economic barriers was crucial to the country's claim of mid-twentieth century renewal. The dramatic transformation of American power-structures, in which Waspism gave way to the so-called meritocracy, is worth pondering not only because it tells a similar "success story," but also because it reminds us of the persistent inequalities that might be concealed just beneath the surface of a new, meritocratic order.[13]

Social science going back decades has examined the uses of higher education to entrench social stratification.[14] Over the past few years, this critique has been picked up by the public discourse in the United States, as the country's institutions of higher education have been criticized for perpetuating an elitist system masquerading as an open invitation to acquire knowledge and its benefits.[15] In reality, the argument goes, these elite institutions normally include only those students who have been adequately socialized and have the resources to achieve the "merit" necessary to gain admittance to the so-called meritocracy. These range from the quotidian test preps, AP courses, and extra-curricular activities which measure and demonstrate carefully constructed "merit," to the deeper inculcation of a certain type of aspirationalism. Once members of these communities have successfully passed through the meritocratic system, they constitute a new class that alleges to be beyond class entirely. *Within* the meritocracy, new distinctions arise based on "merit" which challenge the claim to equality. More dangerously, those who remain *outside* of the new and successful cohorts are branded as failures. In the language of the equality principle, these people are confirmed as not "alike" and thus need not be treated "like" others.

* * *

A similar development is apparent in the formation of the rabbinic movement. Again, the rabbis successfully broke the heredity, priestly monopoly and allowed and encouraged a casteless system of budding scholars, who were ostensibly admitted solely on the basis of piety and the raw desire to engage in religious study. Inevitably, however, this created a class in its own right—the *talmid ḥakham*, literally, a student of the sage(s), who was conceived of in total opposition to the *am ha-aretz*, literally, "people of the land," but essentially, the non-rabbinic, uneducated masses.[16] The growing community of rabbinic sages officially continued to invite into its ranks anyone ambitious enough to commit to the intellectual rigors of rabbinic scholarship. However, the growing divisions between the scholarly and non-scholarly classes made the system function like a modern-day meritocracy that accepted new merit-based members in theory but rarely in practice.

From the Middle Ages on, the nature of the rabbinic "meritocracy" and its achievements and failures have ebbed and flowed.[17] Rather than charting its post-rabbinic fate, the rest of this article stays within the confines of Late Antiquity, but now more closely reads a relevant Mishnah alongside Talmudic discussions about hierarchy and learning. Strikingly, these texts enact and subvert some of the advantages and problems endemic to the rabbinic educational meritocracy.

I begin with a passage from the end of the mishnaic tractate Horayot:

> A man precedes a woman regarding saving a life and returning a lost object; and a woman precedes a man as to clothing [when impoverished] and rescuing her from captivity. When both are at risk of [sexual] abuse [in captivity], the man precedes the woman. A priest precedes a Levite, a Levite an Israelite, an Israelite a "bastard" (*mamzer*, the offspring from an illicit affair), a "bastard" a Gibeonite (a nation that joined the Israelites under fall pretenses; see Joshua 9), a Gibeonite a convert, and a convert a freed [gentile] slave. When [is this rule in effect]? When all of them are equal [in knowledge]. But if the "bastard" is a rabbinical scholar and the High Priest one of the ignorant masses —the "bastard" scholar takes precedence over the ignoramus high priest.[18]

This passage follows a technical discussion about precedence in the sacrificial rite,[19] and opens with an apparently unforgiving—and frankly from a Western perspective, troubling—hierarchical system.[20] According to this scheme, when it comes to assessing rights and "precedence," there are so many distinctions that even within Jewish society, the equality principle is rarely applicable. And yet, when one reads to the end of the Mishnah, the final line proudly upends the entire hierarchical system by declaring that rabbinic learning erases all distinctions, allowing the lowly bastard to take precedence over the most powerful person in the land.

Parallel texts in the Mishnah and tannaitic literature—rabbinic literature compiled in and around the early third century CE—also advance the notion that rabbinic learning has the power to dismantle normal social hierarchies and obligations. One strain maintains that a teacher of Torah gains precedence over one's own father:

> [When] his father's and his teacher's lost object [needs to be returned], his teacher's takes precedence; For his father brought him into This World, but the teacher who taught him wisdom brings him into the life of World to Come. When his father is learned, his father's lost object takes precedence. If his father and teacher were carrying a burden, he helps his teacher and only then helps his father. If his father and teacher were sitting in captivity, he redeems his teacher and only then redeems his father.[21]

Although the conclusion of Mishnah Horayot begins with hierarchy, by the end one suspects that this hierarchical system was only adduced in order to subvert it, with the idea that Torah study, which is even open to "bastards," is the ultimate equalizer. In this way, the end of Mishnah Horayot can be appreciated as foundational in its establishment of the new rabbinic knowledge economy.

And yet, it soon becomes apparent that the establishment of such a meritocracy is incomplete and contains the seeds of future complications. First, note how in the Mishnah's intentionally shocking illustration, it is a learned "bastard" who can take precedence over an ignorant High Priest, even though the "bastard" is not the lowest person in the Mishnah's initial hierarchy. This suggests that perhaps there were unspoken limits as to how much the meritocracy really was "color-blind." "Gibeonites," converts, and freed gentile slaves need not apply.[22]

Second, this Mishnah and other parallel rabbinic texts, demonstrate how the replacement of the old lineage-based hierarchy with the rabbinic meritocracy did not mean that the hierarchical impulse was completely displaced. As the Mishnah makes clear, the old system remains in effect when both bastard and high priest are learned—"When [is this rule in effect]? When all of them are equal [in knowledge]"; likewise, the other Mishnah adduced states "when his father is learned, his father's lost object takes precedence [over his teacher's]."

Furthermore, even once Torah knowledge is established as the great equalizer, we encounter rabbinic discussions that probe which type of learning and teaching was considered sufficient to upend old hierarchies. When considering those situations, when one returns a teacher's lost article before a parent's, the Tosefta—a tannaitic compilation that runs parallel to the Mishnah—first establishes which type of teacher gains privilege over a parent, and rules that "only a teacher who taught Torah, rather than a craft, gains precedence." The Tosefta then further asks, "which kind [of Torah teacher]?" and presents the following responses: "The one who first opened for him [the world of learning]. R. Meir says; his teacher who taught him wisdom (=analysis?) not his teacher who taught him [only] Torah. R. Yehuda says: [Only] when most of his learning is from him [does he take precedence]. R. Yosse says: Whoever enlightened his eyes through his teaching."[23]

As is their wont, the two Talmuds pick up on these tannaitic discussions, expanding and further actualizing them. While the Mishnah had been focused primarily on challenging the prestige of priestly, Levitical lineage, the Talmud takes on royalty, announcing that "a sage takes precedence over the king," explaining that this is because unlike royal power, true wisdom is unparalleled—"[with] a sage who dies we no longer have anyone like him, while a king who dies, all of Israel are able to replace him!"[24]

On the other hand, the Talmuds also attempt to make further distinctions *within* the learning economy. Thus, the Palestinian Talmud records the following discussion:

> It was taught: the arrangers [of oral text] come before the "sharp-pepper" [analysists]... This is what they said: [knowledge of] Mishnah takes precedence over Bible...R. Shmuel b. Nahman says: [Knowledge of] Mishnah comes before Talmud (post-Mishnaic discourse)... R. Yohanan says: [No,] Talmud comes before Mishnah!... R. Shmuel the son of R. Yosse b. R. Bon expounded [the verse]: "A rich man is clever in his own eyes, But a perceptive poor man can see through him" (Proverbs 28:11)—"a rich man is clever in his own eyes"—this is a master of Talmud; "but a perceptive poor man can see through him"—this is the master of Aggadah (non-legal rabbinic learning).[25]

It is not too difficult to imagine how scholastic fights over which type of scholarship was deemed more valuable could create new, even more rancorous inequalities. Indeed, this was the topic of a Talmudic tale recorded in the Babylonian Talmud's discussion of this material.[26] While the story is too long to recount here, its brilliant plot is driven by academic jealousies, and the weapon of choice is shaming someone who is not knowledgeable about obscure and complex sections of the rabbinic canon. By thematizing these tensions, the Talmud both acknowledges and critiques the new hierarchies that can rise within a supposedly meritocratic educational system.[27]

Of course, the reason why the rabbinic meritocracy was so compelling was because despite its potential for academic tensions, officially it opened its doors to everyone. Within its discussion of the material, the Palestinian Talmud quotes the following homily of R. Yohanan: "All forty days that Moses spent on the Mount [during the revelation at Sinai] he would learn Torah and forget it. In the end, it was given to him as a gift. Why was all this necessary? In order to bring back the fools [who might otherwise have been dissuaded from engaging in Torah learning]."[28] Again, this teaching is commendable for its non-elitist encouragement of even those without natural aptitude to join the community in Torah study. Yet there is a dark edge to this powerful notion. In Rabbinic Hebrew, the seemingly playful phrase "to *bring back* the fools (*lehaḥzir et ha-tipshim*)" implies a need for repentance. When it came to the ignorant masses (*amei ha-aretz*) who chose not to join the rabbinic community, the Talmud had incredibly harsh and unforgiving new hierarchical rules in place, which were arguably a legacy of the rabbinic meritocracy: "For R. Yehoshua son of Levi in the name of R. Ḥanina son of Antigonos said: [if in the Mishnah's system of triage there are not enough funds to both take care of] clothing for the wife of a member [of the rabbinic community (*ḥaver*)] and the life of one of the masses (*'am ha-aretz*) clothing for the wife of the member comes first, out of honor for the member."[29]

To sum up, the democratizing, meritocratic formation of rabbinic Judaism, which afforded access to and actively sought out wider groups of Jews to participate in Torah study and enjoy its benefits, also engendered novel hierarchical frictions and new inequalities. On the one hand, even those who were not intellectually inclined were encouraged to join the learned, rabbinic society. And regardless of lineage, the learned were valued more than the most prominent members of the old, priestly elite. Yet, rather than creating a perfect community of equals devoted to Torah study, different intellectual approaches and aptitudes were pitted against each other, leading to new pecking orders. Even more troublingly, the lives of those who, despite rabbinic encouragement, chose not to join the community of learners, were deemed less valuable than that of the intellectuals. If there is a saving grace in the establishment of the new, rabbinic economies of learning, it can be found in talmudic literature's open-ended, "democratic" mode of discourse, where this formative feature of Jewish society was simultaneously constructed and deconstructed.[30]

NOTES

1. The idea is outlined in Aristotle, *Nicomachean Ethics*, trans. Christopher Rowe (Oxford: Oxford University Press, 2002), pt. 1, bk. 5, 3.

2. The story of the ascension of rabbinic Judaism at the expense of the priestly system has been told numerous times. For an influential account, see Shaye J. D. Cohen, *From the Maccabees to the Mishnah* (Philadelphia: Westminster Press, 1987).

3. Gender inequalities in Judaism are critical but beyond the scope of this article. For a feminist critique, see Judith Plaskow, *Standing Again at Sinai: Judaism from a Feminist Perspective* (San Francisco: Harper & Row, 1990). For a somewhat apologetic approach, see Judith Hauptman, *Rereading the Rabbis: A Woman's Voice* (Boulder, CO: Westview Press, 1997). In the present case, it is valuable to note that barring women from rabbinic learning proved particularly resistant, and only shifted relatively recently and not in all Jewish denominations. See Ilan Fuchs, *Jewish Women's Torah Study: Orthodox Religious Education and Modernity* (New York: Routledge, 2014).

4. The rendition of this passage is based on the New Jewish Publication Society translation. Jewish Publication Society of America, *The Torah: The Five Books of Moses*. (Philadelphia: Jewish Publication Society, 1999). All other translations in the paper are mine.

5. On the Mishnah and its significance in the formation of Judaism, see Jacob Neusner, *Judaism: The Evidence of the Mishnah* (Chicago: University of Chicago Press, 1981).

6. For an introduction to rabbinic literature, with discussions of provenance and dating, see Hermann Leberecht Strack and Günter Stemberger, *Introduction to the Talmud and Midrash*, trans. Markus Bockmuehl (Edinburgh: T & T Clark, 1991).

7. Cf. Amram Tropper, *Simeon the Righteous in Rabbinic Literature: A Legend Reinvented* (Leiden: Brill, 2013), 23-68.

8. Sifre Deuteronomy 152-53. See Steven D. Fraade, *From Tradition to Commentary: Torah and Its Interpretation in the Midrash Sifre to Deuteronomy* (Albany: SUNY Press, 1991), 83-87. All rabbinic texts are cited according to standard editions, and are accessible in the original Hebrew or Aramaic, often with English translation, at SEFARIA, "A Living Library of Jewish Texts," https://www.sefaria.org.il/.

9. See Jeffrey L. Rubenstein, *The Culture of the Babylonian Talmud* (Baltimore: Johns Hopkins University Press, 2003).

10. Shaye J. D. Cohen, "The Significance of Yavneh: Pharisees, Rabbis, and the End of Jewish Sectarianism," *Hebrew Union College Annual* 55 (1984): 27-53.

11. Babylonian Talmud Berakhot, 17a.

12. For a recent treatment and reassessment of the sources, see Azzan Yadin-Israel, *Scripture and Tradition: Rabbi Akiva and the Triumph of Midrash* (Philadelphia: University of Pennsylvania Press, 2015).

13. These and some of the following points have been argued at length in William Deresiewicz, *Excellent Sheep: The Miseducation of the American Elite and the Way to a Meaningful Life* (New York: Free Press, 2014), 225-42.

14. Most prominently, see Pierre Bourdieu, *The State Nobility: Elite Schools in the Field of Power*, trans. Lauretta C. Clough (Oxford: Polity Press, 1996).

15. Again, William Deresiewicz' work has been influential; see *Excellent Sheep*.

16. These are the most common terms used in rabbinic literature for these social groups. See Aharon Oppenheimer, *The 'Am Ha-Aretz: A Study in the Social History of the Jewish People in the Hellenistic-Roman Period*, trans. I. H. Levine (Leiden: Brill, 1977); and the more up-to-date work synthesized in Rubenstein, *Culture of the Babylonian Talmud*, 123-42.

17. The rise of the yeshiva in nineteenth-century Eastern Europe, for example, saw a similar "meritocratic" opening-up of access to high-level Jewish learning that also established new, internal hierarchies and entrenched preexisting inequalities. On the yeshiva, see Shaul Stampfer, *Lithuanian Yeshivas of the Nineteenth Century: Creating a Tradition of Learning*, trans. Lindsey Taylor-Guthartz (Oxford: Littman Library of Jewish Civilization, 2012).

18. Mishnah Horayot 3:7-8.

19. Mishnah Horayot 3:6. Although the Mishnah was composed by rabbis after the destruction of the Temple, it still contains a good deal of discussion about priestly and cultic matters—a feature that may represent another aspect of the rabbis displacement of the Levitcal priests.

20. Contemporary Jewish halakhists and ethicists have discussed the matter at some length. For an Orthodox view, see Alan Jotkowitz, "A Man Takes Precedence Over a Woman when it Comes to Saving a Life: The Modern Dilemma of Triage from a Halakhic and Ethical Perspective," *Tradition Magazine* 47, no. 1 (2014): 48-68.

21. Mishnah Bava Metzi'a 2:11.

22. Note, however, that other sources take the Mishnah to its logical, most extreme conclusion. Thus, Rabbi Meir was remembered as saying that "a gentile who engages in Torah study is considered like the High Priest, [for the Bible] states '[You shall therefore keep my statutes and ordinances] which if a man does he shall live by them' (Leviticus 18:5)—it does not say] which if priests, levites, and Israelites' rather 'A Man'—you therefore have learned that even a non-Jew who engages in Torah study is considered like a High Priest" (Babylonian Talmud Sanhedrin 59b).

23. Tosefta Horayot 2:5.

24. Palestinian Talmud Horayot 3:8; 48b.

25. Palestinian Talmud Horayot 3:8; 48b.

26. Babylonian Talmud Horayot 13b-14a.

27. See Jeffrey L. Rubenstein, *Talmudic Stories: Narrative Art, Composition, and Culture* (Baltimore: Johns Hopkins University Press, 1999), 176-211.

28. Palestinian Talmud Horayot 3:8; 48b.

29. Palestinian Talmud Horayot 3:7; 48a.

30. For this feature of rabbinic literature as it relates to the interaction between legal and non-legal material, see Barry S. Wimpfheimer, *Narrating the Law: A Poetics of Talmudic Legal Stories* (Philadelphia: University of Pennsylvania Press, 2011).

REFERENCES

Aristotle. *Nicomachean Ethics*. Translated by Christopher Rowe. Oxford: Oxford University Press, 2002.

Bourdieu, Pierre. *The State Nobility: Elite Schools in the Field of Power*. Translated by Lauretta C. Clough. Oxford: Polity Press, 1996.

Cohen, Shaye J. D. *From the Maccabees to the Mishnah*. Philadelphia: Westminster Press, 1987

———. "The Significance of Yavneh: Pharisees, Rabbis, and the End of Jewish Sectarianism." *Hebrew Union College Annual* 55 (1984): 27-53.

Deresiewicz, William. *Excellent Sheep: The Miseducation of the American Elite and the Way to a Meaningful Life*. New York: Free Press, 2014.

Fraade, Steven D. *From Tradition to Commentary: Torah and Its Interpretation in the Midrash Sifre to Deuteronomy*. Albany: SUNY Press, 1991.

Fuchs, Ilan. *Jewish Women's Torah Study: Orthodox Religious Education and Modernity*. New York: Routledge, 2014.

Hauptman, Judith. *Rereading the Rabbis: A Woman's Voice*. Boulder, CO: Westview Press, 1997.

Jewish Publication Society of America. *The Torah: The Five Books of Moses*. Philadelphia: Jewish Publication Society, 1999.

Jotkowitz, Alan. "A Man Takes Precedence Over a Woman when it Comes to Saving a Life: The Modern Dilemma of Triage from a Halakhic and Ethical Perspective." *Tradition Magazine* 47, no. 1 (2014): 48-68.

Neusner, Jacob. *Judaism: The Evidence of the Mishnah*. Chicago: University of Chicago Press, 1981.

Oppenheimer, Aharon. *The 'Am Ha-Aretz: A Study in the Social History of the Jewish People in the Hellenistic-Roman Period.* Translated by I. H. Levine. Leiden: Brill, 1977.

Plaskow, Judith. *Standing Again at Sinai: Judaism from a Feminist Perspective*. San Francisco: Harper & Row, 1990.

Rubenstein, Jeffrey L. *The Culture of the Babylonian Talmud.* Baltimore: Johns Hopkins University Press, 2003.

———. *Talmudic Stories: Narrative Art, Composition, and Culture*. Baltimore: Johns Hopkins University Press, 1999.

SEFARIA, "A Living Library of Jewish Texts," https://www.sefaria.org.il/.

Stampfer, Shaul. *Lithuanian Yeshivas of the Nineteenth Century: Creating a Tradition of Learning*. Translated by Lindsey Taylor-Guthartz. Oxford: Littman Library of Jewish Civilization, 2012.

Strack, Hermann Leberecht, and Günter Stemberger, *Introduction to the Talmud and Midrash*. Translated by Markus Bockmuehl (Edinburgh: T & T Clark, 1991.

Tropper, Amram. *Simeon the Righteous in Rabbinic Literature: A Legend Reinvented.* Leiden: Brill, 2013.

Yadin-Israel, Azzan. *Scripture and Tradition: Rabbi Akiva and the Triumph of Midrash*. Philadelphia: University of Pennsylvania Press, 2015.

Wimpfheimer, Barry S. *Narrating the Law: A Poetics of Talmudic Legal Stories*. Philadelphia: University of Pennsylvania Press, 2011.

Chapter 10

Equality in Paul of Tarsus—More *and* Less

Bruce Chilton

Paul made a categorical assertion in his Letter to the Galatians, addressing a cluster of churches in Asia Minor with a challenge that has featured in feminist discussion as well as in Liberation Theology (Galatians 3:28): "There is not one Jew or Greek, not one slave or free, not one male or female, because you are all one in Jesus Christ."[1] The context of the statement, in what precedes and follows (Galatians 3:26-4:7), sets out human identity in terms of its relationship to God's Spirit, which Paul believed was established in baptism. His logic is that God sends the Spirit of his Son into the heart of each person, so that he or she becomes a "son" of God who is no longer governed by well-established and often divisive distinctions within the Roman Empire.

Popular though this passage is, it also stands at odds with Paul's reputation. In the popular imagination, Paul opposed Judaism, was a misogynist, and argued for slavery. To a large extent, this impression owes its existence, not to what Paul himself wrote, but to deutero-Pauline letters (chiefly 1 Timothy, 2 Timothy, and Titus): that is, works written in Paul's name after his death. The shadow cast by pseudonymous documents falsely attributed to Paul has been recognized for centuries. Yet the fact is that even his own words, taken from letters he evidently did write, can be cited in support of such characterizations.

PAULINE CONTRADICTIONS

Paul denied the distinction between "Jew or Greek," in a letter composted composed in 53 CE to a cluster of communities in Asia minor, entitled "To the Galatians." Paul fumed in the same letter that he wished those who promoted circumcision according to the Law of Moses among believers would castrate themselves (Galatians 5:12)—an obvious appeal to the anti-Semitism ambient in the Roman Empire. Scarcely two years after he wrote to the Galatians, he sent a letter to churches in Corinth, saying, among other things, that "the women will keep silent in the churches, because it is not appropriate for them to speak" (1 Corinthians 14:34) and that a slave should be content with his lot (1 Corinthians 7:21). Why he said what he did on these occasions is elucidated by the context of the statements, as in the case of Galatians 3:28. Still, we are left with the apparent contradiction that Paul denies three polarities in that statement ("Jew" versus "Greek," "slave" versus "free," "male" versus "female") that he invokes categorically in other passages.

Each of Paul's genuine letters is an episodic communication, a message written to communities with particular interests, concerns, and problems that he addresses from a community with its own challenges and opportunities. The letters to the Galatians and to the Corinthians were composed in Ephesus, a city where Paul enjoyed considerable support, and where he was disposed of a staff that served him as scribes and intermediaries. As a result of his network of communications, an unpredictable variety of topics typically emerges, even within the same letter. They are not intended to be stand-alone works of theology, and were not read as such originally. Many people in his own time disagreed with Paul, and these same letters show that clearly; his opponents were by no means limited to those whom he invited to mutilate themselves in Galatians 5:12. Paul was only considered preeminent, "the Apostle" as he came to be called, long after his death, when his once minority point of view became central within the Catholic Christianity of the second century and later.

The episodic nature of the letters, as well as the opposition to Paul within the communities addressed, can make it difficult to assess his overall position. We need to be aware of when he is speaking to a specific case, rather than about a general position, when he is quoting a point of view only to reject or qualify it, and when—as sometimes occurs—he thinks through a position that he later returns to in order to arrive at an unexpected conclusion. Because his letters are living communications, those judgments are regularly involved in reading them.

Given these variables, an assessment Paul's overall position on any topic cannot be considered adequate unless it deals with the range of his statements on a given issue. In addressing the polarities of Jew/Greek, male/female, and slave/free, both when Paul affirms them and when he denies them, we will uncover a central characteristic of his thought overall.

The polarities in themselves, of course, were by no means Paul's invention. Centuries before Paul wrote his letters, Roman authors derided Judaism as barbaric in many ways,[2] and complained about its diet, its Sabbath-keeping, its practice of male circumcision, and its refusal to worship Hellenistic gods.

Yet the fact of its legality could not be denied from the time of the Maccabean treaty during the time of the Republic. Even after Pompey entered the Temple in 63 BCE and claimed the lands of Judea for Rome, Judaism was practiced in a tension between legal status and social derision. Just that tension was expressed in the polarity between "Judean" (of which the English word "Jew" is a contracted version) and "Greek." In this case, Judeans are the minority in the Roman Empire whose practices were tolerated, not endorsed, and Greeks are not only ethnic descendants from Greece, but also represent the dominant, Greek-speaking culture which defined the Mediterranean world. The fact that there was Roman case law in regard to dealing with Jews meant that the "Jew"/"Greek" polarity was a matter of common sense, and was often seen as a dichotomy. "Jews," in contrast to "Greeks," had become metonymic of minority long before Paul wrote to the Galatians.

Similarly, patriarchy in the Roman Empire was a matter of law, not merely custom.[3] Males headed households, and the paterfamilias had control over the household members as individuals and as a collective. His decisions were binding, so that even his wife's fertility—whether she should bear children, abort a pregnancy, or expose an unwanted newborn—were all within his purview. As Roman citizens, heads of households were also expected to honor the civic gods, to pay for the games of the city in honor of those gods and the emperor, and to serve as magistrates. Marriage and divorce were legally regulated, so that a paterfamilias could also enhance the value of his household by changing his spouse.

Slaves had legal rights, but those rights were not always honored, and recourse to law was much less practical for slaves than appealing to the good will of their masters. Still, the master was understood to act within an authority limited by the knowledge that the slave was a dedicated subordinate, not just property. A legal act of manumission could turn a slave into a freeman, and there were famous cases of that in Paul's time; perhaps the most celebrated freed slave—named Epaphroditus—was a secretary of the Emperor Nero by the time Paul wrote to the Corinthians.[4] The release of slaves was a practice that did not inhibit social life, because new slaves could always be acquired for the Empire. Every territory conquered, every rebellion suppressed, brought new human spoils into the orbit of Rome. Slavery was emblematic of Roman prowess in war, not a racial institution (as in the American case much later), but a benefit of military dominance.

Because warfare was a perennial Roman concern, slaves came into the relationships of the empire on a regular basis. That explains to some extent why the estimates of the slave population reach as high as forty percent, although a more reasonable estimate would be half that.[5] Although precision cannot be expected on the basis of the current state of knowledge, it is clear that slavery's influence reached beyond the period that a slave was owned in the Roman system. Even after a slave had been granted manumission, he relied on his owner as a patron, and continued to be associated with his household. No sector of Roman society remained untouched by the system of slavery.

Given the force and the extent of Roman slavery, Paul's reference to it as an ambient institution appears entirely natural, especially since converts to Jesus' movement in the wider Roman Empire came disproportionately from the slave class. How believers in Jesus should deal with their status as slaves became a pressing concern. Paul's advice in 1 Corinthians 7:21 for slaves to remain in their station accords with Roman law. Yet he says that a slave should take advantage of an offer of freedom, and his explanation applies to the case of slavery and to the other polarities under review (1 Corinthians 7:21-22): "Were you called a slave? Do not let that matter to you, but if you are able to become free, rather make use of the opportunity. For he who is called a slave in the Lord is a freedman of the Lord; similarly, the freeman called is Christ's slave." The conception is that "the Lord" introduces a global qualification in the realm of status identity. One who was called a slave is, in relation to God, a freedman, while obligations impose on those of high status responsibilities commensurate with servitude.

In this same chapter, Paul deals with the question of marriage, urging his readers to remain in their current state, and not to seek to marry. In the case of that institution, as for the case of slavery, he develops a singular policy (1 Corinthians 7:29-31): "This I declare, brothers: the time is constrained. From here on, those who have wives are as those who have none, and those weeping as those who do not weep, and those rejoicing as those who do not rejoice, and those who buy as without possessions, and those dealing with the world as those who had not use for it: because the form of this world passes away." The basis of Paul's advice to slaves is that the current arrangement offers them little prospect of improvement. One might become a freedman, but then continued obligations would be involved, and it was a question of judgment whether the result would be better. Rebellion had been attempted, disastrously in the case of the Third Servile War (73-71 BCE) in which Spartacus played a dramatic role. At its conclusion, Crassus had 600 slaves crucified along the Appian Way from Rome to Capua.

Beyond the current conventions of Rome's global empire, Paul insists that "the form of this world passes away" (1 Corinthians 7:31). Slavery is not a state that will be ended by resistance, but by the observation of its disappearance. At this point, what Paul says about slavery from the point of view of "this world" dovetails with his statement in Galatians 3:28 about there being no "slave or free" in Christ. A person who belonged to the master—in terms of the work owed, the physical services demanded, the allegiance to the gods of Rome required—became by baptism a free agent in relation to Christ.

Conversely, the master, by means of the same baptism in Spirit, acknowledged his kinship with all others who had been baptized, and therefore his mutual obligations with them.

Both aspects of this dynamic, the liberating aspect of baptism and its implications for mutual responsibility, impinge on the issue of women as Paul deals with it. As already mentioned, slavery and marriage are cognate institutions, since both belong to the structure of a world that is passing away in 1 Corinthians 7:31. Seven chapters later in that same letter, he deals with the issue of women speaking in churches. The statement about women keeping silent is so direct, and apparently out of keeping with what Paul says elsewhere, that attempts have been made to argue that the wording of the passage must be corrupt.

Contextually, that effort finds some justification. After all, in the same letter Paul acknowledges that his counterpart in Corinth, a leader of the community who disposed of a staff and hosted a church in her private house, was a woman named Chloe (1 Corinthians 1:11). His letter to the Romans, written just a year after Corinthians, acknowledges a woman "minister" in nearby Cenchreae (Romans 16:1), and that same letter refers to a woman named Junia (Romans 16:7) as an apostle prior to the time of Paul himself. All these references involve women in positions of leadership, which would be difficult to imagine if indeed, women were not to speak, as Paul says in 1 Corinthians 14:34. If we associate the final clause of the previous verse with this statement ("As in all the churches"), the difficulty becomes all the greater.

The passage poses so many difficulties, it is easy to sympathize with the suggestion that it is a insertion into 1 Corinthians by an author other than Paul. There are, after all, entire letters in the New Testament attributed to Paul that in fact come from his followers, and the canon as a whole includes some half a million variants among the ancient Greek manuscripts. But in textual criticism, scholars take their lead from actual manuscripts that suggest alternative readings, not from merely imaginary possibilities.[6] Ancient manuscripts do not justify deleting the passage, although an argument might be made for an adjustment of its order within 1 Corinthians. In any case, even when an ancient manuscript does present a variant, the principle of analysis, when there is a difference among witnesses, is that the more difficult reading is preferable to the easier reading. It is far more difficult to imagine this passage as part of the letter, with its other, positive references to women's leadership, than simply to remove it. The challenge remains to make sense of the best readings of the most ancient manuscripts.

In this, as in other cases in the study of Paul, the disruptive influence is not the transmission of the text, but the impact of a controversy in Paul's time that is difficult to imagine in ours. He wrote 1 Corinthians to a city, and from a city, with which his own background was profoundly out of keeping. A first-century philosopher, Dio Chrysostom, visited Paul's native Tarsus, and reported that the women there were so thoroughly veiled from head to foot that they could not see well enough to walk in the street without assistance.[7] One regard in which Graeco-Roman practice could not find agreement was on the extent to which the human body might be displayed, and standards varied for men and women, as well as from region to region. Paul shows himself to be a typical Tarsan when, in his correspondence with Corinth, he insists that it is a teaching of "nature" that women should only pray or prophesy when veiled, but that men should be unveiled (1 Corinthians 11:3-16). In that way, he argued, a woman's submission to her husband would be symbolized.

In order to buttress his point of view, in a famous remark Paul states that women should veil "on account of the angels" (1 Corinthians 11:10). The remark is fleeting, but appears to refer to the way in which angelic figures in the book of Genesis (called the sons of God, Genesis 6:1-2) saw that human women were beautiful, and had sexual intercourse with them, a corruption that ultimately led to the Noachic Flood. Display of loose hair in cities such as Corinth and Ephesus signaled a woman's sexual availability. In Ephesus, an ancient, crude advertisement remains carved into the paving stones: an arrow with a woman whose hair trails off her head on to her shoulder and breast. It shows the way to the Ephesian brothel, which has been identified archaeologically.

To Paul, a woman should not publicly prophesy, because doing so denied her a veil, since the prophetic act was to be with an unveiled face (see 2 Corinthians 3:18), and the veil was the mark of her submission to her husband. His considerations in this case are comparable to his attitude to slavery, and we have already seen he associated slavery and marriage as institutions of this world.

Finally, his crude remark about those desiring to compel Gentile believers to circumcise in Galatians 5:12 is rooted in his understanding that, while Jews born into the covenant with Moses should continue the practices of which circumcision was the master symbol, non-Jews could not and would not keep all the commandments involved. Rather, all believers, whether Jew or Greek, should pursue the way of faith working by means of love (Galatians 5:6) with differing cultural understandings. Both sides of the divide, Jews and Greeks, were to be understood as Israel (Galatians 6:16), because they were God's people descended from the same faith that Abraham had shown (Galatians 3:29).

The case of the polarity between Jew and Greek invokes a pattern that Paul also applies to the polarity between male and female and the polarity between slave and free. In every case, a real, universally recognized distinction is cited, while in the Roman Empire they amount to dichotomies. Simply denying them brought disruption, and sometimes violence. But in Galatians 3:28, Paul does not deny the polarities; rather, he states that "in Jesus Christ," because the Spirit has been realized in baptism, the polarities disappear.

PAUL'S ANTHROPOLOGY OF RESURRECTION

The key to understanding why Paul can argue for both more and less equality in this way is provided by an anthropology that he sets out in detail in 1 Corinthians. His thinking is distinctive, and unfortunately available translations have confused his views with the theology of later periods, when Christianity was strongly influenced by Stoicism. Stoic philosophers, Graeco-Roman thinkers dedicated to the role of reason in human life, came to see the soul as the seat of this eternal principle. That resulted in the now familiar conception of the soul as immortal and of the body as a passing appearance in the flesh. That, as we shall see, is not Paul's anthropology at all. In order to facilitate discussion, a fresh, more accurate translation is provided at the close of this article, "Translation of 1 Corinthians 15."

When Paul thinks of a person, he conceives of a body as composed of flesh. Flesh in his definition is physical substance, which varies from one created thing to another (for example, people, animals, birds, and fish; 1 Corinthians 15:35-39). On this view, bodies are palpable in the flesh that they inhabit.

But in addition to being physical bodies, people are also what Paul calls a "psychic body," by which he means bodies with souls (1 Corinthians 15:44, from the term *psukhê*). The phrase is badly misconstrued in many English versions, but its dependence on the noun for "soul" (*psukhê*) shows what the real sense is. The adjective does not mean "physical" as we use that word. Although that is a simple point, it apparently requires some emphasis. Scholars of Paul routinely assert that Paul speaks of Jesus' Resurrection as physical,[8] when that is exactly what Paul is about to *deny* in the passage from 1 Corinthians. In other words, people as bodies are not just aggregations of flesh, but they are self-aware and capable of deliberate action. That deliberative self-awareness is precisely what makes them "psychic body."

We might think of Paul's "fleshly body" (*soma sarkikon*) as physical body, what anyone can see and touch, and of his "psychic body" (*soma psukhikon*) as the body people are conscious of when they act on the basis of their agency. The physical body that can be measured and assessed is a fact of biology, while the patterns of activity we learn and follow, as well as the innovative undertakings we might engage in, are facts of history. To Paul's mind, this social, agentive reality is every bit as much "body" as is the physical body. His conception that the body is *not* synonymous with physical substance is among the most challenging aspects of his perspective.

Paul's thought in regard to the physical body and the agentive body has been obscured by the dominance of a later Christian doctrine, current from the time of the Middle Ages, which conceives of "body" as purely physical and mortal, and "soul" as ethereal and (at least potentially) immortal. But for Paul, it is impossible to conceive of a human being, in the flesh or psychic, except as "body." That is the case whether the person is treated physically or the person acts in society as an agent. Paul cannot and does not define a person apart from a body, whether it is "fleshly" (*sarkikon*) or "psychic" (*psukhikon*). He conceived of human bodies as both reflexive (*sarkikon*) and deliberative (*psukhikon*).

Yet even so, the "psychic" or agentive body is *not* immortal. Far from it, because Paul conceives the soul itself, like the act of breathing, to be subject to death. Death for Paul is when living existence ceases both as a breathing physical entity (the initial sense of the Hebrew noun *nephesh* and the Greek *psukhê*) and as an agent capable of deliberative action (1 Corinthians 15:42-44). Immortality does not continue directly from either physical or social life. Immortality derives rather from body in yet a third medium.

In addition to being physical body and psychic body, Paul believes people are (or can become) "spiritual body" (1 Corinthians 15:44). That is, they are not only self-aware; they can relate thoughts and feelings *to one another and to God* (as 1 Corinthians 2:9-16 also shows) in such a way that they can define their purpose in a way that transcends their physical or their personal interests. Paul's understanding of Jesus' Resurrection is that, having died in respect of his flesh and his soul, Jesus became "spiritual body" in a way that reveals human destiny as a whole. Jesus is in that sense the last Adam, a "life-giving Spirit" (1 Corinthians 15:45), just as the first Adam was a "living being" or "soul" (the two words are the same in Greek, *psukhê*). Crucially, people can be physical and psychic and spiritual at the same time: these modes of living are characteristic of being human.[9] In each mode, it is the distinctive reality of a person, a body, which is at issue: reflexive, deliberative, and principled.

For Paul, Jesus is the basis on which people can realize their destiny as God's children, the brothers and sisters of Christ, and know the power of the resurrection in their bodies through his bodily—but also spiritual—Resurrection. "Flesh" and "soul" become, not ends in themselves, but way stations on the course to "Spirit," to which Jesus' Resurrection provides access. Just as sin for Paul marks out the necessity of human transformation in the realm of ethics, so physical death marks out the necessity of human transformation in the realm of its medium of existence. Indeed, the characteristically Pauline tendency to associate death and sin (1 Corinthians 15:56) derives from his three-media conception of what the human body is. For that reason, his conclusion insists that God's Kingdom ultimately is not a matter of flesh and blood (v. 50), but of change into the realm of immortal Spirit (vv. 51-53).[10]

This, for Paul, is the substance of the Resurrection as Christophany. It is more than the angelic warrant that Jesus had been raised, an angelology such as the women at the tomb experienced (Mark 16:1-8), more even than an encounter with the risen Jesus. The Resurrection is the primal offering that signals the full harvest of humanity (1 Corinthians 15:20). At the same time, because sin on Paul's understanding is implicated with the mortality of the flesh (see Romans 7:14-25), overcoming that ethical obstacle is of the same movement as transcending flesh on the way to becoming a spiritual body.

Transcendence characterizes Paul's perspective on Spirit, much as agency explains what he means by "soul," and physicality corresponds to his thinking on "flesh." A person lives by means of body physically and as an agent, but also in relation to purposes beyond considerations of self-interest. That transcendent, "spiritual" body is the only one that Paul conceives of as immortal, and for him Jesus' Resurrection realizes immortality in that sense, not as a survival of physical or social existence.

Because, for Paul, the human body exists in three environments—physical, social, and purposive—it is only to be expected that what we know to be the case in terms of the purpose of human living will be become recognizable in the physical and social worlds. But radical change is implied in that expectation. In the case of the polarities identified in Galatians 3:28, palpable physical signs accompany each: presence or absence of foreskin in Jew/Greek, genital assignment on male/female, presence or absence of constraint in slave/free. Such palpable indicators made the categories evident throughout the Roman world. Yet the categories also involved a social world in which people acted as agents of these distinctions. A Jew is not merely a circumcised person, since some Egyptians were known to keep the practice; the issue was circumcision was a sign of the covenant. Similarly, responsibilities and capacities went with being assigned male or female, slave or free. The "body" of each element in every polarity was a physical as well as a social reality, or "fleshly" and "psychic" in Paul's terms.

But no element of any polarity, and no polarity in itself, could ever be described in Pauline terms as being "spiritual." They belonged to the form of a world that was passing away in favor of Spirit. As they did so, the equality of being "one" was to become the dominant reality. The "more" of equality was the tendency toward the realization of Spirit; the "less" of equality derived from structures of the world as it is, with its physical constraints and social self-interests. Paul did not deny that world or the call for violent action in opposition to it. But he did believe that people had an instrumental role in its effacement in favor of the equality of Spirit

TRANSLATION OF 1 CORINTHIANS 15

1 But I make known to you, brothers, the message that I messaged to you—that you also received. You indeed stand in it, 2 and you are saved through it—in the same terms I messaged to you—if you hold fast, unless you believed uselessly. 3 Because I delivered over to you at the first what I also received, that Anointed died for our sins according to the Scriptures. 4 And that he was buried and that he was raised on the third day according to the Scriptures, 5 and that he was seen by *Kepha'*, then the Twelve, 6 then he was seen by more than five hundred brothers at once (of whom most remain until now, although some sleep), 7 then he was seen by James, then by all the delegates, 8 but last of all as if to the preterm birth, he was seen also by me.

9 Because I am the least of the apostles, who is not worthy to be called apostle, since I persecuted the assembly of God. 10 But by God's grace I am what I am, and his grace has not proved empty in me, but I toiled more than all of them—yet not I but the grace of God in me. 11 Whether I or they, so we announced and you believed.

12 Yet if Anointed is announced, that he has been raised from the dead, how do some of you say that there is not a resurrection of the dead? 13 But if there is not a resurrection of the dead, neither has Anointed been raised. 14 And if Anointed has not been raised, then our announcement is empty and your faith is empty! 15 And we are found God's sham witnesses, because we witnessed against God that he raised the Anointed, whom he did not raise, if indeed the dead are not raised. 16 Because if the dead are not raised, neither has Anointed been raised, 17 and if Anointed has not been raised, your faith is futile, you are still in your sins 18 and therefore also those who sleep in Anointed have perished! 19 If we are hoping in Anointed in this life only, we are the most pitiful of all men! 20 But now Anointed has been raised from the dead, primal offering of those who sleep. 21 For since death is through a man, resurrection of the dead is also through a man. 22 Because just as in Adam all die, so also in Anointed all shall be made alive.

23 But each in his own order: Anointed, primal offering, thereafter those of Anointed in his arrival, 24 then the conclusion, when he delivers over the Kingdom to God, even the father, when he shall abolish all rule and all authority and power. 25 Because it is necessary for him to reign until he puts all enemies under his feet. 26 Death is the last enemy abolished. 27 For he ordered everything under his feet—but when it says that everything has been ordered, evidently that is apart from the one that orders everything for him. 28 Yet when everything has been ordered for him, then the Son himself will be ordered to the one ordering everything for him, so that God might be all in all.

29 What otherwise are those baptized on behalf of the dead doing? If the dead are actually not raised, why are they baptized for them? 30 Why, too, do we confront danger every hour? 31 Every day I die—by your honor, brothers, which I have in Jesus Anointed our Lord! 32 If in human terms I fought animals in Ephesus, what is the advantage for me? If the dead are not raised, Let us eat and drink, because tomorrow we die. 33 Don't be deceived, Bad company corrupts good. 34 Sober up rightly, and don't sin, because some have ignorance of God. I speak to you for shame.

35 But someone will say, How are the dead raised? And in what sort of body do they come? 36 Fool, what *you* sow is not kept alive, unless it dies, 37 and what you sow is not the body that shall be do you sow, but bare germ, it might be of wheat or of some other grain. 38 But God gives to it a body just as he wills, and to each of the seeds a particular body. 39 Not all flesh is the same flesh, but there is one of men, and another flesh of animals, but another flesh of birds, and another of fish. 40 And there are heavenly bodies and earthly bodies, but one is the glory of the heavenly, and another of the earthly; 41 but there is sun's glory, and another glory of moon, and another glory of stars, because star differs from star in glory. 42 So also is the resurrection of the dead. It is sown in decay, it is raised in incorruptibility. 43 It is sown in dishonor, it is raised in glory; it is sown in weakness, it is raised in strength. 44 It is sown a psychical body, it is raised a spiritual body. If there is a psychical body, there is also a spiritual. 45 So also it is written, the first man, Adam, became a living soul, the last Adam a life-making spirit. 46 But the spiritual is not first, but the psychic, thereafter the spiritual. 47 The first man was from the earth, of dust, the second man from heaven. 48 As the man of dust, such also are those of dust; and as the man of heaven, such also are those of heaven. 49 And just as we bore the image of the man of dust, we shall also bear the image of the man of heaven.

50 But this I state, brothers, that flesh and blood cannot inherit God's Kingdom, neither does decay inherit incorruptibility. 51 Look: a mystery I tell you. We shall not all sleep, but we all shall be changed. 52 In a moment, in an eye's flash, at the last trumpet, because it shall blare and the dead shall be raised incorruptible, and we shall be changed. 53 For it is necessary for this corruptible to put on incorruptibility and for this mortal to put on immortality. 54 And when this corruptible puts on incorruptibility and this mortal puts on immortality, then shall be the word that is written, Death is swallowed up in victory: 55 where, death, is your victory; where, death, is your barb? 56 The barb of death is sin, but the power of sin is the law. 57 Thanks to God, who gives us the victory through Anointed Jesus our Lord. 58 So, my beloved brothers, become constant, immovable, always abounding in the work of the Lord; know that your toil is not empty in the Lord.

NOTES

1. For discussion of Galatians and related matters, see Bruce Chilton, *Rabbi Paul. An Intellectual Biography* (New York: Doubleday, 2004). For Liberation Theology, see Gustavo Gutiérrez, *Las Casas. In Search of the Poor of Jesus Christ*, trans. Robert R. Barr (Eugene, OR: Wipf and Stock, 2003). In this paper, translations of the New Testament and other ancient sources are the author's. For the former, see *Novum Testamentum Graece / The Greek-English New Testament* (English Standard Version), 28th ed., ed. Barbara and Kurt Aland et al. (Stuttgart: Deutsche Bibelgesellschaft, 2012), a.

2. The most famous case is Cicero's reference to Judaism as a *barbara superstitio* in his defense of a client who pilfered funds from a synagogue. The speech concerned is presented in *Pro Flacco*, and is described in Peter Schäfer, *Judeophobia: Attitudes Toward the Jews in the Ancient World* (Cambridge: Harvard University Press, 1997), 180-82.

3. See Rodney Stark, *Cities of God: The Real Story of How Christianity Became an Urban Movement and Conquered Rome* (San Francisco: HarperSanFranciso, 2006).

4. See P. R. C. Weaver, "Epaphroditus, Josephus, and Epictetus," *Classical Quarterly* 44, no. 2 (1994): 468-79.

5. See Neville Morley, "Slavery Under the Principate," in *The Cambridge World History of Slavery. The Ancient Mediterranean World*, ed. Keith Bradley and Paul Cartlledge (Cambridge: Cambridge University Press, 2011), vol. 1, 265-86.

6. For principles of criticism, see the Introduction in *Novum Testamentum Graece*, 46-88; and *The Textual History of the Greek New Testament: Changing Views in Contemporary Research*. ed. Klaus Wachtel and Michael W. Holmes, Society of Biblica Literature Text-Critical Studies 8 (Atlanta: Society of Biblical Literature, 2011).

7. Dio Chrysostom, *Discourses 31-33*, trans. J. W. Cohoon and H. Lamar Crosby, Loeb Classical Library 358 (Cambridge, MA: Harvard University Press, 2014), 33.48.

8. So, for example, N. T. Wright, *What Saint Paul Really Said: Was Paul of Tarsus the Real Founder of Christianity?* (Grand Rapids, MI: Eerdmans, 1997), 50.

9. As James Ware argues, this mitigates against the argument that flesh and soul and spirit are completely different substances (Ware, "Paul's Understanding of the Resurrection in 1 Corinthians 15:36-54," *Journal of Biblical Literature* 133, no. 4 [2014]: 809-35, at 832-33). Ware is critical of attempts to claim that resurrection involves a new substance of being in favor of the finding that the spiritual body is "the risen body given life by the Spirit."

10. For this reason, James Ware goes beyond the evidence of Paul in asserting that "the body of flesh and bones" is raised in Paul's understanding (Ware, "Paul's Understanding," 835). Rather, to Paul's mind, the victory of both Christ and the believer (vv. 54-55)—which he expresses as the true meaning of Isaiah's prophecy of resurrection (Isaiah 25:8)—involves a change in the body that had once been only flesh, then soul, and at its best, spirit.

REFERENCES

Chilton, Bruce. *Rabbi Paul: An Intellectual Biography*. New York: Doubleday, 2004.

Chrysostom, Dio. *Discourses 31-33*. Translated by J. W. Cohoon and H. Lamar Crosby. Loeb Classical Library 358. Cambridge, MA: Harvard University Press, 2014.

Gutiérrez, Gustavo. *Las Casas: In Search of the Poor of Jesus Christ*. Translated by Robert R. Barr. Eugene, OR: Wipf and Stock, 2003.

Morley, Neville. "Slavery Under the Principate." In *The Cambridge World History of Slavery. Volume 1: The Ancient Mediterranean World*, edited by Keith Bradley and Paul Cartlledge, 265-86. Cambridge: Cambridge University Press, 2011.

Novum Testamentum Graece / The Greek-English New Testament (English Standard Version). 28th ed. Edited by Barbara Aland, Kurt Aland, Johannes Karavidopoulos, Carlo M. Martini, and Bruce M. Metzger. Stuttgart: Deutsche Bibelgesellschaft; Wheaton, IL: Crossway, 2012.

Schäfer, Peter. *Judeophobia: Attitudes Toward the Jews in the Ancient World.* Cambridge: Harvard University Press, 1997.

Stark, Rodney. *Cities of God: The Real Story of How Christianity Became an Urban Movement and Conquered Rome*. San Francisco: HarperSanFranciso, 2006.

Wachtel, Klaus, and Michael W. Holmes, eds. *The Textual History of the Greek New Testament: Changing Views in Contemporary Research*. Society of Biblica Literature Text-Critical Studies 8. Atlanta: Society of Biblical Literature, 2011.

Ware, James. "Paul's Understanding of the Resurrection in 1 Corinthians 15:36-54." *Journal of Biblical Literature* 133, no. 4 (2014): 809-35.

Weaver, P. R. C. "Epaphroditus, Josephus, and Epictetus." *Classical Quarterly* 44, no. 2 (1994): 468-79.

Wright, N. T. *What Saint Paul Really Said: Was Paul of Tarsus the Real Founder of Christianity?* Grand Rapids, MI: Eerdmans, 1997.

Chapter 11

The Perilous Promise of Equality

Reimagining the Qur'an in Post-Revolution Iran

Tehseen Thaver

Arguments for revival and reform boast a long tradition in Islam, with calls for a moral awakening starting from as early as a few decades after the death of Prophet Muḥammad. More recently, during the nineteenth and twentieth centuries, when all but four Muslim countries (Afghanistan, Turkey, Iran and Saudi Arabia) were under the grip of foreign rule, a number of influential thinkers from Muslim majority societies across the world sought to find explanations for and solutions to their changed realities. Arguments for reform during this period were far from uniform, as their proponents drew from a range of intellectual resources to advance their social and political projects. The different forms of argument and projects of reform at this juncture were at once in response to and constituted by the specific conditions generated by colonial modernity and post-colonial state formation, and the shape that these processes took, in multiple regional contexts. The narrative of modern Muslim reformist thought, especially in relation to new approaches and imaginings of Qur'an interpretation, have taken particularly fascinating and instructive trajectories in contemporary post revolution Iran.

Indeed, in the history of post-colonial state formation in Muslim majority societies, the 1979 Iranian revolution represents a watershed moment that saw the successful overthrow of the monarchical rule of the Pahlavi dynasty, and the establishment of an Islamic theocracy brimming with the promise of popular sovereignty. The overthrow of the monarchy was precipitated by vehement opposition to its governance of domestic affairs, mismanagement of indigenous resources, and perceived servitude to the cultural and economic interests of major Western powers like the United States, in exchange for which they extended the monarchy their political and economic support. It was the common cause of deposing this monarchy, regarded as deeply corrupt and self-serving, that brought together the unusual but formidable alliance of clerics, merchants, left-leaning intellectuals and activists, and the demographically dominant youth of Iran (to name a few of the main players). This alliance presented itself as a boldly defiant and overwhelming challenge that ultimately succeeded in deposing the Shah of Iran, Muḥammad Reza Pahlavī (d. 1980). At the top of the new theocratic power structure stood the Supreme leader (initially Ayatollah Ruḥollah Khomeinī, revered and regarded as the overarching religious authority) and his clerical establishment, which in turn oversaw a parliamentary government. This dramatic series of events was followed by a period of significant political and social turmoil, precipitated by the onset of a debilitating, eight-year long war with Iraq, which led to the further accumulation of power by the clerical establishment.

Throughout the period preceding the revolution as well as during its aftermath, a number of prominent individuals emerged as the authoritative spokesmen for, and architects of, an ideal Muslim society. In this article, I explore the arguments of two such leading contemporary Iranian Shī'ī[1] reformist thinkers, Muḥammad Mujtahid Shabestarī (b. 1936) and Abdolkarīm Soroush (b. 1945). Their arguments form part of the contemporary Iranian reform movement,[2] best described as a tradition of internal critique and an opposition to the clerical establishment as well as a critical and philosophical engagement with Islam's textual tradition. Recently, scholars have pointed out that although the movement (as varied as the individuals and ideas that comprise this movement may be) has not made any significant political gain, reformist discourses have nevertheless represented a dynamic venue for ongoing engagement and debate on a wide range of contemporary sociopolitical issues.[3] Questions ranging from the limits of religious authority and the powers of the state, the relationship between religion, politics, and society, scriptural hermeneutics, and women's rights have all been brought into public view and intensely debated.[4] As historian Said Arjomand points out:

> The movement for the reformation of Islamic thought thus marks the birth of critical theory in modern Shi'ism. It offers a radical critique of contemporary Islamic thought for mistaking the historically contingent forms of Islamic religion for its revealed essence; and for disregarding religious pluralism as the inevitable result of the reading of revealed texts in specific human languages and socio-historical contexts. As more than one reading is inevitable, so there must be more than one straight path to salvation.[5]

The focus of my essay is on Shabestarī's and Soroush's understanding of the Qur'an more broadly. Central to their reformist agendas was a call for what they considered a radically novel view of the Qur'an and its interpretation. Their emphasis on rethinking the Qur'an and hermeneutics is significant for the way it reflects the politics of knowledge and religious authority concerning the custodianship of scripture in modern Islam. Most significant in the writings and lectures of Shabestarī and Soroush is the argument that one must rethink the very nature of scripture itself, and in turn, reorient one's conception of what constitute the authoritative sources for its interpretation. Shabestarī's and Soroush's gesture of grounding their reform project in a rethinking of the Qur'an is amplified by their operation in a discursive landscape in which varied stripes of Iranian Muslim intellectuals, including legal scholars, Qur'an exegetes, and theologians have prioritized the Qur'an in their scholarly agendas.[6] That this refuge in the Qur'an sounds Protestant is not coincidental. In fact, the attempt of scholars like Shabestarī and Soroush to offer a modern Qur'anic hermeneutic was grounded in a particular moment in the intellectual and political history of post-revolutionary Iran in which scholars like them increasingly took inspiration from nineteenth and twentieth century Protestant theologians as a way of curating a response to the anxieties and possibilities of the post-revolutionary moment. One might venture to say that these late twentieth century Iranian scholars imagined their own authority and place in history as analogous to European Protestant theologians from a century or so ago. These intellectual efforts aimed at reconciling religion with the vicissitudes of modernity on the part of Iranian reformers also coincided with the push on the part of Iranian political leaders to forge relationships with the West through campaigns of interfaith dialogue and harmony.[7]

At the heart of Shabestarī's and Soroush's discourses on revelation was the promise of disrupting extant structures of religious authority. Their struggle to dislodge a belief in the infallible and divine nature of the Qur'an as God's Word is inextricably tied to their larger struggle against the established clerical rule which claims authoritative access to the meaning contained within the text. In order to resist the political hegemony of Iran's ruling clergy, Shabestarī and Soroush argued, it was first necessary to challenge the epistemological imperialism that the dogma of "a" singular reified truth accessible to "a" select class of men invariably generates.

In this essay, I argue that while Shabestarī's and Soroush's reform projects are grounded in the democratic impulse of calling for an unmediated and equal access to "truth" and "true religion," their arguments nevertheless bear the imprint of the unequal epistemological terrain in which they are generated. How? The very parameters in which Shabestarī and Soroush engage with the tradition are bound by distinctly secular conceptions of language, history, interpretation, and the human subject. Put differently, as they seek to make the tradition of Islam more democratic, their very desire for hermeneutical equality is interlocked with the conditions and expectations of the modern moment. Their reform projects, directed at freeing "Islam" from the dominant and hegemonic interpretation of the clerical establishment, are grounded in a language of reform that is itself conscripted to a discursive and epistemological terrain dominated by liberal-secular norms.[8] Let me be clear that my highlighting the underlying secular logics sustaining the writings of Shabestarī and Soroush on revelation is not intended to undercut the significance of their contributions to Iranian reformist thought. To the contrary, as I hope to show in this essay, their discourses, charged with thoroughly modern desires and assumptions, are in fact critical in helping us understand the interplay of text and tradition in varying sociopolitical conditions. Thus my objective in this essay is to examine this encounter, whereby distinctly secular philosophies of science, language, and history represent the frame through which premodern discursive artifacts are reimagined and repackaged.

In their discussions on the theme of revelation, Shabestarī and Soroush wrestled with pressing theological and hermeneutical questions. For instance: Who has access to the meaning of the Qur'an? What kinds of inequalities and hierarchies govern the Qur'an's interpretation? Can one imagine a hermeneutic of engaging the Qur'an that is based on equality and equal access? What would such a system do to the religious authority of the scholarly elite? It is Shabestarī and Soroush's navigation of these questions that I explore in the first part of this essay. In the second part, I turn to the underlying assumptions that inform their arguments. More specifically, I examine how the categories "self" and "experience" operate in their hermeneutics. In addition, I explore ways in which their writings mirror a post-enlightenment narrative of "religion," that posits a clear distinction between the public and the private spheres, and that valorizes the interiority of "faith" as the core of religious experience.

PREMODERN DISCURSIVE ARTIFACTS, MODERN REWORKINGS

The sensitive nature of the issues covered by Shabestarī and Soroush, including the questioning of the standard interpretation of the term "revelation" as "speech of God," as well as the obvious challenge that their writings have posed to the foundational logic of the ruling Islamic regime, have led to a string of severe reactions. Their writings and lectures have provoked fierce criticism and even personal attacks from the clerical establishment in Iran; the journals in which their articles were published were shut down. Moreover, Soroush has been forced into exile from Iran after his lectures became a site of recurrent violent protests. Moreover, Soroush's writings were severely censored and he was threatened with assassination. Since both Shabestarī and Soroush were strong supporters of the regime during the Iranian revolution in 1979, they now write in the capacity of disillusioned critics from within, thus rendering their critique even more threatening and alarming.

Let me turn to my first example, Muḥammad Mujtahid Shabestarī. Shabestarī received a traditional seminary education in the city of Qom, Iran—among the preeminent centers of Twelver Shī'ī learning in the world today—and is recognized as a Ḥujjat al-Islām (high-ranking cleric). He also served as director of the Shi'ite Islamic Center in the Imam 'Ali Mosque in Hamburg where he studied German, Western philosophy, and Protestant theology. As a follower of Khomeinī and a defender of the Islamic Revolution, he returned to Iran in 1979 and the following year was elected as representative of the province of Azerbaijan in the first parliament of the Islamic Republic. However he soon retired from politics as he grew skeptical of the Islamic regime. From 1985 onwards, he served as a professor of Islamic philosophy at the University of Tehran until he was forced into retirement in 2005 during the first year of the presidency of Mahmoud Ahmadinejad. The combination of Shabestarī's classical Islamic training and his initial support and service for the Islamic regime have compounded credence to the force of his recent critiques.

The thrust of Shabestarī's discussion on revelation is centered on the distinction between the *core* of the divine message and the social conditions that give that message its specific form. This distinction allows Shabestarī to argue for a historicization of the Qur'an.[9] Moreover, it enables him to ask the following question: What is it that makes the Qur'an—a historical phenomenon—divine? It is in responding to this central question that he turns to the tradition of premodern Sufism. More specifically, Shabestarī's understanding of revelation is heavily informed by the writings of towering Andalusian thirteenth century Sunnī Sufi master Muḥyī al-Dīn Ibn 'Arabī's (d. 1240 CE) discourses on the nature of "God's speech (*kalām Allāh*)." For Shabestarī, Ibn 'Arabī's treatment of revelation, even though from eight centuries ago, was a lot more hospitable to an analytically robust understanding of "God's speech" than what he termed as the dogmatic beliefs that dominate discussion on this subject today. Mobilizing Ibn 'Arabī, Shabestarī claims that the revelatory text in its book form is not to be understood as the eternal word of God. Rather, it only constitutes the word of God insofar as it evokes a religious *experience* in the recipient. Consequently, this Word exists in the present time only within the recipient.[10] This move allows Shabestarī to argue for the revelatory act as a dialectical *process* whereby the individual reading and interpreting the Qur'an plays a primary role in its meaning.

Ultimately, Shabestarī presents his argument as if it were identical to the argument that Ibn 'Arabī put forward eight centuries ago. Namely, that it is not the actual words, or the grammar, or the sounds, or even the content, but rather the *experience* of the individual that determines the revelatory nature of the words.[11] Shabestarī, in his Persian text titled *Hermeneutics, the Book and the Tradition: Process of Interpreting Revelation* (*Hermenutik, Kitab va*

Sunnat: Farayand-e Tafsir-e Vahy) published in 1996 explained this point as follows:

> Ibn 'Arabī's theory was that in order for speech to be revelatory it must come with the quality of producing a [specific] affect in its recipient (*naẓarīya-yi Ibn 'Arabī īn ast keh waḥyānī budan-i sukhan bā chīgūnagī-yi asarguzārī-yi ān dar insān marbūṭ mī shawad*). It is possible for [the same] speech to be revelation for one person and not for another. Accordingly, in order for speech to be revelatory the main question is not whether it conflicts with the laws of nature or not. Rather the key question is this: what does this speech do to one person that it doesn't do to another? What confirms the revelatory nature of speech is the attribute of it being "other than all other speech" (*bi kullī-yi sukhan dīgar*).
>
> According to this view, the Qur'an was revelation for the Prophet, but for others, it becomes revelation when for them too, the Qur'an is other than all non-Qur'anic speech. The notion of revelation as "revelation in itself" (*waḥy fī nafsihi*) at all times and in all places has no meaning.
>
> Ibn 'Arabī does not consider speech to be revelatory because it is an expression that indicates the intended meaning of the speaker [God]. Rather, he considers speech to be revelation because of its razor like speed and power of indication, and because it has an indescribable affect on the recipient that erases the possibility of all thought and reflection on his or her part.[12]

Shabestarī's reading of Ibn 'Arabī's theory of revelatory speech was resoundingly decontextualized. In Shabestarī's account above, one finds little trace of Ibn 'Arabī's effort to link revelation to its affective experience in the recipient, an effort that was part of a broader argument concerning the economy of religious authority. The mystics, for Ibn 'Arabī, occupied a spiritual station that was distinct from that of the masses, thus implying that they too could experience the Qur'anic Words in the way that the Prophet had. What Shabestarī takes away from this however, is not an argument for the preferred spiritual status of the mystics or any other specific group of interpreters. Rather, Shabestarī's argument is driven by the hermeneutical stance that interpretation must rely on the capacity of the interpreter. In other words, it is in the very struggle and engagement between the text and interpreter that meaning is found. To sum up, Shabestarī regarded individual religious experience as indispensable to the interpretive process. This hermeneutical project ultimately sought to democratize access to the Qur'anic text and its meaning. But unlike Shabestarī, Ibn 'Arabī sought to establish the privileged place of a spiritual elite who enjoyed special access to meaning thanks to their advanced status on the spiritual path. So the critical distinction between Shabestarī's and Ibn 'Arabī's normative imaginations was this: for Ibn 'Arabī, in stark contrast to Shabestarī, religious experience did not involve a separation of the individual from the performative choreography of ritual practice. Moreover, the very efficacy of ritual practice in Ibn 'Arabī's thought was inextricably tied to the maintenance rather than the dissolution of spiritual hierarchies governing a religious community.[13]

Turning again to Shabestarī's text, in describing the dialectical encounter between text and interpreter, he invoked a distinct concept of *tawhīd* or unicity of God to explain the role of the individual. He defined *tawhīd* as the negation of divinity for all beings except God, as well as sincere submission to His will and law. Shabestarī is careful to explain that this condition does not lead to the negation of human subjectivity.[14] Instead, this results in a kind of "mediated subjectivity"[15] which, in characteristically Hegelian fashion, first involves a process of negation or alienation from the ego, followed by a consciousness of the sovereignty of the Divine, and finally the stage where this consciousness is then brought back into this world in the form of human agency mediated by God's ultimate sovereignty. Shabestarī sees this ability in humanity as capable of being exercised not necessarily through the "text" of the Qur'an alone but rather as an ever-present human potential.

Shabestarī's more recent writings on the Qur'an and revelation draw more extensively from Western philosophies of language to offer what some might see as a controversial account of the nature of prophecy and the Qur'an.[16] As sociologist Farzin Vahdat has effectively pointed out, Shabestarī argues that the Qur'anic text is not itself revelation. Rather, it is an interpretive understanding of the world by the Prophet, who experienced revelation. Thus in this more recent articulation of his thought, Shabestarī contends that from a Qur'anic point of view, revelation is God's conversation with Muḥammad, which instigated Muḥammad to make certain utterances.[17] As such, the Qur'anic verses are products of revelation, not revelation itself. Shabestarī argues that all that is provided to Muḥammad is a "perspective" (*nigāh*) through which to interpret the world. Vahdat brings attention to Shabestarī's translation of Qur'anic verses from the Arabic "*āyāt*" into the Persian not as signs (*namūd*) but as symbols (*nishān*). In so doing, Shabestarī reinforces the point that the verses should be approached as temporal phenomena, while being rooted in the noumena.[18]

In a quintessentially modern move, by bringing attention onto the individual (in this case, Muḥammad) and away from an autonomous self-speaking text, Shabestarī elevates the subjectivity and agency of the individual, as both the recipient and interpreter of revelation. And in framing his argument for this return of the subject and embrace of the interpreter, Shabestarī was deeply indebted to the philosophy of German theorist Hans-Georg Gadamer. Gadamer's major contribution to the field of hermeneutics was that of removing the stain of "prejudice" from the act of interpretation.[19] An interpreter's prejudice was not an undesirable quality that brought their credibility under fatal questioning. Rather, Gadamer argued, the interpreter's prejudice represented an indispensible, indeed necessary component of any hermeneutical enterprise. Shabestarī was explicit in his invocation of Gadamer's claim that hermeneutical prejudice need not and should not be understood as a negative condition; the active role of the interpreter in deriving meaning from the Qur'an, Shabestarī reasoned, was something to be embraced rather than avoided. So for Shabestarī any form of meaning derived from the Qur'an could not conceivably be external to the God-man relationship from which it is engendered. This view punctuated Shabestarī's larger objective of rehabilitating *faith* as the core of religion in place of a more legalistic understanding of religion. He argued that faith as religious experience should become the core pillar of a "New Theology" and replace or at least supplement the overemphasis on law on the one hand and metaphysical statements about God on the other.[20] In his own words, "According to my interpretation the Qur'an and Sunnah are not the sources of faith for a Muslim … according to Islamic belief, every human being possesses a natural, innate ability to find the path to God. And this does not rely on revelation."[21]

Shabestarī's primary aim was to remove what he saw as an "overemphasis" on the sacred text as the primary source of Truth. He was critical of such privileging of the text, which in his view generated essentialist conceptions of meaning. Shabestarī was equally critical of a strictly jurisprudential approach that remained oblivious to the sociohistorical context of the Qur'an, and that tended to exaggerate legal rulings as the core of religion. In championing this approach, however, Shabestarī resorted to privileging a private faith-based religion that thoroughly undermines the public and embodied dimensions of the Qur'an. More on this soon. Let me next turn though to the thought of Shabestarī's contemporary and contentious Iranian reformist scholar, Abdolkarīm Soroush.

CONTINUOUS REVELATION AND PROPHETIC EXPERIENCE

Abdolkarīm Soroush's writings on the relationship between revelation and religious authority present another important avenue through which to explore the entangled encounter of distinctly modern categories and frameworks with premodern textual artifacts. Soroush's education began with a degree in pharmacology from Tehran University and continued in London in the philosophy of science. A few months after the 1979 Revolution, Soroush returned to Iran and held the position of chair of the department of Islamic culture in Tehran's Teacher's College. He was also appointed as a member of the Advisory Committee on Cultural Revolution. Four years later he resigned from these positions and devoted himself exclusively to teaching and research at the Academy of Philosophy and The Research

Center for Humanities and Social Sciences, also in Tehran. It was soon after the publication of his controversial book in 1990, *The Theoretical Contraction and Expansion of Religious Knowledge,*[22] in which he laid out his theory of the dynamic nature of religious knowledge and its relations to nonreligious knowledge, that Soroush began to come under attack, as he was critiqued trenchantly by prominent members of the clergy. After his exile from Iran, he has been teaching at leading universities in North America and Europe, and has remained a popular and influential figure in Iran despite his physical absence.

A common predicament haunting modern Muslim revivalist currents is posed by the question of how one ought to distinguish between what was permanently sacred and unchanging in the Qur'an from that which was situational and changing. In his hermeneutical program, Soroush does not try to filter the permanent from the temporal in the text. Rather, he takes the Kantian step of distinguishing between the thing itself and its perception, or "religion," as intended by God, as distinct from the temporal human knowledge of it. In positing this distinction, Soroush drew heavily from the thought of philosopher Karl Popper. Having established the changing nature of religious knowledge, he explains that all types of religious knowledge are contingent on external branches of knowledge, which are always in flux.[23] Soroush thus concludes that religious knowledge itself does not embody the Truth, but rather constitutes a struggle that one must strive to attain by means of these other sciences.

In 2003, Soroush extended his discussion of the model of religion vs. religious knowledge to the notion of "revelation" with the publication of what would become one of his most controversial publications, *The Expansion of Prophetic Experience.*[24] In this work, he explains revelation not as a closed Book handed down to the Prophet in one instance, but rather as the result of multiple "prophetic experiences" that were socially and historically situated to his life and time. Of course, this argument shares important parallels with Shabestarī's theory of the Qur'an as a "Prophetic Reading of the World" discussed earlier, though Soroush well preceded Shabestarī in this articulation.[25] Soroush does not limit this revelatory experience to the Prophet. Instead, he argues for the idea of "continuous revelation" by which he means the participation of each generation in the process of lending meaning to the text. Well aware that this view would immediately raise questions about the purpose then, of a prophet, and on the meaning behind the idea of the "finality of prophethood," as is endorsed in Muslim intellectual circles, Soroush is careful to incorporate these questions into his discussion. Thus he explains that the element of guardianship that the task of prophethood constitutes is precisely what is exclusive to the Prophet, and it is this that has come to an end with the cessation of prophethood.[26] Arguing for the continuation of revelation or experience thus reinforces Soroush's position that the Truth is not out there in the form of an unchanging body of rulings exclusively accessible to an elite class of jurists. The continuity of revelation enables for Soroush the egalitarian accessibility of revelation. Moreover, this move also allowed him to consolidate his argument for a thoroughly contextual reading of the Qur'an. In Soroush's view, every generation must extract the Truth from the principles as relevant to its circumstances.

To further bolster his point through reference to Muslim normative sources of authority, Soroush also invoked the Shīʿī doctrine of Imamate (the view that the authority of the hereditary successors [Imams] from the line of the Prophet's daughter are binding) and the Sufi conceptions of sainthood as further evidence of the continuous nature of revelation. This is because through their faith in the successors or Imams, Shīʿīs have "laudably embraced the fine point that the door has not been closed to valid and independent religious experiences, even after the Prophet's demise, and that countless saints may appear and enrich religion with their experiences and discoveries."[27]

Soroush goes on to argue that if one understands revelation through the prism of prophetic experiences, one will be able to recognize that the words of the Qur'an are in fact the words of the Prophet. To justify this provocative argument, Soroush turned to the thought of the magisterial thirteenth century mystic, Jalāl al-Dīn Rūmī's (d. 1273 CE) canonical poetic compendium, the *Mathnavi,* to justify his position: "As Rumi put it, when the sea is poured into a jug, the sea per force complies with the jug. The sea doesn't stop being the sea, but what reaches us is what's in the jug and, unavoidably, the sea complies with the jug's dimensions and capacity."[28]

By asserting that the Qur'anic words were the words of the Prophet, Soroush sought to situate those words in a specific context. Rehearsing a common Muslim modernist refrain, this argument goes something like this: since the Prophet's career and words were contingent to his specific context, so too should all future iterations of Muslim normativity. Despite this historicizing gesture, however, Soroush was still keen to maintain the divine quality of the Prophet's words. In a 2008 interview, for instance, he stated,

> The beloved Prophet of Islam was a human being and he acknowledged and was conscious of his humanity, but this human being had, at the same time, acquired such a divine hue and quality … that whatever he said was both earthly and divine; these two things were inseparable … to say that the Qur'an is Muhammad's word is exactly like saying the Qur'an is Muhammad's miracle. Underlining one is not a negation of the other.[29]

Here Soroush was dealing with a difficult conundrum: how to preserve the integrity of a transcendent divine while also shifting the locus of revelatory authority from the Qur'an to Muḥammad's speech? Soroush responded to this conundrum by presenting a looming yet intangible conception of the "transcendent" whose existence does not undercut the authority of prophetic speech. Moreover as seen in the quote above, in assembling this configuration of the relationship between God and the Prophet, Soroush posited two critical dyads: true religion and fallible religious knowledge, Divine Words and the temporal understanding of those Words. In further emphasizing the normative authority of human prophetic speech, Soroush strategically turned to mysticism. His resort to mysticism was aimed at establishing the intimate interlocking of Divine Presence and Prophetic speech and experience. For this task he turned to the ideas of luminary mystics such as Rūmī and Ibn 'Arabī. Soroush's mobilization of their thought was meant to proffer an understanding of Divine Truth as accessible primarily through human experience, the quintessential model of which was represented by Prophet Muḥammad's experience. His ultimate goal through this exercise was to democratize the accessibility of divine revelation beyond a specialist scholarly elite. This he did by presenting a view of revelation as accessible primarily through experience, as continuously generated, and as tethered to the individual in a dialectical relationship.

RELIGION AS PRIVATE EXPERIENCE: LANGUAGE, HERMENEUTIC, AND SUBJECTIVITY

In a lecture delivered at McGill University in 2005, Soroush confidently exclaimed: "faith is always personal and private, it can be more or less certain, but knowledge cannot be but collective, public and fallible."[30] One can clearly see in this statement the operation of a normative notion of religion that upholds interiority as the most cherished site of "authentic religion." But although Soroush sought to frame his valorization of inwardness as a seamless reproduction of medieval Muslim thought, a closer interrogation of this concept reveals some critical fissures in the coherence of his argument. For this task, I turn to the work of religion scholar Gavin Flood, and in particular to his insights on medieval notions of inwardness. Even though his analysis pertains to non-Muslim contexts, he is nonetheless productive to think with in regard to the intellectual context of modern Muslim reformist thought in Iran that occupies this essay.[31]

Flood argues that in societies of the medieval period, individuals imagined themselves as inseparable to the larger cosmology in which they were embedded.[32] For such a cosmologically-embedded-self, the cultivation of an inner life was rooted in, and shaped by, practice. In other words, the medieval inward self remained connected to community, ritual, and a shared subjectivity. This shared subjectivity was formed through the cultivation of text-informed spiritual practices that overwhelmed or superseded the ego cogito.[33] Put differently, inwardness was formed and performed through textual appropriation, intensive ritual practice, and sustained asceticism.

In contrast, Flood argues, in the West since the Renaissance and through the history of secularization, subjectivity became linked with self-assertion and the self came to be chiefly understood as the possessor of liberty and rights. Thus, the supposedly natural link between subjectivity and individualism is in fact a recent construction that has entailed the stripping of cosmology from subjectivity. In modernity, we have become persons outside of an inherently meaningful cosmos. Whereas previously, cosmology connected a person's subjectivity to a broader community, with secularization, subjectivity emerges as primarily individual and privatized.

Returning to Shabestarī and Soroush, the premodern figures whose writings they frequently invoked as proof texts for their theorizations on revelation—such as Ibn ʻArabī and Rūmī—were also members of what Flood helpfully called "cosmological societies." And, as scholars of Sufism like Shahzad Bashir have long argued, "in Sufi practice the theory of friendship with God pertained both to internal states and social relationships. It mattered most centrally in the perceived necessity of a master who could lead one along the Sufi path."[34] Thus the project of cultivating an inner life, and more specifically, friendship with God through "experience," among other things, was central to the construction of one's authority in broader social settings. This stands in significant contrast to the category of "experience" described by Soroush and Shabestarī. Underlying this "experience" is an understanding of the "self" as an entity that is separable from the embodied practices through which it is cultivated and sustained. In other words, as anthropologist Katherine Ewing has argued in a different context, drawing on the work of Talal Asad: this "conception of 'experience' assumes a particular cultural logic by which the body and spirit are divorced and spirituality is understood as an inner state that does not depend on the condition of the body."[35]

This understanding of the self also diminishes the importance of the distinctly hierarchical relations that characterized an individual's place on the Sufi path, and their cultivation of an inner life in the premodern period. As I have shown above, Soroush's and Shabestarī's reform projects were directed at arguing for a relocation of truth from the text of the Qur'an to the individual experience of the subject. In so doing, they sought to wrest authority away from an exclusive class of clerical interpreters. Yet, the writings of mystics and of scholars whom Shabestarī and Soroush cite as proof texts in support of their arguments were themselves deeply embedded in, and at ease with, a society hierarchically divided into different groups on the basis of their privileged access to truth. Moreover, for premodern mystics, bringing attention to the affective dimensions of religious experience in the individual subject (through hagiography, vision literature, etc.) was critical to the project of forging a clear distinction between different classes of knowers (of the truth).

Thus, quite apart from an individual, private experience disconnected from and invisible to the public gaze and external forms of authority, in the premodern religious imagination there existed a distinctly social dimension to an individual subject's cultivation of friendship with God. The construction of authority in Sufi settings, is never divorced from the articulation and enactment of that authority in society. Shabestarī's and Soroush's deployment of these writings for the purpose of defending a notion of religion that is not subject to forms of authority except that of an internal guide, unmoors these writings from the politico-intellectual conditions that enabled their production.

Further dissonances between the thought of contemporary Iranian reformers and that of the premodern mystics they employ have been highlighted in other recent studies. Kathleen Foody for example, brings to our attention a critical difference in the invocation of "experience" in the work of Soroush and his mystical sources: "While Soroush's writings on Islam arise out of both Ghazali's and Rumi's works—as well as Islamic mystical traditions more broadly—he does not use this language of annihilation; instead, the authority of individual experience replaces the dissolution of the self." Foody further argues: "Soroush locates the center of Muslim practice not as annihilation of the self, but its completion. Muhammad, in a manner that the individual Muslim can and should emulate, grows over time into a more complete personality, not dissolving in the divine but growing through it."[36] Note the act of translation at work here. Soroush and Shabestarī draw on categories and arguments from the mystical tradition and reinvest these older concepts with new meanings for new political projects. But how do they go about doing so? It is to addressing this question that I now turn.

THE SECULAR PRODUCTION OF NORMATIVE RELIGION

In what has preceded I have argued that Shabestarī's and Soroush's mobilization of premodern mystical writings refashion these texts by imagining the individual subject, positioned at the center of the religious experience being described, as separable from the embodied practices in which they participate. Critical to consider here is how this thoroughly modern understanding of the self is enwrapped in a broader imaginary of the normative role and place of religion in the modern world. In the thought of reformers like Soroush, since religion is ultimately a matter of rational choice and deliberation, a properly modern subject must possess the capacity to separate inner belief from the external world of objects, images, and materiality.[37] And this normative notion of religion, as Saba Mahmood has most convincingly argued, advances and is made possible by a particular semiotic ideology. More specifically, in her arresting study of secular pre-commitments driving the Danish cartoon controversy, Mahmood showed that there exist deep ties between a "secular hermeneutic"—one that rests on a secular semiotic ideology whereby language and objects are only arbitrarily related—and the concomitant production of a particular kind of religious subject, unmoored from embodied inhabitations of piety.[38] According to a secular semiotic ideology, she argues, signs are only arbitrarily connected to the concepts they represent. An important upshot of this is that a secular hermeneutic assumes a *contingent* relationship of religious truth to material expressions of religion, including texts and rituals.[39] And underlying this position are the quintessentially modern assumptions of the self as "an autonomous individual believer," of scripture as "historically wrested from traditional methods of reading and their embodied practices," and of "authentic" religion as that which is located in the interior of a person. Mahmood's broader objective of course is to puncture the commonly held assumption that secularism represents a politically neutral cleavage of religion and the state, by showing ways in which the exercise of secular power generates particular understandings of normative religion most conducive to secular governance and state sovereignty. [40]

Mahmood's insights about the interaction between religion, language and secular power shed important light on Soroush's and Shabestarī's reformist program, especially in relation to illumining the secular semiotic logics that undergird their understandings of scripture on the one hand and the prophetic body on the other.

Soroush's project of historicizing the Qur'an – understood as the Prophet's experience of revelation—in order to allow for a more flexible approach to its interpretation—went hand in hand with a dehistoricization of the Prophet's body. How? Soroush, and to a large extent Shabestarī, sought to valorize the Prophet's inner experiences as the foremost aspect of his being worthy of imitation and replication. In so doing, they extirpate the bodily, embodied dimensions of the Prophet that travel in historical time. In other words, they expunge the materiality of his body from the turbulent vicissitudes of time, laying him supine in the atemporal tranquility of inner piety. This move was laced in irony. Because at the crux of their critique of the Iranian clerical establishment was the charge that they de-historicized the Prophet by reducing him to the role of giver of a universally applicable law. I am less interested in evaluating the validity of their critique than in pointing out the resemblance between their own conception of an ideal imaginary of the

Prophet and the conception they accuse the clerics of harboring. If the clerics allegedly reduced the Prophet to a law-giver, Soroush and Shabestarī transformed the Prophet into a quintessentially modern religious subject contained to the vestibule of inner piety. Their argument rests on the assumption that it is not only possible, but also necessary for believers to aspire toward the Prophet's inner experiences, independent from the bodily practices through which they were attained. Here again we see the contingency of bodily practice to the acquisition of religious truth.

Soroush wants to distance himself from an understanding of the Prophet as the messenger of a prepackaged transcendental knowledge handed down to him by God. One might go as far as to say that for Soroush, this would identify the Prophet as lazy—hardly a trait to be celebrated according to a modern logic of labor and virtue! As he revealingly wrote: "it was not as if the Prophet experienced revelation once and ascended to the heavens once, to then rest on those laurels and spend from that treasure for the rest of his life. No. The blessing of revelation rained down upon him constantly, giving him ever-greater strength and flourishing. Hence, the Prophet grew steadily more learned, more certain, more resolute, more experienced; in a word, more of a prophet."[41] Soroush reinforces this point by referring to specific Qur'anic verses, and also to the illustrious medieval philosopher of history, Ibn Khaldūn (d. 1406 CE), whom Soroush positioned as a critical interlocutor for his theory of prophetic improvement. Soroush latched onto a statement by Ibn Khaldūn, in which he stated that the Prophet's endurance for revelation grew over time, and that this explains why the chronologically earlier chapters of the Qur'an were shorter. Soroush mobilized this assertion in an instrumentalist fashion by claiming that there exists a dialectical relationship between the "doer and the deed. The two unmistakably affect one another."[42] But clearly, there is an important difference between Ibn Khaldūn's observation and the argument that Soroush puts forward on the basis of that observation. Soroush uses Ibn Khaldūn's assertion that the Prophet's physical experience of receiving revelation became easier over time to suggest that the Prophet's *interpretation* of that experience became better over time. Soroush adds a normative evaluation to Ibn Khaldūn's descriptive observations.

Soroush's reformist understanding of the Qur'an not only rendered the text into a historical phenomenon based on the individual, interior experience of the Prophet. It also reimagined the Prophet as a deeply rational, modern figure, who must undergo hard work and experience in order to become a better prophet, and to *perfect* religion. For Soroush, the Prophet is an autonomous, reflective, developing, rational subject. In addition, his individual spiritual experiences (reflected in the Qur'an), were informed by the external environment in which he grew and developed as a Prophet. In this way, Soroush connects the subjective expansion of the prophetic experience with the outward expansion of life-experience. Gradualism in the Qur'an, meaning the gradual rather than immediate revelation of the Qur'an's legislative logics and mandate was previously understood by scholars as proof of a responsive divine entity toward humanity's varied situations.[43] In contrast, Soroush interprets this aspect of the Qur'an as an indication of the unfolding *improvement* of Muḥammad in his functional role as prophet-teacher. In short, while in seeking to modernize the Qur'an, Soroush also modernized Muḥammad into a prophet primarily known through his rational and autonomous subjectivity.

CONCLUSION

To conclude, Shabestarī and Soroush took varied approaches while arguing for legal reform. But both enthusiastically shared the premise that the Qur'an and its rulings were culturally and historically specific. Shabestarī adopted a resilient stance on the role of revelation as secondary to the core of religion and drew freely from Western philosophical sources to make a case for a private faith-based religion as opposed to one that is dependent on the authority of the clerical establishment. Despite this controversial argument, curiously, his own standing as a leading jurist has protected him from being subject to severe persecution. Soroush on the other hand, while also inspired by Western thinkers and philosophers, nonetheless couched his discourse in the relatively safer and more familiar intellectual domains of Shī'ī theology and Islamic mysticism. However despite these seemingly mitigating factors, not only have his ideas come under severe attack, often deemed as poisonous, but more seriously, threats to his safety have also compelled him to leave Iran and remain in exile. One might explain this dissonance in the reactions to Shabestarī's and Soroush's agendas on the basis of the former's Muslim traditionalist education and the latter's lack of possessing such traditionalist training. In any case, both these thinkers bring into view important questions and conundrums in relation to the reconfiguration of sources of Muslim normative authority, especially the Qur'an, in decisively modern intellectual and political terrains. The examples of scholars like Shabestarī and Soroush from the Iranian context are especially productive to think with because they show us that even in contexts such as Iran that did not come under the direct control of Western colonial rule, the tentacles of a modern Western imaginary of the normative role and place of scripture nonetheless run firm and deep. What the examples of Shabestarī and Soroush ultimately show us is that achieving radical equality in the domain of scriptural politics represents an aspiration riddled with thorny tensions, ambiguities, and contradictions. Yet still, for all the difficulties it presents, equal access to revelation, especially as a way of overcoming the anxieties of modernity, remains a powerful promise, intimately entangled in profound questions of the self, power, and politics.

NOTES

1. The Shīʻī school represents one of the two major groups within Islam, the other of course being the majority Sunnī school. Their main point of contention primarily revolves around the question of successorship to Prophet Muḥammad, and the normative sources of knowledge constituting the Muslim legal and ethical traditions.

2. For a broad overview of the Iranian Reform Movement, see Said Amir Arjomand, "The Reform Movement and the Debate on Modernity and Tradition in Contemporary Iran," *International Journal of Middle East Studies* 34, no. 4 (2002): 719–31.

3. Omid Safi, "Between '*Ijtihad* of the Presupposition' and Gender Equality: Cross-Pollination between Progressive Islam and Iranian Reform," in *Rethinking Islamic Studies: From Orientalism to Cosmopolitanism*, ed. Carl W. Ernst and Richard C. Martin (Columbia: University of South Carolina Press, 2012), 74.

4. Safi, "Between '*Ijtihad* of the Presupposition' and Gender Equality," 74.

5. Arjomand, "Reform Movement," 724.

6. Note, for example, the Qur'anic turn in the work of leading jurist-theologian Abu'l-Qāsim al-Khū'ī (d. 1992) and influential exegete-scholar 'Allāmah Ṭabāṭabā'ī (d. 1981). See Abdulaziz Sachedina's introduction to Abu'l-Qāsim al-Khū'ī's, *The Prolegomena to the Quran*, trans. Abdulaziz Sachedina (New York: Oxford University Press, 1998), 15.

7. For a detailed study on these overlaps, see Sasan Tavassoli, *Christian Encounters with Iran: Engaging Muslim Thinkers After the Revolution* (London: I. B. Tauris, 2011).

8. For this insight I am indebted to the work of anthropologist David Scott, *Conscripts of Modernity: The Tragedy of Colonial Enlightenment* (Durham, NC: Duke University Press, 2005).

9. It is worth noting that Shabestarī is certainly not alone in making this argument. A similar approach is found in the work of several earlier scholars; the writings of Fazlur Rahman (d. 1988) (from Pakistan) and Nasr Abu Zayd (d. 2010) (from Egypt) for example, have long been associated with approaching the Qur'an as a historical text. Both Rahman and Abu Zayd were unable to continue their scholarly careers in Pakistan and Egypt respectively due to the controversy surrounding their writings on the Qur'an. It may be that Shabestarī's traditional seminary background and his connection to clerical circles by virtue of his intellectual past have spared him a similar fate. Although Shabestarī follows these figures in their approach, of interest to me here are the distinct sources and trajectories of his argument.

10. Muḥammad Mujtahid Shabestarī, "Interview with Mohammad Mojtahed Shabestari (Part 2): Muslims Can Have Democracy without Having to Leave Islam," *Qantara.de* (online), (2008), https://en.qantara.de/node/213 (accessed February 15, 2018).

11. Muḥammad Shabestarī, *Hermenutik, Kitāb va Sunnat: Farāyand-i Tafsīr-i Vahy* [*Hermeneutics, the Book and the Tradition: Process of interpreting revelation*], (Tehran: Tarh-e No, 1996), 140.

12. Shabestarī, *Hermenutik*, 140-41.

13. For more on modern liberal misappropriations of Ibn 'Arabī's thought, see the excellent recent study by Gregory Lipton, *Rethinking Ibn 'Arabi,* (New York: Oxford University Press, 2018).

14. Farzin Vahdat, *God and Juggernaut: Iran's Intellectual Encounter with Modernity*, (Syracuse, NY: Syracuse University Press, 2002), 205. Also see Farzin Vahdat, *Islamic Ethos and the Specter of Modernity* (London: Anthem Press, 2015), 167, where he brings attention to another key passage from Shabestarī: "This view of *tawhid* is a type of relation between God and man. When this relation is 'lively' (*zendeh*) and 'limpid' (*zulal*), man experiences God [...] neither God is negated nor man. In a relation based on pure *tawhid*, God's sovereignty is not competing with man, but gives him meaning and solidifies him" (Shabestarī, *Hermeneutics*, 182).

15. Vahdat, *God and Juggernaut*, 200-211.

16. Muḥammad Mujtahid Shabestarī, *Qirā'at-i Nabavī az Jahān* [The Prophetic Reading of the World], *Madreseh* 6 (2007): 92-100. The publication of this essay by Shabestarī drove the government to shut down the *Madreseh* journal in which it was published. See Vahdat, *Islamic Ethos*, 178.

17. See Vahdat, *Islamic Ethos*, 178.

18. Vahdat, *Islamic Ethos*, 178; "Noumena" (pl. of noumenon), in the philosophy of Immanuel Kant refers to the thing-in-itself, as opposed to what Kant called the "phenomenon"—the thing as it appears to an observer.

19. See Hans-Georg Gadamer, *Truth and Method* (New York: Crossroad, 1989).

20. Muḥammad Mujtahid Shabestarī, "Islam Is a Religion, Not a Political Agenda (Part 2)," *Qantara.de* (online) (July 17, 2008), https://nawaat.org/portail/2008/07/17/islam-is-a-religion-not-a-political-agenda/ (accessed February 15, 2018).

21. Shabestarī, "Islam Is a Religion."

22. Abdolkarīm Soroush, *Qabz o Basṭ-i Teorīk-i Sharī'at—yā Naẓarīya-yi Takammul-i Ma'rifat-i Dīnī* [*Theoretical Contraction and Expansion of Shari'a, or The Theory of Evolution of Religious Knowledge*] (Tehran, Iran: Ṣirat, 2003; first published 1990).

23. Vahdat, *God and Juggernaut*, 201.

24. Abdolkarīm Soroush, *The Expansion of Prophetic Experience: Essays on Historicity, Contingency and Plurality in Religion*, trans. Nilou Mobasser, ed. Forough Jahanbakhsh (Leiden and Boston: Brill, 2009), 10. The original Persian was published even earlier in 2003, *Basṭ-i Tajrubah-yi Nabavī* (Tehran, Iran: Sirat, 2003).

25. Shabestarī, "*Qirā'at-i Nabavī az Jahān*," 92-100.

26. Soroush, *Expansion of Prophetic Experience*, 38.

27. Soroush, *Expansion of Prophetic Experience*, 49.

28. Soroush, *Expansion of Prophetic Experience*, 49.

29. Abdolkarīm Soroush, "Muhammad's Word, Muhammad's Miracle, Interview with AbdolKarim Soroush by Kargozaran newspaper," *drsoroush.com* (online),

(February 9, 2008), http://www.drsoroush.com/English/Interviews/E-INT-MuhammadsWord.html (accessed February 15, 2018).

30. Abdolkarīm Soroush, "The Evolution and Devolution of Religious Knowledge," in *Liberal Islam: A Sourcebook*, ed. Charles Kurzman, (New York: Oxford University Press, 2011), 251.

31. Gavin D. Flood, *The Truth Within: A History of Inwardness in Christianity, Hinduism, and Buddhism* (Oxford: Oxford University Press, 2015).

32. Flood, *Truth Within*, 12.

33. Flood is careful to point out that the binary opposition between individualism and shared subjectivity should not be overdetermined; "there are individualistic dimensions to the shared subjective as there are collective dimensions to modernist individualism." (*Truth Within*, 6).

34. Shahzad Bashir, *Sufi Bodies: Religion and Society in Medieval Islam* (New York: Columbia University Press, 2013), 12.

35. Katherine Pratt Ewing, "The Misrecognition of a Modern Islamist Organization: Germany Faces 'Fundamentalism,'" in *Rethinking Islamic Studies: From Orientalism to Cosmopolitanism*, ed. Carl W. Ernst and Richard C. Martin (Columbia: University of South Carolina Press, 2012), 48.

36. See Kathleen Foody, "Interiorizing Islam: Religious Experience and State Oversight in the Islamic Republic of Iran," *Journal of the American Academy of Religion* 83, no. 3 (2015): 607-8.

37. SherAli Tareen, "Disrupting Secular Power: Saba Mahmood," in *Cultural Approaches to Studying Religion*, ed. Meredith Minister and Sarah Bloesch (New York: Bloomsbury Press, 2018). Here Tareen is engaging Saba Mahmood, "Religious Reason and Secular Affect: An Incommensurable Divide?" *Critical Inquiry* 35, no. 4 (2009): 844.

38. Mahmood, "Religious Reason," 836-62; and Saba Mahmood, "Secularism, Hermeneutics, and Empire: The Politics of Islamic Reformation," *Public Culture* 18, no. 2 (2006): 323-47.

39. "We might suggest here that the project of a secular hermeneutics, and the form of discipline and rule it inaugurates, finds its telos in precisely a subject who recognizes that material expressions of a particular religion—its rituals, observances, laws, and scriptures—are linked only contingently to religious truth" (Mahmood, "Secularism," 342).

40. "Notably, the autonomous individual believer, privileged in the arguments of these thinkers, is a necessary protagonist in the plot of secular political rationality, one who owes his allegiance to the sovereign rule of the state rather than structures of traditional authority. Scripture is accorded a certain place in this secular arrangement of power, but its interpretive authority must be historically wrested from traditional methods of reading and their embodied practices." (Mahmood, "Secularism," 340).

41. Soroush, *Expansion of Prophetic Experience*, 10.

42. Soroush, *Expansion of Prophetic Experience*, 11.

43. Fazlur Rahman, *Major Themes of the Qur'an* (Chicago: University of Chicago Press, 2013), 48.

REFERENCES

Abu'l-Qāsim al- Khū'ī. *The Prolegomena to the Quran*. Translated by Abdulaziz Sachedina. New York: Oxford University Press, 1998.

Arjomand, Said Amir. "The Reform Movement and the Debate on Modernity and Tradition in Contemporary Iran." *International Journal of Middle East Studies* 34, no. 4 (2002): 719–31.

Bashir, Shahzad. *Sufi Bodies: Religion and Society in Medieval Islam*. New York: Columbia University Press, 2015.

Ewing, Katherine Pratt. "The Misrecognition of a Modern Islamist Organization: Germany Faces 'Fundamentalism.'" In *Rethinking Islamic Studies: From Orientalism to Cosmopolitanism*, edited by Carl W. Ernst and Richard C. Martin, 46-60. Columbia: University of South Carolina Press, 2012.

Flood, Gavin D. *The Truth Within: A History of Inwardness in Christianity, Hinduism, and Buddhism*. Oxford: Oxford University Press, 2015.

Foody, Kathleen. "Interiorizing Islam: Religious Experience and State Oversight in the Islamic Republic of Iran." *Journal of the American Academy of Religion* 83, no. 3 (2015): 599-623.

Gadamer, Hans-Georg. *Truth and Method*. New York: Crossroad, 1989.

Lipton, Gregory. *Rethinking Ibn 'Arabi*. New York: Oxford University Press, 2018.

Mahmood, Saba. "Religious Reason and Secular Affect: An Incommensurable Divide?" *Critical Inquiry* 35 no. 4 (2009): 836-62.

———. "Secularism, Hermeneutics, and Empire: The Politics of Islamic Reformation." *Public Culture* 18 no. 2 (2006): 323-47.

Rahman, Fazlur. *Major Themes of the Qur'an*. Minneapolis, MN: Bibliotheca Islamica, 1980; Chicago: University of Chicago Press, 2013.

Safi, Omid. "Between '*Ijtihad* of the Presupposition' and Gender Equality: Cross-Pollination between Progressive Islam and Iranian Reform." In *Rethinking Islamic Studies: From Orientalism to Cosmopolitanism*, edited by Carl W. Ernst and Richard C. Martin, 61-79. Columbia: University of South Carolina Press, 2012.

Scott, David. *Conscripts of Modernity: The Tragedy of Colonial Enlightenment*. Durham, NC: Duke University Press, 2005.

Shabestarī, Muḥammad Mujtahid. *Hermenutik, Kitāb va Sunnat: Farāyand-i Tafsīr-i Vahy*. Tehran: Tarh-e No, 1996.

———. "Interview with Mohammad Mojtahed Shabestari (Part 2): Muslims Can Have Democracy without Having to Leave Islam." *Qantara.de* (online). 2008. https://en.qantara.de/node/213 (accessed February 15, 2018).

———. "Islam Is a Religion, Not a Political Agenda (Part 2)." *Qantara.de* (online). July 17, 2008. https://nawaat.org/portail/2008/07/17/islam-is-a-religion-not-a-political-agenda/ (accessed February 15, 2018).

———. "*Qirā'at-i Nabavī az Jahān*." *Madreseh* 6, (2007): 92-100.

Soroush, Abdolkarīm, "The Evolution and Devolution of Religious Knowledge." In *Liberal Islam: A Sourcebook*, edited by Charles Kurzman, 244-51. New York: Oxford University Press, 2011.

———. *The Expansion of Prophetic Experience: Essays on Historicity, Contingency and Plurality in Religion.* Translated by Nilou Mobasser. Edited by Forough Jahanbakhsh. Leiden and Boston: Brill, 2009. First published. Persian. *Basṭ-i Tajrubah-yi Nabavī.* Tehran, Iran: Sirat, 2003.

———. "Muhammad's Word, Muhammad's Miracle, Interview with AbdolKarim Soroush by Kargozaran newspaper." *drsoroush.com* (online). February 9, 2008. http://www.drsoroush.com/English/Interviews/E-INT-MuhammadsWord.html (accessed February 15, 2018).

———. *Qabz o Basṭ-i Teorīk-i Sharī'at—yā Naẓarīya-yi Takammul-i Ma'rifat-i Dīnī.* Tehran, Iran: Ṣirat, 2003. First published 1990.

Tareen, SherAli. "Disrupting Secular Power: Saba Mahmood." In *Cultural Approaches to Studying Religion*, edited by Meredith Minister and Sarah Bloesch. New York: Bloomsbury Press, forthcoming 2018.

Tavassoli, Sasan. *Christian Encounters with Iran: Engaging Muslim Thinkers After the Revolution.* London: I. B. Tauris, 2011.

Vahdat, Farzin. *God and Juggernaut: Iran's Intellectual Encounter with Modernity.* Syracuse: NY: Syracuse University Press, 2002.

———. *Islamic Ethos and the Specter of Modernity.* London: Anthem Press, 2015.

Chapter 12

Gandhi, Krishna, and Caste

Inequality More or Less

Richard H. Davis

Throughout his life, Mahatma Gandhi relied on the *Bhagavad Gita*, an ancient Sanskrit poem, to reflect on and articulate his own principles and purposes within the very real challenges he faced as leader of the Indian independence movement during the first half of the twentieth century. He spoke of the *Gita* as his "spiritual dictionary" and his "infallible guide to conduct." He translated the text into Gujarati and commented on it at length, and he referred to it repeatedly in his conversations, speeches, and letters. According to the careful study of Y. P. Anand, Gandhi cited the *Gita* 1,406 times in his collected works; this is in addition to his four extended treatments of the text.[1]

Gandhi's reliance on the *Bhagavad Gita*, however, posed several interpretive challenges. In the Indian struggle for liberation from British colonial rule, other leaders had also made the *Gita* a central text, and Gandhi often found himself at odds with them in his own reading of the work. Most notable was his insistence on the principle of non-violence (*ahimsa*). In the *Bhagavad Gita*, the charioteer Krishna (who also reveals himself to be the Supreme God in the course of the conversation) persuades the reluctant warrior Arjuna to take part in the upcoming battle at Kurukshetra. It is a warrior's duty, or *dharma*, he asserts, to fight in a righteous war. Other Indian nationalists like Aurobindo Ghosh and B. G. Tilak accepted Krishna's argument for the employment of violence in a righteous cause, such as opposition to foreign political control. The issue for them was one of strategy: when might it be prudent to take recourse to violence, when foreign rulers maintained a massive superiority in armaments? For Gandhi, by contrast, non-violence was a fundamental principle. He extended considerable effort to argue that the *Gita* in fact endorsed the principle of *ahimsa* implicitly.[2]

Krishna's teachings to Arjuna in the *Bhagavad Gita* also address the question of inequality and social hierarchy. As part of his teachings, Krishna accepts a four-fold hierarchical model of society, common to many other classical Hindu works. The ideal society consists of four basic classes (*varnas*), with distinct duties and capacities, ranked in status from high to low. This four-fold division acted as the template for a more complex hierarchical system of endogamous birth-groups (*jatis*), known in Gandhi's time and still in ours as the "caste system." Along with many other Indian nationalist leaders in the twentieth century, Gandhi struggled with this ancient and still prevalent social model. Was it possible to celebrate both ancient Indian society and the modern value of equality?

GANDHI AND KRISHNA

In a key section of the *Bhagavad Gita*, Krishna begins to reveal his own divine nature to Arjuna. He is unborn and imperishable, lord of all creatures, and the final destination of those who gain liberation. Further, he adds, "I created the fourfold order of the social classes, according to the division of qualities and actions. Although I alone created all this, you should know that I am eternally inactive."[3] We can pass over Krishna's theological paradox of simultaneous divine action and inaction in this passage, and focus here on his basic claim. As Supreme Lord, Krishna is the creator of the fourfold order of social classes, namely the four *varnas*.

The model of four classes was first articulated in a famous hymn from the *Rg Veda* known as the Purusha Sukta, dated to about 1000 BCE. In this hymn of creation, all the fundamental elements of creation come into being from the sacrifice of a primordial being, the *Purusha* or Cosmic Man. Among these elements, the four classes arise from the different parts of this Man's body. "When they divided the Man, into how many parts did they apportion him? What do they call his mouth, his two arms, and thighs and feet? His mouth became the Brahmin; his arms were made into the Warrior, his thighs the People, and from his feet the Servants were born."[4] This early Vedic hymn sets forth both a hierarchy of classes and a functional division of labor, based on the part of the Purusha's body from which each class emerged. From the mouth, the uppermost part of Purusha's body, the Brahmin or priestly class would be responsible for speaking and teaching the sacred Vedas. From his arms, the Kshatriya or Warrior class would be tasked with protecting and ruling society, through force of arms when necessary. The Vaishyas or "People," from the thighs of Purusha, would be the productive class of society, through agriculture and other productive enterprises. (In later Indian society, merchants and traders also belonged to the Vaishya class.) The Shudras or Servants, from the feet, would be the lowest of the four, responsible for serving the other three classes above them.

In classical India numerous works reiterated this model of a proper social order, based on endogamous, occupational, ranked classes. Dharmashastras such as the *Manusmriti* set out the proper codes of conduct for members of the various classes. The great Sanskrit epic poems, the *Ramayana* and the *Mahabharata*, both reinforced the fourfold division of society, even as they reflected on the difficulties of maintaining this order. And many of these texts, following the *Rg Veda*, reified the non-egalitarian social model by giving it a primordial origin. The order of four classes, they stated, was a natural part of the order of things. Krishna's statement in the *Bhagavad Gita*—a portion of the epic *Mahabharata*—follows this legacy. As the Creator, Krishna claims that he also established the order of the four social classes, as part of the original cosmic ordering. Further, he adds, he ascribed to the different classes their own proper capacities and duties. People of different classes, he suggests, are distinct in character.

Gandhi's commentary takes up Krishna's suggestion of innate difference:

> These are the Brahmin, Kshatriya, Vaisya, and Sudra. What should be the character of a Brahmin? What is distinctive of him? He is a Brahmin who knows *Brahman*, who lives most in the consciousness of God. And a Brahmin's work in life is to teach and help people to realize God. Besides this particular gift, he will also have the qualities of character which mark the other *varnas*. The Kshatirya's special dharma is protection of society. He should, above all, be a brave man. The Vaisya occupies himself with commerce. This is his special dharma. If he did not follow it, perhaps the world would not go on as it does. The Sudra's special dharma is service. If he combines with his service the spirit of *yajna* or the motive of public good, he will win the reward of his life. There is here no question of higher and lower. If we regard the person who cleans lavatories as lower and another who reads the *Gita* as higher, that will be the end of us.[5]

Gandhi accepts Krishna's linking of inborn qualities with the four classes, as special duties or *dharmas*. But he asserts that this division of class and occupation does not involve hierarchy or inequality. If one does maintain the inequality of the classes, Gandhi avers, this will have disastrous consequences.

Gandhi's final comment raises a key question. Is it possible to maintain a system of distinct classes, such as the *varna* system, and yet not also retain the inegalitarian hierarchy that was traditionally embedded within it? Can a class society be purged of inequality?

GANDHI AND COLONIAL SOCIETY

In 1920, the Indian National Congress, the principal political organization working towards Indian independence from British colonial control, adopted

Gandhi's program of *satyagraha*, or disciplined non-cooperation. Previously Gandhi had worked in South Africa for over two decades on behalf of the Indian community there. He had developed his two key principles of *swaraj* and *satyagraha*. For Gandhi, *swaraj* denotes the goal of political self-rule, freedom from outside dominion. Yet it also points to the aim of inward self-rule, self-mastery, and the personal liberation from fear. *Satyagraha*, literally "holding firmly to Truth," denotes the practices of disciplined and non-violent civil disobedience aimed at overcoming unjust political rule. For Gandhi *satyagraha* also requires personal discipline and social reform, necessary for creating a just and egalitarian society worthy of *swaraj*.[6] After returning to India in 1915, Gandhi conducted several local campaigns that demonstrated how his methods could be deployed successfully within the pan-Indian independence movement. From 1920 until independence in 1947, Gandhi was the indisputable central figure in the Indian struggle to overcome colonial sovereignty.

As leader of this movement, Gandhi had to confront and seek to overcome numerous divisions and inequalities within India. Colonial India under British rule was a deeply divided society. Foremost was the vast division between British rulers and Indian subjects, within a colonial situation. But also within India, there were major divisions between religious communities, most notably between Hindus and Muslims. And then, there were the long-standing social stratifications. Over the centuries, the ancient four-fold model of social classes, the *varnas*, that Krishna had endorsed in the *Bhagavad Gita*, had given rise to a much more complex hierarchical "caste system" of distinct *jatis*. And this society also included a category of persons who were considered to be outside and below even the lowest rungs of the caste hierarchy. These persons were known as "Untouchables" because it was believed that their touch was inherently polluting, or as "Pariahs." The term Pariah derives from a Tamil language term for one particular low-ranking group in southern India, and had been generalized to refer to all those groups outside and excluded from ordinary caste interactions. The Pariahs were assigned the occupations that Indian society considered the most impure, such as cleaning lavatories and working with animal skins.

So thoroughly was hierarchy integrated into the Indian social fabric that the influential French anthropologist Louis Dumont, for the title of his 1966 study, coined the term *Homo Hierarchicus* to describe the person who lives within the Indian caste regime.[7] The ideological principle of social hierarchy, he argued, is at the heart of the caste system, which in turn has pervaded Indian society throughout its entire history. In contrast, he claimed, those like himself living in modern Western societies had inherited a differing set of ideological premises: those of individualism, democracy, and equality. In Dumont's France, it was the call of "Liberty, Equality, Fraternity," articulated within the French Revolution in the late eighteenth century, and now the national motto of France. (Incidentally, these terms are prominently incorporated into the Preamble of the 1949 Constitution of India.) In the United States, the ideology of equality is embedded in the Declaration of Independence's self-evident truth, that all men are created equal. Dumont suggests the term *Homo Aequalis* to capture the Western diametrical ideological opposite to the Indian *Homo Hierarchicus*, and he observes that this category of human found its best approximation in the American culture described by Alexis De Tocqueville in his 1840 study, *Democracy in America*.[8] Dumont is careful to point out that ideology is not necessarily social reality, and he remained well aware of the most egregious inequalities at the heart of the antebellum American society described by Tocqueville. I do not intend to discuss the vigorous debates over Dumont's broad assertions here. I only mean to point to the idea, found in innumerable Western accounts of India, that Indian society represents a quintessence of hierarchy and inequality.

In the colonial period, British officials, following the policy of "divide and rule," had every reason to reinforce the inequities within Indian society. They worked consciously to exacerbate divisions of religion, ethnicity, region, and social class in order to restrain effective collective actions against the colonial regime. Indian anti-colonial leaders like Gandhi followed an opposite imperative. They needed to overcome those divisions and inequalities, to seek to unite all Indians in shared opposition to a common colonial opponent. This was of course no simple matter. Nor was it a goal they accomplished fully. Many of the colonial period divisions and inequalities continue in contemporary South Asia. In this essay, I focus on Gandhi's responses to the inequities of untouchability and caste within Indian society.

GANDHI AND UNTOUCHABILITY

On untouchability, Gandhi was unambiguous. He declared it a "device of Satan." In January 1921, Gandhi spoke passionately about the prejudices and discrimination directed at Untouchables or Pariahs. "We deny him the use of public wells, we throw the leavings of our plates at him. His very shadow pollutes us."[9] We notice here that Gandhi uses the first person plural: he acknowledges this as a sin of Indian Hindus, in which he and his audience are directly implicated. As Nicholas Dirks has observed, Gandhi pointedly did not hold the British responsible for this particular sin. "Although he blamed the British for a great deal in India," writes Dirks, "he was concerned to take national responsibility for the mistreatment of untouchables and the pride and prejudice of upper-caste Hindus."[10] Accordingly, Gandhi argued that it is necessary "for us Hindus to repent of the wrong we have done, to alter our behaviour towards those whom we have 'suppressed' by a system as devilish as we believe the English system of the Government of India to be."[11] The reparation, he went on, must be "a conscious voluntary effort on the part of the masses." And, he added, this is not something that can be put off until after political *swaraj*. It must precede it.

Gandhi's desire to overcome the social exclusions of untouchability was long-standing. Even in South Africa, long before he became directly involved in the Indian independence struggle, he demonstrated the degree of his determination. Living as a successful barrister in the suburbs of Durban, Gandhi and his wife Kasturbhai employed a Gujarati cook and a Tamil-speaking clerk, Lawrence. The clerk had been born an Untouchable, and had converted to Christianity. Kasturbhai had the job of cleaning the chamber-pots of the household, but she balked at cleaning that of an Untouchable. Gandhi insisted that she do it, and that she do it cheerfully. He imagined that he was his wife's teacher. "I will not stand this nonsense in my house," he commanded. Kasturbhai reacted forcefully, and then, as Gandhi recounts in his *Autobiography*:

> I caught her by the hand, dragged the helpless woman to the gate, which was just opposite the ladder, and proceeded to open it with the intention of pushing her out. The tears were running down her cheeks in torrents, and she cried, "Have you no sense of shame? Must you so far forget yourself? Where am I to go? I have no parents or relatives here to harbor me. Being your wife, you think I must put up with your cuffs and kicks? For Heaven's sake behave yourself, and shut the gate. Let us not be found making scenes like this."[12]

Gandhi goes on to relate that he pulled himself back from his anger just in time. Kasturbhai returned to the house, but his account does not say what happened to Lawrence's chamber pot.

On Gandhi's return to India in 1915, he had to confront the reality of untouchability in a more direct way. His first public action after returning was to found a community of followers, which was named Satyagraha Ashram. Gandhi formulated a set of "vows" that would guide the conduct and activities of this exemplary group, and one of the vows was the erasure of untouchability. As a practical demonstration, Gandhi let it be known that the ashram would accept an untouchable family of worthy reputation into its community, and soon such a family presented itself: husband Dudabhai, wife Danibehn, and infant daughter Lakshmi. The responses both outside and inside the ashram were immediate and profound. The man in charge of the nearby water-lift refused to allow ashram members to share the well, since drops of water from the ashram bucket might pollute the well. A larger social boycott ensued, choking off the necessary funds for the small community. The collapse of the ashram finances was prevented at the last minute by an unexpected donation from a generous local businessman, Ambalal Sarabhai. Worse was the internal dissension. Kasturbhai again took a stand against the inclusion of untouchables in her household, and this time she was joined by Gandhi's nephew Maganlal. Gandhi held firm as the ashram fell on hard times. According to one account:

> When the District magistrate visited the ashram in October [1915] he found it in a rather sorry state, its numbers much reduced by the storm of protest. It consisted of Gandhi and his relatives and virtually no local recruits, though there were still curious visitors who came to see both it and the notable eccentric at its head. There had been a real danger that the group would have to take refuge in the untouchables' quarter of the city and live there by their own manual labour.[13]

Kasturbhai toughed it out, Mangalal eventually returned to the fold, and the ashram survived. In his *Autobiography*, written a decade after these events, Gandhi was able to view this as a valuable lesson. "In the very beginning," he observes, "we proclaimed to the world that the Ashram would not countenance untouchability."[14] For Gandhi, clearly, this was a matter of fundamental principle. Here again, it demonstrates Gandhi's willingness to risk his own family relations over a matter that he considered to have overwhelming priority.

Some critics argued that Gandhi's commitment to this social reform distracted attention from the primary aim, which much be to gain political independence. Yet Gandhi held that the extinction of untouchability was both a strategic and a moral requisite to attain *swaraj*. Since the British colonial government retained its control over India, Gandhi asserted, "through our weaknesses," it would be necessary to remove those weaknesses that divide Indian society in order to work effectively towards independence and to be morally fit to acquire it. Untouchability was a kind of internal colonialism, brought by Indians upon themselves. "In my opinion we have become 'pariahs of the Empire' because we have created 'pariahs' in our midst," he wrote. "The slave owner is always more hurt than the slave. We shall be unfit to gain *Swaraj* so long as we would keep in bondage a fifth of the population of Hindustan."[15]

Accordingly, Gandhi opposed the customs and social reality of untouchability at every level. This began with the intimate community of his ashrams, where he sought to demonstrate on a small scale the kinds of reforms he believed necessary for India as a whole. He made the abolition of untouchability one of the pillars of his Constructive Program, the fundamental social reforms that he argued had to be part of the struggle to gain true independence. In 1932, employing the most powerful of the weapons of *satyagraha*, he undertook a personal fast for the reform of untouchability. Gandhi's efforts on behalf of untouchables were heartfelt, consistent, and sustained.

GANDHI AND CASTE SOCIETY

The challenge of caste society was not so clear cut for Gandhi. To follow his changing position we need to keep in mind the distinction between the two terms for Indian social divisions, namely *varna* and *jati*. Initially, as Dennis Dalton has observed, Gandhi did not differentiate these two terms. But as he assumed leadership within the Indian independence he began to make a distinction. By December 1920, Gandhi was insisting that the two be understood separately. The system of four *varnas* was "fundamental, natural, and essential," while the extrinsic division of *jatis*, which he called the "innumerable subcastes," are sometimes a convenience, but often a hindrance.[16] This enabled Gandhi to criticize the inequities of the current regime of caste society in India and look towards its reform from within, while at the same time celebrating an ancient social institution that has "saved Hinduism from disintegration." It was essential not to confuse these two: "*Varna* has nothing to do with caste," he insisted in 1926.

> Down with the monster of caste that masquerades in the guise of *varna*. It is a travesty of *varna* that has degraded Hinduism and India. Our failure to follow the law of *varna* is largely responsible both for our economic and spiritual ruin. It is one cause of unemployment and impoverishment, and it is responsible for untouchability and defections from our faith.[17]

By adhering to this distinction, Gandhi was able, in his commentary on the *Bhagavad Gita* and many other writings, to accept and even endorse the ancient system of *varna* while criticizing the inequities of the contemporary system of *jati* or castes. Caste is degrading, but the ancient *varna* system of.four classes is somehow free from those defects. Further, he argued, the Vedic concept of four *varnas* point to an organically unified society. For Gandhi, such a traditional society, at least as he envisioned it, was eminently superior to contemporary individualistic Western society as well as to the unequal caste society of contemporary India. In a 1934 booklet titled "Varnavyavastha," meant to collect Gandhi's thinking about the *dharma* of *varna* in a single publication, he asserts:

> The four *varnas* have been compared in the Vedas to the four members of the body, and no simile could be happier. If they are members of one body, how can one be superior or inferior to another? If the members of the body had the power of expression and each of them were to say that it was higher and better than the rest, the body would go to pieces. Even so, our body politic, the body of humanity, would go to pieces, if it were to perpetuate the canker of superiority or inferiority.[18]

Moreover, Gandhi held that the principle underlying the *varna* scheme, not simply an Indian or Hindu phenomenon, has universal application. "The world may ignore it today," he predicted, "but it will have to accept it in the time to come."[19]

Clearly Gandhi sought to idealize the ancient *varna* scheme and to protect it from any criticism as an inherently hierarchical system of social organization. We might ask why Gandhi felt it necessary to proclaim his support for an ancient Indian class system at all, and to continue its praises into the mid-1930s. Why did he not instead advocate simple independence and equality, in the mode of *Homo Aequalis*? What was so wrong with "Liberty, Equality, Fraternity"? Many of his colleagues in the independence struggle, educated in modern ideologies of liberalism, socialism, or Marxism, were comfortable doing so.

Gandhi had several reasons to dissent from this path. One was political, and another was nationalist. A third lay in his long-standing critique of those Western liberal ideas of independence and liberty.

In leading the Indian National Congress and the movement for Indian independence, Gandhi sought to hold together an unruly coalition. This included Muslims and orthodox Hindu conservatives, Marxists on the left, and Hindu nationalists on the right. His endorsement of the ancient Vedic ideas of the system of four *varnas* was one effort to maintain the political support of influential conservative Hindu leaders like M. M. Malaviya and Swami Shraddhananda. Prominent Hindu business leaders, such as members of the Birla and Bajaj families, also valued such reinforcements of conservative Hindu verities. Moreover, the idealized Indian social system of the *varnas* was authentically Indian. It was grounded in the most ancient Vedas. At a time and in a movement that prized all things Indian (or *swadeshi*) over things foreign, from homespun khadi cloth to ancient models of social order, the Vedas and the *Bhagavad Gita* enjoyed a higher status than did John Locke or John Stuart Mill.

The third reason takes us back to Gandhi's notion of *swaraj*. Following earlier Indian theorists like Aurobindo Ghosh, Gandhi considered Western ideas of freedom and independence to be essentially negative concepts, pointing simply to the absence of restraint and regulation. Freedom, in this view, was too often construed in Western thought as warranting an individual's unrestrained pursuit of selfish aims without taking responsibility for others. "Life, liberty, and the pursuit of happiness," from the United States Declaration of Independence, seemed to Gandhi a recipe leading to undisciplined anarchy. Accordingly, in an interview with Indian and foreign journalists, Gandhi linked his definition of *swaraj* or self-rule not only to political autonomy or national independence, but also to individual self-restraint:

> The root meaning of *swaraj* is self-rule. *Swaraj* may, therefore, be rendered as disciplined rule from within.... "Independence" has no such limitation. Independence may mean license to do as you like. *Swaraj* is positive. Independence is negative.... The word *swaraj* is a sacred word, a Vedic word, meaning self-rule and self-restraint, and not freedom from all restraint which "independence" often means.[20]

The Vedic model of the four classes, with its notion of inborn qualities and the responsibilities of each one towards the overall functioning of the whole society, fits within Gandhi's ideal definition of *swaraj*. This would be the model that India should follow as it assumed its inevitable national independence.

But by projecting an ideal social model from the Vedic past as the basis for a future independent Indian nation, does Gandhi get away from the inequalities of hierarchy? His critics thought not.

GANDHI AND AMBEDKAR

Gandhi contended with many critics during his years in the public sphere. One of the staunchest and most effective of these was the Dalit leader B. R. Ambedkar, who engaged in a debate with Gandhi over the question of caste society in 1936. "Dalit," or the "oppressed," was the term chosen by Ambedkar and his followers to replace the negative terms "Untouchables" and "Pariahs", and what Ambedkar considered Gandhi's condescending replacement, "Harijans," "children of God."

Ambedkar sets out his argument in a series of numbered points: (1) caste has ruined the Hindus; (2-3) reorganization of Hindu society on the basis of the four *varnas* is impossible and would be harmful; (4) Hindu society must be organized on a basis that recognizes the principles of "Liberty, Equality, Fraternity"; and (5) to achieve this, the religious sanctity associated with castes and *varna* must be destroyed.[21] Ambedkar recognizes the distinction that Gandhi makes between *jati* and *varna*, but he indicates that there is no real difference. It is caste, the system of the *jatis*, that has ruined Hindu society, and Ambedkar believes that this system grows directly out of the earlier principle of four classes, or *varnas*. Both consist essentially of following in one's ancestral calling. Both involve a division of labor in society which is determined by birth. Both claim a "religious sanctity" for a form of social organization. In Ambedkar's view, both systems are based on profound inequality. There is no way to reconcile the ancient Indian system of *varnas* with the values that Ambedkar endorses, the principles of "Liberty, Equality, Fraternity."

Ambedkar also condemned Gandhi's reliance on the *Bhagavad Gita* as a work relevant to present-day concerns. In his essay on "Krishna and His Gita," Ambedkar asserts that the *Gita* is "neither a book of religion nor a treatise on philosophy," but rather an attempt to defend religious dogmas on philosophic grounds.[22] In contrast to Gandhi's active engagement with the *Gita*, Ambedkar argues that it should be regarded as a part of ancient Indian literature, not as a scriptural work deserving continuing adherence or celebration. Therefore, one should approach the text historically, and explore its role within its own political and religious situation. Among the dogmas it defends is the system of four classes, the Chaturvarnya. The *Gita* "offers a philosophical basis to the theory of Chaturvarnya by linking it to the theory of innate, inborn qualities in men."[23] Why was this important? Ambedkar argues that this was a "counter-revolutionary" effort to blunt the effectiveness of the Buddhist critique of class and caste. The Buddha had preached against Chaturvarnya, and the purpose of Krishna's teachings in the *Bhagavad Gita* was to defend the values of *varna* and the Vedic, Brahmanic values that went along with it.

Gandhi responded to Ambedkar's critique by reiterating his own position. After disavowing caste as harmful to both spiritual and national flourishing, Gandhi restates that the law of *varna* teaches us that we have each to earn our bread by following the ancestral calling. It defines not our rights, but our duties. All individual callings are conducive to the welfare of humanity as a whole. Gandhi then goes on to claim that all callings within the system of *varnas* are equal. "The callings of a Brahmin—spiritual teacher—and scavenger are equal, and their due performance carries equal merit before God and at one time seems to have carried identical reward before man. Both are entitled to their livelihood and no more."[24]

For Ambedkar, an Untouchable/Dalit by birth who had earned a doctorate from Columbia University, was a lawyer by training, and a Buddhist by conversion, there was no possibility of reconciling the ancient system of classes, with its three millennia-long legacy of inequality, to the modern Indian society he wished to see. Ambedkar envisioned a new egalitarian India, with both class and caste, *varna* and *jati*, erased from its social fabric. The proper starting point would be the French Declaration of "Liberty, Equality, Fraternity." As principal architect of the Indian Constitution, Ambedkar was able to insert this motto into its Preamble.

Gandhi, a London-trained lawyer and lifelong ecumenical seeker while remaining Hindu, was also a visionary, and his imagined India accommodated the old Vedic system of classes. In the new era of *swaraj*, he averred, the system of *varna* that had been corrupted into the caste society of the *jatis* could become once again a system of equality:

> When we have come into our own, when we have cleansed ourselves, we may have the four *varnas* according to the way in which we can express the best in us. But *varna* then will invest one with higher responsibility and duties. Those who impart knowledge in a spirit of service will be called Brahmanas. They will assume no superior airs but will be true servants of society. When inequality of status of rights is ended, every one of us will be equal. I do not know, however, when we shall be able to revive true *varnadharma*. Its real revival would mean true democracy.[25]

The struggles of independent India in the years since 1947 to achieve Ambedkar's vision of "liberty, equality, fraternity," or to bring Gandhi's vision on "true democracy" into reality, are beyond the scope of this essay. But varieties of social hierarchy are embedded in the Indic notion of *varnas*, reinforced in sacred works like the *Bhagavad Gita*, and reiterated by revered leaders like Gandhi, and are extraordinarily hard to uproot.

NOTES

1. Y. P. Anand, *Mahatma Gandhi's "Works" & Interpretation of the Bhagavad Gita* (New Delhi: Radha, 2009), in 2 vols.
2. On Indian nationalists and the *Bhagavad Gita*, see Richard H. Davis, *The Bhagavad Gita: A Biography*, Lives of Great Religious Books (Princeton, NJ: Princeton University Press, 2015), 115-53; and K. Nagappa Gowda, *The Bhagavadgita in the Nationalist Discourse* (New Delhi: Oxford University Press, 2011). On Gandhi and non-violence in the *Gita*, see Bradley S. Clough, "Gandhi, Nonviolence, and the Bhagavad-Gita," in *Holy War: Violence and the Bhagavad Gita*, ed. Steven J. Rosen (Hampton, VA: Deepak Heritage Books, 2002), 59-80.
3. *Bhagavad Gita*, 4.13 (cited by chapter and verse), translation mine.
4. *Rg Veda*, 10.90 (cited by chap. and verse), in *Pinnacles of India's Past: Selections from the Rgveda*, trans. Walter H. Maurer (Amsterdam: John Benjamins, 1986)
5. Mahatma Gandhi, *The Bhagavad Gita According to Gandhi* (Berkeley, CA: Berkeley Hills Books, 2000), 59-60.
6. For an explication of these two central terms in Gandhi's thought, see Dennis Dalton, *Mahatma Gandhi: Nonviolent Power in Action* (New York: Columbia University Press, 1993), 1-29.
7. Louis Dumont, *Homo Hierarchicus: An Essay on the Caste System*, trans. Mark Sainsbury (Chicago: University of Chicago Press, 1970).
8. Ibid., 236.
9. Mahatma Gandhi, *Collected Works of Mahatma Gandhi* (Delhi: Publications Division, Ministry of Information and Broadcasting, Government of India, 1958-1984), vol. 19:, 242, quoted in ed. *Sources of Indian Traditions. Volume 2. Modern India, Pakistan, and Bangladesh.* 3rd ed., ed. Rachel Fell McDermott et al. (New York: Columbia University Press, 2014), 363.

10. Nicholas B. Dirks, *Castes of Mind: Colonialism and the Making of Modern India* (Princeton, NJ: Princeton University Press, 2001), 234.

11. Gandhi, *Collected Works*, vol. 19, 242, quoted in *Sources of Indian Traditions*, ed. McDermott et al., 363.

12. Mahatma Gandhi, *An Autobiography: The Story of My Experiments with Truth*, trans. Mahadev Desai (Boston: Beacon Press, 1957), 277. See also Ramachandra Guha, *Gandhi Before India* (London: Allen Lane, 2013), 140.

13. Judith M. Brown, *Gandhi: Prisoner of Hope* (New Haven, CT: Yale University Press, 1989), 101. See also Gandhi's own account, in Gandhi, *Autobiography*, 397-99.

14. Gandhi, *Autobiography*, 399.

15. Gandhi, *Collected Works*, vol. 19, 20, quoted in Dalton, *Mahatma Gandhi*, 55.

16. Gandhi, *Collected Works*, vol. 19, 83-84, quoted in Dalton, *Mahatma Gandhi*, 50.

17. Gandhi, *Collected Works*, vol. 35, 519.

18. Ibid., vol. 59, 65-66. The booklet, published September 1934, is in Ibid., vol. 59, 61-67.

19. Ibid., vol. 59, 65.

20. Ibid., vol. 45, 263-64, quoted in Dalton, *Mahatma Gandhi*, 2.

21. *Sources of Indian Traditions*, ed. McDermott et al., 423.

22. B. R. Ambedkar, *The Essential Writings of B. R. Ambedkar*, ed. Valerian Rodrigues (New Delhi: Oxford University Press, 2002), 193.

23. Ibid., 194.

24. *Sources of Indian Traditions*, ed. McDermott et al., 428.

25. Gandhi, *Collected Works*, vol. 62, 291, quoted in Dalton, *Mahatma Gandhi*, 51.

REFERENCES

Ambedkar, B. R. [Bhimrao Ramji]. *The Essential Writings of B. R. Ambedkar*. Edited by Valerian Rodrigues. New Delhi: Oxford University Press, 2002.

Anand, Y. P. *Mahatma Gandhi's "Works" & Interpretation of the Bhagavad Gita*. 2 vols. New Delhi: Radha, 2009.

Brown, Judith M. *Gandhi: Prisoner of Hope*. New Haven, CT: Yale University Press, 1989.

Clough, Bradley S. "Gandhi, Nonviolence, and the Bhagavad-Gita." In *Holy War: Violence and the Bhagavad Gita*, edited by Steven J. Rosen, 59-80. Hampton, VA: Deepak Heritage Books, 2002.

Dalton, Dennis. *Mahatma Gandhi: Nonviolent Power in Action*. New York: Columbia University Press, 1993.

Davis, Richard H. *The Bhagavad Gita: A Biography*. Lives of Great Religious Books. Princeton, NJ: Princeton University Press, 2015.

Dirks, Nicholas B. *Castes of Mind: Colonialism and the Making of Modern India*. Princeton, NJ: Princeton University Press, 2001.

Dumont, Louis. *Homo Hierarchicus: An Essay on the Caste System*. Translated by Mark Sainsbury. Chicago: University of Chicago Press, 1970.

Gandhi, Mahatma. *An Autobiography: The Story of My Experiments with Truth.* Translated by Mahadev Desai. Boston: Beacon Press, 1957.

———. *The Bhagavad Gita According to Gandhi.* Berkeley, CA: Berkeley Hills Books, 2000.

———. *Collected Works of Mahatma Gandhi.* 90 vols. Delhi: Publications Division, Ministry of Information and Broadcasting, Government of India, 1958-1984.

Guha, Ramachandra. *Gandhi Before India.* London: Allen Lane, 2013.

Maurer, Walter H, trans. *Pinnacles of India's Past: Selections from the Rgveda.* Amsterdam: John Benjamins, 1986.

McDermott, Rachel Fell, Leonard A. Gordon, Ainslie T. Embree, Frances W. Pritchett, and Dennis Dalton, eds. *Sources of Indian Traditions. Volume 2. Modern India, Pakistan, and Bangladesh.* 3rd ed. Introduction to Asian Civilizations. New York: Columbia University Press, 2014.

Nagappa Gowda, K. *The Bhagavadgita in the Nationalist Discourse.* New Delhi: Oxford University Press, 2011.

Part III

PHILOSOPHICAL PERSPECTIVES

Chapter 13

Men of Fortitude

Gender and Combatant Non-Immunity in War

Graham Parsons

It is a glorious and manly thing,
To risk one's life in battle with the foe,
Defending loved ones, wife, and native land.

—Tyrtaeus, quoted by Hugo Grotius
in *The Law of Prize and Booty*[1]

The footage is grainy and silent. The young men squat down in a sunken road and look at the camera quizzically as they simultaneously work to attach bayonets to their rifles. The camera scans the line of soldiers weighed down by helmets, packs, and weapons for a little over a minute. The film ends unceremoniously.[2] The contents of this footage give little indication of the gravity of what is witnessed or why the film has become iconic of the sacrifice of men in war. Captured in the film are members of the First Battalion, the Lancashire Fusiliers Regiment on the morning of July 1, 1916, minutes before they, and tens of thousands like them, attack the German line in Northeastern France on the first day of the famous Battle of the Somme. Within a few hours of the recording of the footage most of the men depicted would be dead or wounded, a tiny fraction of the roughly 57,000 men who would be casualties on that single day.

At 7:30 a.m., "zero hour," the First Lancashire Fusiliers rushed over the top of the sides of the sunken road and trenches further west.[3] As happened across the front that morning they only made it a few steps before they were mowed down by machine gun fire. A survivor later described what he experienced.

> Shouts of pain and calls for help could be heard on all sides.... We stepped over mortally wounded men who tried to grab our legs as we passed, [and] ... we squeezed to one side of the trench while wounded men struggled by us anxious to get gaping wounds dressed.... Men uttered terrible curses even as they lay dying from terrible wounds.... Others sat at the bottom of the trench shaking and shouting, not wounded but unable to bear the noise, the smell and the horrible sights.[4]

As he advanced further, this man witnessed his command trying to maintain control.

> The whole road was strewn with dead and dying men. Some were talking deliriously, others calling for help and asking for water.... Then I heard the Colonel calling out for all fit men to line the bank of the road. He was waving his revolver menacingly.... He called for a signaler. One stepped up ... "Get to the top of that road and signal for reinforcements," he thundered. Without a moment's hesitation, the signaler obeyed. But as he raised his flags to send the first letter ... [he] dropped back into the road, riddled with bullets.[5]

A second wave of men burst forward at 8:15 a.m. only to meet the same fate. Survivors of the now depleted battalion hunkered down where they found themselves and tried to tend to those they could reach. Then, amazingly, at 11:45 a.m., the battalion commander, Lieutenant-Colonel Meredith Magniac, received orders to attack again at 12:30 p.m. "with every man you can raise."[6] Magniac responded by explaining the desperate situation to his commander and giving his opinion that another attack will merely increase their casualties. "If you wish, I will of course attack," he wrote, "I consider it is bound to fail. Machine guns are behind debris in village and rake the front."[7]

To his credit, Magniac's commander, Brigadier General Weir De Lancey Williams, responded to this message by immediately calling off the planned attack. Tragically, Williams' reply reached Magniac too late. At 12:30 p.m., having yet received no response from Williams, Magniac obeyed his orders and commanded his men to go over the top. Yet again, they were cut down. The First Lancashire Fusiliers suffered over 500 casualties that morning.

This story illustrates dramatically an important feature of the ethos and law of military service. Soldiers are treated by their leaders and by themselves as sacrificial instruments of war. They are bound to obey orders even when doing so puts their lives at risk. A soldier's interest in not being killed or maimed does not override the duty to obey orders.

The duty to not put one's life before one's orders is made clear to new soldiers from the start. For instance, the enlistment contract that all US volunteers are currently required to sign specifies that the "enlistment/reenlistment agreement is more than an employment contract. It effects a change in status from civilian to military member of the Armed Forces."[8] Unlike civilian employees, members of the US Armed Forces are, among other things, legally "Required to obey all lawful orders and perform all assigned duties," as well as "Required upon order to serve in combat or other hazardous situations."[9]

While some soldiers have always resisted such demands, the story of the Lancashire Fusiliers shows that many embrace them. Although the Colonel was waving his pistol "menacingly," the signaler, who must have known the danger he was in, nevertheless did not hesitate to rush to the top of the trench to execute his order. And though Lieutenant-Colonel Magniac believed executing his own commander's orders would be fruitless, he nevertheless obeyed and ordered his men to attack. Moreover, his men, even after having experienced the morning's horrors, obeyed him. These appear to be cases where soldiers acted on the belief that it is their obligation to face death upon command. Given the carnage across the front that day in 1916 as well as in the exhausting history of warfare, these cases do not appear to be isolated.

The source of this sense of obligation comes from a vision of the good life that is widely embraced by both members of the military and civilians. Self-sacrificial service in war is seen as profoundly honorable. A good person is willing to put his or her life on the line in battle. Such behavior is courageous, valorous, generous, patriotic, chivalrous, brave, and so on. In general, it is a sign of a flourishing moral character. This was certainly true of many of the soldiers in World War I. Lieutenant Vere Harmsworth, for instance, wrote to his uncle as he contemplated his fate before he went into battle for the first time: "Surely it is a life fulfilled if one dies young and healthy fighting for one's country."[10] Harmsworth was killed in action at the age of twenty-one on November 13, 1916. While the poet Wilfred Owen famously mocked such attitudes toward death in World War I, Hugh Sebag-Montefiore concludes in his recent history of the Somme that this sentiment was common in letters from the front before an attack.[11]

MASCULINITY AND SACRIFICE IN WAR

It is not an accident that the office of military servicemember has, until quite recently, been reserved for men exclusively. Indeed, the exclusion of women and all non-males from the military is nearly a universal, cross-cultural phenomenon.[12] Historically, the presence of women in combat units is extremely rare. In fact, when women were allowed in the ranks it was in a non-combat role, such as the US Army Women's Corps, while women who have served in combat were often believed to be men, as was Deborah Samson, a.k.a. Robert Shirtliff, in the American Revolution.[13] Even so, we should not succumb to the illusion that women are or have been passive in war. Women are often enthusiastic supporters of war, acting as advocates, nurturing the wounded, providing comfort, food, and clothing, and raising future fighters. Still, the business of fighting, of life-risking combat, has been seen as a males-only occupation.

The gender exclusivity of military service reflects the close association of war sacrifice with masculinity.[14] Military service and the burdens it entails are central to the idea of manliness. A good man is not simply physically strong and knowledgeable in the arts of violence, he uses this capacity to protect others, thereby putting his body in harm's way for their sake. Facing fire without fear, or at least without debilitating fear, is a reliable way to affirm one's manhood. The self-sacrificial warrior is what Jean Bethke Elshtain calls, "the exemplary male identity."[15]

That military service is essentially masculine is vividly confirmed by some accounts of women who have served recently in combat units. Revealingly, these women report that they had to become masculine in a broad sense in order to integrate into their units. They changed their hair and grooming habits, the way they talked, and the way they walked. There seemed to these women to be a demand that they become more manly.[16] This suggests that while women may be allowed in combat, femininity is not. Military service is still masculine labor.

Boys are taught from a very early age that toughness and courage are the highest virtues of manhood. Preparing oneself for battle, physically and mentally, is one of their most important tasks. They play with toys that simulate fighting and war. They play sports that prize physical, often bruising, competition. They are discouraged from showing feelings of empathy, fear, and sadness. As Joshua Goldstein says,

> Cultures produce male warriors by toughening up boys from an early age... Although boys on average are more prone to more rough-and-tumble play, they are not innately "tougher" than girls. They do not have fewer emotions or attachments, or feel less pain. It is obvious from the huge effort that most cultures make to mold "tough" boys that this is not an easy or natural task. When we raise boys within contemporary gender norms, especially when we push boys to toughen up, we pass along authorized forms of masculinity suited to the war system.[17]

Crucial to this process of enforcing masculinity is the practice of shaming those who do not conform by feminizing them. Any failure to live up to the demands of masculinity is equated with being feminine. Boys and men receive any of a host of misogynistic or homophobic slurs if they are not "tough" enough. Masculinity thus includes a subordinating vision of women and of womanliness. Manhood and womanhood are therefore not isolatable.[18]

This helps explain the hostility toward the inclusion of women in combat roles. General William Westmoreland captured the problem well when he said, "No man of gumption wants a woman to fight his nation's battles."[19] In other words, manliness requires the exclusion of women from combat. The inclusion of women would be to feminize and thereby destroy the masculine character of military service.

We can conclude then that one of the origins of the idea that sacrifice in war is honorable concerns gender, specifically the notion of masculinity. In as much as we endorse masculine virtues, we endorse the goodness of military service. And in as much as we endorse the goodness of military service, we endorse masculine virtues.

GENDER AND DISCRIMINATION IN WAR

Gender norms can influence how we think and act in many ways. Often they cause us to apply principles, rules, or laws in biased ways. We might, for instance, weigh the testimony of a woman differently from that given by a man. If we do this because we implicitly assume women are less trustworthy than men, then we are applying epistemic standards in a gender-biased way.

But there is a more disturbing way gender bias can affect our thinking. As feminist philosophers have shown for centuries, gender bias can infect the very principles, rules, or laws that we apply to the world.[20] Our standards themselves can be gender-biased, which has occurred in many cases. Certainly our notions of marriage and divorce, paternity, and reproductive rights, and of the difference between the public and the private have been shaped by gender. This is a disturbing form of bias that requires a deeper form of change in order to overcome or mitigate it. We are forced to rethink our standards of fairness, justice, rights, equality, or liberty.

I want to show that this form of gender bias is at work in the traditional standards of military ethics. In particular, I will focus on what is known in traditional Just War theory as the *principle of discrimination*, which holds that combatants in war, no matter which side they are on, are legitimate targets of deliberate attack whereas noncombatants are not. This principle is based, in part, on an implicit appeal to the norms of warrior masculinity. Purging the principle of discrimination of this gender influence will require reforming how we think about who is a legitimate target in a war and who is not. In particular, it will require adopting a more restrictive notion of who may be deliberately attacked in war.

The traditional view of discrimination in war divides human communities into two relevant groups—combatants and noncombatants—and demands radically different treatment of them.[21] On the one hand, noncombatants are never to be deliberately attacked. They can, in certain circumstances, be willingly subjected to the risk of unintentional harm, or collateral damage, but cannot be intentionally killed or maimed. The permissibility of endangering the lives of noncombatants unintentionally is governed in part by the principles of necessity and proportionality in accordance with the traditional *theory of double effect*. This theory stipulates that noncombatants can be put in danger of unintentional harm only when it is necessary in order to achieve a military objective, when the objective itself is of sufficient importance, and when the mortal harm brought to the noncombatants is not a means to the fulfillment of that objective. In effect, the theory of double effect applies the other principles of the conduct of war, namely necessity and proportionality, to the moral conundrum of willingly making noncombatants vulnerable to unintentional harm. I will return to this important matter. For now, I want only to emphasize that, according to the traditional principle of discrimination, even where necessity and proportionality dictate otherwise, it is impermissible to subject noncombatants intentionally to direct attack.

On the other hand, the principle of discrimination permits relatively unrestricted attacks on combatants. Regardless of how they came to be combatants (for example, whether they volunteered or were conscripted), and regardless of the justice of their cause (for example, whether they are participating in a colonial conquest or defending others from aggression), those fighting in war are legitimate targets of deliberate attack. To be sure, there are elaborate restrictions on the treatment of captured or surrendered combatants and there are also restrictions on the sort of weapons that may be used against them. Yet, as Michael Walzer puts it, combatants in war are "subject to attack at any time."[22] Even when not currently engaged in combat (for example, asleep, on leave, or retreating), combatants are considered as "fair game." Necessity and proportionality are the ruling principles. As Gabriella Blum concludes, "The striking feature of the mainstream literature is its general acceptance (albeit at times with some moral discomfort) of the near-absolute license to kill all combatants and of the law's view of combatants as nothing more than instruments of war."[23]

The vast majority of the philosophical literature on discrimination in war has focused on the prohibition of attacks on noncombatants. This literature is rich and valuable. Moreover, I suspect that there a fruitful gender analysis to be done on this side of the discrimination coin.[24] However, I will focus on the unqualified permission to attack combatants. There is a small body of literature critical of the traditional permissiveness regarding attacks on combatants.[25] I wish to add my voice to this literature. Unlike the other critics, however, I will try to show the role that gender has played in legitimating the traditional view.

Consider an incident in World War II: The Battle of the Bismarck Sea off the northeastern coast of New Guinea. On the morning of March 3, 1943,

Allied planes closed in on Japanese ships transporting the entire Fifty-first division, roughly 7,000 men. The Allied planes attacked at low-altitude with 0.50 caliber guns and bombs. Japanese soldiers were gunned down as they tried to escape ships hit by bombs. Many Japanese made it into the water and climbed onto lifeboats. Still, they were strafed by planes over and over again. As one account described it, "The water was whipped into a bloody froth, the blood mixing with chunks of flesh and the oil from the sunken ships. There was no respite for the survivors, who now floated defenseless, naked and exposed to machine gun fire. The grisly business continued into the night. When nothing was seen to move in the water, the strafing runs ended."[26] Reportedly, "some allied pilots and crews became sick and vomited at the low-level sight of the carnage their bullets and cannon shots were causing."[27] Almost 3,000 Japanese soldiers were killed in the attack.

As was the case throughout the war in the Pacific, and as is typical in conventional warfare generally, Allied forces adopted the policy that any Japanese combatant may be attacked without hesitation. There appears to have been no effort to rescue, to capture, or to solicit the surrender of Japanese forces even when they were floating in the open ocean. Although there is good reason to doubt that Japanese soldiers would have allowed themselves to be captured or to surrender, even to save themselves from drowning, allied forces appear to have had no sense of an obligation to try to avoid killing or maiming their enemies even when they were so vulnerable and defenseless. As long as they were classified as combatants they were treated as fair game. Prior to attacking combatants, one need not first determine if the attack is necessary to attain a military objective or if the attained military objective is sufficiently valuable to be worthy of the attack. It is presumed to be the responsibility of the combatants to declare their surrender in order to avoid being attacked. Until that time, they are subject to attack.

As the nausea of Allied airmen might indicate, many of us sense that the treatment of the Japanese in the Battle of the Bismarck Sea is morally questionable. However, the incident does not appear to violate the traditional principle of discrimination.

THE DEFENSE OF COMBATANT NON-IMMUNITY

Many reasons are offered to justify the traditional view of the non-immunity of combatants. Two arguments have been very influential:

The Argument from Moral Non-Innocence

The concept of *innocence* (whose root meaning is *not causing harm*) has been central to debates focus about discrimination. For many commentators, innocence is what distinguishes those who are not legitimate targets in war from those who are. The innocent are not liable to attack and they retain their right not be harmed. The not-innocent (those causing harm) are liable to attack. Moreover, the same commentators commonly treat the innocent as noncombatants and the not-innocent are combatants. Thus, the concept of innocence in war has provided an important moral criterion for distinguishing between combatants and noncombatants and for supporting the permissibility of attacking combatants.

However, a deep dispute has grown about the relevant meaning of "innocence." One side of this dispute holds that we ought to apply a strictly *moral* conception of innocence to the issue of discrimination in war. That is to say, those who are innocent in war are those who have done nothing morally wrong that makes them liable to attack, while the not-innocent in war are those who have committed, or currently are committing, a moral wrong and thus are liable to attack.

According to proponents of this view, the traditional view of the non-immunity of combatants is correct because combatants are committing a moral wrong by virtue of their prosecuting an unjust war. Noncombatants, on the other hand, are not prosecuting a war at all and so have done nothing wrong to make them liable to attack. On this view, a combatant is like a person who attacks you on the street in order to steal your wallet. The attack makes the assailant liable to defensive violence in order to stop it. Noncombatants, however, are like bystanders who happen to be in the vicinity of your assault on the street. Since they have done nothing to make themselves liable to attack, it would be wrong for you to attack any of them, even if it would help you thwart the assault. This view has become extremely popular in recent decades and forms the heart of what is known as "revisionist just war theory."[28]

However, the sixteenth century theologian and philosopher, Francisco de Vitoria, was also an exponent of this view.[29] By "innocent" Vitoria appears to mean "not morally responsible" and by "not innocent" he means the opposite, referring to the not-innocent in war as "wicked." He argues that, just as it would be wrong to punish a person for a crime for which he is not responsible, it be wrong to defend oneself by deliberately injuring a person who is not morally responsible for the threat one is attempting to repel.[30] Accordingly, Vitoria regards combatants in war to have done wrong by participating in an unjust war, for which reason they are legitimate targets of deliberate attack, whereas noncombatants are not.

One problem with this argument is that, even if correct, it does not prove as much it intends. Even if combatants are legitimate targets because they are doing wrong by prosecuting an unjust war, it would only follow that the combatants serving in an unjust war are legitimate targets. Combatants in a just war would not be doing anything that would make them liable to attack. But the traditional view holds that combatants on all sides in a war, just or unjust, are legitimate targets. Consequently, the argument from moral non-innocence does not offer an unqualified defense of the traditional principle of discrimination. This, of course, is precisely what the revisionist just war theorists want us to recognize. Many of them believe we ought to abandon the traditional principle of discrimination altogether.[31]

But there is a bigger problem for the argument from moral non-innocence. The claim that combatants in an unjust war are personally acting wrongly contradicts other basic commitments of traditional just war theory as well as the ethos and law of military service. Traditional just war theory, as well as the culture and law of the military, embrace the *theory of public war* which holds that soldiers act as the moral instruments of their political sovereigns. Soldiers are not responsible for the justice of the wars they fight but are obligated to fight upon the command of their sovereign. The obligation to serve upon command is not absolute because, according to the traditional view, soldiers should refuse to participate when the war is patently unjust, but if they are uncertain whether the war is just or unjust, they are obligated to participate if so ordered by their sovereign.[32]

This is how Vitoria treated the question of uncertainty. He writes that "lesser subjects who are not invited to be heard in the councils of the prince nor in public council are not required to examine the causes of war, but may lawfully go to war trusting the judgment of their superiors."[33] Thus, even when a soldier doubts the morality of his sovereign's war, he is still obligated to obey. To think otherwise is to assume that, "If I am in doubt whether the prince's war is just or whether the cause of a particular war is just, it follows immediately that I must doubt whether or not I may lawfully fight."

Here is his argument:

> I admit that it is never lawful to act against a conscientious doubt, so that if I am in doubt whether I should act or not it is a sin to act. But it is incorrect to deduce that if I am in doubt as to whether the cause of war is just, I must therefore doubt whether I may lawfully make war, or fight in that war. In fact, we must deduce just the opposite: If I am in doubt about the justice of war, it follows that it is lawful for me to go to war at the command of my prince. In the same way, if an officer of the law is in doubt whether the judge's sentence is just, it is quite invalid to conclude that he must doubt whether he may lawfully carry out that sentence; on the contrary, indeed, he knows very well that he is required to carry out the sentence of his superior.[34]

But Vitoria also contends that soldiers fighting an unjust war are "wicked," acting immorally, which makes his position inconsistent. He cannot have it both ways. If soldiers are bound to participate in war upon command, then they are not necessarily doing anything wrong by participating in an unjust war. If soldiers who do serve in an unjust war are necessarily acting immorally, then they cannot be obligated to participate in war upon command.

The Argument from Material Non-Innocence

Another defense of the traditional principle of discrimination has also been influential. According to it, combatants in war are liable to attack, not because they have done something wrong, but because they are currently threatening their enemies, rightly or wrongly. According to this view, in as much as they are engaged in fighting, combatants are thereby liable to attack by their opponents. It is by becoming combatants as such that they lose their right not to be attacked. Noncombatants, however, are not threatening their enemies and are therefore not liable to attack.

The turning point of this argument, as with the previous one, is the meaning of "innocence." The word is here used in a non-moral sense. The innocent, according to this view, are those who are simply not threatening others. The reasons for threatening others are irrelevant. To threaten others is simply to give up one's innocence. The seminal articulation of this position is to be found in Michael Walzer's classic work, *Just and Unjust Wars*. Noncombatants are never legitimate targets since, Walzer maintains, they are "innocent…, a term of art which means that they have done nothing, and are doing nothing that entails the loss of their rights."[35] The same cannot be said of combatants. Combatants are liable to attack because "simply by fighting, whatever their private hopes and intentions, [combatants] have lost their title to life and liberty, and they have lost it even though, unlike aggressor states, they have committed no crime."[36]

This view does a better job producing a defense of all the aspects of the traditional principle of discrimination than the previous argument. In particular, if true, it would follow from this argument that the combatants on all sides of a war are liable to be attacked. The argument from moral innocence only justified attacks against combatants fighting in an unjust war.

Nevertheless, the second argument also significant weaknesses. To begin with, it seems unconvincing as a theory of justified violence. As Walzer himself admits, this view of liability to attack does not apply to other areas of social life. The person who attacks me on the street to take my wallet is liable to attack. However, if I were to engage in defensive violence against this assailant, I do not in turn become liable to attack simply because I now constitute a threat to the assailant. Surely I maintain my right not to be attacked even when I use violence to protect myself in situations like this. But the view of liability to attack presupposed by the present argument would seem to entail that people become liable to attack merely by defending themselves against unjust violence. This seems indefensible. It is simply wrong to assert that one's liability to attack is independent of the morality of one's actions.[37]

But there is a further problem for this argument. As with the previous one (the argument from moral non-innocence), the present argument runs into trouble when we try to reconcile it with the theory of public war, in particular with the principle that soldiers are obligated to threaten their enemies when so ordered by their commanders. But according to the present argument, soldiers by so doing lose their right not to be attacked. This invites an objection on the grounds of fairness (or something like it). It seems like a cruel trick to hold that it would be wrong for one not to engage in an activity *and* that one forfeits the right not to be harmed by engaging in that very activity. Soldiers caught in that position might well complain that they have no way to preserve their right not to be harmed. But beyond this concern, the problem with this argument is that it seems to over-determine the soldiers' liability to attack in war. If they are obligated to engage in combat despite its life-risking character, they have *already* lost their right not to be harmed. Being bound to fight upon command has rendered them able to be sacrificed in war. For this reason, the theory of public war embraced by traditional just war theory seems to make the second argument superfluous.

Gender, Public War, and Discrimination

I have tried to show that the typical defenses of the traditional principle of discrimination are inadequate. One reason they are inadequate comes to light when we try to reconcile them with the theory of public war, that is, with the idea that soldiers are obligated to serve in war upon command. This tension between the traditional defenses of the principle of discrimination and the theory of public war is revealing. If we examine classic arguments in defense of public war and the obligation of soldiers to serve in war upon command, we find that at their core are appeals to norms of masculinity. Hence, gender grounds the traditional reasoning about the obligations of soldiers to serve in war. Revealing the role of gender in traditional military ethics opens the possibility that gender also grounds the traditional principle of discrimination.

The appeal to gender in traditional just war theory is subtle yet unmistakable. When traditional military ethicists attempt to explain how it is that a political subject is bound to engage in life-risking battle upon command they appeal to the virtues of masculinity. The theory of public war is based on the idea that it is good for men *as men* to risk their lives in war for the sake of their communities. However, early modern military ethicists struggled more than their predecessors (such as Vitoria) to justify the duties of military service, because in the early modern period the rights of individuals began to form the foundations of political justice. Since the obligation to risk one's life for the sake of the community implies that the community is more important than the individual, it was a distinct challenge for these theorists to justify the obligations of military service. They thus worked hard to justify military service, offering substantive discussions of the basis of the obligations of soldiers. To illustrate, I will briefly describe the efforts of four such theorists: Grotius, von Pufendorf, Hobbes, and Vattel.

For Hugo Grotius, the duty to face danger in combat arises from natural virtue. He writes that "some Acts of Virtue may by a human law be commanded, though under the evident Hazard of Death. As for a Soldier not to quit his Post."[38] The relevant virtue for Grotius here is charity.[39] While charity is not immediately associated with masculinity, an early work of his appeals more clearly to gender. In this work, Grotius praises risking one's life for the state as an expression of the natural virtue of fortitude, one of the two virtues "most beneficial [to others], both in private and in public life."[40] Indeed, Grotius genders the virtue. In the same passage, he quotes approvingly a passage from Tyrtaeus: "It is a glorious and manly thing, / To risk one's life in battle with the foe, / Defending loved ones, wife and native land."[41]

Samuel von Pufendorf appeals directly to the virtue of bravery on which to base the duty to risk one's life in war. According to him, it would simply be cowardly for a man to refuse to engage in combat out of fear of injury or death. In fact, Pufendorf claims that a good man will praise his commander for ordering him to risk his life: A soldier "is bound to defend the Post his Commander appoints him to, tho' perhaps he foresees he must in all probability lose his Life in it.... And no man of Bravery or Spirit will ever complain that he is commanded upon such a Duty, but will rather commend his General's Judgment and Conduct in it."[42] Bravery and spirit are central to masculinity and help form the foundation of Pufendorf's theory of public war.

Thomas Hobbes, who struggled mightily in his *Leviathan* to justify the obligations of soldiers, clearly presupposes a warrior's masculinity as natural. He excuses women and feminine men from the duty to serve in war upon command. He declares that "there is allowance to be made for natural timorousness, not only to women (of whom no such dangerous duty is expected), but also to men of feminine courage."[43] As we can see, the basis of the exception here is a presumed character deficiency in women and some men. Feminine people are timorous; they have inadequate courage; they lack the moral character that would enable them to put their lives on the line in war upon command. This sort of character is to be expected of women but not of men, whereas the deficiency in men must be rare enough that, not only can we burden men with the political obligation to serve in war, we also can be confident that the commonwealth will have a sufficient pool of soldiers on which to rely in the event of war. Hobbes also relies on gender difference when he defends his claim that the succession of the throne should go to the monarch's male over his female offspring. This is because "men are naturally fitter than women, for actions of labor and danger."[44]

Emer de Vattel also relies on gender division when setting out the duties of military service. "Every man capable of carrying arms should take them up at the first order of him who has the power of making war.... Although there be some women who are equal to men in strength and courage, yet such instances are not usual; and rules must necessarily be general, and derived from the ordinary course of things."[45] Only men have the political obligation to participate in military service, Vattel claims, because men, by nature, are inclined to have the moral character suited to "supporting the fatigues of war." In particular, men tend to have the courage to risk their lives in battle upon command. For a man to fail to do this is a peculiar kind of moral failure, far worse than the same failure in a woman.

Each of these authorities reveals that norms of masculinity ground the obligations of military service in the theory of public war. Also, it should be no surprise that the gender norms endorsed by many cultures, which encourage boys and men to find honor in self-sacrificial service in war, have also percolated through our theories of military ethics. Gender bias has therefore infected the standards we have been accustomed to use in the evaluation of military conduct.

How has this affected the traditional principle of discrimination in war? Suppose for the moment that the theory of public war with its gender foundation is true. That is to say, suppose that legitimate political authorities have the right to raise military forces, whether through voluntary enlistment or through conscription, and have the right to command them in life-risking combat. Given the gender foundation of military policy, the soldiers in these forces (all assumed to be men) are dispensable in war *as men*, because it is honorable for them to give their lives in war for their communities. Now suppose that two public bodies, each with their own legitimate political authority, are at war with each other, deploying their respective forces. Under the theory of public war, the soldiers on either side engaged in combat would be obliged to obey the commands of their superiors. And they would have this obligation because, as men, they become sacrificial in war.

Against this background, we can ask ourselves: "Which members of the communities are legitimate targets of deliberate attack and which are not?" The answer jumps immediately to the fore: only the soldiers are legitimate targets and everyone else is not. In other words, the traditional principle of discrimination seems like the right answer. This is because, according to the theory of public war, all members of the military have been rendered sacrificial in war, independent of the reasons for that particular war. Each political community has exercised its rights to take away the rights of certain members not to be killed, namely those who are naturally bound to give their lives in war. No other members of the community have such a natural duty. Thus, it seems that the theory of public war neatly produces the traditional principle of discrimination. In view of the inadequacies found in the typical defenses of the traditional principle, we should ask ourselves if this principle is really being supported by the assumption of gender norms in the theory of public war.[46]

"DEGENDERING" DISCRIMINATION IN WAR

The traditional principle of discrimination in war allows for relatively unrestricted attacks on combatants in war, presuming them by default to be legitimate targets. There is no expectation that, prior to attacking, it be determined that a particular combatant needs to be attacked in order to attain a strategic goal or that a particular combatant's life is worth taking in order to achieve a given goal. One can kill or maim combatants without hesitation. We have struggled to find a good justification for this permission. In fact, it appears that a false assumption of gender norms explains the sacrificial status of combatants.

I would like to close by proposing a *Revised Principle of Discrimination* that is more defensible:

> Noncombatants in war are never to be deliberately attacked whereas combatants may be deliberately attacked only when (a) the attack is necessary in order to achieve a strategic goal, and (b) that goal is of sufficient significance to merit the attack.

The important change is that the revision establishes conditions on attacks against combatants. In particular, the principles of necessity and of proportionality now govern strikes against combatants. According to the revised principle, combatants are not simply "fair game." They may be attacked only when there is good reason to believe they need to be attacked in order to achieve the mission at hand and the mission must be worth taking the combatant's lives or limbs. Combatants should not merely be thought of as the sacrificial instruments of war. In effect, the revised principle adopts an approach similar to that taken by the traditional principle of double effect regarding noncombatants. Recall that the traditional principle permits risking unintentional harms to noncombatants only when those risks are necessary to achieve the mission and when they are proportional to the value of the mission. The revised principle of discrimination asks us to think of deliberate attacks against combatants in the same way.

Returning to the Battle of the Bismarck Sea, the revised principle would question the permissibility of the Allied attacks on Japanese combatants, especially those combatants adrift in the open ocean. It is at least arguable that strafing the ocean surface in order to kill as many defenseless Japanese soldiers as possible served no significant military purpose or, if it did, the purpose was of limited value compared to the number of Japanese lives at stake. I will not claim that the attacks were not in fact necessary or proportionate. It might turn out that they were. The point is that we cannot simply presume that, because the victims were classified as combatants, the lethal attack on them were permissible. It must be shown first that the attack is necessary and proportionate. This was not done in the Battle of the Bismarck Sea, despite the fact that a reasonable person could doubt the attack was necessary and proportional.

The revised principle of discrimination which I propose is not based on the liability of combatants to deliberate attack. Instead, it is based on the value of the military objective, or the just cause of the war. The revised principle simply asserts that when it is necessary to achieve the military objective, and when it is proportionate to the value of that objective, combatants may be deliberately attacked. On this view, combatants have done nothing to make themselves liable to attack. They may be killed nonetheless because they need to be in order to attain the just cause. Certainly, many philosophers will object to the absence of an appeal to liability in this account.

One issue of concern here is that without an appeal to the liability of combatants as such there is nothing to prohibit deliberate attacks against noncombatants. What happens if deliberately attacking noncombatants is necessary and proportionate to achieve the objective of the war? It would seem that the rationale behind the revised principle would have to permit such attacks on noncombatants in such circumstances. Despite the revised principle's prohibition of attacks on noncombatants, there seems to be no substantive defense of this prohibition. This is a serious objection. I agree that without full substantiation the revised principle cannot offer a meaningful prohibition of attacks against noncombatants. Still, I believe some substantiation can be offered.

The reason that the revised principle of discrimination can prohibit attacks on noncombatants is that, in the vast majority of cases, such attacks are in fact not necessary in order to achieve a just cause for war. Presuming that the only just cause for war is to thwart aggression consistent with the rights of the enemy to political autonomy, just wars should harm the enemy as little as possible in order to thwart their aggression. The goal of a just war is simply to force the enemy to abandon their aggressive project. This should be done with as little injury to the enemy as possible.

I submit that deliberate attacks on noncombatants fail to live up to the demand that we minimize injury to our enemies. Unlike much traditional thinking, this is not because combatants are subject to being sacrificed whereas noncombatants are not. Rather, it is because attacks on noncombatants will escalate the war and make the enemy less likely to capitulate, thereby prolonging the fight and leading to greater harm. Attacks on noncombatants make communities less likely to capitulate because they foster resentment and heighten fear that the enemy's war aims exceed the limited ends of a just war. Communities during a war are quite vulnerable. Their very survival is at stake, or at least is feared to be, and fear encourages a tendency to find evidence of the worst possible intentions on the part on the enemy. Deliberate attacks on noncombatants are taken by their victims as evidence that their enemy seeks to destroy or exterminate their community, which in turn galvanizes their resistance and undermines their willingness to negotiate. They increasingly see the enemy as people with whom peace is impossible.[47] But limiting attacks only to combatants can provide them possibly convincing evidence that peace consistent with their rights as a political community is the ultimate goal of the war. For this reason, it is not necessary to deliberately attack noncombatants in a just war. However, it could be necessary and proportionate to attack combatants.

Such is what a "degendered" principle of discrimination could look like.

NOTES

1. Tyrtaeus, *Elegies*, quoted in Hugo Grotius, *Commentary on the Law of Prize and Booty* (1603), ed. Martine Julia van Ittersum (Indianapolis: Liberty Fund, 2006), http://oll.libertyfund.org/titles/1718 (accessed April 21, 2018).
2. Geoffrey Malins, "Sunken Lane," YouTube video, 0.51, posted July 19, 2016, https://www.youtube.com/watch?v=3Sb7urnjEaE (accessed April 21, 2018).
3. The following account is drawn from Hugh Sebag-Montefiore, *Somme: Into the Breach* (Cambridge, MA: Harvard University Press, 2016), 92-106.
4. Sebag-Montefiore, *Somme*, 96.
5. Sebag-Montefiore, *Somme*, 96.
6. Sebag-Montefiore, *Somme*, 97.
7. Sebag-Montefiore, *Somme*, 97.
8. U.S. Department of Defense, "Enlistment/Reenlistment Document Armed Forces of the United States," DD Form 4/1, October 2007, at 2, http://www.esd.whs.mil/Portals/54/Documents/DD/forms/dd/dd0108.pdf (accessed April 21, 2018).
9. U.S. Department of Defense, "Enlistment/Reenlistment Document."
10. Sebag-Montefiore, *Somme*, 518.
11. Sebag-Montefiore, *Somme*, 518.
12. Joshua S. Goldstein, *War and Gender: How Gender Shapes the War System and Vice Versa* (Cambridge and New York: Cambridge University Press, 2001), 10-22.
13. Jean Bethke Elshtain, *Women and War* (Chicago: University of Chicago Press, 1995), 174-75.

14. See Tom Digby, *Love and War: How Militarism Shapes Sexuality and Romance* (New York: Columbia University Press, 2014); Goldstein, *War and Gender*; and Elshtain, *Women and War.*

15. Elshtain, *Women and War*, 205.

16. Anthony C. King, "The Female Soldier," *Parameters* 43, no. 2 (Summer 2013): 13.

17. Goldstein, *War and Gender*, 287-88.

18. See Digby, *Love and War*; and Goldstein, *War and Gender.*

19. General William Westmoreland, quoted in Goldstein, *War and Gender*, 283.

20. For a sense of this literature see Jean Bethke Elshtain, *Public Man, Private Woman: Women in Social and Political Thought* (Princeton, NJ: Princeton University Press, 1982).; Susan Moller Okin, *Justice, Gender, and the Family* (New York: Basic Books, 1989); and Carole Pateman, *The Sexual Contract* (Stanford, CA: Stanford University Press, 1988).

21. For some classic statements of this principle see Francisco de Vitoria, "On the Law of War," in *Vitoria: Political Writings* (1528), ed. Anthony Pagden and Jeremy Lawrance (New York: Cambridge University Press, 1991), 293-327; Francisco Suárez, "A Work on the Three Theological Virtues," in *Selections from Three Works* (1621), ed. Thomas Pink (Indianapolis, IN: Liberty Fund, 2015), 829-989; Samuel von Pufendorf, *The Law of Nature and Nations: Eight Books* (1672), 4th ed., trans. Basil Kennett, ed. and corr. Jean Barbeyrac (Clark, NJ: Lawbook Exchange, 2005); Emer de Vattel, *The Law of Nations* (1758), ed. Béla Kapossy and Richard Whatmore (Indianapolis, IN: Liberty Fund, Inc., 2008); and Michael Walzer, *Just and Unjust Wars: A Moral Argument with Historical Illustrations*, 5th ed. (New York: Basic Books, 2015).

22. Walzer, *Just and Unjust Wars*, 138.

23. Gabriella Blum, "The Dispensable Lives of Soldiers," *Journal of Legal Analysis* 2, no. 1 (Spring 2010), 69-124, at 72, https://dash.harvard.edu/bitstream/handle/1/4324405/dispensiblelives.pdf?sequence=1 (accessed April 21, 2018).

24. For an attempt to show the role of gender here see Helen M. Kinsella, "Gendering Grotius: Sex and Sex Difference in the Laws of War," *Political Theory* 34, no. 2 (2006): 161-91.

25. See Blum, "Dispensable Lives of Soldiers."

26. Quoted in Arthur Herman, *Douglas MacArthur: American Warrior* (New York: Random House, 2016), 469.

27. Quoted in Herman, *Douglas MacArthur*, 469.

28. For examples of this school see Jeff McMahan, *Killing in War* (New York: Oxford University Press, 2009); Helen Frowe, *Defensive Killing* (New York: Oxford University Press, 2014); Seth Lazar, *Sparing Civilians* (New York: Oxford University Press, 2015); and Lazar, "Evaluating the Revisionist Critique of Just War Theory," *Daedalus* 146, no. 1 (Winter 2017): 113-24; and Cécile Fabre, *Cosmopolitan War* (New York: Oxford University Press, 2012).

29. Vitoria, "On the Law of War," 314-15. Hugo Grotius is arguably another classical defender of this view of discrimination. See his *Rights of War and Peace* (1625), ed. Richard Tuck (Indianapolis, IN: Liberty Fund, 2005).

30. Vitoria, "On the Law of War," 282-83.

31. See especially, McMahan, *Killing in War*; and Frowe, *Defensive Killing*.

32. See Vitoria, "On the Law of War"; Suarez, "Work on the Three Theological Virtues"; Grotius, *Rights of War and Peace*; Pufendorf, *Law of Nature and Nations*; Vattel, *Law of Nations*; and Walzer, *Just and Unjust Wars*. For discussion see my "Public War and the Moral Equality of Combatants," *Journal of Military Ethics* 11, no. 4 (Winter 2012): 299-317.

33. Vitoria. "On the Law of War," 308.

34. Vitoria. "On the Law of War," 312.

35. Walzer, *Just and Unjust Wars*, 146.

36. Walzer, *Just and Unjust Wars*, 136.

37. For more thorough articulations of this objection see Jeff McMahan, "Innocence, Self-Defense, and Killing in War," *Journal of Political Philosophy* 2, no. 3 (September 1994): 193-221; and David Rodin, *War and Self-Defense* (New York: Oxford University Press, 2002).

38. Grotius, *Rights of War and Peace*, bk. 1, chap. 4, sec. 7, 357.

39. Grotius, *Rights of War and Peace*, bk. 2, chap. 25, sec. 7, 1158.

40. Grotius, *Commentary*, ed. Ittersum, 440.

41. Grotius, *Commentary*, ed. Ittersum, 441.

42. Pufendorf, *Law of Nature and Nations*, bk. 8, chap. 2, sec. 4, 759.

43. Thomas Hobbes, *Leviathan* (1651), ed. Edwin Curley (Indianapolis, IN: Hackett Publishing, 1994), chap. 21, sec. 16, 142.

44. Hobbes, *Leviathan* (1651), ed. Curley, chap. 19, sec. 22, 126.

45. Vattel, *Law of Nations*, bk. 3, chap. 2, sec. 10, 474.

46. For one scholar who argues that gender plays a role in legitimating combatant non-immunity, see Helen M. Kinsella, *The Image Before the Weapon: A Critical History of the Distinction between Combatant and Civilian* (Ithaca, NY: Cornell University Press, 2011).

47. This appears to be how Germans responded to Allied terror bombing in World War II. See Nicholas Stargardt, *The German War: A Nation Under Arms, 1939-45* (New York: Basic Books, 2015).

REFERENCES

Blum, Gabriella. "The Dispensable Lives of Soldiers." *Journal of Legal Analysis* 2, no. 1 (Spring 2010), 69-124. https://dash.harvard.edu/bitstream/handle/1/4324405/dispensiblelives.pdf?sequence=1 (accessed April 21, 2018).

Digby, Tom. *Love and War: How Militarism Shapes Sexuality and Romance*. New York: Columbia University Press, 2014.

Elshtain, Jean Bethke. *Public Man, Private Woman: Women in Social and Political Thought*. Princeton, NJ: Princeton University Press, 1982.

———. *Women and War*. Chicago: University of Chicago Press, 1995.

Fabre, Cécile. *Cosmopolitan War*. New York: Oxford University Press, 2012.

Frowe, Helen. *Defensive Killing*. New York: Oxford University Press, 2014.

Goldstein, Joshua S. *War and Gender: How Gender Shapes the War System and Vice Versa*. Cambridge and New York: Cambridge University Press, 2001.
Grotius, Hugo. *Commentary on the Law of Prize and Booty* (1603). Edited by Martine Julia van Ittersum. Indianapolis: Liberty Fund, 2006. http://oll.libertyfund.org/titles/1718 (accessed April 21, 2018).
———. *Rights of War and Peace* (1625). Edited by Richard Tuck. 3 vols. Indianapolis, IN: Liberty Fund, 2005.
Herman, Arthur. *Douglas MacArthur: American Warrior*. New York: Random House, 2016.
Hobbes, Thomas. *Leviathan* (1651). Edited by Edwin Curley. Indianapolis, IN: Hackett Publishing, 1994.
King, Anthony C. "The Female Soldier." *Parameters* 43, no. 2 (Summer 2013): 13-25.
Kinsella, Helen M. "Gendering Grotius: Sex and Sex Difference in the Laws of War." *Political Theory* 34, no. 2 (2006): 161-91.
———. *The Image Before the Weapon: A Critical History of the Distinction between Combatant and Civilian*. Ithaca, NY: Cornell University Press, 2011.
Lazar, Seth. "Evaluating the Revisionist Critique of Just War Theory." *Daedalus* 146, no. 1 (Winter 2017): 113-24.
———. *Sparing Civilians*. New York: Oxford University Press, 2015.
Malins, Geoffrey. "Sunken Lane." YouTube video, 0.51. Posted July 19, 2016. https://www.youtube.com/watch?v=3Sb7urnjEaE (accessed April 21, 2018).
McMahan, Jeff. "Innocence, Self-Defense, and Killing in War." *Journal of Political Philosophy* 2, no. 3 (September 1994): 193-221.
———. *Killing in War*. New York: Oxford University Press, 2009.
Okin, Susan Moller. *Justice, Gender, and the Family*. New York: Basic Books, 1989.
Parsons, Graham. "Public War and the Moral Equality of Combatants." *Journal of Military Ethics* 11, no. 4 (Winter 2012): 299-317.
Pateman, Carole. *The Sexual Contract*. Stanford, CA: Stanford University Press, 1988.
Pufendorf, Samuel von. *The Law of Nature and Nations: Eight Books* (1672). 4th ed. Translated by Basil Kennett. Edited and corrected by Jean Barbeyrac. Clark, NJ: Lawbook Exchange, 2005.
Rodin, David. *War and Self-Defense*. New York: Oxford University Press, 2002.
Sebag-Montefiore, Hugh. *Somme: Into the Breach*. Cambridge, MA: Harvard University Press, 2016.
Stargardt, Nicholas. *The German War: A Nation Under Arms, 1939-45*. New York: Basic Books, 2015.
Suárez, Francisco. "A Work on the Three Theological Virtues." In *Selections from Three Works* (1621), edited by Thomas Pink, 829-989. Indianapolis: Liberty Fund, 2015. 829-989.
Tyrtaeus. *Elegies*. In *Commentary on the Law of Prize and Booty* (1603), edited by Martine Julia van Ittersum. Indianapolis, IN: Liberty Fund, 2006. http://oll.libertyfund.org/titles/1718 (accessed April 21, 2018).
U.S. Department of Defense. "Enlistment/Reenlistment Document Armed Forces of the United States." DD Form 4/1. October 2007. http://www.esd.whs.mil/Portals/54/Documents/DD/forms/dd/dd0108.pdf (accessed April 21, 2018).

Vattel, Emer de. *The Law of Nations* (1758). Edited by Béla Kapossy and Richard Whatmore. Indianapolis, IN: Liberty Fund, Inc., 2008.
Vitoria, Francisco de. "On the Law of War." In *Vitoria: Political Writings* (1528), edited by Anthony Pagden and Jeremy Lawrance, 293-327. New York: Cambridge University Press, 1991.
Walzer, Michael. *Just and Unjust Wars: A Moral Argument with Historical Illustrations*. 5th ed. New York: Basic Books, 2015.

Chapter 14

Minding Gibbon's Manners

Unwritten Rules and the Rhetoric of Equality

Hugh Liebert

How do we know when a democracy is no longer a democracy? More broadly, how do we know when *any* regime has changed? Is regime change a political fact having to do with the definition of citizenship, a legal fact one can trace in jurisprudence, or an economic fact having to do with the distribution of income? To some extent, regime change can be all of these. But it is also a change in the way individuals relate to one another.

Consider neighborliness, or how we treat the people that we meet each day.[1] If people we once encountered as equals—speaking frankly, looking them straight in the eye, shaking hands—come, over time, to seem significantly superior or inferior to us, such that we can no longer be as free and easy around them as we had been, what has changed? Nothing overt in our political, legal, or economic situation has necessarily changed. No written, legally binding code detailing social behavior has been revised in committee. The rules of neighborliness are not those sorts of rules. Nor are they moral duties, at least by most understandings of moral duty. I may be obliged to respect, even love my neighbor, but I am not obliged in quite the same way to smile and wave when we pass each other on the sidewalk. The rules of neighborliness are not codified, yet everyone knows them. To the extent they are enforced, it is through opinion, or with praise and shame. When I consider what happens when I do not treat a neighbor as we both understand that I should, I can recognize that my life is governed by a host of rules that are not "laws." They are not written down, not publicly deliberated in a body designated for that purpose, not enforced through coercion or penalty—but they are nevertheless binding on me. Although it feels more fitting to call them customs and ascribe to them a social rather than political meaning, these rules clearly have political significance. When I encounter neighbors as equals, I share one kind of life with them; when they are encountered as superiors or inferiors, I share with them another sort of life.[2] We can imagine a neighborhood or a nation changing from one way of life to another.

If the unwritten rules governing neighborliness merely mirrored political, legal, or economic facts, such that a change in the latter necessitated a change in the former, these unwritten rules would not constitute a particularly interesting field of study. But there is reason to think that the development of unwritten rules has its own tendencies, sometimes lagging behind developments in other areas, sometimes anticipating them, and sometimes moving in an opposite direction entirely. In one neighborhood, increasing economic inequality might lead to a breakdown or redefinition of neighborliness; in another, an egalitarian conception of neighborliness might seem all the more binding in response to emerging inequalities in other areas. If we wanted to understand the difference between these neighborhoods, we would not begin by studying economic facts, for the same reason we would not begin to explain a change in the economy by reference to a legal change. Although these spheres of life are not entirely autonomous, they are sufficiently so to be studied apart from one another. If the realm of unwritten rules has this sort of autonomy, we should begin to understand it by considering its own laws.

Several writers in the eighteenth century pioneered this approach to what I have called unwritten rules and which they called *mœurs* and *manières*, "morals" and "manners." These terms included, but were not limited to, matters of social etiquette. J. G. A. Pocock has argued that the development of commerce in the eighteenth century led philosophers to think about the qualities of character that allow one to be sociable, or to interact amicably and profitably with other people—qualities that were not exactly virtues (certainly not in the sense associated with the austere ancient republics), but were nevertheless (as an ethical matter) important for living a happy life and (as a philosophical matter) seemed important for distinguishing one nation or civilization from another.[3] When for instance Edmund Burke claimed that the French Revolution threatened modern civilization, he spoke often of its effect on manners:

> When to these establishments of Regicide, of Jacobinism, and of Atheism, you add the correspondent system of manners, no doubt can be left on the mind of a thinking man, concerning their determined hostility to the human race. Manners are of more importance than laws. Upon them, in a great measure, the laws depend. The law touches us but here and there, and now and then. Manners are what vex or sooth, corrupt or purify, exalt or debase, barbarize or refine us, by a constant, steady, uniform, insensible operation, like that of the air we breathe in. They give their whole form and color to our lives. According to their quality, they aid morals, they supply them, or they totally destroy them.[4]

Burke's conception of "manners" evokes the basic texture of our social interactions which, insofar as we are social beings, we can never live without. This, I take it, is the point of the analogy between manners and "the air we breathe." Sometimes the air we breathe is healthy, other times polluted; sometimes the basic texture of our social interactions is respectful, peaceable, and pleasant; other times it is harsh, crude, and brusque. Just as air quality is of concern to one who cares about physical health, so the quality of manners is of concern to one who cares about moral and political health.

In what follows, I will take as a guide the eighteenth-century English historian Edward Gibbon, a contemporary of Burke's and a friend, who took a similar view about the social significance of manners.[5] The first volume of Gibbon's *History of the Decline and Fall of the Roman Empire* is in fact of special relevance to present day discussions about equality. It charts the unlikely but, in Gibbon's view, salutary survival of egalitarian manners in Rome during a period when economics and politics grew less egalitarian, even though the inequalities long-established in other spheres of life eventually exerted a destructive influence on social manners. My goal here is not to describe Gibbon's own intellectual context, nor to offer a fuller study of volume 1 of the *Decline and Fall.* I want instead to focus on Gibbon's portrayal of the evolution of manners from the time of Emperor Augustus to that of Diocletian, which I believe can help us to understand how changes in manners influence changes in regime.

Gibbon's account of Rome's fall also helps illuminate some problematic assumptions underlying our own worries about increasing inequality in the United States. Contemporary concerns about inequality are anchored to democratic principles. In the eyes of those who are committed to the fundamental principle that all men are created equal, equality forms the core of justice, so that growing inequality seems synonymous to growing injustice. Scholars who write about inequality often assume that truths set us free—that frankly facing up to and talking about unjust inequalities in our society is the best way to correct them. They also assume that the inequalities that matter most are real, material inequalities like unequal wealth or income. But I think that both assumptions are at best only partially true. Studying Gibbon's account of manners can help us to recognize that egalitarian forms of social interaction—democratic manners—might be the most important form of equality for defenders of democracy to hold onto, even (perhaps especially) when there is something clearly false or even hypocritical about them.

TRUTH AND PROPAGANDA IN GIBBON'S ROME

The first volume of Gibbon's *History of the Decline and Fall of the Roman Empire* begins with Augustus, whose forty-year reign as emperor ended in 15

AD, and ends with Diocletian, whose twenty-year rule ended in 305 AD. Like Augustus, Gibbon writes, Diocletian was "a founder of a new empire" but his view differed on how political life should reflect the inequalities of real power (*DF*, 1:359).[6] Augustus thought that such inequalities should be covered up; Diocletian thought they should be displayed and enhanced. Gibbon contrasts the two in this passage:

> Like the modesty affected by Augustus, the state maintained by Diocletian was a theatrical representation; but it must be confessed, that of the two comedies, the former was of a much more liberal and manly character than the latter. It was the aim of the one to disguise, and the object of the other to display, the unbounded power which the emperors possessed over the Roman world. (*DF*, 1:389)

For Gibbon, disguising unbounded power is preferable to displaying it, inasmuch as "liberal and manly character" is preferable to servility.[7] Gibbon suggests later that covering over inequality—to speak plainly: lying—can be the better part of prudence, whereas emphasizing inequality serves as a symptom, perhaps even a cause, of a civilization's decline. The truth does not set one free, or not always.

What is most remarkable about Gibbon's portrayal of the early empire is that he is as unflinching in his negative judgment of its hypocrisy as he is clear-sighted regarding the beneficial effects of that hypocrisy. This paradoxical evaluation shows itself in the way Gibbon describes both the imperial regime and its founder, Augustus.

Let us begin with the regime. Gibbon exposes the lie at the heart of the early empire. "The system of the Imperial government," he writes, "as it was instituted by Augustus, and maintained by those princes who understood their own interest and that of the people,... may be defined an absolute monarchy disguised by the forms of a commonwealth" (*DF*, 1:93). Presumably the princes' interest has to do with maintaining their own power, but in what sense does this sort of governance serve the people's?

Gibbon answers this question when he explains why the senate refused Augustus's (insincere) offer to abdicate his kingly role and thereby return Rome to the status of a republic. "The present greatness of the Roman state, the corruption of manners, and the license of the soldiers," Gibbon says, "supplied new arguments to the advocates of monarchy" (*DF*, 1:87)

Once Rome had grown too large, its manners too corrupt, its soldiers too licentious, to maintain the old regime, the interests not only of the princes but also of the people demand a monarch.

Gibbon might have portrayed the founder of this new regime as a principled but realistic republican, eager to preserve, by means of hypocrisy if necessary, as much of the old way as the size, manners, and military might of Rome would allow. Instead, his Augustus is a "subtle tyrant" whose character, to the extent we can speak of his having a character, is defined by fear and the absence of principle: "A cool head, an unfeeling heart, and a cowardly disposition, prompted [Augustus] at the age of nineteen to assume the mask of hypocrisy, which he never afterwards laid aside" (*DF*, 1:96). On Gibbon's interpretation, all that might appear noble about Augustus is artifice, rooted ultimately in the genuine but base motive of fear. The only ennobling quality that Augustus seems to possess, in fact, is a skill or an intuition which enables him to recognize so clearly the "various dictates of his interest." Gibbon calls this quality "a cool head"; we might call it intelligence or prudence, the last being a virtue Gibbon grants Augustus and his successors (*DF*, 1:96, 99).

Whatever the nature of Augustus's virtue, its effect is not only a new government but also a new theory of government. "Augustus was sensible that mankind is governed by names," Gibbon writes (*DF*, 1:96). This insight opens the way for all of the propaganda and artifice that, in these passages, Gibbon seems to condemn. Augustus's "names" hide a reality that is not an approximation of or an aspiration to the ideal, but its exact opposite. The Romans are not nearly-free or as free as they can be under the circumstances. They are slaves. And here Augustus is not limited in any meaningful sense by the names he must speak. His is an "*absolute monarchy* disguised by the forms of a commonwealth" (*DF*, 1:93 ; emphasis mine). Augustus, the master, seems no less a master for pretending not to be one.

While Gibbon's Augustus is unconcerned with the genuine interests of the Roman people, Gibbon nevertheless assures us that, despite its founder's intent, his government of deceptive names serves the people's interests as well as those of the emperor. Yet, for all of his power, Augustus is not free to speak just any names. He is not free, in particular, to speak the truth. He must speak like a republican, creating a "more liberal and manly" comedy than the facts justify.

GIBBON'S "MANNERS"

As we have seen, Gibbon presents three reasons for monarchy as serving a popular, not solely princely, interest: Rome has grown too large, its manners too corrupt, and its soldiers too licentious to maintain a republic. Much can be said about each of these reasons for the new regime, but I would like here to focus on the central one, which strikes me as the most interesting and perplexing of the three. What exactly does Gibbon mean by the corruption of manners? Since he speaks of corrupt manners on only two other occasions in the first volume of *Decline and Fall*, we can consider these cases in some detail.

The first instance links corrupt manners with flattery and indiscriminate obedience. "The corruption of Roman manners would always supply flatterers eager to applaud, and ministers prepared to serve, the fear or the avarice, the lust or the cruelty, of their master" (*DF*, 1:103-4). This passage alludes to a lost time, when Romans spoke frankly and resisted tyrants. The change that marked the corrupt present from that purer past was not one of law or even regime, however, insofar as Augustus maintained the republic's forms and formalities. It was rather a change in the sort of behavior that was considered permissible or respectable. At one time, a citizen could not conceive of himself praising without admiring, or obeying without respecting; later on, however, the pairing became disconnected, and the absence of either admiration or respect triggered no shame. Such is the change that the corruption of manners seems to entail.

Gibbon speaks again of corrupt manners when describing Elagabalus, the cross-dressing and sexually voracious Syrian who held the Roman throne for four bloody but colorful years early in the third century. Once Elagabalus's appointed successor, Alexander Severus, starts to win public esteem—Elagabalus being an easy act to follow—Alexander "excited the tyrant's jealousy, who resolved to terminate the dangerous competition, either by corrupting the manners, or by taking away the life, of his rival" (*DF*, 1:169). Gibbon only gestures at the details of Alexander's corruption, making them seem perhaps more salacious than is justified. Herodian, whom Gibbon cites, says that Elagabalus taught his heir "dancing and prancing" as well as superstitious rites.[8] In any event, Elagabalus' education does not take, Alexander emerges unscathed, and soon the Praetorian Guard murders the emperor and places Alexander in the imperial chair. Here again we see corrupt manners linked to reluctance to resist a tyrant, as Elagabalus recognizes (rightly, Gibbon has led us to think) that a corrupt Alexander would not challenge his rule.[9] But in this passage we also glimpse an aspect of "manners" that we had not seen hitherto: manners link private and public behavior. Gibbon suggests that the sort of person who dances and prances and oversees superstitious rites, even away from the public eye, is not likely to take a public stand.

From these two case studies of what Gibbon means by corrupt manners, we gain some clarity on how he uses the concept more broadly. "Manners" are unwritten social rules enforced primarily by praise and blame. Corrupt manners allow tyrants to be flattered rather than resisted; subjects are not legally bound to flatter an emperor, but they know that they are meant to do so, and do not anticipate being shamed when they do. For Gibbon, "manners" also represent an element of character. One can be said *to have* the manners of a servile subject or a spirited citizen, in something like the way we say one has good or bad manners. Since manners are an element of character, they are evident in private as well as public life, and changes to one (private or public) may carry implications for the other. If Alexander acts shamelessly in private, he is less likely to act honorably in public life. Manners, then, describe our internal, personal disposition towards an external, interpersonal realm regulated by praise and blame.

MANNERS AND THE IMPERIAL SYSTEM

Such a concept has significant explanatory value for Gibbon when considering not only Rome's republican past but also its confrontation with non-Roman civilizations. Compared with the manners of people to their north and west, those of the Romans appear "soft" (*DF*, 1:147) and "elegant" (1:243-44); non-Romans manners seem "fierce" (1:107), "savage" (1:186, 293, 440), and "rustic" (1:360, 402). When compared to more ancient civilizations to their east, however, it is the Romans who seem "unpolished" (*DF*, 1:62; compare 1:166, 313). Manners are among the social phenomena—along with language, religion, institutions, and complexion—that Gibbon uses to distinguish one nation or civilization from another (*DF*, 1:49, 62, 231, 258, 370, 440, 499). National manners are placed along a continuum of hard to soft: savage northerners have the hardest manners, refined easterners have the softest, and Rome falls somewhere in between.

Gibbon's evaluation of national manners involves a theory of history. Manners start hard and get progressively softer. When Gibbon speaks of "the progress of manners" (as at *DF*, 1:67), he has in mind greater gentleness towards one's fellow man. His reason seems to be that the very experience of social relations governed by unwritten rules (as distinct from law or force) shapes character; the more one engages others peacefully, without appealing to force, the more peaceable one becomes. Barbarism entails constant violence; civilization, constant peace, at least within the bounds of civilization. Insofar as the coordinated action of individuals also generates power, civilization tends to predominate over barbarism. While manners therefore tend over time towards softness, the normative weight of Gibbon's evaluative categories falls on the mean. "Humanization" entails softening hard manners (*DF*, 1:59, 274; compare 1:67), but "restoring" or "reforming" manners means making excessively soft manners harder (*DF*, 1:262-4, 274, 475). As these last examples suggest, manners are sufficiently fixed to define national character, but they are not for that reason static. Indeed, Gibbon understands the Roman empire to be not only the site of relatively moderate manners—neither too hard nor too soft—but the cause and overseer of great shifts in national manners.

Just as the Roman economy brings the goods of the west and east into contact with each other for the benefit of both (see esp. *DF*, 1:78-84), so it uses the hard manners of westerners to defend the empire as a whole, in the process softening or humanizing western manners and giving soft easterners more security than they could win with their own arms. "The rougher trade of arms was abandoned to the peasants and barbarians of the frontiers, who knew no country but their camp, no science but that of war, no civil laws, and scarcely those of military discipline," Gibbon writes. "With bloody hands, savage manners, and desperate resolutions, they sometimes guarded, but much oftener subverted, the throne of the emperors" (*DF*, 1:186; compare 1:146). Romanity spread the relatively soft manners of the city into the provinces, pushing the hard manners of the barbarians further towards the frontiers. Thus Gibbon can speak of the empire being "coalesced into one great nation" by the "powerful influence of laws and manners" (*DF*, 1:62, 31; compare 1:168). But as Roman manners are extended, the soldiers who are stationed in the city of Rome also come from farther afield, leading ultimately to a point where a Roman can be shocked by a "Roman" soldier who strikes him as not Roman at all. The pace at which hard provincials are incorporated into the military exceeds the rate at which their manners are softened to resemble those of the Romans themselves.

By attending to Gibbon's use of "manners" alone, then, we discern an important element of his theory of how the Roman Empire maintains itself. The empire uses the goods of the east to soften the hard barbarians of the north and west; it uses the hard barbarians of the north and west to man the legions that rule in the east. In between are the Romans, who maintain this system as long as their manners are not excessively soft, but who become excessively soft, since this is how manners tend. To slow the progress or decline of manners requires that the tendency of manners to soften over time be reversed, or that more and more "hard barbarians" enter into the system as soldiers and leave as moderately soft Romans. However, the emperors' wariness of glorious generals limits the incorporation of new territories and populations; in Gibbon's words, the emperor did not aspire to "conquests which might have proved no less fatal to himself than to the vanquished barbarians" (*DF*, 1:33). The primary mode in which emperors may avert decline, then, is the reversal or forestallment of manners' natural tendency towards softening. When Gibbon's narrative reaches Diocletian, the founder of a Roman empire superseding that of Augustus, it becomes clear that the hypocritical preservation of the republic's empty egalitarian forms was one such device, slowing, though no more than slowing, Rome's decline.

GIBBON'S DIOCLETIAN

Gibbon draws a close parallel between Augustus and Diocletian. "Like Augustus, Diocletian may be considered as the founder of a new empire. Like the adopted son of Caesar, he was distinguished as a statesman rather than as a warrior; nor did either of those princes employ force, whenever their purpose could be effected by policy" (*DF*, 1:359). As this last sentence suggests, Augustus and Diocletian share a set of characteristics: both are characterized as artful (*DF*, 1:92, 361, e.g.), prudent (1:99, 386), and crafty (1:87, 386).[10] Both of them think policy is generally preferable to force, and they agree regarding the objects that policy should pursue. In settling Rome's war with Persia rather than expanding the empire eastwards, Diocletian adheres to "the moderate policy of Augustus and the Antonines" (*DF*, 1:380).

These similarities serve to heighten the starkest point of contrast between the two founders. For, as we have seen, both maintain states that are "theatrical representation[s]," but Augustus's aims to disguise while Diocletian's to display "the unbounded power which the emperors possessed over the Roman world" (*DF*, 1:389). It is in light of Diocletian's new display of the imperial power that the significance of Augustus's earlier disguises comes to light. Diocletian removes the imperial court from Rome, with grave consequences for the remnants of the old regime. The people and senate of Rome, for all that their "corrupt manners" inclined them towards flattery, still treated their emperors in a more egalitarian spirit than the stark superiority of the emperor's power would seem to demand. "The emperors … disdained that pomp and ceremony which might offend their countrymen, but could add nothing to their real power," Gibbon writes. "In all the offices of life, they affected to confound themselves with their subjects, and maintained with them an equal intercourse of visits and entertainments" (*DF*, 1:93-4). The forms of the republic, however empty and false they might sometimes seem under the empire, preserve a certain egalitarian spirit with modest but not meaningless consequences. Prudent emperors are "in some measure obliged to assume the language and behavior" of one who rules over equals (*DF*, 1:386-7).

Diocletian preferred to reside in the city of Nicomedia (in today's Turkey) to Rome, where he passed just two months of his long reign. He cut short his first and only visit to Rome because he was "disgusted with the licentious familiarity of the people" (*DF*, 1:385).[11] Diocletian's reforms to Augustus's version of the empire serve to erase such remnants of republican equality. Prominent among these reforms is the inversion of Augustus's government of names. Whereas Augustus had knitted together republican offices to form a monarchy in fact but not in name, Diocletian retains only the name *imperator* from the republic, and adds to it the title *dominus*, which under the republic, Gibbon notes, was restricted to describing the relationship of master to slave, and *deus*, which emperors previously had accepted from their eastern subjects but only posthumously from Romans (*DF*, 1:387-88, 94-95). The manners of Diocletian's court change to reflect the "stately magnificence of the court of Persia" rather than the familiarity of Rome. A subject approaching Diocletian would proceed through a large retinue of officers and eunuchs into the inner reaches of an ornate palace, where he was to "fall prostrate on the ground, and to adore, according to the eastern fashion, the divinity of his lord and master," a man or god who like the Persian kings wore a diadem and "sumptuous robes" of silk and gold paired with gem-studded shoes (*DF*, 1:389). This was all a far stretch from the simplicity of the court of Augustus. Gibbon assures us, however, that Diocletian was very much on his rocker. The change in manners was an artful policy formed from "a just estimate of himself and of mankind." Diocletian "flattered himself, that an ostentation of splendor and luxury would subdue the imagination of the multitude... and that habits of submission would insensibly be productive of sentiments of veneration" (*DF*, 1:389).

Augustus had centralized real power in response to the civil wars of the late republic and to the large size, corrupt manners, and insolent troops that were part cause and part effect of those wars. But the egalitarianism of the republic survived, in form if not in substance, in the way individuals related to one another and to their leaders. Diocletian, having emerged from a fifty-year crisis during which some thirty emperors ruled and Augustus's "artful edifice" nearly crumbled, concluded that even the hollow remnant of republican equality was a luxury too costly for the empire to maintain. It was better, he thought, to bring manners into line with reality—to alter the formalities, the theater, of political life to reflect the emperor's preeminence. Diocletian intended to root the subjects' acceptance of authority, not in the provisional permission to rule that one grants to a peer with the assurance he will not become more than that, but in the veneration one feels for a being who belongs to a higher order. Diocletian's theatrical representation was not "more liberal and manly" than Augustus's, but it was not intended to be. Diocletian wanted Roman manners to more honestly reflect the realities of Roman politics in order to make political life more stable and sustainable, if less free.

In Gibbon's view, it was Diocletian, not Constantine, who was most responsible for the "new system of Imperial government" (*DF*, 1:386). But it was Constantine who would turn the sentiments of veneration that Diocletian artfully inspired in the Romans towards a new divinity, with the paradoxical effect of renewing a certain egalitarianism of manners among men. As Christians, the Romans became more equal than they had been even under the rule of Augustus. But that is a matter for the next chapter—the next volume—in Gibbon's "history of human manners" (*DF*, 1:70).[12]

CONCLUSIONS

Rome, even under the republic, did not declare itself to be committed to the truth of human equality. The social distances separating men and women, masters and slaves, patricians and plebeians, citizens and non-citizens, were all of them far too great for human equality to seem plausible, much less a self-evident truth.[13] Nevertheless, among Romans who belonged to many or all of the privileged categories, a certain form of equality, particularly in access to political rule, came to be an important principle. This civic equality was so important that a "subtle tyrant" like Augustus had to speak the words of the old regime in establishing the new imperial regime, in which citizens would not share equally in rule. Such words became mostly but not completely meaningless, at least on Gibbon's understanding. Mere formalities, like whether the emperor was addressed as *princeps* [the first among equals] or *dominus et deus* [master and god], mattered. They linked the Romans of the empire to their republican past, and they served also to create their own reality. A subject who must be treated like a citizen need not see himself to be quite as servile, and so is not as servile, as a subject treated like a slave.

One should hesitate to draw parallels between Gibbon's time and our own, and more than just hesitate to suggest that we share something with Augustus, Diocletian, and the people they ruled. So let us conclude modestly, by taking stock of what Gibbon might help us to recognize about manners in their relation to equality. We tend often, perhaps too readily, to think of equality as an economic phenomenon—something that can be captured, measured, and compared with precision, as when we make use of a numerical index. It also comes easily to us to think of equality as a political or legal phenomenon, having to do, for instance, with how many people have access to the ballot or have standing to defend their rights in court, or face barriers. These are all important aspects of what equality means to us, to be sure. But Gibbon helps us to appreciate that many inequalities can exist without impacting the fundamental facts of our regime—how we understand ourselves, live our own lives, and relate to those around us. A rich man whom I can look in the eye when we shake hands, and who will do the same to me, is my superior along one dimension but perhaps not the decisive one. Are our manners preserving the equality that matters to us? That is a question that is hard to answer concretely and precisely, but it is an important question for all of that.

NOTES

1. For a penetrating analysis of neighborliness, see especially Nancy L. Rosenblum, *Good Neighbors: The Democracy of Everyday Life in America* (Princeton, NJ: Princeton University Press, 2016). Rosenblum argues that neighborliness is an important part of the "democracy of everyday life ... the enduring substrate of democracy, which we fall back on at crucial moments to maintain our democratic bearings" (247); nevertheless, she distinguishes the neighbor from the citizen, who must necessarily engage in partisan struggles with strangers.

2. Compare Rosenblum, *Good Neighbors*, 238, on the difference between rough equality among neighbors in a democracy and neighborliness "regulated by social rank or hierarchy or tribe or tradition or clientelism."

3. J. G. A. Pocock, "Virtues, Rights, and Manners: A Model for Historians of Political Thought," *Political Theory* 9, no. 3 (August 1981): 353-68; repr. *Virtue, Commerce, and History: Essays on Political Thought and History, Chiefly in the Eighteenth Century* (Cambridge: Cambridge University Press, 1985), 37-50. Pocock has developed this idea with a view to Edward Gibbon in his, *Barbarism and Religion*, 6 vols. (Cambridge: Cambridge University Press, 1999-2015), see esp. 1:107-34, 2:19-21, 2:120-36 (on Voltaire's *Essai sur les Mœurs*), 3:413-14, 4:92-93.

4. Edmund Burke, "Letters on a Regicide Peace," in *Selected Works of Edmund Burke*, ed. Francis Canavan, 4 vols. (Indianapolis, IN: Liberty Fund, 1999), 3:126. Pocock discusses this passage in "Virtues, Rights, and Manners," 366; for context see esp. his "Introduction," in *Reflections on the Revolution in France*, by Edmund Burke (Indianapolis, IN: Hackett, 1987), xxxv-xxxvi.

5. David Womersley has shown how Gibbon's sympathy with Burke's critique of the French Revolution influenced the writing and revision of several drafts of Gibbon's *Memoirs*. See Womersley, *Gibbon and the "Watchmen of the Holy City": The Historian and His Reputation, 1776-1815* (Oxford: Oxford University Press, 2009), esp. 209-40.

6. I shall refer parenthetically to volume and page number of David Womersley's edition of Edward Gibbon, *The History of the Decline and Fall of the Roman Empire (DF)*, ed. Womersley, 3 vols. (London: Penguin Press, 1994).

7. Note, however, that even though Diocletian is said "to display" rather than disguise the emperors' unbounded power, his is still a "theatrical representation." We will discuss below the trappings and rituals that Diocletian enacts; it is to these that Gibbon immediately refers when he presents Diocletian as a dramaturge. Nevertheless, the fact that neither Augustus nor Diocletian presents a vision of politics free from some sort of distortion suggests to us that politics (or just the imperial regime?) requires some form of dishonesty or misrepresentation, such that one is left to distinguish lies that disguise the truth (Augustus) from those that display the truth (Diocletian).

8. Herodian,*History of the Empire*, 2 vols., trans. C. R. Whittaker, Loeb Classical Library 454-5 (Cambridge, MA: Harvard University Press, 1969), 1:60-1 (5.7.4).

9. If we imagine Alexander's education under Elagabalus taking place in private, we can take Alexander's corruption to entail a diminishment in his willingness to assume the risks of revolt. If we imagine the education to take place in public—or to be publicly known—we might add to Alexander's own personal corruption, the practical difficulty of maintaining the support of those disgruntled with Elagabalus's extravagance, once the alternative (Alexander) ceases to differ from the status quo. The balance of the evidence Gibbon cites supports the first interpretation, but the two are not incompatible with one another.

10. Compare David Womersley, *The Transformation of* The Decline and Fall of the Roman Empire (Cambridge: Cambridge University Press, 1988), 75-76.

11. Compare the "rude license of the people and the soldiers" at *DF*, 1:389.

12. Edward Gibbon explored the notion of manners (*moeurs*) as the proper subject of "philosophical history" in his first published book, the *Essai sur l'étude de la littérature*. See especially chaps. 2 and 55 of the *Essai*, ed. Robert Mankin (Oxford: Voltaire Foundation, 2010), 94, 128. For comment on this work's significance with a view to Gibbon's *The History of the Decline and Fall of the Roman Empire*, 6 vols. (London: Strahan & Cadell, 1776-1789), see in particular Peter Ghosh, "Gibbon's First Thoughts: Rome, Christianity, and the *Essai sur l'étude de la littérature*," *Journal of Roman Studies* 85 (1995): 148-64, and Pocock, *Barbarism and Religion*, 1:208-39.

13. We might want to add an exception for Roman philosophers such as the stoics. For all of the Stoics' capacity to dissolve most of the distinctions we mention here, the distinction between the virtuous and non-virtuous remained, in such a way as to preclude the democratic conclusions that Jefferson and others would draw from their own egalitarianism.

Chapter 15

A Kantian Approach to Recognizing Privilege

Courtney Morris

Immanuel Kant advanced a political theory centered on equality, freedom, and independence. These political virtues stem from his ethical theory, which is based on the "categorical imperative," or the command that one should act only on principles that would be rational for everyone to act on. Kant's idea is that moral choices should be untainted by anyone's desires or situations. If a principle is a moral one, he thinks, it is so for everyone, regardless of one's social, historical, or personal context. The moral law, for Kant, is blind the same way the justice of the United States purports to be. Moral principles are, in turn, founded on Kant's belief that "every human being has a legitimate claim to respect from his fellow human beings and is *in turn* bound to respect every other."[1]

And yet, Kant also expressed views which we now recognize as sexist and racist, and seem deeply tainted. Here are two excerpts from his writings, *On the Feeling of the Beautiful and Sublime*:

> Laborious learning or painful grubbing, even if a woman could get very far with them, destroy the merits that are proper to her sex, and on account of their rarity may well make her into an object of a cold admiration, but at the same time they will weaken the charms by means of which she exercises her great power over the opposite sex.[2]
>
> ...
>
> The **Negroes** of Africa have by nature no feeling that rises above the ridiculous. Mr. **Hume** challenges anyone to adduce a single example where a Negro has demonstrated talents, and asserts that among the hundreds of thousands of blacks who have been transported elsewhere from their countries, although very many of them have been set free, nevertheless not a single one has ever been found who has accomplished something great in art or science or shown any other praiseworthy quality, while among the whites there are always those who

> rise up from the lowest rabble and through extraordinary gifts earn respect in the world.[3]

While these sentiments are particularly repugnant, they do not misrepresent his considered published views on women and blacks. Although Kant also expressed stereotypical views about the French, the English, the Spaniards, the Italians, the Germans, the Greeks, and the Russians, none were as blatantly dismissive as those of women and of people of African descent.[4]

As a feminist, a Kant scholar, and a person who cares deeply about inclusion, I am uncomfortable with this tension in Kant's work. One problem is how to judge Kant himself. But there is a more pressing problem: Kant's own ethical theory should have *ruled out* his sexist and racist views. What good is an ethical theory that cannot?

The typical response from a Kant scholar, whether consciously adopted or not, is that Kant was a product of his times and that his prejudices do not affect the validity of his arguments. These apologists do for Kant what some do for the whole discipline of philosophy: although western philosophy's history of sexism and racism is embarrassing and open for correction, it alone does not invalidate whole fields of thought. A philosophical view, even if presented by a racist or sexist, can still be considered on its own merits. Indeed, these defenders claim we do philosophy a disservice by discounting a philosopher's arguments just because they happened to have offensive personal views.[5] Kant's views of women and blacks, it is conceded, were more than personal; they were part of his theory on the nature of the beautiful and sublime. Nevertheless, the defense goes, we can reject them without concluding that they cripple his core arguments. The general tenets of Kant's ethical theory remain as valid or invalid as they ever were. We simply update the theory with our more enlightened views about gender and race. Another possible response, put forward by some feminists, is to investigate the whole nature of reason as set forth by Kant to see if *it* is gendered or racist—that is, whether it implicitly favors masculine or white over feminine or oppressed ways of thinking. Scholars who take this approach have the burden of defining what it means for thinking to be "masculine" or "feminine" or "white" or "oppressed."[6] They also must decide if "reason," as it stands after their analysis, is worth defending or if it is instead the source of the trouble.[7]

In this essay, I will not directly address whether reason, in Kant's sense, is gendered or racist, though I do not think that it is obviously not. My aim is to investigate whether Kant's ethical theory has the capacity to exclude reprehensible views or can be consistently supplemented. Does it have the resources that would enable a moral agent today to recognize judgments grounded on racial or gendered privilege in a way that Kant did not? Or does it allow such judgments even when the categorical imperative is correctly applied? Does Kant's own sexist and racist views indicate a flawed understanding of his own theory or is the problem with the theory itself? However, the answers to these questions touch on the broader issue of whether reason, as Kant understood it, is gendered or otherwise privileged. For if his ethical theory is unable to block racist, sexist, or otherwise offensive judgments, then perhaps it does privilege the white male perspective and hence ought to be rejected for a more inclusive theory.[8]

I argue that Kant's theory does have the tacit resources to address the moral obligations that stem from privilege. By "privilege," I mean the societal advantages one receives thanks to membership in a group whose defining characteristics are irrelevant to one's moral value as a human being. In fact, Kant himself maintained that people do have a moral obligation to be sensitive to how their judgments and actions affect members of marginalized groups. He identified two moral duties: (1) the duty to be sympathetic towards others, and (2) the duty to not be contemptuous of others.[9] Although Kant does not show how these duties might ground moral sensibilities so as to block racist or sexist judgments, my aim is to show how they can. Hence, I contend that Kant's theory has the tools to expose sexist and racist views. His failure was in not uncovering the further duty to recognize his own privilege.

THE UNIVERSAL NATURE OF KANT'S MORAL THEORY

Although many ethical theories have been put forward by philosophers who were themselves racist and sexist, Kant's bigotry is especially troublesome because his theory purports to be "universal," which means that its proper application is supposed to generate moral judgments that are valid for any moral agent, regardless of contingent facts about that agent. It should not matter, morally speaking, if one lives in a "backward" time, or was raised in a prejudiced community, or was born with selfish genes. One should supposedly have access to the same moral judgments as another person differently situated, since by virtue of this theory everyone can access pure reason, untainted by empirical facts.

Indeed, the theory's insistence on disregarding particularities and differences is part of what makes it appealing. Kant is concerned with an individual's selfish desires interfering with moral judgment and action. He was well aware that factors of this kind can easily distract us. I know I should return a wallet, but I could use its several hundred dollars. I know I should report that my classmate cheated on an exam, but doing so will likely expose me to ridicule and isolation. I know I should admit an honest mistake that will cost the company thousands of dollars, but doing so will cost me my job. I know I should not convict someone I do not believe is guilty, but the rest of the jury is pressuring me and I do want to go home. And on and on. In every such case, our desires threaten our resolve to do the right thing. But a moral system that permits doing otherwise is not moral at all: you *should* return the wallet, report your peer, admit your mistake, and not convict those whom you believe are innocent, regardless of what you want. Morality does not care what you want; it cares about what you should do. Neither does it matter that you are placed in circumstances entirely beyond your control where you would arguably need to lie, cheat, or steal. The woman in a war-torn city who steals bread to feed her child is subject to the same moral judgment as the thief who steals to take revenge on a competing business; the woman's circumstances and intentions make no difference. The theory's universality erases such differences.

Kant's treatment of morality clearly has a sharp edge: moral laws carry the force of *orders* to perform an action (or to refrain). Perhaps they are better understood as *standing orders*, in the way that "*Love thy neighbor*" and "*Do not steal*" put demands on our conduct, not merely once, but whenever circumstances require. Borrowing terminology from the area of grammar, Kant called these orders or commands *imperatives*, which he classified in turn as either *hypothetical* or *categorical*. A hypothetical imperative is conditional in nature, taking the form of an "*if–then*" statement.[10] If I am eagerly hoping to get a reward, I should return the wallet. If I want to get back to my family as soon as possible, I must go along with the other jurors.

In fact, hypothetical imperatives ground most of our rational choices. If I do not want my grade to drop, then I had better get to class. If I do not want dinner to burn, then I had better take it out of the oven. We could not survive without hypothetical imperatives; they are the hallmark of rational planning and acting. But Kant wanted to focus our attention on cases where the "*if*" half of a hypothetical imperative expresses motives or desires that may distort our moral thinking. Consider a different example: suppose that a charming cat showed up on my doorstep and now resides comfortably in my home. A few days later I spot a photo of this very cat at my supermarket under a Cat Missing sign. Now, I consider myself a good person, and I know I should not take, or keep, things that do not belong to me. But this is a very special cat. I would also like to have the posted reward money. I am experiencing a clash of feelings. If I want to retain my self-respect, I ought to return the cat. The same holds true if I want to get the money. But I really like this cat and the cat seems very pleased with me, which prompts me to keep it despite the reward.[11] My decision, in short, lies in the hands of my desires and feelings, the conditions mentioned in the "*if*" part of the "*if–then*" statement. What follows in the "*then*" half of the statement depends on these conditions. On some, I do the right thing; on others, I do not. They point me in opposite directions.

Kant was much bothered by such variability. He thought that if I do the right thing on the basis of merely my feelings or my wishes then my decision lacks moral worth. Kant's point is that hypothetical imperatives, and hence desires, cannot *ground* moral commands. If an action is wrong, it is so for everyone; a lie is a lie. Similarly, if my action to return the cat is the right thing to do, it is not *made* right because of my wanting to receive a reward or keep my self-respect. Morality makes claims on all humans, not just on those who happen to have certain desires. Moral commands are not hypothetical; their nature is to be *unconditional*. They apply universally—to everyone—regardless of circumstances. Instead of saying "Don't lie *if* you don't want a bad reputation," a moral command says "Don't lie, period." However, Kant was not interested in compiling a list of particular moral commands. His aim was to locate the moral force that underlies them.[12] Like our capacity to reason, this force—the moral law, he calls it—distinguishes us as human beings. It is capable of withstanding the distracting impulses of desire and self-interest, though it may often fail to do so.

Kant's moral philosophy can easily strike one as stoical, abstract, and obscure, as well as so cerebral and demanding as to serve no practical purpose. On the contrary, he sought to show how the moral law embedded in human nature can be put to work as a guide to our conduct. He provided a formula to help us decide the right thing to do and to perform actions that have genuine moral worth. This is the celebrated (and notorious) *categorical imperative*, which he thinks underlies specific universal commands such as "Do not lie" and "Love thy neighbor."[13] For Kant, it captures the *pure form* of any such moral law, with no specific content. The categorical imperative says: "*Act only in accordance with that maxim* [that is, *plan of action*] *through which you can at the same time will that it become a universal law*."[14] The categorical imperative counts as a "test" for determining the rightness of a planned action. It directs us, before we carry out the plan, to contemplate a world in which that plan has become a universal law, a law according to which everyone acts in the same way. It demands that we imagine a world whose own moral laws require everyone to act as we plan to act. And then it challenges us: Would it be rational for you to will (that is, to bring) that world into existence?[15] If not, then you have your answer about what is the right thing to do in this case.

One of Kant's own examples is that of a man who is considering whether to lie when negotiating a loan. Although needing the loan, the man also knows full well that he will not be able to repay it. The "maxim" or plan in this case is: "When I believe myself to be in need of money I shall borrow money and promise to repay it, even though I know that this will never happen."[16] But when the man imagines a world in which everyone follows the same rule, he realizes that the bank would not lend him money, nor anyone else for that matter, and hence that to carry out the plan in such a world would be fruitless. This means that his plan, when universalized as the moral command, "Lie for the sake of getting a loan," is irrational and consequently that for him to negotiate a loan in this way would be the wrong thing to do. However, it is important to keep in mind that, although using the categorical imperative can point us to the right thing to do, it cannot *make* us do it. Kant's moral law leaves us the freedom to choose and, it might be, make the wrong choice.

So that, in a small nutshell, is Kantian ethics. Many are attracted to its ability to ground objective, universal judgments in what most humans share and value: the capacity to reason, which enables them to judge whether their maxims (the possible plans of action facing them) can be rationally universalized and defended.[17] But the universality of Kant's theory comes at a cost. Undoubtedly, selfish desires do sometimes threaten the ability to act on moral duties, and the categorical imperative opens the way to block them. But in so doing, it blocks others too. Yes, lying is generally wrong, one might say, but in *this* case it is obviously permissible, since I want to protect the Jews in my attic from being seized by the Nazi officers at the door.[18] Yes, breaking my state's laws is generally wrong, but what about defying a racist law to publicize its absurdity?[19] Furthermore, the theory's very universality cannot seem to accommodate the fact that different moral reasoners live in different eras. That Kant was writing in the eighteenth- century when it was still acceptable to believe that women were not capable of full rationality should not matter. Kant's capacity to reason during his time, according to his own theory, should not be different from ours today, so he should not have arrived at moral judgments differently. But of course, he did: he judged women to be less rational than men and people of African descent to be incapable of contributing to culture.

Perhaps Kant has a possible defense here. He could say that his judgments, as despicable as they sound, express opinions only and are not *moral* judgments, nor do they indicate how one should treat women or those of African descent. Indeed, he could argue that his theory requires one to ignore one's racist or sexist desires or beliefs and to treat all people with respect regardless of how one feels about it. Let us say that you are a racist who wants to show your superiority over black people. Go ahead and have that desire, but at the same time recognize that the moral law requires you to restrain it and treat them with respect anyway. Or suppose that you are a misogynist who believes women to be the lesser sex. Go ahead, hold that belief, but recognize that the moral law demands that you to treat them with respect. In this sense, Kantian ethics seem designed to override and correct for illegitimate desires and false beliefs. Even a sexist and a racist can be moral, it seems to say; regardless of their personal beliefs and desires, the moral realm obliges that their actions follow the moral law.

This response would be convincing if the theory were robust enough to counter any moral agent's despicable desires and beliefs. But even if Kant thought that his theory could accommodate such problems on a theoretical level, its actual application cannot. Our beliefs and desires are not so easily separated from the actual moral judgments we make and the actions we take. In fact, Kant's view of women influenced him to make questionable moral judgments. His own political theory contends, for instance, that women should remain passive members of society, and hence not be allowed to vote.[20] This seems telling evidence against the idea that the categorical imperative, especially when deployed by an expert like Kant, will ward off wrong judgments or actions. But perhaps this is not so much the fault of the theory as of the humans who must execute it. We humans are remarkable self-deceivers who can be influenced in our own favor even when pretending to make objective moral judgments. Kant recognized the tendency of the "dear self"—the selfish, greedy, superior self—to rear its head, especially at times when the moral law demands we ignore it.[21]

The general problem, then, is that despite Kant's intention to make the categorical imperative relevant to making moral decisions, he seems to have ignored the messy, prejudiced conditions of human life in which it very much needs to be implemented.[22] And so the question remains whether or not his theory can be shown to navigate those conditions. I will argue that Kant was aware of the difficulty and that his theory can. But first it will be necessary to give the problem greater detail.

RULES OF MORAL SALIENCE

I have acknowledged that Kant's moral theory, owing to its universality, seems to erase the very details that might allow people to recognize bias in their moral judgments. What I mean is this. Granted that the categorical imperative does ground specific moral duties (for example, "Never lie" or "Give to charity"), the fulfillment of such duties can create the impression that one is moral yet fail to provide any impetus to recognize or address the unequal and often immoral treatment of unprivileged groups. I have focused here on the inequalities that stem from race and gender, but of course, there are many more. Kant's theory seems to leave a moral agent with no sense of duty or obligation to confront such inequalities, thus allowing their continuance. Meanwhile, the same agent, even one who is not personally sexist or racist, can enjoy the societal benefits that come with privilege, ignorant of the fact that not everyone is so positioned.[23] Not only that, the agent might possess the warm self-assurance of being moral.

A related issue is whether an ethical theory based on reason can genuinely spur moral progress within a society. Is it well suited for conservatives? Can it ground the type of political activism that is often the catalyst for moral change and progress? Or would it block the very things necessary to do so?—Awareness of history as seen from another's perspective, the resentment and indignation that often motivates people to change it, the passion to rally support for a cause. Factors such as these would appear to be more at home in a theory based on the "moral sentiments."[24]

Barbara Herman has addressed a broader version of the problem. The charge against Kant's theory, she says, is that it is "forced to discard those particular features of texture and detail which give actions their moral significance to agents."[25] "In short," she continues, "the difficulty with a conception of morality that ties moral judgment to rules is that it ignores details (particular facts about individuals and cases) that are morally relevant."[26] She responds to this problem by arguing, quite persuasively, that the practice of moral judgment, in the Kantian sense, must be understood to operate against a background of "rules of moral salience" that indicate to an agent what he or she must pay attention to, morally speaking, when deliberating proposed actions. Even though Kant does not make this explicit, she argues that an agents must have "some moral understanding of their actions before they use the CI [categorical imperative] procedure," and it is rules of moral salience that "structure an agent's perception of his situation … and enable him to pick out those elements of his circumstances or of his proposed actions which require moral attention."[27] These rules of moral salience (hereafter RMS) do not themselves generate duties (only the categorical imperative does that), but they do serve to guide an agent in understanding when to test a maxim against the categorical imperative. RMS represent the "moral understanding that in part defines a 'moral community.'"[28] One gains them in one's moral education. But importantly, they are separate from the formal elements of any rule-based ethical theory, though they can serve to fill out the content of one's maxims.

Herman's concept explains how context can legitimately play a role in applying the categorical imperative. To see this, we return to the example of a man considering whether to lie for the sake of getting a loan. If Herman is correct, then RMS operate in the background of this man's situation to show that it is one which requires moral deliberation. The function of RMS, she writes, is to "guide in the recognition of those areas where the fact that persons are moral persons ought to instruct agents' deliberations and actions."[29] In this case, RMS would guide the man to recognize the lender as a moral agent whose own ends and goals are features of the situation to be considered.[30] RMS, in other words, are rules that guide us in our understanding of the moral features of human beings, namely, that they are "ends in themselves" and not to be used as mere means.[31] They help us recognize when a person should be treated as autonomous, our moral equal possessing his or her own ends and goals, and therefore ought not to be violated or manipulated.

The case of lying to get a loan contrasts with many everyday ones. We commute to our jobs, sit at our desks, do our grocery shopping, and text with our friends—all actions that do not normally require moral deliberation. But wanting to lie does call out for moral deliberation precisely because we know, through RMS, that it involves manipulating and taking advantage of another rational agent. Of course, what sorts of situation call out for moral deliberation depends deeply on context: if a certain grocery store is being boycotted for racist treatment of its employees, RMS would hopefully inform us that the humanity of a person or a group of people, whose agency is morally relevant, is in danger of being violated. That fact will then highlight the case as one that calls for moral deliberation. In this way, RMS allows a theory like Kant's to take advantage of particular, non-universal facts while still maintaining its universality and formal character.

In light of Herman's argument, we can presume (although my historical support will be limited to Kant's own comments) that he himself lived in a society with defective RMS; the rules failed to make salient the fact that women and blacks have full moral agency and hence deserved equal moral treatment. Even worse, the RMS operating in the background of eighteenth-century German society (and undoubtedly of many, many others) did nothing to highlight the oppression of either group as worthy of moral sensitivity. Of course, this is all arguable; it is hard to believe that there were not some parts of his society attempting to make such facts salient. How much an individual, as opposed to a society, is to blame for individual or institutionalized racism or sexism is a difficult question worth much more examination than I can offer here. The point is that the introduction of RMS allows us to say that Kant's mistake was not with reason or his capacity to use it, but rather with defective RMS.

But this distinction raises a difficulty. If certain facts do not reveal themselves to an agent as relevant, especially if one lives in a society that takes no special care to highlight such facts, then it is hard to blame the agent for his or her ignorance of them. A moral system should not require an agent to be omniscient in order to apply a moral rule correctly. Herman agrees.[32] That would require too much—and since Kant adheres to the "ought implies can" rule, it follows that if one *cannot* for any reason perform an action, then one certainly cannot be *obligated*, morally or otherwise, to perform that action. The same seems to apply in the case of thoughts and judgments that involve one's own privileged status: if such a judgment or insight is inaccessible to someone, whether for psychological or other reasons, then that person cannot be faulted for failing to see it as relevant to moral reasoning. This does not excuse the person, however, from taking every effort to make such insights accessible to oneself.

Jeffrey Gauthier finds a deeper problem with Herman's proposed solution to the problem of particularity. According to him, "judgments following from the test of the categorical imperative must not merely accommodate moral progress but be able to serve as the *mainspring* for moral progress."[33] In other words, the possibility of moral progress, in a Kantian-like system, must be rooted in the theory itself rather than in something outside it, as the rules of moral salience are considered to be:

> In acknowledging that *RMS* are necessary for reaching moral judgments on the basis of the categorical imperative, Herman puts a new spin on this doctrine [of duty]. If treating all persons as ends-in-themselves is morally required, and if ideologically grounded defects to the *RMS* systematically impede our capacity to perceive whole classes of persons as ends-in-themselves, then the motive of duty must be sufficient to induce what is necessary to correct those defects.[34]

Gauthier's point seems to be that, unless the categorical imperative itself is the mainspring for progress, its application is perfectly compatible with immoral judgments. His point is noteworthy. If one lives in a time when the rules of moral salience are defective, given their failure to recognize oppressed people as human, then we must be motivated by *duty* to fix those defects. But "duty," for Kant, is just what is based on the categorical imperative. And, as we have already seen, "agents who rely exclusively on that test as a guide for action may be unaware of the manner in which racism and sexism inform their judgments."[35] Thus, Gauthier's critique is that "rules of moral salience" are inadequate to block a universal theory like Kant's from allowing sexist and racist judgments.

I believe that Gauthier is partly correct—the introduction of rules of moral salience does not provide an absolute safeguard against immoral judgments.[36] (I will return to this point in my conclusion.) He is wrong, however, in claiming that the "motive of duty" is not sufficient for one to recognize possible ideological defects in rules of moral salience. Indeed, there is textual evidence that Kant himself thinks that we have the positive duty to be self-aware in precisely this way—a duty to reveal and discover faults in RMS. Although discharging this duty can only go so far in illuminating one's own privilege, it can go farther than Gauthier claims. Moreover, since this duty is based on other duties that Kant himself already recognizes, they are firmly grounded in the categorical imperative.

THE DUTY TO "SEEK, LISTEN, AND RECONSIDER"

I contend that the duty to make one's privilege salient is found in what I call the duty to "seek, listen, and reconsider." I mean this to be one duty with three parts: the first, to be proactive about seeking other perspectives and not allowing oneself to simply rest content with one's world-view; the second, to listen to what others say directly and indirectly about their experience with an attempt at understanding their stories or arguments; and the third, to reconsider one's own arguments and judgments accordingly. Reconsideration does not require one to change one's mind, only for one to be humble and open to doing so.

Ideally, this tripartite duty is designed to illuminate one's privilege and to reveal how one's irrelevant societal advantages may bias one's judgments. A moral agent who strives to fulfill this duty will at least make progress towards becoming a more moral human being. Significantly, the duty is already found in duties that Kant has identified. The first is to be sympathetic.[37] For Kant, "sympathy," insofar as it is considered a receptive feeling, cannot be considered a duty, since one cannot be required to acquire feelings one simply does not have. But if we consider "sympathy" to be a capacity that one can will, that is, the free capacity to "share in others' feelings," then we do in fact have a duty to "sympathize actively in [another's] fate." He continues: "It is therefore a duty not to avoid the places where the poor who lack the most basic necessities are to be found but rather to seek them out, and not to shun sickrooms or debtors' prisons and so forth in order to avoid sharing painful feelings one may not be able to resist."[38]

Two features of Kant's description are worth noting. First, he includes the requirement to be proactive. We must "seek out" the places that will provide opportunities to be sympathetic. It is what Kant calls an "imperfect" duty, which means that there is no definitive rule about how to fulfill it, unlike the duty not to lie, which one is required to follow always. Thus, the extent to which one must seek such opportunities is open. But clearly one cannot stand by passively.

Second, Kant's tone is superior and condescending. Be sympathetic towards those you recognize as inferior, like the poor (especially those too poor to pay their debts!) and the sick. This tone infects Kant's statements of his other duties too—and it is, I believe, what damaged his own moral judgment the most. But there is no reason why we should only sympathize with those who we judge to be below us; if we have the duty to sympathize, we have it toward everyone. Thus, the duty is to be proactive about seeking out those who have different experiences and perspectives, especially when they differ from our own. This would include a requirement that one be proactive about learning how historical conditions, contingent though they are, have led to inequality and privilege, especially when one has benefited from those conditions. Thus, the duty to "seek" is implied by Kant's duty to sympathize. The duty to listen and reconsider—the last two steps of the duty I am suggesting—is found in Kant's explication of the duty to respect other human beings:

> To be *contemptuous* of others (*contemnere)*, that is, to deny them the respect owed to human beings in general, is in every case contrary to duty; for they are human beings. At times one cannot, it is true, help inwardly looking down on some in comparison with others (*despicatui habere*); but the outward manifestation of this, is nevertheless, an offense.... On this is based a duty to respect a human being even in the logical use of his reason, a duty not to censure his errors by calling them absurdities, poor judgment and so forth, but rather to suppose that his judgment must yet contain some truth and to seek this out, uncovering at the same time the deceptive illusion (the subjective ground that determined his judgment which, by an oversight he took for objective), and so, by explaining to him the possibility of his having erred, to preserve his respect for his own understanding.[39]

Once again, the passage contains an insight but presented condescendingly. First the insight: we have a duty to respect another's "logical use of reason," which is to treat another as though that person has good reasons for believing what he or she does. Second, the condescension: you do that person a favor by supposing that his or her "judgment must yet contain some truth." The purpose, however, is to point out another's errors so that he can preserve his "respect for his own understanding." But again, I see no reason why one does not have the duty to both listen *and* reconsider. After all, it might be one's own arguments that are subject to illusion and error, and thus one's own understanding to need correction. If we expect another to be open to such corrections, we too are similarly obligated. Hence the duty to respect another's "logical use of reason" includes the duty to listen humbly, with an open-mind, willing to change one's views.

The duty to seek, listen, and reconsider entails two corollary-duties: first, a pedagogical duty to teach developing moral agents, likely children, but perhaps adults, successful ways of learning and practicing this duty. The duty to be morally sensitive entails a duty to make educational systems, public or private, more diverse and inclusive, *not less*. Kant agreed that we had duties to teach children the necessities of moral reasoning, including the duty to sympathize with others.[40] I am merely suggesting that they be implemented in a certain way. This means—and it is no doubt a controversial claim—that school systems, including home schools, which deliberately or accidentally omit certain perspectives are morally suspect. A teacher is morally obligated to expose a student to different interpretations of historical events, though, of course, there is no duty weighing on anyone, teacher or student, to adopt any view or interpretation as the truth. The important point is that moral sensitivity requires a robustly diverse and inclusive education involving different perspectives and experiences. The second corollary-duty implied by the duty to seek, listen, and reconsider, is that a person in an oppressed, marginalized, or unprivileged group has the duty to share his or her perspective in a public way, especially directed at those in power.[41] Most of us are privileged in some ways but not in others and hence are obligated to both recognize how privilege might bias our views and to highlight for others the ways in which it might work against us.

MORE THAN COOL REASON?[42]

The core of Kant's ethical theory is that moral duties are based on "pure reason," that is, untainted by empirical desire or contingent fact. Although an ethical system should be expected to draw the line between acting for the right reasons and letting emotions decide for us, Kant's theory seems to create a high barrier. In the attempt to found moral judgment on nothing but "cool reason," without any reference to emotion, desire, particularity, and history, it seems we block our ability as moral reasoners to take into account facts intuitively relevant to the making of moral judgments. Ideally, we would like a theory that can be universal *and* sensitive to the contingencies of the imperfect human beings who implement the theory.

I have shown that Kant's theory can indeed do both of these things. But there is bound to be a severe objection against my attempt to ameliorate it. An ardent defender of Kant might complain that, by encouraging sensitivity to contingencies, I am debasing his theory. Why focus on the moral blindness of Kant's era? After all, we in twenty-first century are undoubtedly blind in ways that for some reason or other we do not see. Every age is blinkered to moral wrongs that are pointed out only later. The problem for my own approach, the objection continues, is that I have introduced *too many* contingencies, to the point that the theory cannot succeed in leading different moral reasoners to the same judgments based on nothing but their cool, unemotional reason. So, while my *improvements* to Kant's theory might succeed in making reasoners more morally sensitive, it also succeeds, to its detriment, in making moral reasoning less *Kantian*. Why embrace a "universal" ethical theory at all, if one must depend on particularities for it to work?

I believe that part of this objection is correct; it is true that an ethical theory must reference more than "cool reason" and account for the messy human conditions in which we all make moral judgments. I disagree, however, that this is any objection to Kant's theory. Indeed, I think Kant himself would entirely agree that responsible, free moral agents are morally obliged to be aware of and take into account their own historical situation. As Herman points out, Kant does not require his moral reasoners to be morally naïve or ignorant.[43] Kant himself offers examples of moral agents applying the categorical imperative in which they *are* sensitive to their surrounding conditions.[44] He argues, for example, that "casuistical questions," that is, questions about how to apply the moral law in particular cases, are "most helpful to the pupil's moral development" to help "test their understanding."[45] Knowledge of the peculiarities of one's case, therefore, does not interfere with the basing of moral judgments on reason alone; it merely guides one to understand what is morally relevant.

Without doubt, no matter how carefully a person follows the duty to "seek, listen, and reconsider," morally suspect judgments are still possible. I have agreed with Herman that the formal elements of Kant's theory only operate against a background of RMS. But because those rules depend on one's moral community, and hence on one's time in history, the duty to seek, listen, and reconsider will be manifested in different ways for different communities and the individuals within those communities. The details that were morally salient for Kant included one's class and one's health, as we can see in his insistence that we sympathize with debtors and the sick. We might think Kant then fulfilled his duty to seek, listen, and reconsider because he brought attention to the mistreatment of *those* people. Hence, it could seem that he fulfilled the tripartite duty I described while simultaneously maintaining his sexism and racism. Because the duty to seek, listen, and reconsider is an "imperfect" one, there is no certain way to know whether one has sufficiently examined one's own views.

Casting this point as an objection, however, is based on what I believe is a false assumption about Kant's ethical system: that because it emphasizes "pure reason," it will, *in its application*, lead to unquestionable, absolutely objective results. I do not think this is true, and I do not think Kant thought it to be true. While I do think he would agree that pure reason, in its *perfect* application, would lead every human, no matter their circumstance, to the same conclusions, I think he would acknowledge and be perfectly comfortable with the fact that the actual application is always imperfect, given one's RMS. Kant's emphasis on pure reason and objectivity in moral judgment, I maintain, was meant as an *ideal*—an end or goal that he thought humans should attempt to approximate the best they can.[46] I do not believe that he understood our considered ethical judgments as settled knowledge, the way that he thought the laws of Newtonian physics were. The "good will," which he says every agent should act in accordance with, is not a finished product that we can point to; rather, it is the ethical standard by which we judge human action as morally praiseworthy or blameworthy.

Granted, Kant often talks as though he believes that application of the categorical imperative will lead unerringly to objective judgments. But there is also much evidence he was fully aware that human reasoners will not actually execute pure reason in a perfect way. Kant insists that one has a duty to improve oneself,[47] which of course includes the duty to strive for moral perfection. But a "morally perfect" being would be one who always acts on the right motives, motivated only by respect for the moral law.[48] Yet he recognizes that one can never fully know one's true motives. "The depths of the human heart are unfathomable," he admits.[49] To be sure, the inaccessibility of one's motives is not the same as the ignorance or bias that might lead one to make questionable moral judgments. The former consists of doing the right thing but possibly for the wrong reasons (selfish reasons, that is, rather than out of respect for the moral law). The latter consists of not having sufficiently investigated one's own beliefs about what features of the world or of other persons are morally relevant. But they have this much in common: someone who is unaware of selfish motives can also be unaware how bias and privilege might affect the content of maxims. The possibility of either sort of case helps explain why Kant would accept that moral judgment, despite its basis in "pure reason," is not *in any case* perfect. Otherwise, the duty to strive for moral perfection would not make sense. Indeed, Kant thinks that moral perfection is impossible in a human life-span, which incidentally proves, he thinks, that we are immortal, since if it were impossible, we could not be obligated to strive for it.[50]

Further evidence that Kant knows that human moral judgment is imperfect is found in his argument that one has the moral duty to "know oneself," that is, to know one's tendencies toward selfishness and one's moral weaknesses.[51] Such a requirement would appear unnecessary, if to follow the categorical imperative is merely a matter of following cool and objective reason. Also, notably, Kant thinks that history morally progresses, which again would not make much sense unless Kant allowed for different ages to be led by reason to different moral judgments. In short, Kant does not regard "reason" and its application in the categorical imperative as faulty for not actually leading to absolutely objective judgments. Rather, the evidence shows that he considers the categorical imperative to yield perfect results only under ideal conditions, which we know is not the nature of our world. But a world in which it becomes possible to identify, then ignore, and ultimately overcome one's selfish motives and biases is worth striving for.

Admittedly, the tripartite duty I have described is not a perfect solution, and it might not have corrected Kant's own racism and sexism. But he was human: a being endowed with reason and needing to make moral judgments in a world of emotion, desire, distorted information, unfair presumptions, and unjust histories. We are all so human. Kant's theory, I believe, motivates us to be humans in a morally richer sense: beings endowed with reason who can self-reflect, recognize the plights of others, and *change*. That is the part of our humanity worth fighting for.

NOTES

1. Immanuel Kant, *The Metaphysics of Morals*, 6:462, in *Practical Philosophy*, trans and ed. Mary J. Gregor (Cambridge: Cambridge University Press, 1996), 579.

2. Kant, *On the Feeling of the Beautiful and Sublime*, 2:244-55, in *Anthropology, History, and Education* ed., Günter Zöller and Robert B. Louden, trans. Mary Gregor et al. (Cambridge: Cambridge University Press, 2007), 52-62.

3. Kant, *On the Feeling of the Beautiful and Sublime*, 2:253, in *Anthropology, History, and Education*, ed. Zöller and Louden, 59; Kant's use of boldface.

4. See Kant, *Anthropology From a Pragmatic Point of View*, 7:314-20, in *Anthropology, History, and Education*, ed. Zöller and Louden, 409-15.

5. Allen W. Wood provides this defense of Kant—or rather, indicates that Kant's philosophy needs no defense against his personal views. As Wood says,

> It is a sometimes uncomfortable fact that the philosophers of the past whose thoughts we study with most profit were not especially fine human beings. The only way to deal with this fact is to face up squarely to the cognitive dissonance it occasions and then to resolve to set it aside as irrelevant to anything that could be of legitimate interest in deciding which philosophers to study. It displays a deplorable misunderstanding of what philosophy is—and what may be gained by studying it—to treat past philosophers as gurus at whose feet we are to sit in order to absorb their wisdom, or alternatively, to find in their unattractive personal traits and characteristics an excuse for not studying them at all. If a past philosopher, Kant for instance, was an admirable person, that still gives us no reason to study his philosophical thoughts if they were unoriginal or mediocre and do not repay our careful investigation and critical reflection. If the philosopher was a thoroughly unattractive character, or even if some of his opinions on morality or politics offend enlightened people today, it may still be true that his contributions to philosophy are indispensable to our understanding of philosophical problems and of the history of people's reflections on them. (Wood, "Kant's Life and Works," in *A Companion to Kant*, ed. Graham Bird [West Sussex: Wiley-Blackwell, 2010], 20.)

6. See, for example, Sally Sedgwick, "Can Kant's Ethics Survive the Feminist Critique?" in *Feminist Interpretations of Immanuel Kant*, ed. Robin May Schott (University Park: Pennsylvania State University Press, 1997), 77-100.

7. For a particularly engaging discussion of this question, see Robin May Schott, "The Gender of Enlightenment," in *Feminist Interpretations of Immanuel Kant*, ed. Schott (University Park: Pennsylvania State University Press, 1997), 320-37.

8. Whether that means that the theory is *inherently* white and male is then a separate question. But at the very least, such an analysis would show that the theory privileges those in power, which happen to be white men.

9. See Kant, *Metaphysics of Morals*, 6:456-57 and 6:463, in *Practical Philosophy*, trans and ed. Gregor, 574-75 and 579-80.

10. See Kant, *Groundwork for the Metaphysics of Morals*, 4:414, and 4:441-45, in *Practical Philosophy*, trans and ed. Gregor, 67-68, and 89-93.

11. Thanks to Robert E. Tully for the wonderful example.

12. Kant, *Groundwork*, 4:446-48, in *Practical Philosophy*, trans and ed. Gregor, 94-96.

13. Kant, *Groundwork*, 4:416, in *Practical Philosophy*, trans and ed. Gregor, 68-69.

14. Kant, *Groundwork*, 4:421; emphasis in the original, in *Practical Philosophy*, trans and ed. Gregor, 73.

15. Here I follow John Rawls's interpretation in *Lectures on the History of Moral Philosophy*, ed. Barbara Herman (Cambridge, MA: Harvard University Press, 2000), 167-70.

16. Kant, *Groundwork*, 4:422, in *Practical Philosophy*, trans and ed. Gregor, 73-74.

17. Kant cannot clearly accommodate humans who seem to lack rationality (e.g., babies, small children, those with advanced dementia). This is seen by some to be a decisive objection against his theory.

18. Kant, of course, came before the Third Reich, so did not talk of Nazis at the door. But he does eerily anticipate the type of case that became only too real for those who lived under Hitler's regime: a murderer is at the door asking if the victim is in your home, which he is. Kant argues one is not allowed to lie in such a case. See *On a Supposed Right to Lie from Philanthropy*, 8:425-30, in *Practical Philosophy*, trans and ed. Gregor, 611-15.

19. This is a case of civil disobedience. Kant did not believe a citizen to have such a right (*Metaphysics of Morals*, 6:321-22, in *Practical Philosophy*, trans and ed. Gregor, 464-65).

20. *Metaphysics of Morals*, 6:314, in *Practical Philosophy*, trans and ed. Gregor, 457-58.

21. Kant, *Groundwork*, 4:407, in *Practical Philosophy*, trans and ed. Gregor, 61-62.

22. This objection is a regular one against Kantian ethics. George Wilhelm Frederick Hegel perhaps made it most forcefully. See *Natural Law: The Scientific Ways of Treating Natural Law, Its Place in Moral Philosophy*, trans. T. M. Knox (Philadelphia: University of Pennsylvania Press, 1975), 77.

23. As Jeffrey A. Gauthier puts it, "one of the features of systems of oppression such as racism and sexism that makes them so difficult to change is the fact that even thoughtful and perceptive moral agents can perpetuate the systems without consciously willing any racist or sexist principles at all." ("Hegel and the Problem of Particularity in Moral Judgment," in *Women's Philosophy Review* 22 [Autumn 1999]: 70).

24. Examples of moral "sentimentalism" includes Hume's and Adam Smith's ethical theories. Kant quickly dismisses Frances Hutcheson's version, saying it is "without exception empirical and obviously not at all qualified for the universal principle of morality" (Kant, *Critique of Practical Reason*, 5:41, in *Practical Philosophy*, trans and ed. Gregor, 172-73).

25. Barbara Herman, "The Practice of Moral Judgment," *Journal of Philosophy* 82, no. 8 (August 1985), 414-15.

26. Herman, "Practice of Moral Judgment," 415.

27. Herman, "Practice of Moral Judgment," 415.

28. Herman, "Practice of Moral Judgment," 425.

29. Herman, "Practice of Moral Judgment," 428.

30. In this way, RMS are not arbitrary or conventional, Herman says, but rather based in what Kant calls the "moral law" (Herman, "Practice of Moral Judgment," 428-29). They force the deliberating agent to ask questions about who is a moral agent or end in himself, what the conditions of agency are for those moral agents, and what the "marks of reasonable claims and restraints" are accordingly.

31. Kant, *Groundwork*, 4:428, in *Practical Philosophy*, trans and ed. Gregor, 79.

32. Herman, "Practice of Moral Judgment," 431.

33. Hegel, *Natural Law*, trans., Knox, 59; emphasis mine.

34. Hegel, *Natural Law*, trans., Knox, 68.

35. Hegel, *Natural Law*, trans., Knox, 68.

36. Herman agrees, "Practice of Moral Judgment," 432.

37. Kant, *Metaphysics of Morals*, § 34-35, in *Practical Philosophy*, trans and ed. Gregor, 440-43.

38. Kant, *Metaphysics of Morals*, 6:457-58, in *Practical Philosophy*, trans and ed. Gregor, .

39. Kant, *Metaphysics of Morals*, 6:463, in *Practical Philosophy*, trans and ed. Gregor, .

40. See esp. *Lectures on Pedagogy*, 9:487, in *Anthropology, History, and Education*, ed. Zöller and Louden, 474-75.

41. Indeed, Carol Hay argues that Kant's theory entails that the oppressed person must also stand up for themselves in the face of injustice. See "A Feminist Kant," *New York Times*, December 8, 2013, *Opinionator* (blog), https://opinionator.blogs.nytimes.com/2013/12/08/a-feminist-kant/?_r=0 (accessed April 15, 2018).

42. I borrow this title from George Lakoff and Mark Turner's *More Than Cool Reason: A Field Guide to Poetic Metaphor* (Chicago: University of Chicago Press, 1989). They argue that the whole Enlightenment's goal of "cool reason," of which Kant was the most forceful advocate, is a ruse, since judgment involves relying on metaphors based on human embodiment.

43. Herman, "Practice," 419.

44. Kant, *Groundwork*, 4:421-23, in *Practical Philosophy*, trans and ed. Gregor, 73-75.

45. Kant, *Metaphysics of Morals*, 6:483, in *Practical Philosophy*, trans and ed. Gregor, 595-96.

46. It is technically what Kant would call an "idea," which is a concept that is incongruent with experience, meaning that nothing in experience will ever be congruent with it (see *Critique of Pure Reason*, ed. and trans. Paul Guyer and Allen W. Wood [Cambridge: Cambridge University Press, 1998], A313/B370, 395-96).

47. Kant, *Metaphysics of Morals*, 6:444-47, in *Practical Philosophy*, trans and ed. Gregor, 564-67.

48. Kant, *Metaphysics of Morals*, 6:446, in *Practical Philosophy*, trans and ed. Gregor, 566-67.

49. Kant, *Metaphysics of Morals*, 6:447, in *Practical Philosophy*, trans and ed. Gregor, 567; and *Groundwork*, 4:407, in *Practical Philosophy*, trans and ed. Gregor, 61-62.

50. See Kant, *Critique of Practical Reason* 5:110-111, in *Practical Philosophy*, trans and ed. Gregor, 228-29.

51. Kant, *Groundwork*, 4:407, in *Practical Philosophy*, trans and ed. Gregor, 61-62.

REFERENCES

Gauthier, Jeffrey A. "Hegel and the Problem of Particularity in Moral Judgment." *Women's Philosophy Review* 22 (Autumn 1999): 5-105.

Hay, Carol. "A Feminist Kant." *New York Times*, December 8, 2013. *Opinionator* (blog). https://opinionator.blogs.nytimes.com/2013/12/08/a-feminist-kant/ (accessed April 15, 2018).

Hegel, George Wilhelm Frederick. *Natural Law: The Scientific Ways of Treating Natural Law, Its Place in Moral Philosophy*, trans. T. M. Knox. Philadelphia: University of Pennsylvania Press, 1975.

Herman, Barbara. "The Practice of Moral Judgment." *Journal of Philosophy* 82, no. 8 (August 1985): 414-36.

Kant, Immanuel. *Anthropology, History, and Education*. Edited by Günter Zöller and Robert B. Louden. Translated by Mary Gregor, Paul Guyer, Robert B. Louden, Holly Wilson, Allen W. Wood, Günter Zöller, and Arnulf Zweig. Cambridge Edition of the Works of Immanuel Kant. Cambridge: Cambridge University Press, 2007.

———. *Critique of Pure Reason*. Edited and translated by Paul Guyer and Allen W. Wood. Cambridge Edition of the Works of Immanuel Kant. Cambridge: Cambridge University Press, 1998.

———. *Practical Philosophy*. Translated and edited by Mary J. Gregor. Cambridge Edition of the Works of Immanuel Kant. Cambridge: Cambridge University Press, 1996.

Lakoff, George, and Mark Turner. *More Than Cool Reason: A Field Guide to Poetic Metaphor*. Chicago: University of Chicago Press, 1989.

Rawls, John. *Lectures on the History of Moral Philosophy*. Edited by Barbara Herman. Cambridge, MA: Harvard University Press, 2000.

Schott, Robin May. "The Gender of Enlightenment." In *Feminist Interpretation of Immanuel Kant*, edited by Robin May Schott, 320- 37. University Park: Pennsylvania State University Press, 1997.

Sedgwick, Sally. "Can Kant's Ethics Survive the Feminist Critique?" In *Feminist Interpretations of Immanuel Kant*, edited by Robin May Schott, 77-100. University Park: Pennsylvania State University Press, 1997.

Wood, Allen W. "Kant's Life and Works." In *A Companion to Kant*, edited by Graham Bird, 10-30. West Sussex: Wiley-Blackwell, 2010.

Chapter 16

Inequality in Skepticism

Robert E. Tully

In these days of truthiness, fake news, alternative facts, and the constant stirring of partisan passions inside social bubbles, skeptics provide a convenient target. The logic of social commitment is simple: if you are not with me, then you are against me. Committed believers—whatever the belief—easily suspect a skeptic's refusal to endorse their claim as equivalent to accepting its denial, and the rejection of a pair of contrary claims as irrational. Dismissal of the skeptic has a long pedigree. Among truth seekers, skeptics have long been called scoffers and truth-deniers. Dismissed by the herd, skeptics are not considered as fellow-travelers in the pursuit of truth but simply as laggards. Indeed, since ancient times this has been their reputation even among philosophers, except of course among professed skeptics. The skeptic has been conveniently treated as antagonistic towards truth, a relentless opponent to be either refuted or rejected, and never as its guardian. The idea therefore that skepticism itself might be needed to protect truth seems comparable to a farmer's entrusting his chickens to a fox.

Nevertheless, I aim to elaborate and defend this idea. More exactly, I intend to promote a form of skepticism which I will argue is essential to Philosophy and adds value to it. But my purpose is not to bring skepticism in from the cold and give it a place with other "-isms" in the web of beliefs. The skepticism I have in mind is neither a theory nor an ideology. What I call *prudential* skepticism does not station itself alongside religion, politics, atheism, agnosticism, or natural science, nor does it promote the views of their adherents. In other words, it stands in contrast to what I will call *dogmatic* skepticism. Although skepticism of the sort I want to defend does place *reason* and *truth* at the center, the commitments it makes to them, once these have been explained, might strike many as thin, abstract, and unappealing, perhaps so remote as to seem beyond the fringe.

Indifference would not be surprising. Since the time of David Hume (1711-1776), skepticism in Philosophy has represented a robust opposition to traditional metaphysical and theological claims about, for instance, the status of the self or the existence and nature of God. It has become virtually a doctrine in itself, a sort of negative metaphysics whose adopted framework is modern science. Hume's own views were rooted in an ancient tradition he called *academical* or *mitigated* skepticism, traceable to the successors of Plato, but Hume also rejected an extreme version he called "*excessive* skepticism," or Pyrrhonism, associated with Pyrrho of Elis, who predated both Socrates and Plato. The form of skepticism I want to develop, prudential skepticism, is even more mitigated than Hume's. Given the framework of science, the dogmatic skepticism associated with his philosophy has an abundance of truths in its grasp which are the received truths of natural science. Indeed, it is a doctrine dominated by assurance rather than by doubt. I intend to challenge neither those truths nor the entitlement of modern skeptics to rely on them. The basic philosophical question I raise is whether there are facts and truths to be found *outside* this framework. However, before turning to examine the relationship between "fact" and "truth," and the role that skepticism has played in the Empiricist tradition, I want to distinguish skepticism of any sort in philosophy from mere cynicism. My final topic will be to consider the limits of the framework of truths Hume has bequeathed us.

SKEPTICISM VS. CYNICISM

The word "cynic" has endured far longer than the philosophical school known as Cynicism. The Cynics traced their origin to Socrates but lacked a Plato to immortalize their doctrines and arguments. Unlike the Sophists, however, the Cynics do not seem to have sold their services as teachers, or to have been targeted by other schools in Athens for advancing skeptical views about knowledge. According to the fragmentary record of their views the Cynics offered a philosophy of life that stressed self-discipline, strength of character, independence, living in accordance with nature, and maintaining social detachment. Nevertheless, ancient accounts tell us that Cynics such as Diogenes aimed to be part of the world. He defied social conventions, insulted the rich and famous, chastised politicians, and interpreted the principle of living according to nature to include practices not normally performed in public. Anecdotes about this philosopher suggest he was also a mixture of hippie and performance artist. He doubtless would have had many followers on Facebook. Unfortunately, love of gossip about Diogenes seems to have distracted historians' attention from recording his philosophical arguments. The school itself disappeared in the sixth century AD.

What we call cynicism today is not a descendant of the ancient school and should be distinguished from any brand of philosophical skepticism with regard to truth. A skeptic's proper concern is where to draw the line between knowledge and belief and what should count as a criterion of certainty. Some skeptics may even conclude that no such criterion exists. But a cynic disparages the task itself. Skeptics argue that what is ordinarily considered knowledge does not pass the test, that truth is elusive if attainable at all, and that the persistence of conflicting beliefs is a sure sign that the so-called edifice knowledge is no more than a set of accepted beliefs which have earned only a temporary right to be called true. Cynics by-pass the argument. Truth for the cynic is in the eyes of the beholder, or at the beholder's convenience. The cynics' attitude to truth corresponds to the ethical view that the meaning of notions like *justice*, *right*, and *wrong* varies from person to person and, if fixed at all, is decided by the person with the power to enforce what these words mean. Plato long ago sought to expose and refute such a view in Socrates' reported encounters with famous Sophists.[1] Unfortunately, while Plato's arguments are philosophical accomplishments in themselves, they probably never converted the Sophists, nor would they likely persuade anyone else, then or now, whose commitments are dominated by self-interest. The tendency to subordinate morality to political power is a social constant.

The perennial challenge to Philosophy, including skepticism, is to reach a deeper level than that of self-interest. Even a skeptic needs a starting point for this purpose, some assumed truth or other, before deploying reasons for rejecting it. Arguments are what determine whether or not a belief is true and therefore worth holding. Arguments test beliefs. A cynic, however, adopts beliefs on different grounds and with enough self-assurance to give them the appearance of being true. The beliefs might be sustained by the force of emotion, including a feeling of righteousness; or they might nest comfortably with prejudices held by family or friends; or catch a wave of "woke" opinions trending in the media. A cynic's beliefs are held so firmly that arguments for them seem unnecessary, while criticisms against them are treated as offensive. Human society is fertile ground for rumors, half-truths, propaganda, and disinformation. Cynics and willing followers have existed for as long as there have been political parties, agenda-heavy newspapers, taverns and salons, pulpits and soap boxes, and local water wells. In Hume's words: "Ambition, avarice, self-love, vanity, friendship, generosity, public spirit; these passions, mixed in various degrees, and distributed through society, have been, from the beginning of the world, and still are, the sources of all actions and enterprises, which have ever been observed among mankind."[2] News sites and social media are merely the most effective outlets to date.

In pointing at the cynic I mean to be pointing into a mirror. The distance is negligible. Cynics are not other persons but another part of ourselves.

Emotions permeate our beliefs, and the words we find to express them are rarely unaffected by a rhetorical tinge of approval or disapproval. The real difference between the cynic and the non-cynic within us is one of degree, but at the extremes the difference is substantial. A belief held with reason may never be free of emotion, but emotions without reason can form the hard core of prejudicial beliefs. The cynic in us sometimes takes the mere strength of conviction to be a measure of its truth. Skepticism, especially of the dogmatic form, is not free of this tension. There is always the risk that the achievements of a skeptical argument become detached from the impulse of doubt that drove them and are then allowed to harden into the convictions of a closed mind. The duty of prudential skepticism is to keep creative doubt alive and, as much as possible, to balance the tension by argument. But that effort requires some sense of what is to count as truth.

FACTS VS. FICTION

Fake claims are new in name alone.[3] What causes them to be fake has never changed. It is essentially a simple matter, as simple as the difference between true and false. A knowledge of this fundamental difference is built into our use of language and is no less natural than pointing to things. However, human language is not neutral between the two poles of truth and falsity. The intended *default* meaning of the statements we make is that they are true. For instance, if we tell someone that the President tweeted an abusive message last night, we may disbelieve *what* the tweet says but at least we intend it to be taken as true that there *was* such a tweet. That is the way reports are meant to be taken. Communication functions on the basis of this default setting. Liars exploit it.

Fake claims are false though usually not completely detached from reality if they are meant to deceive others into accepting them as true. It is not the deception itself, however, which renders a claim false. A claim is fake if it is false but not false because it is fake. A serial liar can succeed in deceiving others by telling them something the liar knows full well to be *not* true. A claim is false because there is no fact which makes it true. The absence of a fact is not marginal or incidental. Fake claims can be politically effective and psychologically compelling but fundamentally they are irrational. They violate the logic of language and a semantical rule of communication. A claim with no fact to support it is gaseous. At best it expresses merely someone's feeling or attitude without delivering any fact to us, even though we might want to accept it. Or the claim might be an instance of self-deception, willful or not. At worst, a fake claim expresses a false belief that someone is inclined to hold *despite* the facts and perhaps also wants us to accept. Fake claims are the common currency of cynics. Some cynics are also liars.

Claims represent facts to us. They point to them, direct our attention to them. If we understand a claim then we understand what fact is meant, that is, what would *have* to be the case *if* the claim is true. But a claim does not make itself true; what makes it true is the existence of the fact it represents. One way of describing the relationship between claims and facts is to say that the former *correspond* to the latter. A more vivid description is that true claims *picture* or *mirror* facts.[4] False claims are warped or broken mirrors—in other words, there is no fact corresponding to them.

True and false claims are relatively tangible items. They comprise the statements we make in words or in writing, and the statements we encounter when we hear or read them. In a broad sense, therefore, claims are physical (sentences spoken, words on a page, text on a screen). We use them to assert facts. But what, then, are facts? Since we regularly speak of *making* statements, what sort of product is involved? What exactly is being reflected? Consider two examples: Donald Trump was elected 45th U.S. President in November, 2016; the color of his hair is golden (a word hairdressers might avoid). Both of these claims are true; we are dealing with facts. Yet at this very point the metaphor of picturing facts seems to fail us. The relationship between a true claim and its fact is nothing like that of a landscape painting to the landscape, or of a selfie to the face of the person holding the iPhone. We can point *at* Donald Trump—many do—and at televised events we can see *that* his hair has a golden color. We can see the color and also his head and face, etc., but in addition to these details we do not literally *see* a further item, the particular fact we assert. The countless claims people have made that Trump was elected are not fake, since they all point to the same fact. But where then is that fact? Words like "*pointing*" and "*represent*" bring us only to a threshold, beckoning us towards something not visible.

One way to approach this question is to ask what the natural world would contain if there were no human beings. Such a world would have eruptions and eclipses, hurricanes, the seasons, diseases, births and deaths among all the other species, global warming as well as global cooling—all the different sorts of objects and events that humans could talk about if they too were on the planet. But a world without humans is a world without facts. Facts enter the scene with language, however primitive the language. Facts are the sophisticated means by which humans process their experience of things and convey that experience to others through language, at times merely through gestures. What we perceive now or remember perceiving furnishes evidence for our claims. The claims we make closely tie us to the world by means of such evidence. Facts are the way in which humans package the evidence of their senses; and claims—the statements we formulate in language—are the wrapping of the package. It is one thing to *see* the color of the President's hair, another to *say* what color it is.

Human language, I suggest, should be regarded as a complex form of perception. Given our current technology and understanding of physiology, we are comfortable enough with the idea that the eyes (along with the whole optical mechanism of the brain) process wavelengths into well-formed patterns of color that we identify as familiar visual objects (like rainbows and road signs). We take it for granted that the world we see is, somehow, *there* to be seen. However, if people universally were blind, their world would lack visual objects. There would be no colors for humans to perceive, to pick out, name and describe. Of course, we could speculate about what sorts of sensory content might be associated with particular stimuli, analogous to what sharks might experience through their specialized faculty of electroreception, or could try to imagine what ultraviolet colors would look like if we had the right sort of receptors in our eyes. But we do not see ultraviolet colors, and if the human species were eyeless none of us would see colors at all. Equally, there would be no visual facts to communicate, literal facts involving colors on which to agree or to dispute. But even if there were no visual facts there would still be perceptual facts of some kind or other to be encountered, if there is anything at all that our experience of the natural world delivered to us. For the contents of all such experiences would be—as they are with seeing—the raw material for our claims about that world. The world is a constant source of factual content for such claims.

Not only do facts enter the world with language, so also does truth. The color of Trump's hair itself is not true, but a claim about it is true (or fails to be true) only because of a fact. To verify a claim, that is, to establish its truth, is thus to locate whatever fact the claim directs us to. Just as we depend on experience in order to obtain facts, we depend on facts in order to be able to say something true about the world. What we call human knowledge, then, is the continuing product of this process.[5] It is constrained by extremes. An absolutely factless world, one with which we had no contact whatever, could not be a source of knowledge since it would not be a source of experience. An absolutely subjective world, on the other hand, would be devoid of communicable claims and facts, if any such facts exist. True claims are anchored to the evidence of experience and built upon it. False claims—including fake news—are language adrift. Between these two limits is a sliding scale whose fulcrum is balanced by the results of appealing to evidence. There is a constant need to demand facts and to weigh claims by recognized standards of evidence, to render doubtful claims more certain, and occasionally to show that what has been accepted as indubitable is no longer so. The growth of scientific knowledge is probably the most refined example of this process, though it is clearly not an algorhythmic one. Human communication is uneven in its results and more or less fragile in the degree of its acceptance of truths. Robots would likely manage the process more smoothly.

What I have just described is an idealization of a very imperfect world, but it is the common world which even deceivers inhabit. Skeptics, whatever their popular reputation, play by the rules of this world. They are concerned with facts. There would be no point disputing a claimed truth if it could not be shown to be false or at least not worth holding. Both prudential and dogmatic skeptics are defenders of truth despite disagreeing over the scope of truths to defend. But if truth were conceded to lie only in the eyes of the beholder, the very concept of truth would become hollow. Skepticism in Philosophy therefore represents a healthy commitment to connecting claims with facts, respect for evidence, and the need to test arguments for soundness. Contrasted with cynicism, it does not attack the logical framework of human knowledge. The tradition of skepticism is to scrutinize whatever facts philosophers claim to be available within that framework; for their part, the efforts philosophers have made to preserve those facts after close scrutiny reveal the homage they have been willing to pay that tradition. The central question emerges, then: what sorts of facts survive the closest scrutiny?

SKEPTICISM'S PROGRESS

The history of modern Empiricism, which began to flourish in the early seventeenth century, contains three supreme ironies generated by the philosophical quest for stability against a skeptical undertow:

(1) The first irony is that the doctrines designed by early philosophers to combat extreme skepticism were accused by later ones of promoting it. René Descartes (1596-1650) was firmly convinced that his arguments drove a stake into the heart of skepticism of the kind that was popularized a generation earlier by Michel de Montaigne (1533-1592).[6] John Locke (1632-1704), although Cartesian in many respects, nevertheless contended that Descartes' ambitious method was based on false claims about the existence of innate and indubitable truths. Moreover, he contended that so ambitious a method only led philosophical speculation "into the vast ocean of *being*, as if all that boundless extent, were the natural and undoubted possession of our understandings." No wonder then, Locke continued, that philosophers "raise questions, and multiply disputes, which never coming to any clear resolution, are proper only to continue and increase their doubts, and to confirm them at last in perfect skepticism."[7]

But George Berkeley (1685-1753) argued with considerable ingenuity that Locke's own approach, which distinguished between sensory ideas (directly experienced) and the physical causes of those ideas (never directly experienced), in fact created an insurmountable barrier between perceivers and the external world. Consequently, if we take those ideas as images that refer "to *things* or *archetypes* existing without [outside] the mind," Berkeley wrote, if we "suppose a difference between *things* and *ideas*, and that the former have a subsistence without the mind, or unperceived," then "we are involved all in *skepticism*."[8]

Yet Hume regarded Berkeley himself as prince among skeptics, remarking that "most of the writings of that very ingenious author form the best lessons of scepticism, which are to be found either among the ancient or modern philosopher." In Hume's opinion, Berkeley's skepticism does not qualify as *mitigated* (or moderate): "that all his arguments are, in reality, merely sceptical, appears from this, *that they admit of no answer and produce no conviction*. Their only effect is to cause that momentary amazement and irresolution and confusion, which is the result of scepticism."[9] The ability to stun the mind and render it confused about the very possibility of attaining truth is the signature of the extreme and virulent type of skepticism which Hume called Pyrrhonism.

The final section of Hume's *Enquiry* was meant not only as an epitaph for metaphysics but also as a call to philosophers to redirect their efforts "to such subjects as fall under daily practice and experience; leaving the more sublime topics to the embellishment of poets and orators, or to the arts of priests and politicians."[10] The results of genuine philosophical research, he declared, are only aspects of "common life, methodized and corrected." Hence such enquiries, if not concerned with mathematics and similarly abstract domains, should deal only with ordinary matters of fact and existence, which are "incapable of demonstration." Hume thus presents the framework of what I call dogmatic skepticism. He has no doubt whatever about whether there are facts, what the facts are, and where to find them. The dogmatic skeptic's truths include those of modern "natural philosophy" [Physics] and "chemistry," which have abandoned the aspirations of traditional metaphysics. Philosophical claims cannot be organized under the heading of "Principles," as Berkeley had done, nor can truths about the world be deduced from self-evident truths of reason, as Descartes had attempted. From Hume's standpoint, Philosophy's progress, even ignoring all of the bumps encountered along the way, can hardly be described as linear. Its path has circled back to a starting point predating Descartes.[11]

(2) A perhaps greater irony in Empiricism is that its founders endorsed in their own work a major tenet of traditional skepticism: that our senses, and generally our whole physiological nature, constitute unreliable sources of knowledge. The ancient views of Sextus Empiricus, rehearsed in the late sixteenth century by Montaigne,[12] provided posterity constant reminders of such deficiencies. The early skeptics remind us that what we see varies according

to distance, lighting, time of day, age, and the condition of our eyesight, so that two people often do not see literally the *same* shapes and colors, even if they agree in the words they use for them. We see that straight objects (like oars) appear bent when inserted in the water; that the very same water is warm when felt by a cold hand but cool when felt by a warm one; and that a tower, roundish from afar, is seen closer up to be straight-sided rather than curved. Although we do not believe such objects really change their shape or do have incompatible temperatures at the same moment, and although common sense is comfortable with such cases without being plunged into skepticism, the traditional examples drawn from everyday experience force us to recognize that our senses and our bodies are the permanent medium through which we apprehend the world. Its variability is partly thus a function of ourselves, which directly affects our ability to form true beliefs. The prevailing assumption of common sense, that mere transparency separates us from the outer world, that we see things *directly* and *as* they are, cannot therefore be true. But if all knowledge begins with sensation, as philosophers since the time of Aristotle have contended, then the medium must always distort the message, more or less.

Seventeenth century scientists developed a more radical version of skepticism about the senses which reached back to a physical theory known as *atomism.*[13] Common sense conveniently decides which color counts as the "real" color of an object, but according to the new scientific theory color *itself* is not a property of physical objects at all. Science and common sense perceive the same world but parse it differently, and science has the superior grammar. To the atomist, the genuine properties of matter are few. Galileo limited those properties to *size*, *shape*, spatio-temporal *location*, *motion*, and *mass*. They are what define matter down even to the level of imperceptible atoms. The rest of what we sense belongs elsewhere or not at all:

> I think … that these tastes, odors, colors, etc., so far as their objective existence is concerned, are nothing but mere names for something which resides exclusively in our sensitive body, so that if the perceiving creatures were removed, all of these qualities would be annihilated and abolished from existence. But just because we have given special names to these qualities, different from the names we have given to the primary and real properties, we are tempted into believing that the former really and truly exist as well as the latter.[14]

The distinction Galileo makes between two kinds of quality, in effect demoting one kind by relegating it to the world of experience, and assigning the other kind to an independent physical world, became fundamental to the metaphysical doctrines of both Descartes and Locke. These two (among others) appropriated a traditional name for the contents of experience, *ideas*. The word usefully distinguished them the uneven border between the physical world and our representations of it. Only those ideas relating to the genuine properties of physical matter, the so-called primary qualities, engage a part of the real world, and these qualities themselves are parts of facts. Ideas of the other kind of qualities mentioned by Galileo, the so-called secondary qualities, are defective representations. To describe an apple as green and tasting bitter may have common sense on its side, but from the side of science the description is false. The so-called evidence of the senses with regard to colors and tastes is trumped by stronger evidence. Physical theory thus provided Descartes and Locke a new vantage point from which to view the world as well as a bulwark against skepticism about the senses. Berkeley would later challenge this barrier, not because he was hostile to science, but because he believed that Physics granted itself privileged access to both sides of the barrier. Berkeley's rejoinder was simple: "But I do not see how the testimony of sense can be alleged, as a proof for the existence of anything, which is not perceived by sense."[15]

(3) The third irony of modern Empiricism is that even the scientific "escape" from skepticism falls prey to similar objections. Why should ideas of primary qualities be any less deceptive than ideas of color? Ideas of *any* kind are subject to the vagaries of perception. Locke was confident that ideas of primary qualities really do resemble their counterparts, to which a skeptic can reply: the question is not whether ideas of primary qualities resemble anything better but whether they resemble anything at all, for a distorted idea which has been set up as a standard bearer for truth leaves us no less detached from the world than do ideas of secondary qualities. It also leaves us a dilemma. Either scientific knowledge should be recast in terms of systematic relationships among ideas themselves or the scientific description of the world should accept the limits on objectivity which skepticism forces it to recognize. Berkeley promoted the first alternative as a radical solution to the problem of skepticism. In his doctrine, known since as Idealism,[16] the raw material for science consists of ideas themselves, systematically classified and organized. By attempting to reconfigure science on a basis of predictable patterns of ideas, Berkeley sought not only to defeat the residual flaws he identified in his predecessors' doctrines but also to vindicate common sense. He was "not for having any man turn *skeptic*," he declared, "and disbelieve his senses."[17] The apparent incompatibility of these two goals might explain why Hume considered Berkeley himself an exemplary skeptic. Berkeley's doctrine made God rather than physical matter the supreme cause of all ideas, the laws of nature being interpreted as God's laws, and thus made Physics subordinate to Theology. His Idealism was therefore unlikely to win converts among those seeking independent truth in the universal objectivity of science. Instead, it offered science a

foundation not merely based on experience but consisting of it, thereby rendering facts subjective.

Hume did not solve this dilemma but preferred to avoid it. He positioned himself between the mind and the world it perceives, not so much as gatekeeper than as omniscient observer. The observed world for Hume contains the familiar objects of sense perception—the sun, snow, mountains, paintings, animals, and all the facts of common sense whereby we encounter them. Hume did not divide the world between the primary qualities outside and the ideas within by which the mind makes sense of the perceived world. In Hume's epistemology, ideas are reckoned to be *copies* of impressions, and impressions lie very much at the safe physical interface between our bodies and the other objects we encounter. His doctrine remains very much on the side of common sense in its relation to the scientific account of the world. Their co-existence is peaceful. Hume allows no wedge to force them apart.

Yet the claims that common sense makes about the facts of perception are the very ones contested by both traditional skepticism and seventeenth century scientific atomism, not to mention by the sciences Hume commends to us in the *Enquiry*. Consequently, if metaphysics in the Empiricist tradition since Descartes has indeed led back under Hume's guidance to a pre-Cartesian era, it has traveled not merely a bumpy road but has arrived with dignity lost. Common sense and what I have called dogmatic skepticism are the survivors. Hume seems to have been sanguine about this outcome, which suggests a fourth great irony about Empiricism that I shall mention at the conclusion.

SKEPTICISM, METAPHYSICS, AND COMMON SENSE

The skeptical attitude found in the natural sciences, despite professional disagreements, is benign and productive. As facts gradually accumulate and settle (though unevenly), and as theories become corroborated, a bedrock of agreement forms among scientists. Truth is gained, achievements are lauded, and scientific knowledge progresses. In Philosophy, however, the natural condition appears to be one of perpetual disagreement and resistance to progress, and the virtue of learning from mistakes sometimes degenerates into the vice of repeating them. I have described discord of this kind in the history of Empiricist metaphysics, where skepticism came to achieve the status of doctrine. Owing to its inveterate antagonism towards claims about certainty and the existence of facts lying outside the framework of the natural sciences, skepticism of this kind is the evil twin of metaphysics. Yet, because the very identity of Philosophy incorporates metaphysical questions, it seems that *radical inequality*—doctrinal divisiveness rather than mere diversity—afflicts metaphysical enquiry, and perhaps much else in the enterprise of Philosophy.

Skepticism itself has multiple personalities. Hume identified more than six varieties, but his main contrast is between "excessive" or Pyrrhonian skepticism and the moderate variety he recommends (*academical* or *mitigated*). The contest between these two is not settled by reason. According to Hume, the Pyrrhonian's triumphs—irrefutable arguments such as those he attributes to Berkeley—only show the limits of human understanding. Reason itself can therefore offer no solution. Rather, the antidote to Pyrrhonian doubt is the "strong power of natural instinct" to reject it. Rejection does not equal refutation, however, and denial of this kind is not a logical move but merely refusal, a turning away. Is reason then a slave to instinct? When reason in the guise of Empiricist metaphysics deeply conflicts with the instinct of common sense, Hume's answer is clear. The alternative is excessive skepticism. Hume's preference for mitigated skepticism makes it clear he does not consider the natural sciences to be a comparable source of conflict, presumably because the beliefs of common sense stand to be "methodized and corrected" by them. Mitigated skepticism and common sense thus are allies in their understanding of objectivity. Whatever differences are marked out between them, they share a broad framework of empirical facts which science in its continuing research will extend. This framework defines for Hume the limits of empirical knowledge. What makes his mitigated skepticism dogmatic is that he saw neither reason not need to extend those limits.

The *Enquiry* gave only brief attention to the abstract sciences such as arithmetic and geometry. Truths concerning the "relations of ideas" (as Hume called them) are logically certain either intuitively or demonstratively, and their certainty is based on the law of contradiction; that is, their denial entails a logical contradiction, the polar opposite of necessary truth. Hume claimed that they are "discoverable by the mere operation of thought, without dependence on what is any where [*sic*] existent in the universe."[18] Being only formal truths, they lack empirical content. Hume promptly relegated them to the sidelines and later on confirmed their limited role: "It seems to me, that the only objects of the abstract sciences or of demonstration are quantity and number, and that all attempts to extend this more perfect species of knowledge beyond these bounds are mere sophistry and illusion."[19] As is well known, Kant thought Hume had made a major blunder by classifying the truths of mathematics as purely analytic, and by failing to investigate what is involved in that "mere operation of thought" by which their truth is discovered. Mathematical truths do not indeed depend on what exists "in the universe," as Hume contended, but Kant insisted that understanding their truth requires a more complicated cognitive exercise than appealing to the law of contradiction. It requires a process whereby the mind recognizes their necessity, one that is carried out by what he called the *intuition*. Such truths have a dual character. They are formally certain (like analytic truths) but the process whereby the mind brings together their constituent concepts generates new information. Kant thus proclaimed a new class of truths. The mind does not await the test of sense experience to recognize their certainty. They have their basis in reason, outside the context of sense perception, and yet they apply with certainty to any such experience. Kant labeled all such truths *synthetic a priori*. He meant the phrase to capture this dual role which joins certainty with the discovery of conceptual data.

With evident condescension, Kant remarks that if Hume had examined a simple truth of addition, like *7 + 5 = 12*, he would have proceeded to ground its truth on empirical verification, just as he had done in his famous analysis of the relation of cause and effect. But then, Kant says, Hume would have had to do the same for the axioms of mathematics, "which he was far too acute to do."[20] The mortal thrust which Hume intended for metaphysics would necessarily also "have reached mathematics, which was not and could not have been Hume's intention." Kant supposes that Hume would have spotted the flaw in his own doctrine. Having sidelined formal truths, however, Hume preoccupied himself with perceptual experience. He thus failed to notice the richness of cognitive experience and "did not suspect such a formal science" (as Kant calls his own doctrine), but instead deliberately ran his ship aground "on skepticism, there to let it lie and rot."[21] Kant declared that his formal science is replete with synthetic *a priori* truths, a whole new domain of facts to be charted, which provide the real basis of metaphysics, and one that is meant to show the limits of Hume's skepticism.

Although Kant's method of investigation is deeply introspective, the direction it took was not new. The method was first given philosophical prominence more than a century earlier by Descartes. The celebrated first truth of which Descartes had no doubt concerned his own existence, his self, which initially he associates with mental acts such as doubting, willing, and perceiving, not with his own body. Such acts are episodes which warrant true statements like, "I doubt," "I am willing," etc., when they occur. Although hardly mathematical in content, these statements describe facts which, he says, "I think I see utterly clearly with the mind's eye." The truths that such facts support are counted as indubitable. This was Descartes' recipe for dealing with the challenges of traditional skepticism. Deny anything you wish about the material world, he contended. Even when I doubt that what I call my body exists as a material thing, it is impossible for me to deny that my act of denying is occurring. And against the supposition he had made previously, that his thoughts are manipulated by a supreme deceiver who ensures that nothing is indubitable, Descartes declares:

> whenever I turn my attention to those very things that I think I perceive with such great clarity, I am so completely persuaded by them that I spontaneously

> blurt out these words: let anyone who can do so deceive me; so long as I think that I am something, he will never bring it about that I am nothing. Nor will he one day make it true that I never existed, for it is true now that I do exist. Nor will he even bring it about that perhaps two plus three might equal more or less than five, or similar items in which I recognize an obvious contradiction.[22]

Descartes sought to anchor his basic truths to a pair of moorings: common sense about the self-validating immediacy of his own experience, and the laws of logical certainty. He used both of these to construct arguments, the truth of each premise being consciously affirmed, and each conclusion demonstrably true from such premises, not only for Descartes himself but also for anyone whose own "mind's eye" is directed toward them. The plan of the *Meditations* was intended to lead attentive readers willing to repeat the stages, first to their own existence as thinking beings, then to God, but ultimately back to the empirical world, freed finally from the skeptical doubts that might subvert a firm metaphysical foundation for scientific knowledge. Many philosophers since Descartes have doubted that he was justified in claiming to have reached his destination. Kant himself kept his distance. However, my focus is not on Descartes' goals but on the introspective method he introduced to Philosophy, which influenced Empiricist metaphysics until Hume. The focal point is the gaining of knowledge from the standpoint of the knower.

Descartes once challenged the ancient tenet that nothing reaches the understanding unless it has first passed through the senses, in short, that *all* our knowledge originates in perception. This principle is true as far as it goes, he allowed, but doesn't go far enough. Descartes insisted in his *Discourse on Method* that the idea of the self, of what he called the *thinking thing*, did not reach the understanding through the senses but was already waiting there to be encountered.[23] Yet his metaphysics treats the self as a special type of object, modeled on material objects perceived by the senses, except for being remote, private, and also immaterial, which means that Descartes' thinking thing is an object in form only, perhaps in name as well, since every relevant aspect of its identity seems to have been lost in translation. What is ordinarily meant by "I" is the person speaking. The self not only includes the body, it is a social object that expresses its feelings and interacts with others. Descartes does not seem to have recognized the considerable asymmetry. The thinking thing he takes to be his self was not encountered like a valley or a cloud. Although discovered introspectively it was never literally *observed* at all, however attractive the metaphor of introspection (looking within) is. The mind's eye is never seen. Nevertheless, the paradox is that what Descartes misleadingly sought to identify as an inner object is essential to *any* instance of observing. Even introspecting to that extent is a kind of observing. Descartes' method deals with what might be called cognitive facts, with emphasis on the cognitive. Each cognitive act of sensing, imagining, doubting and willing carried for Descartes its own truth-making, distinct from the formal certainty of simple arithmetical truths, but no less certain. This certainty arises not from the object observed but from the fact of its being observed. The self-evident truth of a cognitive act lies in its being evident, not *to* a self but *in itself.*

The self-evidence of direct experience stressed by Descartes became the core of Empiricist metaphysics. Descartes intended his *Meditations* partly as a manual of exercises to enable readers to conduct their own introspection and to discover some level of certainty in their own experience. Introspection became a metaphysical trope. Locke and Berkeley routinely supported their claims about knowledge by asking their readers to look within, and Kant duly informed his own readers about what they would find. Perhaps inevitably, this tradition imbued the very concept of objective empirical knowledge with an inescapably subjective dimension. Hume's response to the whole tradition was to eliminate the dimension itself. He portrayed the mind in quasi-mechanical terms: a device for receiving *impressions*, copying and storing them as *ideas*, sorting them by his three *laws of association* according to the demands of experience, thereby enabling the person whose mind it is to recognize and anticipate patterns of events in future experience, under the protective guidance of instinct. Unsurprisingly, when Hume introspected, he reported being unable to discover a self of any kind whatever among his ideas.[24]

This sea change in philosophical outlook is the fourth great irony. Empiricist metaphysics began with an effort to integrate scientific knowledge into the world of experience (the world of ideas) and ended up being cashiered from the framework of science. Not that natural science today would lament the loss. The language of seventeenth century atomism is quaint. The Physics on which it relied is an ossified relic. The traditional language of selves and ideas is unacceptably personal, whereas contemporary science has developed objective standards for describing psychological phenomena. Introspection itself is not a decisive source of data, and not infrequently is an unreliable standard of truth. When science approaches the mind it increasingly studies the brain. From this standpoint, the need for a subjective dimension is considered as relevant today as the theory of phlogiston. Nevertheless, experience is presupposed as much in common sense beliefs as in the empirical truths compiled in science. They are a record of observations. However much science objectifies facts, they constitute the permanent products of experience. There is no scientific observation of the brain, directly or more likely through instruments, which does not begin with the record of what is observed as a recordable episode in the experience of the scientist. If that episode should itself be observed in the observer's brain, it will involve a further episode in another's (or the same person's) experience. The possibility of knowledge entails this priority, which belongs to the act of observing and, thus, to the cognitive fact of observing.

Truths depend on facts, facts are expressible in language, and language (I've suggested) is a complex form of perception. Whether the fact concerns the number of planets detected in a remote, invisible galaxy, or the very visible color of Donald Trump's hair seen at a rally or in a Saturday Night Live skit, or my own hand held before my eyes, or even my doubting that what I see is my hand, it originates with and is ultimately tied to a perceptual record of observation. But natural language was never designed to uncover the metaphysical truths related to such overt cognitive facts. Common sense operates with generous assumptions. We take names for things to refer to the *same* objects for every observer; the regularity of perception encourages confidence that the world we perceive is completely *independent*, that its continuity does not require our presence; and we speak comfortably of *sharing* experiences, as though a feeling were a drink to be passed around. While the old empiricists made the same common-sense assumptions, they also accepted that the possibility of gaining scientific knowledge depends on encountering the world only through the medium of ideas. They never rejected scientific facts outright, although in Berkeley's case these facts were radically reinterpreted. Berkeley's Idealism was a systematic effort to make ideas the common source of empirical knowledge both for common sense and for natural science. Although there are many reasons why Berkeley failed to persuade his contemporaries, one was that he used plain common sense language in seeming conflict with assumptions favored by both sides. Metaphysics promoted as common sense had far less a chance of prevailing than skepticism itself.

The truths of common sense and science tell us about the objective world but also, in much subtler ways which philosophers from Descartes to Kant have sought to capture, about *our* world. These are the facts of experience that prudential skepticism catches in its net and that neither Descartes nor Berkeley sifted out. To describe such facts as the *foundation* of knowledge is misleading, for it suggests something that can be planned, installed, and then modified when needed. A less misleading metaphor for their role is as the *bedrock* of knowledge, something taken for granted and so deep in the structure of knowledge as to be impervious to skepticism. However, the facts of experience themselves are not buried. They are pervasive and they are also the unassuming stuff of metaphysics. For practical purposes and in most circumstances, mentioning such facts would be redundant, in much the same way that saying *It is true that Donald Trump was elected President* says semantically no more than that he was elected. Yet, in matters of both knowledge and language, what is conveniently treated as redundant is nevertheless always present as a distinct fact.

NOTES

1. An example is Plato's dialogue, *Gorgias*, where Socrates interrogates the celebrated sophist, Gorgias and his pupil, Polus, on the nature and value of rhetoric.

2. David Hume, *An Enquiry Concerning Human Understanding*, ed. Eric Steinberg, 2nd ed. (Indianapolis, IN: Hackett Publishing, 1993), sec. 8, pt. 1, 55.

3. I am using "fake claim" in a semantic sense, which relates claims to evidence. President Trump often uses it in a rhetorical sense when referring to views unfavorable to him which are therefore to be dismissed.

4. The semantical trope that true claims (propositions) picture facts, that facts have a form which is mirrored in them, was given prominence by Ludwig Wittgenstein in a work he completed in 1918: *Tractatus Logico-Philosophicus*, trans. D. F. Pears and B. F. McGuinness (London: Routledge & Kegan Paul, 1961).

5. I admit that this is a highly simplified account, for we customarily speak of facts which are beyond our reach, such as in the past, or are at a level of physical matter beyond our senses, as in the case of photons, or which have nothing at all to do with sensation, as in the case of numbers, formulas, and computer code. Some facts have restricted access, as in the case of feelings and emotions, and many facts are based on other facts, as in the case of generalizations. Nevertheless, it provides both a model and a starting point, as well as a useful focus on the logical relation between claims and facts.

6. Descartes' method of doubt aimed to reveal a class of indubitable truths, the most famous being that his very act of thinking, even doubting, established the fact that he existed as a thing that thinks. This is the topic of his second meditation, "Meditation Two: Concerning the Nature of the Human Mind: That It is Better Known Than the Body". See his *Discourse on Method and Meditations on First Philosophy*, trans. Donald A. Cress, 4th ed. (Indianapolis, IN and Cambridge: Hackett Publishing, 1998), 63-69.

7. John Locke, *An Essay Concerning Human Understanding,* ed. Kenneth P. Winkler (Indianapolis: Hackett Publishing Company, 1996, bk. 1, chap. 1, sec. 7, 6. Although Locke's work appeared a half-century after Descartes' *Meditations on First Philosophy*, and his remarks seem intended to cover a range of philosophers (such as Spinoza, Leibniz and perhaps the Cambridge Platonists), his principal target was Descartes' doctrine of innate ideas.

8. George Berkeley, *A Treatise Concerning the Principles of Human Knowledge* (Indianapolis, IN and Cambridge: Hackett Publishing, 1982), pt. 1, sec. 87, 57; Berkeley's emphasis. The word "all" of course includes Locke.

9. Hume, *Enquiry*, sec. 12, pt. 1, 107n64; Hume's emphasis.

10. All the quoted phrases in this paragraph are from Hume, *Enquiry*, sec. 12, pt. 3, 111-14.

11. Hume's focus in sec. 12, pt. 1 of the *Enquiry* is on the Empiricist tradition since Descartes. Earlier sections of the *Enquiry* (for instance, sec. 7, pt. 1) allude to the doctrines of Continental philosophers, such as Malebranche. Hume's criticisms of metaphysical systems were doubtless also meant to include those of others such as Leibniz.

12. In my opinion the best example is Michel de Montaigne's *Apology for Raymond Sebond*, trans. Roger Ariew and Marjorie Greene (Indianapolis, IN and Cambridge: Hackett Publishing, 2003), which details vast discrepancies in cultural as well as perceptual beliefs.

13. The doctrine of atomism dates from the teachings of the classical philosophers Democritus and, later, Epicurus. The Epicurean universe was given a systematic and didactic presentation by Lucretius (c. 99BC-c. 55BC) in his *De Rerum Natura* ["On the Nature of Things"] whose lengthy poem was influential during the sixteenth century and serves as a sort of prologue to seventeenth century physics. From ancient times, atoms were understood to be the smallest particles of matter. The essential properties of matter, however, were not catalogued until the modern period. Seventeenth-century physicists such as Robert Boyle (1627-1691) referred to their version of the doctrine as *corpuscularianism*, which sought to identify the properties belonging to the smallest parts of matter, corpuscules (minute bodies).

14. Galileo Galilei, *The Assayer* (1623), trans. Roger Ariew, in *Modern Philosophy: An Anthology of Primary Sources*, ed. Roger Ariew and Eric Watkins, 2nd ed. (Indianapolis, IN and Cambridge: Hackett Publishing, 2009), 22.

15. Berkeley, *Treatise*, pt. 1, sec. 40, 38.

16. Berkeley's preferred name for his doctrine was "Immaterialism" and was meant to contrast with the materialistic views he associated with Thomas Hobbes (1588-1679).

17. Berkeley, *Treatise*, sec. 40, pt. 1, 40; Berkeley's emphasis. Skeptical challenges about the possibility of drawing the line between knowledge and belief concerning material objects might seem to apply equally to Berkeley's ideas. However, Berkeley was not concerned with skepticism in the comparatively traditional sense, since he was certain that *all* of our experience puts us in touch with reality in the first place, which he regarded therefore as immune to any fundamental skeptical challenge. His doctrine of Idealism (or Immaterialism) did not claim omniscience with regard to the reliability of perceptual experience.

18. Hume, *Enquiry*, sec. 4, pt. 1, 15.

19. Hume, *Enquiry*, sec. 12, pt. 3, 112.

20. Immanuel Kant, *Prolegomena to Any Future Metaphysics*, trans. James W. Ellington (Indianapolis, IN and Cambridge: Hackett Publishing, 1977), Preamble, §2, 13.

21. Preface, in Kant, *Prolegomena*, 6.

22. Descartes, "Meditation Three: Concerning God, That He Exists," in *Discourse on Method and Meditations on First Philosophy*, trans. Cress, 71.

23. Descartes, *Discourse*, pt. 4, 21. The same also holds true, he claimed, for the idea of God.

24. David Hume, *A Treatise of Human Nature*, ed. David Fate Norton and Mary J. Norton (Oxford: Oxford University Press, 2000), pt. 4, sec. 6, "Of Personal Identity," 165.

REFERENCES

Berkeley, George. *A Treatise Concerning the Principles of Human Knowledge*. Indianapolis, IN and Cambridge: Hackett Publishing, 1982.

Descartes. *Discourse on Method and Meditations on First Philosophy*. Translated by Donald A. Cress. 4th ed. Indianapolis, IN and Cambridge: Hackett Publishing, 1998.

Galileo Galilei, *The Assayer* (1623). Translated by Roger Ariew. In *Modern Philosophy: An Anthology of Primary Sources*, edited by Roger Ariew and Eric Watkins. 2nd ed. Indianapolis, IN and Cambridge: Hackett Publishing, 2009.

Hume, David. *An Enquiry Concerning Human Understanding*. Edited by Eric Steinberg. 2nd edition. Indianapolis, IN: Hackett Publishing, 1993.

———. *A Treatise of Human Nature*. Edited by David Fate Norton and Mary J. Norton. Oxford: Oxford University Press, 2000.

Kant, Immanuel. *Prolegomena to Any Future Metaphysics*. Translated by James W. Ellington. Indianapolis, IN and Cambridge: Hackett Publishing, 1977.

Locke, John. *An Essay Concerning Human Understanding*. Edited by Kenneth P. Winkler. Indianapolis, IN: Hackett Publishing Company, 1996.

Montaigne, Michel de. *Apology for Raymond Sebond*. Translated by Roger Ariew and Marjorie Greene. Indianapolis, IN and Cambridge: Hackett Publishing, 2003.

Wittgenstein, Ludwig. *Tractatus Logico-Philosophicus*. Translated by D. F. Pears and B. F. McGuinness. London: Routledge & Kegan Paul, 1961.

Epilogue

Bruce Chilton

The extent to which "more" or "less" equality is desirable has been taken up by the contributors to this volume as a challenge. Each of their articles reflects awareness both of the stances of the sources they analyze and of the perspectives the authors themselves deploy in the task of understanding. The act of interpretation requires a knowledge of self as well as a knowledge of the source that is studied. This dual knowledge, articulated with evident consistency across a variety of idioms, animates this volume, just as it came to life during our conference, which convened on the campus of Bard College in 2017.

HISTORICAL PERSPECTIVES

"Equality Deferred: A Litany of Discrimination" opens our discussion, taking up the ways in which *de facto* discrimination in the Unites States today prolongs the inheritance of the *de jure* discrimination of slavery. A gifted legal thinker, Robert J. Goldstein explains that the events surrounding the killing of Michael Brown by a police officer in Ferguson, Missouri catalyzed his interest. His experiences during a period of five years for the West Point Civil Rights Staff Ride constitute the data arranged in his litany that presents a nexus of problems in which "none of us are outsiders," because it is an American dilemma.

The setting of preparations for the Ride during the tenure of President Obama makes all the more painful Goldstein's description of the clash of optimism with the realities of a continuing imbalance of power and wealth. Political underrepresentation, inequality in employment opportunities and conditions, exclusion from the range of choice in home ownership that the white majority enjoys, continuing restriction of educational opportunities, disproportionate exposure to environmental risk, endemic poverty, inordinate rates of incarceration, and the experience of official violence—that amounts to a dreadful litany and all the more so as all the elements are connected. In response, Goldstein makes a careful case for institutional reparation in the shape of changes "focused on achieving real equality." American society itself is at risk, in his argument, until that challenge is met.

George W. Gawrych takes up an analysis of another culture and time in "Equality and Diversity in the Late Ottoman Empire and Modern Turkey." It is especially instructive to consider his analysis of Ottoman policy for accommodating ethno-religious diversity in the wake of Goldstein's account of the American failure to overcome its greatest challenge in that regard. The *millet* system at the beginning of the nineteenth century protected Jews and Christians as religious communities within a dominantly Muslim state. Between 1839 and 1876, *Tanzimat* (or "Reorganization") increasingly extended an equality of individual rights to all the Sultan's subjects. Legislation, some drafted with consultation with British and French advice, resulted even in the accession of Christians and Jews into imperial administrative positions.

Gawrych identifies two factors that ultimately defeated these measures, and saw the demise of the Ottoman Empire. Within its administration, the attempt at constitutional reform exposed, but did not restrict, the power of the Sultan. Perhaps more fatally, nationalistic movements among Serbs, Greeks, Bulgarians, Macedonians, and Armenians resulted in territorial losses. As Gawrych puts the matter, by 1913 "Ottomanism had thus failed to triumph over the ethnic nationalism of the various *millets*." Nationalistic tendencies also and inevitably affected Muslim populations, as well. During World War I, government policies of ethnic deportation and repression completely reversed earlier laws, and did nothing to forestall the end of the Ottoman Empire.

That end did not bring finality, however. Gawrych provides a lucid explanation of the Kemalist revolution as one of national resurgence for both Turks and Kurds. The Republic of Turkey, founded in 1923, was to be a secular state, but Atatürk (the name Mustafa Kemal took in 1934) aimed at homogeneity rather than pluralism as a principle of strength. The extent and difference of the Kurdish population, however, made that an impossible aim. Since 1978 the Kurdistan Workers' Party has championed both a nationalist and social agenda, and the question of how to deal with such demands are today an existential question not only for Turkey, but also for Iraq and Syria. If the threat to the Ottoman Empire at the outset of World War I came from the regions to its west, today the east and south pose their dangers, as issues of Kurdish identity are interwoven with civil war, competing nationalisms and nation-states, and conflicting religious ideologies. Unlike the American case detailed by Goldstein, Gawrych's expositions serves as a reminder that the progress of equality depends upon more than good will. Forces outset the control of a reforming culture can leave its strategy in tatters and its existence in doubt.

Unlike contemporary America or Ottoman and Turkish Anatolia, the Third Reich has seen few defenders of its social system. David S. Frey caries no brief to do so in "The Social Practice of (In)equality in Nazi Germany." His aim, on the contrary, is to use this instance to illustrate "how the oppression, denial of freedoms, and even murder enable privileged groups and individuals to develop and accept defective notions about the nature of equality." During the opening of World War II, equality became defined in terms of the destructions of Jews. That definition was a matter of social practice in Frey's analysis.

Nazi ideology claimed to be aimed at forming an egalitarian racial state, where "Ayran" privilege becomes the norm at the expense of others. He poses the disturbing question "do people only experience equality when they realize advantages, privileges, rights, and opportunities which others do not enjoy?" The *Volksgemeinschaft* (the "people's community") was to remove class distinctions, on the understanding the *Volk* were Ayran. But to remove the distinctions, what did not belong to the *Volk* needed to be excluded, including Jews as well as non-Ayran groups and allegedly defective people. Exclusion was legal, but also included social elimination (from rights to marry Ayrans, for example), and commercial boycott. Party and state (in the infamous *Gleichschaltung*) were synchronized, but even more effectively, so were state and culture. Popular aspiration and law conspired to present empowering the *Volk* as necessarily entailing the disenfranchisement and eventual elimination of Jews.

The outbreak of World War II, with its militarization of social relations, meant greater apparent and felt autonomy and freedom for those who identified with the *Volk.* Frey especially focuses on women drawn into the war effort who traveled east, and shared in confiscated property; "It is this social practice of inequality that gave German women in the East the palpable sense of equality as national comrades (*Volksgenossen*)." Active mistreatment of alleged inferiors, whether by soldiers or those associated with the Nazi campaign, fed a social construction of superior equality. So committed was the *Wehrmacht* to the ideology, it endorsed and even encouraged summary executions and other atrocities. Frey reads these actions, not simply as related war crimes, but as a network in which social practice—left to treat equality as the prize of a select group to be exacted at the expense of alleged parasites, opponents, and weaklings—can be shown to result in genocide.

The sobering insight that equality might be used as a motivation to produce inequality, even to the point of destroying those deemed unfit to be equal, shows how interpretation needs to be aware of itself as decisions are made and choices adjudicated. In this historical section of the work as a whole, the profoundly practical impact of *hermeneutics* becomes apparent. The term, from the Greek word for interpretation as such (*hermeneia*), has been taken within humanistic learning to refer in particular to the self-criticism of the interpreter, engaged even as the text or other source is subjected to criticism.

Morten G. Ender and Betsey Lucal focus on repeated inequalities that come to expression in public discourse, "(1) race and ethnicity, (2) sex and gender, (3) socio-economic class, (4) sexuality, (5) physical ability, (6) age, and (7) religious affiliation." These issues have a particular history in their chosen institution, as they explain in "Social Inequality and the United States Army: The (Un)lucky Seven." After detailing key cases, the authors trace how changes in the Army track along the lines of the revolution in the definition of citizenship within the industrialized West. At this point, the article moves into fresh territory. Following on the work of David Segal, Ender and Lucal point out that the Army has served to take once marginalized groups fully into citizenship and legitimacy, in symbolic and actual terms. The influence of the American and French revolutions appears to the authors a significant factor in this process, such that "the US military has become one of the most diverse organizations in US society."

This picture, however, requires further analysis in order to be appreciated. Although the Army may be diverse, that does not mean that it is inclusive, and inclusivity is the particular characteristic that Ender and Lucal wish to test. This requires careful definition, and they suggest that diversity should be understood as valuing people from varied backgrounds, so that their difference does not become the exclusive interest, but a point of leverage that enables each person to join in the process of social interaction. American society is famously diverse, but that very phenomenon has given rise to categorical constructions of groups, which are often taken as having value in themselves. Everyone, the authors suggest, experiences the seven categories that they refer to. The question is, how determinative are they of how we are perceived? The seven categories themselves exist generally in public discourse, but they become enhanced as the result of hierarchical application. Because the Army is a hierarchy, that produces social inequality by definition. That is what produces "difference," understood as a real distinction.

In a way reminiscent of Frey's analysis, Ender and Lucal use a relational model of inequality, in which a privileged group exists only because oppression exists. Hegemonic ideologies confirm the status quo. Yet the authors close their contribution by documenting recent changes in the hierarchical definition of difference and their accompanying ideologies, provocatively asking whether the winds of change blow in the direction of giving children brought into the United States without full documentation access to the status of full citizenship.

Military pensions have occupied both a progressive and a controversial place in American history. They recognize service to the nation at the risk of one's well-being, and sometimes one's life, and yet they also have been subject to preferential judgments. Brandon Jason Archuleta argues that the Civil War has proven to be a formative influence in the American form of the institution in "Civil War Pension Policy: The Politics of Policy Subsystems." Given the crucial role of the Civil War in the history of racism in the United States, the argument in itself is intriguing. Archuleta portrays pensions as exercises in redistribution bringing together social, economic, and defense policies within a subsystem of control.

Sectional interests are documented within the period of Reconstruction; that and other factors meant that selective veterans and their dependents could be advantaged for many years. Quoting Theda Skocpol, Archuleta uncovers "an open-ended system of disability, old-age, and survivors' benefits for anyone who could claim minimal service time on the northern side of the Civil War." He argues, however, that a new lens is necessary to understand the process behind this outcome. Using the conception of a policy subsystem, he then traces interactions among congressional committees of jurisdiction, bureaucracies dedicated to veterans' services and pensions, powerful veterans' lobbies and influential private interests, an attentive media, and the presidency. Using the typology of Daniel McCool, but also correcting McCool's analysis, Archuleta finds that the pension subsystem became "autonomous" in the late twentieth century; earlier it had been "dominant." A skillful analysis of the historical conditions follows, including the rise of patronage and special-interest maneuvering in the provision of benefits. By 1893, Archuleta finds that 41.5 percent of federal income was devoted to pension benefits, an amount not only disproportionately large, but disproportionately provided to the North at the expense of the South. The drift from recruiting soldiers to rewarding certain sectors of the society is one that Archuleta observes continuing in current practice.

Pensions need not be unequal, but courts martial might be inherently so, in that an element of hierarchy is necessarily present that is not a formal factor in civilian courts. Nonetheless, the military justice system, despite its unique nature, honors recourse to a jury. In "Selecting a Military Court-Martial Panel: A Study of Inequality," Christopher Jacobs argues that a crucial inequity needs to be overcome for military courts to live up to their aspiration for justice. Under the Uniform Code of Military Justice, courts martial are not settled authorities, but are convened by a military commander authorized to do so. This convening authority "determines whether or not to proceed with a court-martial, the level of court-martial to which the case will be referred, the charges to be leveled against an accused (known as the 'defendant' in the civilian criminal justice system), and which officers and enlisted Soldiers of his command will serve as members of the court-martial panel (the jury)."

That degree of latitude would be difficult to match in a civilian setting, and Jacobs concentrates on the last element. In his opinion, this makes courts martial "inferior to an impartial civilian jury." The setting of the controversy is the acknowledged difficulty of balancing discipline and justice within the post-War Uniform Code of Military Justice, which replaced the much-amended Articles of War that already attempted a compromise. Yet the guarantee of the Sixth Amendment of an impartial jury continues to be abrogated.

The legal precedent that permits the accusation is curious. The Fifth Amendment, which addresses a different concern, "excepts cases arising in the land or naval forces, or in the militia, when in actual service, in time of war or public danger." Oddly, that enumerated exception in the Fifth Amendment has been applied to the interpretation of the Sixth Amendment. Archuleta details attempts, by courts and military practice, to mitigate the problem, but he finds them unsatisfactory. In the end, he calls upon the Supreme Court to rule in accordance with the plain meaning of the Fifth and Sixth Amendments.

Where Archuleta is concerned with the protection of service personnel, Darya Pushkina takes up a task of another organization, the United Nations, to protect civilians. The issue has become increasingly fraught, as the number of peace missions increases and therefore partnerships with regional organizations becomes necessary. In "United Nations Peace Missions and Protection of Civilians: Equality versus Efficiency?" Pushkina argues that "peacekeeping missions should be evaluated not only on the performance of peacekeepers on the ground [mandate evaluation], but also on whether violence was limited, human suffering reduced, conflict spread prevented, and progress was made towards positive peace."

She argues that, because mandate evaluation has been used as a sufficient criteria, the formation of state entities under UN patronage is often taken to spell success. But if signs of growing violence are not factored into consideration, the result is that the UN itself appears neo-colonial, and in the case of Croatia for example, negotiated settlement of local violence became impossible. In Pushkina's judgment, extending concern to the protection of civilians implies guardianship of rights as well as security, preferably by the State, and if necessary the international community. The Kigali Principles on the Protection of Civilians (2015) is cited as a model, but Pushkina calls attention to lack of resources: expenditure is required for peace keeping to become more subtle as well as more robust, as the Principles would demand. Partnerships between the United Nations and the African Union and the United Nations and the European Union have emerged as a potential solution to the problem, but Pushkina cites difficulties of coordinating purposes and agreeing on aims. The present, unsatisfactory situation can be addressed, however, if issues of equality in protecting civilians are joined with an understanding of the measurable evaluation of resources deployed.

THEOLOGICAL PERSPECTIVES

Historical study necessarily involves hermeneutical reflection. The perspective of the researcher engages with that of source, so that self-awareness is necessarily involved. Historians do not always operate explicitly with that understanding, but the contributions to this volume represent their discipline admirably in this regard. The critical study of religion, a type of historical engagement, also requires hermeneutical awareness, but in a sense that is enhanced in comparison. A religious system by its definition involves a relationship among what people do (their ethics), how people worship (their ritual), and how people account for meaning (their theology). As a result, analysis of any given religion or event within religion brings the interpreter to take account, not only of her or his self-awareness, but also of the account of meaning which the religion deploys in that case. Religious are natural engines of hermeneutical perspective, which then feeds into the process of interpretation.

Because religions involve a self-awareness that the interpreter needs to account for within the act of interpretation, a double hermeneutic is regularly in play. In "Ultimately Equal and Relatively Complicated: Questions about Equality in Teaching Buddhist Studies, " Dominique Townsend adds another dimension of hermeneutical concern: that of her students. In her experience, students often arrive for the study of Buddhism "thirsting for a system that will exemplify peace, equanimity, simplicity, and goodness," and soon come up against what they understand as inequality.

Issues of gender arise when Townsend discusses cases in which the Buddha is portrayed as refusing women's requests to be accepted as *bhikṣuṇī*, or nuns, and then as hedging acceptance with qualifications. Alongside that discrimination, Indian and Tibetan systems of Buddhism commonly differentiate the intellectual ability of students, in order to determine which practitioners may approach the highest teachings. Townsend then introduces the teaching of the Two Truths, a fascinating doctrine, since it represents a hermeneutical adjustment within Buddhism that is applicable to the cases to hand. By this principle, relative truth reflects appearance while ultimate truth reflects insight of the emptiness of all things. Townsend is well aware that the applicability of the teaching to the cases of gender and intellectual discrimination does not mean that they are similar. In fact, she experiences them as quite different. But they draw similar responses from students, and so may be approached together. In any case, their reactions reflect commonly held views in regard to Buddhism, but Townsend also spells out the profoundly egalitarian assertions of classic Buddhist texts and practices.

The dynamic Townsend sets out illuminates how texts deal with the issue of misogyny within the precept that "In all things, there is neither male nor female." She also deals with current controversies revolving around the ordination of women. The issue of intellectual hierarchy, on the other hand, is trenchant in view of "basic Buddhist hermeneutical and pedagogical assertions that Buddha taught different levels of truth to suit the needs of students with varying capacities or levels of intelligence and readiness to learn." At this point, a fruitful contrast to current expectations in regard to education as a whole is evident. In fact, Townsend goes on to commend the doctrine of the Two Truths, when not applied in order to justify inequality, as a means of "critical analysis of complex topics, within and beyond Buddhist studies."

The expectations brought to Buddhism by students differ radically from those brought to Rabbinic Judaism. Yet Shai Secunda begins his essay "The Rabbinic Meritocracy and Its Discontents," by reminding the reader that the rabbinic movement in the wake of the destruction of the Second Temple in 70 CE replaced priestly authority with that of "biblical and legal interpreters based in the Galilee." In effect, this "looks like a democratic, intellectual society," albeit a society defined by men. Even the issue of hierarchy, raised in Townsend's article on Buddhism, seems to be addressed, for example in the teaching that "one who accomplished much [in his learning] and one who accomplished little are equal, as long as they direct their heart towards heaven."

But here Secunda engages in an explicitly comparative move in order to raise the central issue of his article. In the United States, the educational system has been vaunted as a meritocracy that helps fulfil egalitarian dreams, but recent critiques portray it as entrenching social stratification. An analogous feature emerges in an assessment of the texts of Rabbinic Judaism, where a well-known use of language shows that the system of religion "created a class in its own right—the *talmid ḥakham*, literally, a student of the sage(s), who was conceived of in total opposition to the '*am ha-aretz*, literally, 'people of the land,' but essentially, the non-rabbinic, uneducated masses." This new class was held to supersede the system of castes within Judaism, but then those of the lowest castes "need not apply," as Secunda explains. Moreover, when learning is used as a measure of standing, hierarchies of the kind and quality of learning naturally emerge, as they do within the texts. Most disturbingly, "the lives of those who, despite rabbinic encouragement, chose not to join the community of learners, were deemed less valuable than that of the intellectuals."

Positing a single principle of equality, when it might be taken up or not taken up by others, leaves those who adhere to the principle in a position of advantage. There is a hierarchy implicit in the application of the principle, even when people are left to choose whether to apply it. Secunda discovers in the Rabbinic case not a transcendence of the problem, but a literature so lucid that "this formative feature of Jewish society was simultaneously constructed and deconstructed."

The conundrum that ultimate truth is expressed by ordinary, relative beings is in no sense limited to Buddhism. The Buddha might say "there is neither male nor female," and St. Paul—despite his reputation—could also teach that "There is not one Jew or Greek, not one slave or free, not one male or female, because you are all one in Jesus Christ" (Galatians 3:28). To a considerable extent, as Bruce Chilton discusses in "Equality in Paul of Tarsus—More *and* Less," Paul's reputation is not merited, the product of works attributed to him that he did not write. More interestingly, however, Paul does seem to contradict himself in letters that he did compose. He was not irenic when it came to those who promoted circumcision among Gentile believers, saying they should castrate themselves (Galatians 5:12). He urged women to remain silent in congregations of believers (1 Corinthians 14:34), and advised slaves to be content in their positions (1 Corinthians 7:21).

Each of the polarities Paul engages ("Jew"-"Greek," "slave"-"free," "male"-"female,") was an established principle in the time he wrote, a matter of law as well as custom, seemingly a part of nature. For this reason what is surprising in what Paul says is not when he upholds or ignores them, but when he contradicts them. The basis of his contradiction is even more instructive. He asserts that "the form of this world passes away" (1 Corinthians 7:31). That disappearance of the world with its conventions is the basis of his claim, grounded in his conviction of its replacement by a better reality.

The remainder of the article focuses on Paul's treatment of the issue of resurrection in 1 Corinthians 15. The matter for him is not simply a question of what happened to Jesus after his death, nor is it even limited to the fate that humanity is heading towards. Rather, Paul conceives of a new humanity emerging in resurrection. This is neither a matter of physical existence nor of individual souls, but of "spirit." At that level, unconstrained by the weakness of flesh and the self-interest of soul, Paul conceives a person as a "spiritual body:" alive to purposes that are transcendent, determined by neither physical need nor social convention. "But no element of any polarity, and no polarity in itself, could ever be described in Pauline terms as being 'spiritual.' They belonged to the form of a world that was passing away in favor of Spirit."

Current discussion of Muslim interpretation typically concentrates on established patterns of classical interpretation and how they are taken up within modern settings. Tehseen Thaver crafts a different approach in "The

Perilous Promise of Equality: Reimagining the Qur'an in Post-Revolution Iran." The Iranian revolution of 1979 followed an agenda of revival and reform, in which the two thinkers Thaver has selected occupy distinctive places. Together, they are part of a reform movement "best described as a tradition of internal critique and an opposition to the clerical establishment as well as a critical and philosophical engagement with Islam's textual tradition." That is, their efforts are self-consciously hermeneutical. In both cases, they argue for a new understanding of the Qur'an.

Another commonality between Soroush and Shabestarī is that they challenge the infallible and divine nature of the Qur'an as part of an attempt to dislodge the purchase of clerical authority. Thaver problematizes their contributions from the outset, even as she values them, because they are "bound by distinctly secular conceptions of language, history, interpretation, and the human subject." Shabestarī makes a distinction between the core of the divine message and the social conditions in which it is articulated. This leads to an argument "that the Qur'anic text is not itself revelation. Rather, it is an interpretive understanding of the world by the Prophet, who experienced revelation." In this embrace of the active role of the interpreter Thaver calls attention to the influence of the Protestant theologian, Hans-Georg Gadamer. Soroush, on the other hand, draws on Karl Popper's use of the Kantian distinction between the thing in itself and its perception to urge acknowledgement of "independent religious experiences."

Within both thinkers, Thaver traces what she describes as a modern construction of the self and its authority apart from a wider, cosmological society (as in the pre-modern period). (The shift is consonant with the move that Krister Stendahl identified as the Reformation's dedication to "the introspective conscience of the West."[1]) To Thaver this seems evidence that for all the apparent isolation of Iran from colonization "the tentacles of a modern Western imaginary of the normative role and place of scripture nonetheless run firm and deep."

The *Bhagavad Gita* is, at one level, a war poem. For that reason. Indian nationalists could and did resort to its text in order to endorse the use of violence. Yet Richard H. Davis shows that Mahatma Gandhi's life and work were also bound up with the *Gita*, which he read as an infallible guide that in fact endorsed the principle of nonviolence (*ahimsa*). But Gandhi faced quite another interpretative challenge, as Davis goes on to demonstrate in "Gandhi, Krishna, and Caste: Inequality More or Less." In the *Gita*, Krishna explains to Arjuna not only his duty as a warrior, but the place of all "birth-groups" (*jatis*) within the caste system. This breaks society down into the classes of the Brahmins or priests, the warriors, the people, and the servants.

Gandhi's own commentary on the *Gita*, as explained by Davis, attempts to use the text to explode inequality: "If we regard the person who cleans lavatories as lower and another who reads the *Gita* as higher, that will be the end of us." That is because, just as the *Gita* means the pursuit of non-violence when it speaks of war, so it refers to inborn qualities and their associated duties rather than to caste when its speaks of the classes. The boldness of the hermeneutical move, as well as its character, is apparent in dealing with both war and class. David then situates Gandhi's thought within the setting of India, his own biography, and the characterization of Indian society in the West as essentially hierarchical.

Gandhi's response was to characterize "untouchability," the most egregious aspect of the caste system as a "device of Satan," which demanded repentance. To his mind, and in his practice, the whole concept needed to be eradicated, even at the cost of slowing the campaign for the independence of India from British colonialism. Davis quotes him as saying, "In my opinion we have become 'pariahs of the Empire' because we have created 'pariahs' in our midst." Caste was clearly his enemy, yet he upheld and even celebrated the scheme of *varnas*, on the gounds that it was not a birth-group but a matter of inborne character. In his idealized scheme, the *varnas* were to be recognized as a universal principle.

Davis attributes pragmatic motives to Gandhi's defense of the *varnas*, including political and nationalist considerations. Moreover, Davis observes, in a remark akin to Thaver's, that Western constructions of equality warrant "an individual's unrestrained pursuit of selfish aims without taking responsibility for others." He concludes this section by saying, "The Vedic model of the four classes, with its notion of inborn qualities and the responsibilities of each one towards the overall functioning of the whole society, fits within Gandhi's ideal definition of *swaraj*."

B. R. Ambedkar, the leader of the "Dalit" (as they preferred to call themselves, rather than "untouchables" or "pariahs") objected to the deployment of the *varnas* in the *Gita*, to the *Gita* itself, and to Gandhi's resort to it. Davis closes with a contrast between Ambedkar's thorough historicism and Gandhi's analogical reading. While the former might be at home in a secular university in the West, the latter would find ready company in the hermeneutics of St Augustine.

PHILOSOPHICAL PERSPECTIVES

"Soldiers are treated by their leaders and by themselves as sacrificial instruments of war." That is the finding Graham Parsons takes from his description of the opening of the Battle of the Somme. His generalization hearkens back to a contribution to our previous conference, which explained how sacrifice has been mainstreamed in warfare since biblical times and before.[2] The interest here, in "Men of Fortitude: Gender and Combatant Non-Immunity in War," takes us to the link between military service and masculinity. Parsons cites records of women in the field of war who imitated male behaviors, and the aim of upbringing to socialize boys to become warriors.

Part of the process of socialization often includes shaming boys who do not conform to the masculine image by treating them as feminine. The move proceeds in such an undifferentiated way that homophobic language and misogynistic language blurs together. Gender, applied as a normative principle, has that effect, in that all that is not masculine, in this military case, is subordinated. Parson argues that this bias has had a particular influence in military ethics.

The definition of who may be a target in war derives from "norms of warrior masculinity." Traditionally, non-combatants may not be attacked, although they can be put in danger of unintentional harm in order to achieve a military objective. The calculation demands judgments of necessity and proportionality, but that is a relatively straightforward qualification of a rule against targeting non-combatants. Yet combatants remain "fair game" even when they are asleep. They acquire rights when they are captured. But not when they are present as what Gabriela Blum calls "nothing more than instruments of war."

Parsons shows that the traditional view depends on finding that combatants are "non-innocent," or even "wicked." But he observes that this depends upon the evaluation of the particular war, and the extent to which a combatant is acting on the orders of sovereign authority. Even the modified formulation of Michael Walzer, in terms of the threat a combatant poses rather than his or her moral sanding, seems dubious to Parsons. At base, it justifies the removal of threat by soldiers who "have been rendered sacrificial in war ... [when they were] bound to give their lives in war."

The deeper problem with the traditional view of limited targeting is not those it includes, but those it would exclude. Combatants are treated indiscriminately because the masculinized definition of those who are in the ranks defines them as those who are sacrificial. This leads Parsons to revise the principle in respect of *combatants*, so that "combatants may be deliberately attacked only when (a) the attack is necessary in order to achieve a strategic goal, and (b) that goal is of sufficient significance to merit the attack." As Parson observes, the revision might lead to greater exposure to non-combatants, in that it removes the automatic liability of combatants. But at least this discussion brings the issue of the justice of war into the field of battle, and does not limit it to questions of statecraft. By de-gendering the applicability of that effort, this proposal offers genuine progress.

Hugh Liebert investigates an intimate field of equality—neighborliness. How we relate at that level is a matter of daily experience, and yet has profound significance: "When I encounter neighbors as equals, I share one kind of life with them; when they are encountered as superiors or inferiors, I share with them another sort of life." Unwritten rules seem to govern these relationships, and they appear to have a relative degree of autonomy. Edmund Burke saw the importance of "manners' in this sense; his friend Edward Gibbon took up the political significance of manners, which Liebert traces in "Minding Gibbon's Manners: Unwritten Rules and the Rhetoric of Equality."

The particular importance of Gibbon's approach lies in his observation that equality can be put into practice even under conditions of growing economic and political inequality. The contrast between Augustus and Diocletian is the pivot of interest. In Gibbon's description, "It was the aim of the one to disguise, and the object of the other to display, the unbounded power which the emperors possessed over the Roman world." Between the two, Gibbon prefers Augustus, in that foregrounding inequalities can provoke civilizational decline.

The provocative feature of Gibbon's preference is that Augustus' duplicity is in his analysis anything but subtle. He came to the conclusion, "His virtues, and even his vices, were artificial; and according to the various dictates of his interest, he was at first the enemy, and at last the father, of the Roman world." In Liebert's analysis, a loosening of Roman manners, which had devolved into flattery, signaled the need for monarchy to replace the Republic. Augustus' represents the use of political duplicity, in effect, to address moral duplicity. The underlying drama of this trajectory comes from Gibbon's contention that the manners that had united the civilization could no longer do so.

Diocletian in this analysis "wanted Roman manners to more honestly reflect the realities of Roman politics in order to make political life more stable and sustainable, if less free." He did not succeed in his attempt, but in a certain way Constantine did, by deflecting veneration to a new divinity rather than the person of the emperor. That adjustment did not reverse the problem of manners, but Liebert suggests that the equality they represented did not need to fall victim to political or economic inequality in a way that may be instructive to us.

Where Liebert concerns himself with the power that can be worked out by means of apparently egalitarian manners, Courtney Morris confronts the opposite relation in Immanuel Kant. In his case, while the categorical imperative involved mutual respect, the philosopher himself was openly sexist and racist. In "A Kantian Approach to Recognizing Privilege," she wonders why his ethics did not rule out his prejudice. Rather than appeal to the prejudice of Kant's milieu (which he seems in any case to have exceeded) or attempt to determine whether his view of reason was implicitly gendered, Morris decides to ask another question: "Do Kant's own sexist and racist views indicate a flawed understanding of his own theory or is the problem with the theory itself?"

Morris argues that Kant's theory does have the resources to correct itself, on the basis of recognizing privilege. His understanding of the duty to be sympathetic and not to be contemptuous can be developed to recognize one's own privilege and to correct for it. To begin with, however, Morris identifies both the strength and the weakness of Kant's approach: its universality. Attractive although the categorical imperative is, it does not account for ethical judgments in morally chaotic circumstances, such as when disobedience of civic authorities is called for. Further, the universal character of the imperative *should* have corrected the racism and sexism that Kant flaunts.

Here Morris deploys Barbara Herman's argument for rules of moral salience in deploying the categorical imperative. Such rules determine when to test a moral course by the imperative. In doing so, the rules allow a consideration of context, and particularly of the moral status of other people, "when a person should be treated as autonomous, our moral equal possessing his or her own ends and goals, and therefore ought not to be violated or manipulated." On this basis, Morris believes that Kant's approach can be contextualized and humanized. She proposes making one's privilege salient by means of the duty to "seek, listen, and reconsider." The solution, she acknowledges, is not "perfect," and by its revision of Kant may be said to be less Kantian, in the sense of being universal, than his appeal to reason. But reason for Morris is human before it is universal, and "the part of our humanity worth fighting for."

Robert E. Tully argues for another part, the part of us that is skeptical. But his skepticism is "prudential," a matter of how we evaluate, rather than "dogmatic," in which skepticism takes the form of overt denial. David Hume is taken as an example of the latter, because he denies metaphysics but accepts received truths of natural science. There is indeed an "Inequality in Skepticism." Tully wants to ask whether facts and truths might exist outside of the Empiricist tradition. In order to accomplish that task, he needs to distinguish skepticism from cynicism, carefully disambiguating the ancient school from the modern phenomenon. The modern cynics are more like sophists in their facile approach; for them truth "is in the eyes of the beholder, or at the beholder's convenience."

The problem, however, is that the self-interest that propels the cynic propels us all: "Emotions permeate our beliefs, and the words we find to express them are rarely unaffected by a rhetorical tinge of approval or disapproval." The degree of difference from person to person might be vast in this regard, but the issue of governing self-interest remains. That is just where prudential skepticism balances the tendency for arguments "to harden into the convictions of a closed mind." Even dogmatic skepticism, by what it denies as well as what it affirms, stands in need of this balancing factor.

For that balance to be achieved, some sense of "facts" seems necessary, and Tully deploys the early Wittgenstein to say that "true claims *picture* or *mirror* facts." To this extent, language is "a complex form of perception." Facts enter the world by means of that gateway. By means of those facts, we can "say something true about the world." Human knowledge is the outcome of the whole process, and false claims—"fake news" in particular—set the process adrift. The role of skepticism is to keep it on track.

What follows is a history of skepticism since the seventeenth century, set out at first as a set of ironies connected with Empiricism, which skeptics generally embrace. The first is that skeptics have accused one another of skepticism. The second is that the tradition of Empiricism finds that the senses are unreliable sources of knowledge, and the third is that ideas, rather perceptions, offer no more reliability.

The result of these self-cancelling ironies is that what Tully calls Hume's dogmatic skepticism endorses only science but cannot not say precisely why it does so. "Owing to its inveterate antagonism towards claims about certainty and the existence of facts lying outside the framework of the natural sciences, skepticism of this kind is the evil twin of metaphysics." But then there is the last, fourth irony about Empiricism. It had set out to integrate scientific knowledge within its own metaphysics, but natural science went its own way so that dogmatic skepticism is left with making a compromise between common sense and its resort to science. Prudential skepticism, then, proves to be a gently constructive force, identifying facts that are "the unassuming stuff of metaphysics."

In Tully's article, as well as in all the philosophical contributions, hermeneutical reflection occurs not as a choice, but as a constitutional principle of the discipline. There is always a skeptic behind skepticism, so that when discussion of that topic (and *mutatis mutandis* the others) refers to an intellectual option, human decision is also implicated. Scholars of religion have long known that their subject matter involves claims of meaning, but they have not always—as they have here—risen to that challenge by evaluating the meaning concerned. Historians' commitment to hermeneutics is volitional, but at times their subjects engage in actions that require not only critical analysis, but self-critical reflection. The topic of equality drew us all in to this productive self-criticism, in a way that meant we met as practitioners of common crafts in the humanities, and discovered affinities that transcend institutional setting.

NOTES

1. Krister Stendahl, "The Apostle Paul and the Introspective Conscience of the West," *Harvard Theological Review* 56, no. 3 (1963): 199-215.

2. See Bruce Chilton, "Poisoned Virtue: Child Sacrifice in Abrahamic Scriptures and Interpretation," in *Intolerance: Political Animals and Their Prey*, ed. Bruce Chilton and Robert E. Tully, Dialogues on Social Issues, Bard College and West Point (Lanham, MD: Hamilton, 2017), 147-71.

REFERENCES

Chilton, Bruce. "Poisoned Virtue: Child Sacrifice in Abrahamic Scriptures and Interpretation." In *Intolerance: Political Animals and Their Prey*, edited by Bruce Chilton and Robert E. Tully, 147-72. Dialogues on Social Issues: Bard College and West Point. Lanham, MD: Hamilton, 2017.

Stendahl, Krister. "The Apostle Paul and the Introspective Conscience of the West." *Harvard Theological Review* 56, no. 3 (1963): 199-215.

Name Index

Ancient Sources Index

About the Editors and Contributors

Bruce Chilton is a scholar of early Christianity and Judaism. He wrote the first critical translation and commentary for the Aramaic version of Isaiah, *The Isaiah Targum* (T&T Clark, 1987), as well as academic studies that analyze Jesus in his Judaic context, *A Galilean Rabbi and His Bible* (Wipf & Stock, 1984); The *Temple of Jesus* (Bard College, 1992); and *Pure Kingdom* (Eerdmans, 1996). He has taught in Europe at the Universities of Cambridge, Sheffield, and Münster, and in the United States at Yale University, as the first Lillian Claus Professor of New Testament, and at Bard College. Currently Bernard Iddings Bell Professor of Philosophy and Religion at Bard College, he also directs the Institute of Advanced Theology there. Principal publications include *Rabbi Jesus: An Intimate Biography* (Doubleday, 2000); *Rabbi Paul: An Intellectual Biography* (Doubleday, 2004); *Mary Magdalene: A Biography* (Doubleday, 2005); *The Cambridge Companion to the Bible* (Cambridge University Press, 2007); *The Way of Jesus* (Abingdon Press, 2010); *Visions of the Apocalypse* (Baylor University Press, 2013); and *Christianity—The Basics* (Routledge, 2015).

Robert Edmund Tully retired in 2017 as Professor of Philosophy at the United States Military Academy and is Professor Emeritus of Philosophy both at West Point and at the University of Toronto. He is the coauthor (with Frederic Portoraro) of a textbook on symbolic logic and coeditor (with Bruce Chilton and Jacob Neusner) of *Just War in Religion and Politics* (Lanham, MD: University Press of America, 2013), to which he also contributed an essay. He is the author of numerous articles on Bertrand Russell, G. E. Moore, and Ludwig Wittgenstein, and on a range of topics in the fourth edition of the *Cambridge Dictionary of Philosophy*. His research interests include Natural Logic (the cohabiting of logic and rhetoric in natural language); the doctrine of Neutral Monism; the evolution of Russell's metaphysics; and the development of George Berkeley's Idealism from *Towards a New Theory of Vision* (1709) to *Alciphron*, written during the philosopher's three-year stay in Newport, Rhode Island, starting in 1729, and published on his return to London.

* * *

Brandon Jason Archuleta, currently active duty as a U.S. Army Strategist, taught for three years as Assistant Professor of American Politics in the Department of Social Sciences at West Point. A veteran of the wars in Iraq and Afghanistan, Brandon's research interests and expertise focus primarily on the public policy process, specifically as it relates to defense, national security, and foreign affairs. He is a Term Member of the Council on Foreign Relations and a Clements Center National Security Fellow at the University of Texas at Austin. He is currently completing a book-length manuscript, provisionally titled *Twenty Years of Service: The Politics of Military Pension Policy and the Long Road to Reform.* He holds a BS in American Politics from the U.S. Military Academy at West Point, an MPA in International Affairs from the Lyndon B. Johnson School of Public Affairs, and a PhD in Government from the University of Texas at Austin.

Richard H. Davis is Professor of Religion and Asian Studies Programs at Bard College, Annandale-on-Hudson, New York. Formerly he taught as assistant and associate professor at Yale University. His most recent publication is *The Bhagavad Gita: A Biography* (Princeton University Press, 2014). He is author of four other books: *Ritual in an Oscillating Universe: Worshiping Siva in Medieval India* (Princeton, 1991), *Lives of Indian Images* (Princeton, 1997), *Global India, circa 100 CE: South Asia in Early World History* (Association for Asian Studies, 2010), and *A Priest's Guide for the Great Festival* (Oxford, 2010). He has edited two volumes, and also wrote the text for a catalog of Indian religious prints, *Gods in Print: Masterpieces of India's Mythological Art* (Mandala, 2012). Currently he is continuing work on the reception history of the *Bhagavad Gita,* and on a history of religions in early South Asia.

Morten G. Ender is Professor of Sociology in the Department of Behavioral Sciences and Leadership at West Point, New York. A multiple award-winning teacher, his courses at West Point include: Organizational Culture and Socialization; Qualitative Research Methods; and Armed Forces and Society. He also co-chairs the new Diversity and Inclusion Studies Minor.

His research appears in *Teaching Sociology, Journal of Adolescence, Death Studies. Military Psychology, Journal of Homosexuality*, and *Armed Forces & Society*, among other journals. His books include *Inclusion in the American Military*, with David Rohall and Michael Matthews (Lexington, 2017); *The Millennial Generation and National Defense*, with Rohall and Matthews (Palgrave, 2014); *The Routledge Handbook of War and Society*, with Steve Carlton-Ford (Routledge, 2011); and *American Soldiers in Iraq* (Routledge, 2009). The latter two books received back-to-back (2010 and 2011) Outstanding Book Awards from the Peace, War, and Social Conflict Section of the American Sociological Association.

David S. Frey is Professor of History and Director of the Center for Holocaust and Genocide Studies (CHGS) at West Point. He is the author of *Jews, Nazis, and the Cinema of Hungary: The Tragedy of Success, 1929-44* (I. B. Tauris, 2017). He has published articles and chapters on, among other topics, the Rwandan Genocide, early warnings of mass atrocity, and Hungarian history. In 2014, with four coauthors, he published *Ordinary Soldiers: A Study in Ethics, Law and Leadership* (United States Holocaust Memorial Museum). At West Point, he offers courses on Genocide, the Holocaust, and the History of Race, Nation, Ethnicity, and Gender, and has won awards for teaching and innovation. He is cocreator and co-Chair of West Point's Diversity and Inclusion Minor. As Director of the CHGS, Dr. Frey has spearheaded efforts to increase the Academy's and US Armed Forces' awareness and understanding of the phenomenon of genocide, its history, and means of prevention. This effort has won him national citations from President Obama and the United States Holocaust Memorial Museum.

George W. Gawrych is Professor of Modern Middle East and Military History at Baylor University. He taught in the Combat Studies Institute at the U.S. Army Command and General Staff College from 1984 to 2001, and held the visiting position of Charles Boal Ewing Chair in Military History at the U. S. Military Academy, West Point, 2016-2017. Among his book publications are *The Albatross of Decisive Victory: War and Policy between Egypt and Israel in the 1967 and 1973 Arab-Israeli Wars* (Greenwood Press, 2000), and *The Young Atatürk: From Ottoman Soldier to Statesman of Turkey* (I. B. Tauris, 2013) for which he received the 2014 Distinguished Book Award for Military Biography from the Society for Military History. Currently, he is researching for a second volume on Ataturk which covers the period as President of the Republic of Turkey, 1923-1938.

Robert J. Goldstein is Professor in the Department of Law at West Point where he teaches Constitutional Law, Civil Rights Law, and Environmental

Law. He is also Director of the Center for the Rule of Law. He created and leads the West Point Civil Rights Staff Ride. As general counsel for Riverkeeper, Inc., he managed many high-profile environmental cases related to the Hudson River PCB Superfund, as well as power plant pollution cases that culminated in *Entergy v. Riverkeeper*, decided by the U.S. Supreme Court.

Christopher W. Jacobs, Lieutenant Colonel in the U.S. Army, is an Assistant Professor in the Department of Law at West Point, where he has served on the faculty for four years. He has also served as a Staff Judge Advocate; Associate Staff Judge Advocate at United States Central Command; Regional Defense Counsel; Associate Professor at the Judge Advocate General's School of the Army; Administrative Law Attorney; Trial Counsel; Legal Assistance Attorney; and Defense Counsel. Lieutenant Colonel Jacobs deployed to Kosovo in 1999 as the Deputy Task Force Legal Advisor, and to Afghanistan in 2007 as the Chief of the Rule of Law for Combined, Joint Task Force 82 and its successor, CJTF-101. He currently teaches both National Security Law and Advanced Law of Armed Conflict.

Hugh Liebert is Associate Professor in the Department of Social Sciences at West Point, where he teaches political theory and American politics. He received his BA from Harvard University, and his MA and PhD from the University of Chicago. He is the author of *Plutarch's Politics* (Cambridge University Press, 2016), and the forthcoming *Religion Around Gibbon*. He has edited several volumes and published numerous journal articles.

Betsy Lucal is Professor of Sociology at Indiana University South Bend, where she also directs the First Year Experience program and teaches in the Women's and Gender Studies program. She formerly served as a Deputy Editor for *Gender & Society* and currently edits the Gender & Sexuality Section of *Sociology Compass*. She has won multiple teaching awards, including the Hans O. Mauksch Award for Distinguished Contributions to Undergraduate Teaching from the Teaching & Learning Section of the American Sociological Association. The second edition of her textbook, *Food & Society: Principles and Paradoxes*, co-authored with Amy E. Guptill and Denise A. Copelton, was published by Wiley in 2017. She teaches courses on gender and sexuality, sociological theory, the sociological imagination, and making sense of college life.

Courtney Morris is Assistant Professor in the Department of English and Philosophy at West Point. She received an MA in English from SUNY Buffalo, an MA in Philosophy from University of Wisconsin, Milwaukee, and a PhD in Philosophy from University of California, Riverside. Her research interests include Kant, Early Modern Philosophy, and Nineteenth-century Philosophy. She is particularly interested in Kant's metaphysical views and his critique of his predecessors. Her most recent article is "The Logical Root of the Transcendental Ideas of Pure Reason," published in *History of Philosophy Quarterly* 35, no. 2 (2018). Her current work focuses on Kant's neglected theory of education.

Graham Parsons is Associate Professor in the Department of English and Philosophy at West Point. He completed his PhD in Philosophy from The Graduate Center, City University of New York in 2012. He has published articles on the philosophy of war and peace, and the obligations of soldiers, in journals such as *Social Theory and Practice*, *Philosophia*, and *Journal of Military Ethics*. He is currently working on a book examining the role that gender has played in the development of just war theory. He teaches a variety of philosophy courses at West Point, including electives for philosophy majors and the ethics course required for all cadets. He also regularly lectures in the Bard Prison Initiative. Among all his activities, he is most proud of serving as the coach of West Point's Ethics Bowl team, currently reigning as national champion.

Darya Pushkina is Associate Professor at the Faculty of Liberal Arts and Sciences at St. Petersburg State University. She earned her BA from Reed College in 1995, and her PhD University of Maryland in 2001. She is a specialist in international relations and comparative politics, and examines the issues of war and peace from both perspectives, specifically concentrating on the United Nations peace missions. She has published a number of articles on the topic and currently is working on a book-length manuscript. She is teaching a variety of courses in both Russian and English, including: The 3 C's of War: Causes, Cures and Consequences, and International Security, International Humanitarian and Criminal Law.

Shai Secunda is a scholar of late antique Judaism and other Eastern late antique religions, especially Zoroastrianism. His first book, *The Iranian Talmud: Reading the Bavli in its Sasanian Context* (University of Pennsylvania Press, 2014), illustrates how to read the Babylonian Talmud alongside neighboring Zoroastrian Middle Persian literature. He studied at Yeshiva and Harvard Universities, and occupied posts at both Yale University and the Hebrew University of Jerusalem. He is now the Jacob Neusner Associate Professor in the History and Theology of Judaism at Bard College.

Tehseen Thaver was Assistant Professor of Religion at Bard College at the time of the conference, and is now Assistant Professor of Religion at

Princeton University. Her work centers on multiple forms of Muslims' engagement with scripture—pre-modern and modern, oral and textual, interpretive and performative. She is currently working on a monograph titled *Beyond Sectarianism: Text, Hermeneutics, and the Formations of Religious Identity in Medieval and Early Modern Islam.*

Dominique Townsend is Assistant Professor of Buddhist Studies at Bard College. She is a scholar of Buddhism with a focus on early modern Tibet. Her current research concerns Tibetan Buddhist cultural production and aesthetics. She is also conducting preliminary research for a book on Tibetan Buddhist poetics and translation theory.